Horrors of *a* Voice (object *a*)

Tristam Adams

Horrors of *a* Voice (object *a*)

Vox-Exo

palgrave
macmillan

Tristam Adams
Dudley, UK

ISBN 978-3-031-62049-2 ISBN 978-3-031-62050-8 (eBook)
https://doi.org/10.1007/978-3-031-62050-8

Cover illustration: Kohl-Illustration / Alamy Stock Photo

This Palgrave Macmillan imprint is published by the registered company Springer Nature Switzerland AG.
The registered company address is: Gewerbestrasse 11, 6330 Cham, Switzerland

Paper in this product is recyclable.

With thanks to Mark Fisher, Lynn Turner, and my family.

Contents

Introduction

> In a philosophical sense, that demons choose to present themselves via voice and sound—at once present and absent—is noteworthy.
>
> —Thacker[1]

> If it was successfully murdered, why does it recur? *Does it not know that it is dead?*
>
> —Dolar[2]

The above aside of Eugene Thacker's in *In the Dust of This Planet: Horror of Philosophy Vol. 1* is one prompt for this project, for in it there is an implicit recognition of the question of voice in terms of horror. Voice, in this sense, can be taken up to announce the horror of the subject: a confrontation with a lacuna, an epistemological—or ontological—crisis.

A second spark, and the most referenced text within, is Mladen Dolar's *A Voice and Nothing More*. This small book, from the Slovenian School in 2006, brought the question of voice attention after gaze had been a focus for so long. In explicating the concept of 'the object voice' Dolar, amongst others, makes frequent recourse to a horror vocabulary.

[1] Eugene Thacker, *In the Dust of this Planet: Horror of Philosophy Vol. 1.* (Winchester, UK: Zero Books, 2011), 28.

[2] Mladen Dolar, *A Voice and Nothing More (Short Circuits)* (Massachusetts, USA: MIT Press, 2006), 44, emphasis added.

T. Adams, *Horrors of* a *Voice (object* a*)*,
https://doi.org/10.1007/978-3-031-62050-8_1

These two books have little in common. Firstly, Lacan is not mentioned in Thacker's book, whereas Dolar's book came from the school that re-ignited interest in the flamboyant Frenchman, who seated himself on the throne as heir to Freud. *In the Dust of This Planet: Horror of Philosophy Vol. 1* turns to a nihilist philosophy to decentre human experience. *A Voice and Nothing More* is a psychoanalytical engagement with voice in relation to the signifier wrapped up in a treatise that explicates what Dolar calls 'the object voice'.

This project takes up Thacker's opening gambit in the horror of philosophy but utilizes it along the way of staging an intervention. The intervention contests Dolar's posit of 'the object voice'. This text seeks to not only explore the gnomic line of Thacker's to elucidate horrors in voice but crucially departs from Dolar's conceptualization of voice. The turn away from Dolar's stratagem resituates the question of voice in Lacanian psychoanalysis to be an urgent concern of the body and the ear. This reframing of voice as a tableaux vivant of flesh, cartilage and membrane warrants a different term to that employed by Dolar and the Slovenian school. Thus, the corporeal and aural horrors of voice will be articulated as a question of 'object *a* voice'. It is this departure—of exploring voice in terms of corporeality and audition, of listening, being open to the plurality of object *a* voice (not merely *hearing* the definite article of the object voice)—where horror abounds.

Dolar's work has certainly ignited discussion on voice, yet extant commentaries seldom develop criticality.[3] John Mowitt's brief but insightful reading of Dolar's project (in *Radio: Essays in Bad Reception*) is an exception. The work presented here does not pursue the omission of the acoustic that Mowitt detects in *A Voice and Nothing More;* instead, two gripes of neglect—corporeality and aurality—are levelled. In this sense a key contribution is to take up the questions Dolar skilfully circumvents in order to provide a sustained rearticulation of Lacan's voice qua object *a* as an object of horror. This departure from Dolar contributes to the significance Lacan's work continues to hold for voice yet also addresses and articulates the concept of voice qua object *a* as a pressing question of corporeality and aurality. Such an addressal impresses the distinct relevance Lacan's work still holds for considerations and discussions of voice and body (or voices and bodies).

On one level the turn towards the body is part of demonstrating an intrinsic entanglement that Lacan's object *a* is of and from the trauma

[3] Mowitt's careful detection of Dolar's recalcitrance to consider the acoustic qualities of voice is a conspicuously measured criticism.

bodies are subjected to; it is at such a confluence where voice is emerged. Voice too is similarly of and from various types and registers of trauma; these are articulated consecutively by the themes of violence, physical transformation and insidious contagion. In each instance, the question of voice and body is afforded a scrutiny that errs close to clinical in its sustained attentiveness to flesh, cartilage, membrane and tissues. This bent of the clinical, this turn towards the body, does not solely elucidate an application of Lacan's voice qua object *a* to questions of the body; it also impresses the prevalence and significance of the body in Lacan's work.

On a further level, the sustained consideration of the body as integral to voice qua object *a* proposes a more prominent and significant role Lacan's work offers for the tableaux of voice and body in the frame of psychoanalysis and interdisciplinary voice studies. Lacan has more to contribute to the question of the body in voice than contemporary exponents, such as Dolar, allow space for. In this sense the project seeks to contribute to a historiographical revision of the figure of Lacan. Contra the dominant and popular sketch of Lacan as an intellectual maverick who succumbed to algebraic and topological abstractions in later life, whose 'work' has been received as seminars from a pedagogical context over and above his psychoanalytical practice, this text partly seeks to underscore and evidence the attentions he paid to the body.[4,5] This is one reason why issue is taken with

[4] Note the remark: 'analysis can be distinguished from everything that was produced by discourse prior to analysis by the fact that it enunciates the following, which is the very backbone of my teaching – I speak without knowing it. I speak with my body and I do so unbeknownst to myself.' Jacques Lacan, *On Feminine Sexuality, The Limits of Love and Knowledge: Encore, The Seminar of Jacques Lacan, Book XX*, Trans. Bruce Fink, Ed. Jacques-Alain Miller (New York/London: Norton and Company, 1998), 119.

[5] See also Suzanne Hommel's touching recollection in Gérard Miller's film'Rendez-vous chez Lacan': 'I was telling Lacan about a dream I had. And I told him "I wake up every morning a 5 o'clock,' " and I added "It's at 5 o'clock that the Gestapo came to get the jews in their houses." At that moment Lacan jumped up from his chair, came towards me, and gave me an extremely gentle caress on my cheek. I understood it as 'geste à peau', the gesture…' Miller interrupts her account to 'explain' that 'He had transformed Gestapo in 'geste à peau'. Hommel continues to describe the tactile break with analytic protocol as a 'very tender gesture, it has to be said – an extraordinarily tender gesture […] it didn't diminish the pain but it made it something else […] 40 years later, when I recall that gesture, I can still feel it on my cheek. It was a gesture as well which was an appeal to humanity, something like that.' Leo Bersani, in *Receptive Bodies*, notes that Miller's emphasis and attention is on the master's 'play' with signifiers, yet Hommel's account focuses resolutely on tactile qualities (51–53). The instance is presented here to highlight that Hommel's presented account does not mention Lacan 'saying' 'geste à peau'. The homophonic play is a silent voice emerging from the interaction of two bodies, from the tender attention Lacan paid to Hommel's cheek.

Dolar's too quick move to psychoanalysis. Whereas, as he declares, his methodology of enquiry is 'Army, Opera—Psychoanalysis' the intervention here insists on a thorough appraisal of the question of the body within this trajectory. The considerations, scrutiny and sensitivity that Lacan afforded the body will be fostered here.

The intervention in Dolar's scheme of 'the object voice' and the synthesis between voice qua objet petit *a* is established in the first chapter, 'Beyond the Veil of Our World'. It is here where the boldest criticisms of Dolar's vernacular and strategy are outlined. The following three chapters—'Violence', 'Changes' and 'Insidious'—operate as subsequent explicatory drives. Overall, the first chapter details Dolar's avidity to leapfrog to psychoanalysis to elucidate 'the object voice' without recourse to the body. Whereas his schema is army (language), opera (aesthetics), psychoanalysis, here the trajectory is language, aesthetics, the body (including the ear). The first chapter establishes the significance of corporeality and audition whilst uncovering Dolar's recalcitrance to addressing such questions. 'Violence', 'Changes' and 'Insidious' all turn to the question of what voice means for the body it comes from or goes into.

The context of this work within wider fields warrants some explication, for it is not merely a retort to *A Voice and Nothing More;* the text contributes to several dialogues ignited by various texts predating 2006. A plethora of texts have contributed to the interdisciplinary field of 'voice studies', whilst this project is perhaps an atypical voice studies text it does engage in particular facets of enquiry that are progenitors of the field.

Considerations of voice within music videos contribute to many discussions that emerged from Kaja Silverman's *The Acoustic Mirror: The Female Voice in Psychoanalysis.* The extensive ruminations on the significance of voice in terms of Michael Jackson's subjectivity in 'Changes', attended to via a stereo methodology of film theorizing and psychoanalysis, underscore the continued relevance and urgency of Silverman's argument that materials such film continue to operate from an ideology of gendered vocalities. In this case, it is argued to be a construct that male subjects such as Jackson panders, plays, subverts and parodies. The critical auditions of feminine vocalities in ancient texts, folklore and myth in 'Insidious' impress the deeply gendered hearings of voice in cultural materials prior to cinema: contributing to outlining a continuum of engendering narratives via recourse to the work of Nancy. A. Jones, Leslie C. Dunn and Barbara Engh in the two formers' edited anthology *Embodied Voices: Representing Female Vocality in Western Culture.*

More recent discussions of voice have murmurated in new materialist and posthumanist frameworks. Whilst this text is not explicitly claimed to be a direct confrontation with the possibilities and questions raised in these emerging projects, it does contribute to how the concept of voice can be thought beyond the immediate and acute definition of human vocalization. 'Violence', despite its foci on vocalization, poses the question of voice as a register of exogenous violence wrought on the human subject. 'Changes' and 'Insidious' both take up a concept of voice that is located beyond the horizon of the human animal's subjectivity and body. Certainly, in the sense of the project's interdisciplinary methodology there are similarities with new materialism's 'transversality across "feminist theory, science and technology studies, and media and cultural studies" to which, Norie Neumark, adds 'media and the arts' as ways of 'thinking, doing and producing knowledge'.[6] A claim of this text—one that differentiates the project from others working in new materialist and/or posthumanist frameworks—is rather than posing arguments for voices beyond a narrow anthropocentric conception but to insist 'the human voice' never was: that voice is defined by its excess beyond the human's body and thought. This claim is where the project departs from the trajectories of enquiry in works such as Dominic Pettman's *Sonic Intimacy: Voice, Species, Technics (or How to Listen to the World)*. [7] The claims here impress not the possibilities of voices beyond the human but illustrates that 'human voices' are distinctly inhuman.

The title should be explained. *Vox-Exo* refers to an always other, an always outside, what Thacker would term 'the-world-in-itself' the objective beyond we never really grasp. Thacker argues that when this world paradoxically makes itself 'known'—or perhaps a better term might be sensed—horror abounds. Here, in terms of voice, it is a voice, as a foreign object, from within or without that confounds the subject and brings horrors. The plural 'horrors' of *a* voice registers the demonic voices referenced in Thacker's book: 'we are legion.' Here the ambivalence of a voice being always in excess of 'a voice', being more than one voice, is taken up. That is to say, the voices explored here, whilst singular in example, are never singular in essence: there is always plurality. Additionally, to say a

[6] Norie Neumark, *Voicetracks: Attuning to Voice in Media and the Arts* (Cambridge, Massachusetts/London, England: The MIT Press, 2017), 8.

[7] Dominic Pettman, *Sonic Intimacy: Voice, Species, Technics (Or, How to Listen to the World)* (Stanford, California, USA: Stanford University Press, 2017).

voice implies voice without specificity. A voice that is irreducible to the subject, to sound, to the human and to its source. It is precisely in voice's irreducibility to such terms where horror emerges as unresolvable questions. This plurality and non-specificity of voice has more fealty with Lacan's objet petit *a*—of which voice is one—than the overtly singular and specific term 'the object voice'. *The voice is not the focus of this book.* To add a line that sounds distinctly Lacanian in its gnomic aplomb we could say, the voice does not exist, and there is no human voice. This is the ineradicable alterity of voice, *a* voice that sounds from within and without: an 'extimate' voice.

In addition to Thacker's text, two other horror theory texts are employed. Each was published after Thacker's. Dylan Trigg's *The Thing: A Phenomenology of Horror* is employed to confront phenomena that confound and destabilize paradigms of what the human body is; it seeks the horror of the other side of the body, a horrific and unhuman facet.[8] Ben Woodward's *Slime Dynamics* is utilized to detail the possibility of a life that continues beyond an anthropocentric presupposition of what life is. This text introduces themes of corporeal incursion and a slippery inexactitude concerning the limits of life and death. [9]

A more detailed explanation of each chapter will be provided in a moment. Before continuing, some recalcitrance and methodological choices warrant explanation: firstly concerning the treatment of technology and secondly concerning the roles sound studies play. In terms of technology, vocalization and the interactions of bodies and voices are given privileged attention before any consideration of recorded voices, amplified voices or modulated voices. This distinction bears upon a definition of technology in the plainest, lay, sense.[10] There is already a well-blossomed range of critical texts that pursue questions of voice and

[8] Dylan Trigg, *The Thing: A Phenomenology of Horror* (Winchester, UK: Zero Books, 2014).

[9] Ben Woodward, *Slime Dynamics* (Winchester, UK: Zero Books, 2012).

[10] Not in the wider sense of technology as established in continental philosophy and postructuralism. To put it differently, one might say voice is taken as already being technology in this sense, but the text does not concern itself with lengthy ruminations of phonographical questions, technics, questions of recording and replication. These themes are touched on at times, but the body is afforded (overdue) primacy.

technology, the relationships, the implications, the cultures and vocalities.[11] Indeed, such a seam of enquiry is so established that texts that consider voices and bodies apart from technology are hard to find amidst the cacophony that has resulted from Edison's toying with the human ear. Such enquiries are necessary, but one symptom of a focus on technologically formulated and/or reformulated voice is a tendency to ignore the body, the flesh and cartilage that gives and is given to voice. Technology raises a question of a disembodied voice that depletes foci from questions of the corporeal. This methodological decision has not been taken lightly; a cursory glance over the genre horror fiction nestled in the bibliography shows a wealth of texts that detail the horrors of a disembodied voice. But such technologically disembodied and orphaned (to supernatural presence) voices open questions that are already well explored over and above the body. Rather than seek to add further commentary to this field, here the body is considered and takes precedence over its resonance in the myriad technologies that re-voice and disembody.

Many of the examples presented here are diegetic examples portrayed within a medium. Some of the voices here are technologically voiced. The music videos and records of Michael Jackson are given a lot of attention. Jackson's voice is a technologized voice; it is given to the viewer/listener by virtue of a great recording-mixing-disseminating apparatus. Indeed, many listeners only hear the voices of such performers by technological proxy. However, can it not be contested that the diegetic implications of these voices can be considered without recourse to the technology that serves their reception? Might a wilful deafness to the question of technology serve to cultivate a greater sensitivity, attunement, to the body and voice it records and sounds? To the retort that this close listening of the body, this unhearing of the noise of technics, is a theoretical *take* one maintains whilst at once allowing one's ears to benefit from its phagic

[11] For example, Michel Chion, *The Voice in Cinema*, Trans. Claudia Gorbman (New York, USA: Columbia University Press, 1999); Brian Kane, *Sound Unseen: Acousmatic Sound in Theory and Practice* (Oxford, UK: Oxford University Press, 2014); John Mowitt, *Radio: Essays in Bad Reception* (Berkeley, California, USA: University of California Press, 2011); Neumark, Norie; Ross Gibson and Theo van Leeuwen, eds. *Voice: Vocal Aesthetics in Digital, Arts and Media* (Cambridge, Massachusetts/London, England: The MIT Press. 2010); Dominic Pettman, *Sonic Intimacy: Voice, Species, Technics (Or, How to Listen to the World)* (Stanford, California, USA: Stanford University Press, 2017); Jeffrey Sconce, *Haunted Media: Electronic Presence from Telegraphy to Television (Console-ing Passions)* (Durham and London, UK: Duke University Press, 2000); Jonathan Sterne. *The Audible Past: Cultural Origins of Sound Reproduction* (Durham and London, UK: Duke University Press, 2003).

reception, the following question may be levelled: does a reading, theorizing or utilization of Plato, Freud, Lacan, Edgar Allen Poe or Stephen King require a robust—to the point of fixation—rumination on the technics and consequences of the emergence of the Gutenberg press up to its cyan-glowing cybernetic zenith? This book takes as a given the negative and pursues the horrors of voice in terms of body and aurality with the liberty a literary theorist is afforded for their readings. A literary theorist is not required to address the Gutenberg press; thus, a theorist of voice should not be required to address the phonograph.

For the sake of maintaining fidelity to the body, the threads of this project turn away from extensive commentaries of sound and/or listening. One reason for this is that by engaging in discussions of, say, Thoreau or Schaeffer, a phenomenological prospect is opened up. What is listening, the experience of listening over and beyond the rudimentary process of audition? There are two reasons to circumvent this question and the wealth of literature addressing it. Firstly, listening presupposes subjective experience of sonic phenomena. Yet, as any dealings with voice quickly arrive at, and as is key to object *a* voice, voice is by no means sound. Voices can be auditioned: aural hallucinations are a key example, but that does not mean one is dealing with sound. On the other hand, just because a voice is listened to does not dispel the issues of active and passive listening explored so well by Schafer. A way to strafe this conundrum is to make distinctions between questions that consider how voice is sounded out—vocalization—and questions that explore how sounds and voices are *attended to*. This book takes the former question as priority over recourse to lengthy ponderances of how one attends to voice that, one way or another, gets inside the head. Vocalization is framed as violence in the chapter of the same name. 'Changes' builds on that concept and suggests that violent corporeal changes are evoked by voice. The examples here are the genre horror narratives of Michael Jackson's work. Of concern here are horrors of voicing and voicings, not horrors of listening or hearing. The foci on voicings over how voice is attended to do, however, run into a tension: how to discuss the effects of voicing without succumbing to the question of listening. This tension is most closely navigated in the final chapter, 'Insidious', that explores voice as analogous to bacteria, slime, virus and parasites before travelling near Sirens on its way to voice in ancient Greek pedagogy. The foci on voice in these contagious formulations resist lapsing into questions of how sound is received. How a voice spreads is considered, and the evidence of its affect upon the bodies of those who hear it is considered. But the question of what it sounds like, how we hear it, how we experience it—attend to it—is not. How a voice *comes to be* heard is as close as this book strays to the question of listening. The Sirens and earworms (INMI) are certainly limits of this position.

Concerning Methodology. As should already be clear, an intervention in a very specific articulation of a particular Lacanian concept is the impetus for articulating an intrinsic corporeal horror in voice. The argument is then articulated in three distinct modes—'Violence', 'Changes' and 'Insidious'. Each chapter contains a distinct methodology. 'Violence' draws heavily on scientific texts, texts from social evolution, developmental studies and, also, literary sci-fi and theory-fiction. This is a mode of enquiry that utilizes the impressions of creative works to articulate the imports that empirical texts pose. This is not a common methodology, surprisingly. Especially in the Slovenian's school's psychoanalytical commentaries recourse to empirical data is occasional and scant. 'Violence' seeks to underscore the corporeal horrors of voice by way of alloying object *a* to empirical knowledge sets. Imposing a coherence between Lacanian intellect and the endeavours of science, the clinic.

'Changes' is quite different. This chapter bears a methodology not too dissimilar to the close readings of popular culture by members of the Slovenian school, in particular that of Žižek. Žižek tends to elaborate via an array of popular culture materials—Scott's *Alien* franchise, Hitchcock films and science fiction—whereas Dolar's cultural materials (in terms of voice) tend to err on less popular European materials such as classic texts, opera and modernist literature. Despite Jackson being a figure of which there is a wealth of commentary, and despite his vocalizations being highly idiosyncratic, not many texts focus on the role voice played in his work. Secondly, psychoanalytical readings of Jackson are also, strangely, lacking despite his persona being a curious knot, a thrilling Matryoshka, of paradox, tensions, ironies, thrills of delight and horror. 'Changes' takes up these two wanting avenues and posits Jackson as a conduit of voices at once horrific and of indeterminate corpus.

The methodology of 'Insidious' contains stratagems from both the previous chapters. On one level its argument is made of a continuum of explicatory readings that run from genre horror to classic Greek philosophy (resonating the explicatory penchants of both Dolar and Žižek). On another level, this continuum incorporates several scientific texts to underscore the contagious natures of earworms; using empirical studies in amalgamation with close readings develops a methodology that shares the employments of discipline in both 'Violence' and 'Changes'. In this sense it is a methodological composite of both the previous chapters.

Now, each chapter in turn will be outlined in detail. Welcome to orientation. 'Beyond the Veil of Our World' contains some introductory detail that continues the claims made here in greater detail. This opening chapter is where an intervention is staged. The opening tone is introductory (hence the brevity of this text) and lays out the positioning and contributions to the omissions and troughs of Dolar's work. The chapter could stand as a retort to Dolar's book. Subsequent chapters are more illustrative and comprise a trio of examples that argue, with persistent foci on the body, for the horror of object *a* voice defined contra Dolar's 'the object voice'.

The opening section, 'Acquiesce to (H)ear: How's It Sound?' refers to vocalization; it asks—over and above aesthetic appreciation or linguistic articulation—what is required of the body that sounds? This opening section takes up the contention that methodologies and causes of sounding can be attended to without recourse to subjective ruminations on the phenomenological imports of experiencing sound. The passage draws up the argument that Dolar neglects to address questions of audition and corporeality. That Dolar attends to aesthetics and linguistics (the latter much more so) over the acoustic qualities of the sounding body. It closes by claiming a more clinical approach should not neglect the sounds emitted from the body that voices.

The following section, 'The So-Called Object Voice', makes two claims. Firstly, that the 'the object voice' is an inexact phrase for voice as it is located within Lacan's schema. This move is supported by reference to Stijn Vanheule's works that delineate the difference between the partial object and the objet petit *a*. Secondly, the similitudes of horror and voice qua objet petit *a* are articulated. This is conducted by way of Vanheule's text and by highlighting the vocabulary and metaphorical choices of the Slovenian school's most significant commentators on voice. Žižek and Dolar tend to opt for a vernacular that would be at home in pulp genre horror.

'Speaking of the Object *a*' addresses voice in its relation to language, its post-signifier status as a non-signifying excess or residue. The genre horror theme of ghosts and undead is carried through. The overriding drive is to further underscore Dolar's recalcitrance to addressing the body. If voice is the excess of a subject within language, then what should one make of additional sonic emissions? This thread is articulated via some biographical details of Lacan (graphed from Roudinesco's superb biographies) and Alice Lagaay's essay 'Between Sound and Silence: Voice in the History of Psychoanalysis'. Voice, here, is couched not as a disturbance of speech but as an excess of the body over its application to language.

'Aphonic Voice' continues the trajectory of focusing on the structural context of object *a* voice. This contribution to the thread marks out an antinomy: voice is posited to be an audible object, but not necessarily a sonic object. Voice, it is posited, may resonate where sound waves do not pass. Throughout this presentation of readings of voice as object *a* (this section utilizes Jacques-Alain Miller's text 'Jacques Lacan and the Voice') physical horror is writ large. The example of the aural hallucination Lacan speaks of—'Sow!'—is exemplary insofar as it is a voice heard without sound: a voice of horror, a horrific incursion, a register of the libido's traverse across flesh.

'Synthesis: Object Horror (Demon Voices)' provides a synthesis of object *a* voice with the work of Thacker. Thacker's opening thought in *In the Dust of This Planet: Horror of Philosophy Vol. 1* is presented as a lead into the quote concerning demon voices presented above. This synthesis then moves through Freud's reading of a case of demonological possession and a passage from Dylan Trigg's in *The Thing: A Phenomenology of Horror*. Object *a* voice is framed as an object that announces horrors for the subject.

'Unknown Horrors' returns to the ears of the body, detailing instances and formulations of voices announcing an epistemological lacuna, a crisis that evokes horror in the subject. The acousmatic voice is pitched via readings of David Toop, Freud and Otto Rank's *The Trauma of Birth*.

'Freud's Vacuum' is a primer for the following section. It illustrates how Freud's treatment of voice does not attend to sounding but instead listens for the significance of sounds. That is to say, Freud focused on what the body said or failed to say but not on the noises it produced and how it produced them. This is provided by way of an appraisal of Dolar's division of aesthetics and language in the chapter 'Freud's Voices'. It is argued that both Dolar and Freud impose meaning on the sounds of the body, that each has a tendency towards a *hyperphasic* ear. That each, in the question of voice in terms of aesthetics and language, tends to listen *for* each in voice rather than being sensitive to the body and listening *to* its voice.

'Beyond *Beyond the Pleasure Principle*' focuses on two examples of Freud's ear. The text presents Lagaay's survey of voice in psychoanalysis and Irigaray's close reading of Ernst's vocalization in *Beyond the Pleasure*

Principle. [12] It is argued that Freud, in the writing of Ernst's 'expression of interest and gratification, emitting a loud long-drawn-out 'o-o-o-oh' ' moves too quickly to assume it meant *fort/*go away.[13] Irigaray's argument is that Freud does not consider the body in this turn; its distinct orality is 'overlooked'. The additional gloss here is that on top of this subtle repudiation of the body there is a lack of consideration of vocalization. The second example of Freud's problematic treatment of voice in the famous text is argued to be his reading of Torquato Tasso's *Gerusalemme Liberata* (1581). Here, voice resounds in a moment of horror, yet Freud takes it up as a marker of repetition. These examples serve to illustrate voices from without, that whilst coming from traumatized and brutalized bodies, also announce horrors, unknowns. This thread is the incorporation of horrors of the vocalizing bodies into the prospect of object *a* voice: *vox-exo*.

The second chapter, 'Violence', opens with a return to Dolar's opening premise of *A Voice and Nothing More,* whereby he pitches a joke that draws the binary of aesthetics and language being the two obfuscatory paradigms concealing 'the object voice'. Dolar's line in his introduction is that to get past these two veils of voice one must turn to psychoanalysis. It is argued that this is too quick, that one must be sure to turn to the body first, like a good clinician that appraises physical maladies and symptoms first. The chapter then shifts, in contrast to the previous chapter, to a disciplinary kaleidoscope; it moves from texts considering voice in evolutionary, biological, anthropological, psychological and neuroscientific terms. It also uses fiction and theory-fiction to illustrate imports from these fields. This is not a scatter-shot methodology employed to support an argument. It is a way to re-ground voice, as a horrific object *a* voice, in the body. Disciplines are brought in to not only elucidate the Lacanian schema of object *a* voice, but to illustrate that the high structuralism of Lacan's thought continues to find resonance in findings in the empirical sciences: in this acute case, horrors of *a* voice in bodies.

In the second section 'Exquisite Delicacy and Barbarism' voice is described to be a delicate orchestration that brutalizes, co-opts and asphyxiates the body from which it issues. 'Spinal trauma and throats torn

[12] Luce Irigaray, "The gesture in psychoanalysis" Trans. Elizabeth Gould, *Between Feminism & Psychoanalysis*, ed. Teresa Brennan, 127–138 (Abingdon, UK, New York, USA: Routledge, 1989).

[13] Sigmund Freud, *Beyond the Pleasure Principle*, (Connecticut, USA: Martino Publishing, 2009). 12.

with the talk sickness' extend this vocal inhumanism to a number of levels, phylogenetic, evolutionary and developmental. This malady of voice is then amalgamated into Lacan's comment that the subject is 'captured and tortured by language'.[14] This move retroactively frames the preceding empiricism of vocalization qua torture with *a* horror sheen. It also alloys Lacanian conceptions of voice to the suffering body. The chapter culminates in a close reading of Lacan and his commentators and argues that voice in his schema was always a locus of corporeal horror wrought from without.

'Changes' takes another shift of tone. Here, close intertextual reading of voice horror moments in popular music and music videos illustrates voice as a register of corporeal transformation. The first section, 'Dreadful Symptoms: *Corpaural Sleuthing*', picks up the delicacy of vocalization detailed in 'Exquisite Delicacy and Barbarism' but argues that, by virtue of the virtuosic requirements of vocalizing, voice sounds out transformations, shifts and changes in the voicer. This priming text brings in Lagaay's comments about the stethoscopic view of voice and speech that emerged from psychoanalysis to play alongside Anne Karpf's wealth of details concerning 'What the Voice Can Tell Us' from *The Human Voice: A Story of Remarkable Talent*.[15] After this grounding, the chapter admittedly plunges into a reading of Michael Jackson's music video *Thriller*. Using texts from Kobena Mercer and Margo Jefferson, *Thriller* is read as an exercise in horror-erotic double valence: a Janus-faced *thrill*. This reading incorporates Roland Barthes' concept of the grain of the voice from the synonymous essay. The subsequent section, 'Get Away!', provides a close reading of a small moment at the start of *Thriller* when 'Michael' transforms into a lycanthropic being. Just before the transformation takes hold he looks up and snarls 'Get Away!' The scene is argued to be an illustration of the horrors of puberty, corporeal changes wrought from without. Voice is considered as a harbinger of change. 'Inhuman Noise and Interspecies Grain in *Black or White*' provides a close reading of Jackson's *Black or White* music video. Here, voice is posited to be evocation of human limits—a chimerical, pan-species, voice of plurality, torsions and horror.

'Insidious', in methodology, is a mix of chapters "Beyond the Veil of Our World" and "Violence". Recourse to empirical studies, fiction and

[14] Jacques Lacan, *The Psychoses: The Seminar of Jacques Lacan Book III 1955–1965*, Trans. Russell Grigg, Ed. Jacques-Alain Miller (London, UK: Routledge, 1993), 243.

[15] Karpf, *The Human Voice: A Story of Remarkable Talent* (London, UK: Bloomsbury, 2007).

close intertextual readings are all employed to explore the incursions and contagions of voice. 'Slimy and Wormy' grounds voice as analogous to slime and pose their equivalence with the vital, horrifying, excess of slime Woodward elaborates in *Slime Dynamics.* This section encompasses contagion and earworms (involuntary musical imagery [INMI]) and finishes on the point of voice's incursion into bodies. Texts from Žižek and Dolar that exploit a horror vocabulary are employed. This weaving not only underscores the argument of an implicit horror in voice but also performs the necessity to explore the question of horror in the object *a* voice. 'Crazy' develops the contagion of voice in terms of a parasitic pathogen.

'Parasites and Earworms' surveys several INMI as agents of torment and horror in literature and film. Mark Twain's *A Literary Nightmare*, comments from Stephen King concerning earworms, the 'Cuban Pete' character in Charles Russell's *The Mask*, E.B. White's short story, *The Supremacy of Uruguay* and Alfred Bester's *The Demolished Man* are all deployed to illustrate this concept. Nestled within this piece is a sketch of *Ophiocordyceps unilateralis*, a parasite that compels a host body to behaviours expediting proliferation. It is claimed that INMI is structurally (for the subject/host) analogous to parasites and the aural hallucinations Lacan describes. Each is an agent of torment and horror that move through bodies.

'Sirens' Spell' pivots on the double meaning of spell: to order symbols correctly and the act of casting a magical force. The section focuses on the latter modality of spell as a register of gendered vocalities in the history of the Siren figure. Several texts, including the editors' introduction from Leslie C. Dunn and Nancy A. Jones' *Embodied Voices: Representing Female Vocality in Western Culture*, are employed. The reading of the Sirens then extends to incorporate *The Voyage of Máel Dúin*, an ancient Irish text circa 700AD. These readings continue to elaborate the contagious and corruptive potency of voice, but they also introduce, in the seam of interspecies voice, a distinct question: for whom are such voices horrifying? The text concludes that these 'spells' spell out a particular subject's fears and horrors: a male subject's.

'Sounds Like Us: Vivisection' addresses the treatment of voice in Aristotle's writings. The passage returns to the question of vocalization and underscores the partition of man, the male human animal, from other animals. The section considers Lacan's comments, running along the same annexation of man in terms of intentionality. This section is very much a lead into the following section. Aristotle's distinctions rest largely on empirical observations and a small synthetic leap concerning the presence of soul; the larger implications of the question of gender and species in voice are most insidiously laid by Plato. 'Bacchic Frenzy: Forgetting How to Walk and Speak' continues the thread of division in voice in terms of music. The political drive to control voice is illustrated. Early examples of states controlling the insidious nature of voice—guarding against the horrors of corrupting earworms—are explored. Questions of gender and species within this division of voice continue to be addressed. The piece argues that patrician man has guarded (from the ancient Greeks fretting over music modes and the Dionysian dithyramb to the review board that suggested lowering BPMs in Fabric might prevent drug use) against musical enjoyment lest it led to a 'hell of unending misery'. Here, enjoyment in music and voice are presented as prospects of horror that man has legislated and sought to control.

'Flauting Sense' takes up this notion of man guarding against the horrors of voice but adds a twist: the horrors are pleasure. This twist is explicated with a debt to Adriana Cavarero's nuanced reading of Plato's Symposium in *For More Than One Voice: Toward a Philosophy of Vocal Expression*. It is argued that Alcibiades and Plato are plagued by the contagious and spellbinding nature of Socratean voice; their love of this voice is unrequited: it is a torment. The former's reaction is to flee the voice. Plato's move is to devocalize logos, meaning and soul, from voice by reducing it to script. In each case, these are responses to the physical insidiousness of voice, methods of bearing the horrifying corporeality of voice: the horrors, the jouissance, the *thrill*, of voice.

Beyond the Veil of Our World

Acquiesce to (H)ear: How's It Sound?

If voice is the object of enquiry, then what is the nature of this object? What is voice? To begin let us consider voice as it is commonly understood in lay terms, as it is immediately thought of when one sounds the word, 'voice', in conversation: a sound from a body.

There is no way around this; voice is generally taken to be a type of sound, we might call it a sound object, a sonic phenomenon; something with empirical traits, physics: something that moves air as well as moves through air and other materials. Audition of voice is contingent on a series of physics: force, movement, of the body, the mouth and the ear. These facets of voice, the physics of voice, couch our object in sonic and empirical terms. It is in this sense that sound studies and scientific texts concerning voice contribute significantly to the discussion. Exploring what the human corpus undertakes when vocalizing—what voice requires of the body that produces it—is a key part of this chapter. How voice comes about must not be skipped over, but it is by no means the whole story. Curiously, one might say a focus on *how* voice sounds can neglect how voice *sounds*. An opera lover is keen to know about a new tenor's recent performance. He is good friends with another opera lover, someone who was lucky enough to see this recent performance that is the talk of the town. This friend is an otolaryngologist. Over dinner together one day, he asks his good friend the otolaryngologist how the tenor *sounded*.

T. Adams, *Horrors of* a *Voice (object* a*)*,
https://doi.org/10.1007/978-3-031-62050-8_2

The physics of sound and the particularities of human vocalization fall short of some crucial nature of voice. It resists reduction to both the physics of its production and the phenomenon of its sonic and acoustic after life. This is one problem Pierre Schaeffer addresses in *Solfrege de l'objet Sonore*, albeit with a focus on music. Recourse to dry empiricism, acoustics and mathematics frame the subject of voice scientifically, but this is then no different a treatment than might be applied to any other sound within nature. Voice, like music, is not merely another sound within nature. Wouldn't most agree with the claim there is something different about voice and music over the din of the world? We might think of voice as different to other sounds, we might *feel* it sounds different, but the scientist can always claim that, at least in terms of physics, it is much like other sounds. So, it might be more accurate to say voice *sounds* different even if it sounds in *the same way* as other sounds.

We are creeping up on the question of audition. Schaeffer, in the same text (a transcription of his audio essay), counter-poses the other side of this theoretical conundrum. He writes of the sound object: 'the sum of the psychological phenomena of perception'.[1] There is a pointed English pun here whereby 'sound object' twists into an ironic term—there is nothing 'sound' (as in secure, safe, robust) about an object. One immediate avenue of thought is the phenomenology of audition, listening. However, this line quickly results in a general concern of sound studies—asking the grand question, what is it to listen?

There are two broad lines of flight from this bind—either a phenomenological endeavour encompassing psychoacoustics with consistent recourse to voice or an engagement with sound studies. The former, although perhaps useful for contemplating how voice may be heard without physical sound (i.e. aural hallucinations), would not leave time for any appreciation of the voice, its aesthetic, 'texture' or context.[2] We may return to our opera lovers' dinner where the two men listen to a record of this infamous tenor. Here we might sympathize with our opera lover's perplexity and exasperation when his good friend the otolaryngologist

[1] Pierre. "Solfrege de l'objet Sonore" *UbuWeb Papers*, accessed January 29, 2019, http://www.ubu.com/papers/schaefer_solfege.pdf.

[2] Our opera lover then asked a phenomenologist—much to his regret—before acquiring a recording of the performance. After some evenings spent rapt in his apartment listening to the tenor's voice he looked forward to expressing his enthusiasm with a visiting sound studies scholar. They were affable enough, but the conversation quickly resulted in torsion, cross-purposes.

explains how the tenor's voice is 'perfectly normal'. 'It cannot be a normal voice,' explained our aesthete, 'it's magnificent!'

To ask of voice, 'how's it sound?' opens a tension along a continuum from the concealed larynx, mouth, the ear, perception and experience, with myriad other physics, such as acoustics, along the way. A way to formulate this tension, a way of articulating the bind, might be by way of the term *phenomenon*. The secondary definition of the noun is for something special; this applies to voice well. But the primary definition is more germane. Phenomenon is a fact that exists, or is observed to exist, particularly when its cause or explanation is in question. The empirical traits of vocalizing and audition both fall short of the essence of voice, its phenomenon the empirical sciences chart well, but the question of voice is by no means exhausted by observations of vocalization, audition or the physics of sound. The details of each might go some way to provide a basis from which thought can spring, but voice is by no means reducible under such modes. How best to conduct a consideration of voice beyond mere phenomenon?

Dolar's proposition of the Lacanian 'Object Voice' in *A Voice and Nothing More*, '[d]oubtless the most sustained recent reflection on the voice', is a particular mode of conducting a pursuit of such an essence beyond the disciplines mentioned thus far.[3] The book opens with an anecdote about Italian soldiers listening to the beautiful voice of their leader rather than heeding the semantic content it carries:

> There is a story which goes like this: In the middle of a battle there is a company of Italian Soldiers in the trenches, and an Italian commander who issues the command "Soldiers, attack!" He cries out in a loud and clear voice to make himself heard in the midst of the tumult, but nothing happens, nobody moves. So the commander gets angry and shouts louder: "Soldiers, attack!" Still nobody moves. And since in jokes things have to happen three times for something to stir, he yells even louder: "Soldiers, attack!" At which point there is a response, a tiny voice rising from the trenches, saying appreciatively "*Che bella voce!*" "What a beautiful voice!"[4]

[3] John Mowitt, *Radio: Essays in Bad Reception* (Berkeley, California, USA: University of California Press, 2011), 25.

[4] Mladen Dolar, *A Voice and Nothing More (Short Circuits)*, (Massachusetts, USA: MIT Press, 2006), 3.

Dolar writes of a 'third level: an object voice which does not go up in smoke in the conveyance of meaning, and does not solidify in an object of fetish reverence, but an object which functions as a blind spot in the call and as a disturbance of aesthetic appreciation.'[5] Dolar states that one might show fidelity to meaning by running to attack, fidelity to aesthetics by running to the opera and fidelity to the third level by turning to psychoanalysis.[6] Language and meaning on the one hand, beauty and aesthetics on the other, and a third level, psychoanalysis. Notice that physics are absent from each turn of Dolar's claimed premise. The body is passed over, acoustics fall on deaf ears: flesh, cartilage, membranes and waves never made the edit.

A later chapter in *A Voice and Nothing More* is titled 'The "Physics" of the Voice'. It glides over corporeality deftly and charmingly. Nonetheless, despite such delicacy, the text is lacking a certain side of voice: its passion and voluptuousness—its body. Dolar's treatment is more dentist than disco. The warmth or moisture, the breath of voice, is eliminated to the point of being an antithesis to Barthes' enraptured essay, 'The Grain of the Voice'.[7]

The bulk of 'The "Physics" of the Voice' focuses on 'The Acousmatics of the Voice'. There is more to be said about Schaeffer's reinvigorated term 'acousmatic' than can be included in this consideration of Dolar's treatment (or not) of physics. A brief definition: acousmatic refers to a sound whose source cannot be identified. Thus, an acousmatic voice would be heard without the body being seen. Dolar, here, is of course discussing the nature of voice's capacity for disembodiment and the uncanny and haunting effects of hearing a voice coming from nowhere. But there is an irony here: the chapter of *A Voice and Nothing More* that addresses the "physics" voice does so by focusing mostly on an acousmatic voice whereby the source body is hidden, concealed, out of sight.

Dolar recounts the philosophical origin of the term provided in the Larousse dictionary: '"The Acousmatics were Pythagoras' disciples who, concealed by a curtain, followed his teaching'.[8] Later in the section he discusses the veil that conceals the powerful wizard in Lyman Frank

[5] Ibid., 4.

[6] Ibid., 4.

[7] Roland Barthes, *Image-Music-Text* (London: Fontana, 1977), 179–189. Barthes' text restlessly yearns for the body in voice.

[8] Dolar, *A Voice and Nothing More*, 61.

Baum's *Wizard of Oz* and goes on to speculate how Pythagoras' students felt as their master was the disacousmatized. He writes:

> It may well be that, once the lifted screen uncovered a pitiable old man, the disciples' main concern was to maintain the illusion, so that the disillusionment which they must have experienced did not affect the big Other. Another screen had to be raised to prevent the big Other from seeing what they saw, and this second veil entailed a dividing line between the initiated and the uninitiated. Perhaps it is no coincidence that the Pythagorean school was the first to institute the division into esoteric and exoteric knowledge, the esoteric being reserved for those who had seen the Master, and the exoteric for those who knew his teachings merely by his voice, so that the line concerned not the doctrine itself, only its form. Does not the term esoteric imply *maintaining the veil after the veil has been lifted*?[9]

Concerning the second sentiment regarding esotericism, particularly the final line emphasized above, it is tempting to pose a question: does this divulge the methodology Dolar subscribes to? Some pages previously, Pythagoras' veiling is declared 'a stroke of genius which stands at the very origin of philosophy'.[10] A veil behind the veil, the pedagogical stroke of genius at the birth of 'philosophy'—are such sentiments merely coincidental asides in this "physics" chapter that skirts around with such reticence to both the acoustics and corporeality of voice?

Perhaps it is no coincidence, then, that the cover of *A Voice and Nothing More*, the mouth, the corporeal aperture of voice, is hidden behind Michael Redgrave's hand?[11] The corporeal physical aperture, the mouth, is given due consideration in 'Violence'. And then there is the chapter title, 'The "Physics" of the Voice'. Why the quotation marks? Is this some grammatical register of how, for the question of voice, physics are a bit … awkward? Do the quotation marks, not acknowledged or justified in the chapter, betray of smidge of irk? Or even annoyance … is this a textual tell, a slip, of wanting to hold physics at arm's length? Or is this caution? Ought

[9] Ibid., 68, emphasis added.

[10] Ibid., 61: 'The Teacher, the Master behind a curtain, proffering his teaching from there without being seen: no doubt a stroke of genius which stands at the very origin of philosophy—Pythagoras was allegedly the first to describe himself as a "philosopher," and also the first to found a philosophical school.'

[11] And Steven Connor's *Dumbstruck: A Cultural History of Ventriloquism*.

one to handle carefully, or best avoid, the corporeality of voice? What horrors does it harbour?

Dolar's neglect of physics does not just apply to the corporeal interpretation of the term; it also extends to acoustics—the physics of sound. Voices are commented on as being beautiful or loud; they are described enough to give the reader some sense of the voices in question—but the physics of sound are only explored as far as disembodied voices, how voice jettisons the body from which it issues. Dolar writes that 'the object voice' is silent and mute—but he must, nonetheless, access his elucidation of this object via heard voices, voices with meaning (speech) or voices of aural beauty—voices that are discussed in terms of how they might sound or have sounded, voices that, most certainly come from a body (even if such a body is concealed). John Mowitt, in 'Facing the Radio', observes that Dolar 'avoids wrestling with precisely the acoustic character of the void within which the voice as object is said to resonate'.[12] This book affords foci to the acoustic and corporeal physics of voice. Although this is by no means an empirical text, such observations are utilized as ways into the question of voice beyond phenomenon, object *a* voice, its horrors: *vox-exo*.

The So-Called Object Voice

To begin understanding object *a* voice with any precision some vagaries need to be addressed. This can be conducted via consideration of how the object *a* emerges within Lacan's schema. The subject of *jouissance*, as Vanheule writes in *The Subject of Psychosis: A Lacanian Perspective*, is 'a crucial starting point' for interpreting object *a*.[13] Vanheule, in 'The Object *a* and Jouissance in Psychosis', outlines a tripartite structure of Drives, Partial Objects and Object *a*. He also provides a useful table listing, in turn, Drives, Partial Objects and Object *a*. The text begins by detailing Lacan's shift of schema in the 1960s, particularly how 'aspects of being cannot be grasped via language and that the registers of libido and drive cannot simply be reduced to the Symbolic.'[14] This then leads to a survey of the dynamic of the subject of jouissance and the Other before focusing on the 'significance' the object *a* has for this revised schema.[15] Vanheule

[12] Mowitt, *Radio: Essays in Bad Reception*, 26–27.

[13] Stijn Vanheule, *The Subject of Psychosis: A Lacanian Perspective* (London, UK: Palgrave Macmillan, 2011), 131.

[14] Ibid., 125.

[15] Quotation marks because a defining facet of object *a* is its alterity to the signifying chain, the Symbolic.

conducts this with reference to Lacan's matheme of the field of the Other and the field of the Subject. Considering Lacan's revised dialectical paradigm and the object *a's* emergence from this schema is necessary. Its omission from the Slovenian school's works on voice and object *a* is, at the very least, a moot point. Here, through charting Lacan's post-1960s' schema, the complexion of object *a* emerges as one of alterity and corporeality.

Let's begin by way of the difference between the subject of the signifier and the subject of jouissance. The former "exists', to the extent that its position and identity in the world are articulated via the Other.'[16] Whereas the subject of Jouissance:

> refers to the libidinous corporeality of being. It designates a state of being that is not (yet) determined by the signifier. The subject of jouissance 'is' but does not exist. It designates the human being qua Thing, before it is differentiated by means of the signifier. Its identity and its position in the world are not articulated.[17]

Vanheule states that the relationship between the Other and the subject of Jouissance was conceptualized by Lacan in dialectical terms.[18] Most salient, for our question of voice, is the character of object *a* that emerges from this dialectic of the Other and the subject of Jouissance.

> [I]n the tension between jouissance and Other an *Aufhebung* or upheaval is realized, which gives rise to a new component of subjectivity: the object *a*. The object *a* is a component of libidinous corporeality that is created by using signifiers, but that is not represented by means of the signifier. It is an element of being that persists in the subject of the signifier, but is not transformed into Symbolic existence.[19]

There are two points of comment to be made here. Firstly, the sentiment expressed here runs along the lines of Lacan's famous graph of desire where voice shoots out like a 'spectral apparition' (as Žižek is wont to say) as an effect of the signifying operation.[20] The object *a* emerges from the signifying operation but is in no way compatible with the Symbolic—it is

[16] Ibid., 127.

[17] Ibid., 127.

[18] Vanheule goes on to describe how Lacan's topological and logical approach did not adhere to developmental psychology, histories or causation via a dialogue between Lacan and Piera Aulagnier in the latter's 1961–1962 guest lecture.

[19] Ibid., 127.

[20] Slavoj Žižek, "I Hear You with My Eyes" *Gaze and Voice as Love Objects*, Eds. Renata Salecl and Slavoj Žižek, (Durham and London, UK: Duke University Press. 1996), 103.

irreconcilable, incompatible, with any mode of expression via signifiers. Secondly, note the term 'libidinal corporeality': we have flesh here. The dialectical transition between the Other and the subject of Jouissance, the 'central terms Lacan puts forward in his dialectical model', is what 'gives rise' to the object *a*, our outbreak of libidinous corporeality—'an uncanny life of an undead monster'.[21]

The subject of Jouissance is spoken of in terms that recall Freud's vesicle of organic matter—a sensible subject. Lacan speaks not only of the pleasure principle, but of the organism that is sensible to pleasures (which risk overwhelming the organism and being experienced as pain). There is a particular sense of the sensitive flesh, the fragile corpus, threaded through his writing. Regard Vanheule's quotation of Lacan, from 1970:

> If the living being is something at all thinkable, it will be above all as subject of the jouissance; but this psychological law that we call the pleasure principle (and which is only the principle of displeasure) is very soon to create a barrier to all jouissance. If I am enjoying myself a little too much, I begin to feel pain and I moderate my pleasures. The organism seems made to avoid too much jouissance.[22]

Vanheule turns to how Lacan proposes a 'quasi-arithmetical explanation' to understand the transformation the 'dialectical tension' produces in the Other and the subject of jouissance: the matheme of the division of the Other in Seminar X. A reproduction from within *The Subject of Psychosis: A Lacanian Perspective* is presented below:

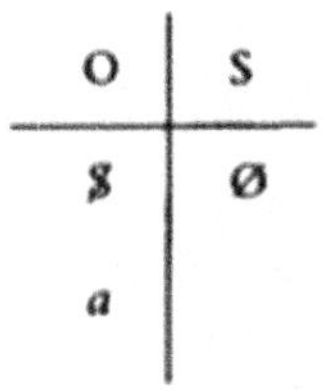

The matheme of the division of the Other

The matheme of the division of the other

[21] Vanheule, *The Subject of Psychosis: A Lacanian Perspective*, 128; Žižek, "I Hear You with My Eyes", 103.

[22] Vanheule, *The Subject of Psychosis: A Lacanian Perspective*, 128.

This presents two fields. On the left there is the field of the Other, on the right the field of the subject of jouissance. The field of the Other is experienced as the external world, whereas the field of the subject of jouissance is experienced as internal.[23]

Moving down a level there are lines over the symbols. Looking to the left we see the field of the Other. Notice that, as Vanheule writes, the fact that O 'is presented as the element that will be divided makes clear that Lacan still brings into play the primacy of the Other: a is the system through which bodily jouissance is transformed.' The subject of jouissance can only be, partly, articulated via the Other.'[24] The S, the subject of jouissance, is divided, hence the overlaid dividing line, via the 'treasure trove' of signifiers, language, from which it is articulated, partly expressed, in the realm of the Other.

Moving to the right we see the 'barred Other'. This is what constitutes the unconscious, the 'Other in so far as I do not reach it'.[25] We could say this is the gravity between the signifiers the divided subject has taken from the treasure trove, or, what unknown, and unknowable, signifiers are taken as remaining beyond the subject. To get at this doomed partial nature of the dynamic Vanheule's closing line in the text, and his embedded quotation from Lacan, provides nuance and elaborates the scrappy (in that it results in bars, division and remainders—not inexact), Sisyphean, schema of the subject and their unconscious:

> The idea is that no matter how much speech is produced about S, some aspects of jouissance cannot be articulated via the Other. This idea brings Lacan to the conclusion that in our use of language, 'The whole existence of the Other suspends on a guarantee that is lacking, hence the barred Other' (Lacan 1962–3, p. 136). The only thing the Other provides to the living being is a medium by means of which a subject can be articulated. What it does not offer is a standard against which this articulation can be tested, nor does O supply a set of ultimate signifiers through which S can be fully named. The bar drawn on O indicates that irrespective of how much signifying articulation takes place, something remains unsaid. There is no final signifier that can hook up the true signification of speech. No so-called 'Other of the Other' gives consistency to the signifiers that are actually articulated as a result of this division.[26]

[23] Ibid., 130.
[24] Ibid., 130.
[25] Lacan, 1962, quoted in Vanheule, Ibid., 130.
[26] Ibid., 130–131.

But wait. There is something else, something that bleeds out of this dialectic; it is the small *a*, bottom left. This is the object *a*, the remainder of the dialectical tension that produces the barred other and the divided subject of jouissance. In the sub-section 'The object *a*' Vanheule writes that the object *a* 'refers to the element of the living being that cannot be inserted into the order of the Symbolic; a component of flesh and blood that remains inert in relation to the signifier'.[27] He then quotes Lacan's comment that it is being 'in so far as it is essentially missing in the text of the world' before suggesting that as object *a* is a remainder of the division between O and S, this basic dialectical dynamic is a necessary prelude for interpreting it.[28]

It is here where resonance with Freud and the import of partial objects comes in. Notably, and again, to underscore the absent body in Dolar's formulation, it is also here where the body's subjection to libidinous drives, its vicissitudes, is brought in.

> In operationalizing the object a Lacan starts from Freud's idea that the libidinous drive is expressed in specific erogenous zones, and from Melanie Klein's and Donald Winnicott's theory on the partial object which says that object relations don't necessarily focus on people, but can just as well be concentrated on body parts such as a mother's breast.[29]

Vanheule continues to say that, Lacan, 'in line with Freud [...] argues that the object a is manifested in specific registers of the drive, which in their turn are connected to specific erogenous zones'[30] and that manifestation of the object *a* can be located in the 'oral, anal, scopic and invocative registers'.[31] Vanheule suggests that to grasp the precise manifestation of object *a* in these registers of drive, a lucid distinction between 'the object *a* and the partial object' is warranted.[32] He then details various partial objects, working in turn through the four registers Lacan speaks of. He writes, concerning the invocative register of the drive, that 'the ear is the erogenous zone and the object it relates to is sound.' But also the 'object *a*, in its turn, is what remains of the partial object upon its transformation

[27] Ibid., 131.
[28] Ibid., 131.
[29] Ibid., 131.
[30] Ibid., 131–132.
[31] Ibid., 132.
[32] Ibid., 132.

by using language.'[33] This object *a*, that remains of the partial object, is not tangible but a 'pastiche that covers up the Real of being'.[34] Quite how the term 'tangible' is to be interpreted is one of the tensions that both Vanheule and Dolar leave unattended. Synonyms for tangible such as physical, material, corporeal,—these terms do not sit as harmoniously with Vanheule's previous sentiment of the object *a* being a libidinous corporeality, nor Žižek's horror-laden exclamation of it being 'an uncanny life of an undead monster'.[35] Is this symptomatic of the voice's troublesome status in philosophy? Something referred to as tactile, textured, bodied yet at the same time, disembodied—at once bodily and of the body?

After this brief prime of the Other and the subject of jouissance and how it leads into the question of object *a*, a turn to Vanheule's table may well be useful. Not least because it will assist in explicating *why* the term 'object voice' might be prone to misinterpretation but also because it will elucidate the tensions and ambiguities that are beginning to be touched on.

In the below table there are two entirely distinguished arrays of objects within the Lacanian schema.[36]

Drive	*Partial object*	*Object a*
Oral	Nipple	Taking in nothing
Anal	Scybalum	Giving nothing
Scopic	Image	Gaze
Invocative	Sound	Voice

Given that the term voice, or experiences, narratives and treatises on the subject invariably evoke a sounding thing and audition of such a thing, a term like 'Object Voice' is potentially prone to misinterpretation between the 'Partial Object' and 'Object *a*'. Statements like Salecl and Žižek's 'Lacan added to Freud's list of partial objects (breasts, faeces, phallus) two other objects, voice and gaze' gloss—smudge—the categorical distinction between partial objects and object *a*.[37] Dolar's, *A Voice and Nothing More*,

[33] Vanheule, *The Subject of Psychosis: A Lacanian Perspective*, 132. This is a structural definition Dolar also emphasizes.

[34] Ibid., 132.

[35] Ibid., 127; Žižek, "I Hear You with My Eyes", 103.

[36] Vanheule, *The Subject of Psychosis: A Lacanian Perspective*, 133.

[37] Salecl and Žižek eds. "Introduction" in *Gaze and Voice as Love Objects* (Durham and London, UK: Duke University Press. 1996), 3. Breast and faeces can be taken as merely less exact, more general, terms for nipple and scybalum. Such a difference may be symptomatic of translation.

argued for voice as a Lacanian object-cause, referring to it as 'the object voice'.[38] This phrasing is certainly prone is misinterpretation. It is with an aim for impressing greater precision that the 'object voice', as it is generally referred to by the Slovenian school thinkers (and subsequent responding and elaborating texts that emerged from the intellectual nexus), will be referred to in this book as the 'object *a* voice'. It is clear that voice and gaze do not stand in the same structural context as breasts or faeces. There are consistent conflations of partial objects with object *a* and umbrella references to both categories as 'objects' in commentary and literature. An example of this is in the introduction to *Sound Effects: The Object Voice in Fiction*.[39] A footnote in Stephanie Swales' *Perversion: A Lacanian Psychoanalytical Approach to the Subject* also qualifies a move with the umbrella term of 'psychoanalytic objects' before exploring in much more precise detail, via Jacques-Alain Miller, the gaze and voice with correct terminology—objet petit *a*.[40] Jacques-Alain Miller, by contrast, in *The Later Lacan: An Introduction*, repeatedly references voice as object *a*. When describing the nipple Vanheule writes 'partial object' but subsequently drops the specificity when referencing scybalum, image or sound: 'at the invocative level the ear is the erogenous zone and the object it relates to is sound.'[41] A slightly more precise formulation might read: at the invocative level the ear is the erogenous zone, and the partial object it relates to is sound.

It cannot elude notice that voice, the object *a* beyond the phenomenological partial object of sound, is not something one hears, sings or speaks. But at once, the overarching definition of the object *a*, qua remainder, residue, irreducible to symbolic existence, necessitates that voice—even if it is silent—is, for the subject, contingent to sound; the partial object relating to the invocative drive and the erogenous (h)ear. This component of libidinous corporeality, as much as it is mute, is only mute 'after', sound. It is in this passage, of sounding partial object to silent object *a*, where ambiguity may arise. Voice immediately evokes a sounding thing, but the structural residence of object *a* is a remainder of the sounding partial

[38] Although he produced earlier texts exploring the same subject the book is certainly the most established and thorough treatise on this topic. An earlier edited collection, *Gaze and Voice as Love Objects*, contained just two chapters featuring voice, one of which all too briefly.

[39] Jorge Sacido-Romero and Sylvia Mieszkowski. *Sound Effects: The Object Voice in Fiction*. Leiden (The Netherlands: Koninklijke Brill/ Rodopi, 2015).

[40] Stephanie Swales, *Perversion: A Lacanian Psychoanalytical Approach to the Subject* (New York, USA: Routledge, 2012), 112.

[41] Vanheule, *The Subject of Psychosis: A Lacanian Perspective*, 132.

object. To unfold a narrative of a subject's experience of voice, qua object *a*, there is a necessary perambulation through sound, the partial object.

Perhaps it is this structural context of object *a* that elicits the Slovenian school's leitmotif of referring to the 'object voice' as inaudible, silent, stuck in the throat after a necessary excursion through the experience and aesthetic characteristic of heard 'voices'.[42] The presence of such a refrain in the texts of Dolar and Žižek at once underscores a sense of corporeality and embroilment in the act of vocalization as it attests to its silence. One can regard the repeated deployment of Munch's *The Scream* (1893) in a similar sense. It is an impressive illustration of the silent corporeal object *a* voice concept's contingency to the aural partial object in both Dolar's, *A Voice and Nothing More*, and Žižek's, 'I Hear You with My Eyes.'[43] It is in these discussions of the silent scream where horror creeps in. Žižek, in this turn, couches the aesthetic appreciation of music as the partial object which prevents the horror or the object *a*. '"Why do we listen to music?": *in order to avoid the horror of the encounter of the voice qua object.* [...] it is a lure, a screen, the last curtain, which protects us from directly confronting the horror of the (vocal) object.'[44]

Speaking of the Object *A*

Lacan, in his introductory speech to the 'Names-of-the-Father' seminar in *Television: A Challenge to the Psychoanalytic Establishment*, is quite explicit in placing voice as that of the Other, as an object *a*. The *a*, stands for *autre*, other. But he is also clear in saying that this voice 'speaks':

> The voice of the Other should be considered an essential object. Every analyst is solicited to accord it its place. Its various incarnations should be followed, as much in the realm of psychosis as at that extremity of normal functioning in the formation of the superego. Through seeing the petit *a* source of the superego, it is possible that many things will become more clear. The relation of voice to the Other is solely a phenomenological approach. If it is truly, as I say, petit *a* as fallen from the Other, we can exhaust its structural function only by bringing our inquiry to bear on what

[42] Žižek, "I Hear You with My Eyes", 93, and Dolar, *A Voice and Nothing More*, 61.
[43] Dolar, *A Voice and Nothing More*, 69; Žižek, "I Hear You with My Eyes", 93–94.
[44] Ibid., 93. Original emphasis.

the Other is as a subject, for voice is the product and object fallen from the organ of speech, and the Other is the site where "it"—ça—speaks.[45]

How are we to interpret this speech? Does this voice speak like you and me? Does it sound? What does it say? The Slovenian theorists describe 'the object voice' as silent, stuck in the throat and structurally irreducible to the signifying matrix of language. What, then, is the import of Lacan's declaration that such a voice speaks?[46] Does it speak without word or sound?

The voice Lacan speaks of—as a voice that speaks—ought to be, he declares, accorded its place by the analyst. But to say 'the voice' is not quite right here, for the following line plunges this voice into plurality, *legion*.[47] The voice we have here is one of various 'incarnations:' '*ses incarnations diverses*'. The phrase immediately evokes the ghoulish, uncanny or undead.[48] Incarnations might be interpreted as iterations, guises, as the previous term various (or *diverses*) alludes to. There is also a theological implication in the word: the embodiment(s) of a deity, spirit or quality in flesh.

From this invocation of voice manifesting as myriad, incarnations, with all the connotations of supernatural, plural, shifting avatars, the methodology of uncovering its relation to the Other is proposed as being a resolutely phenomenological question: what the Other is *for* the subject. The context and experience of its existence for the subject is a way into fathoming its relation to the Other (and by extension its significance for the analysand).[49] It is here where the horror and strangeness of object *a*, its

[45] Jacques Lacan, *Television: A Challenge to the Psychoanalytical Establishment*, Trans. Denis Hollier, Rosalind Krauss, Annette Michelson and Jeffrey Mehlman. Ed. Joan Copjec (New York, USA: W. W. Norton & Company, 1990), 87.

[46] The original: 'La voix de l'Autre doit être considérée comme un objet essentiel. Tout analyste sera appelé à lui donner sa place, ses incarnations diverses, tant dans le champ de la psychose que dans la formation du sur-moi. Ceci, abord phénoménologique, ce rapport de la voix à l'Autre, le petit a comme chu de l'Autre, nous pouvons en épuiser la fonction structurale à porter l'interrogation sur ce qu'est l'Autre comme sujet. Par la voix, cet objet chu de l'organe de la parole, l'Autre est le lieu où ça parle.'

[47] Such a pluralism resonating with 'Legion'—see Thacker.

[48] Žižek, "I Hear You with My Eyes", 103.

[49] Lacan as Ghostbuster: 'tell me what the ghosts say'.

horrific alterity, a voice of the Other incurring into the subject's experience begins to unfold on a number of levels.[50]

Let's return to the question of a voice that speaks. As Lacan states, voice is the product, a 'fallen object from the organ of speech', *par la voix, cet objet chu de l'organe de la parole, l'Autre est le lieu où ça parle.* Dolar, in *A Voice and Nothing More* opens 'The Metaphysics of the Voice' by presenting Lacan's graph of desire, whereby voice runs out, like a protruding limb, as the outcome of the signifying operation. [51] Presented below is the version Dolar uses from Alan Sheridan's translation.[52]

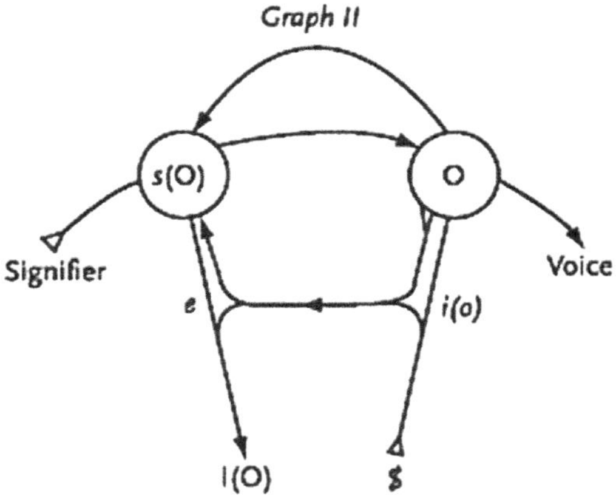

[50] In Adrian Lyne's psychological horror Vietnam veteran film *Jacob's Ladder* (1990) there is an impressive evocation of the Other's speech. The only moment of nondiegetic speech in the film arrives when Jacob is lying in bed. His wife, from whom he is estranged, visits and tells him she 'still loves him' after he softly exclaims 'I'm not dead.' A voice pierces the scene: "dream on…." It is not a voice recognizable as any character in the film. The viewer hears the voice, but it evokes an aural hallucination within the diegesis. Within the scene a voice is not sounding, his wife and children do not react to it. Is this the voice of the Other, erupting, piercing the plain of language, with speech to suggest that Jacob is, in fact, dead and that his wife does not love him?

[51] Dolar, *A Voice and Nothing More*, 35.

[52] Jacques Lacan, *Écrits: A Selection,* Trans. and Ed. Alan Sheridan (London: Routledge, 1989), 234. It should be noted that Bruce Fink's translation provides a slightly different algebra. The difference is of little import for the questions at hand here—it only departs insofar as the 'O' is replaced by 'A' and *a*, maintaining more fidelity to the original French: *autre.*

Dolar asks: 'So why is there the voice as the outcome? Why does the signifier run out into the voice as its result?'[53] Voice, in the diagram, is a remainder after the signifying operation, an excess that cannot be incorporated into the 'binary logical web'.[54] This is the perplexing tension Dolar presents us with: is it to be thought of in terms of being pre-reduction to the avatars and symbols of the signifier by virtue of the signifying operation? No, its nature must be understood as an ineradicable non-signifying excess, a structural outcome, resultant, of the signifying operation.

Dolar couches this as a question of phonology: with a flourish of genre horror narrative, he asks 'which voice do we find there—the one that phonology has killed? If it was successfully murdered, why does it recur? Does it not know that it is dead?'[55] It is hard to dispose of a body too. This claim is in the second chapter, 'The Metaphysics of the Voice'. Michel Poizat's works are a heavy influence here. Dolar, in a note at the back of the book, writes: 'For a detailed account, see Poizat's remarkable book on sacred music, *La voix du diable* (1991). I draw a lot of the information in this section from this source.'[56] Indeed, Poizat's *The Angel's Cry: Beyond the Pleasure Principle in Opera* is a significant psychoanalytical investigation of voice in the Anglophone world that predates Dolar's work.[57] *The Angel's Cry* contains horror themes writ large; death cries, thrills—jouissance—of ecstasy and horror. The diagram Poizat presents in the 'Words and Music' chapter not only places silence/cry in a similar structural context as Dolar's 'object voice' (post speech, signifying linguistic message, and beyond aesthetic/singing) but also couches this silence as invocatory: referencing Lacan's 'invocatory drive'.[58] Dolar's aforementioned deployment of Edward Munch's *The Scream* (1893) strikes a silent resonance with Poizat's thesis in 'The Silence That Screams, the Other Silence'.[59]

Returning to voice's subjection to phonology. It is in the opening chapter, 'The Linguistics of the Voice', where Dolar writes:

[53] Dolar, *A Voice and Nothing More*, 35.

[54] Ibid., 35.

[55] Ibid., 35.

[56] Ibid., 194. Dolar also provides a list of 'important work, wholly or partly inspired by Lacan' in an endnote to his essay 'Voice after Lacan' in *After Lacan: Literature, Theory, and Psychoanalysis in the Twenty-First Century*. The first five works listed are Poizat's.

[57] Michel Poizat, *The Angel's Cry: Beyond the Pleasure Principle in Opera*, Trans. Arthur Denner (Ithaca, New York/London, UK: 1992).

[58] Poizat, *The Angel's Cry: Beyond the Pleasure Principle in Opera*, 90–91. Footnote 79.

[59] Ibid., 87–92.

> The inaugural gesture of phonology was thus the total reduction of the voice as the substance of language. Phonology, true to its apocryphal etymology, was after killing the voice—its name is, of course, derived from the Greek *phone*, voice, but in it one can also quite appropriately hear *phonos*, murder. Phonology stabs the voice with the signifying dagger; it does away with its living presence, with its flesh and blood.[60]

Dolar, in claiming that phonology dismantled the voice into 'elementary structures of kinship', or 'mere bundles of differential oppositions,' rehearses how voice—surplus to communication or not—was reduced to differences, presences and absences under a phonological project.[61] He writes: 'the prosody, the intonation and the accent, the melody, the redundant elements, the variations, and so forth. Bones, flesh, and blood of the voice were diluted without remainder into a web of structural traits, a checklist of presences and absences.'[62]

Dolar is deliberately too quick. For he goes on to say that phonology never quite completes its reduction of voice into a differential matrix. Despite the phoneme being 'the way in which the signifier has seized and molded the voice [...] it can never quite be tamed into the simple transparent matrix of differential oppositions'.[63] Dolar uses the example of the Wachowskis' *The Matrix* film, to demonstrate that 'The signifier needs the voice as its support, just as the Matrix needs the poor subjects and their fantasies, but it has no materiality in itself: it just uses the voice to constitute our common "virtual reality"'.[64] He goes on to say the phonological operation always 'produces a remainder which cannot be made a signifier or disappear in meaning; the remainder that doesn't make sense, a leftover,

[60] Dolar, *A Voice and Nothing More*, 19. This scene of murder strikes a harmony with Poizat's comment of the double valence of thrill of a penetrating cry beyond language and aesthetic: 'Are those tears, then, tears of joy, or tears of loss [...] And those shivers: people call them shivers of pleasure. Perhaps they are. But the shivers are also the visceral expression of a feeling of dread. And is there really a fundamental difference between the thrill that comes at the climax of the love duet in Act II of *Tristan und Isolde* and the shudders of dread—experienced explicitly as such when Lulu screams her death cry under Jack the Ripper's knife—that unfailingly overcome us no matter how familiar we are with this work, no matter how prepared we may be for that rending cry?' Poizat, *The Angel's Cry*, 4. See also Poizat, *The Angel's Cry*, 40 and extensive commentary on Lulu pages 201–207.

[61] Ibid., 19.

[62] Ibid., 19.

[63] Ibid., 19–20.

[64] Ibid., 20.

a cast-off—shall we say an *excrement* of the signifier? The matrix silences the voice, but not quite.'[65]

Dolar's first avenue of pursuit for this unsilenced facet of voice, which is seemingly recalcitrant to the signifier, is accent, intonation and timbre.[66] This is a strawman; it goes up in signifying smoke on pages 20–23. What follows is perplexing. After a line concerning the "prelinguistic" and "postlinguistic" classification of intonation, timbre and accent, the focus segues to physiological emissions such as coughing and hiccups. This thread is then woven into Aristotle's partitioning of sounds, voices and speech by the presence of soul in various species.[67] Coughs and hiccups are acknowledged as a break in speech, a 'disruption of the ascent toward meaning' before suggesting that such corporeal noises 'are hardly ever simply external to the structure—quite the opposite, they may well enter into its core or become its double. We can easily see that there is a whole "semiotics of coughing": one coughs while preparing to speak.'[68]

To elucidate this point, that the cough or hiccup, that corporeal interruption *of* voice we share with animals, Dolar turns to Lacan's reference to Aristophanes' hiccupping fit in Plato's *Symposium*. He writes of Lacan's *Transference* seminar, where Lacan recounted Alexandre Kojève's advice: 'since Kojève is a very superior sort of person, namely a snob, he answered me: "In any case you will never interpret the Symposium if you do not know why Aristophanes had a hiccup!"'[69] Lacan then presses the significance of Aristophanes' spasm and highlights the line, in his copy,

[65] Ibid., 20. Emphasis added.

[66] Ibid., 20.

[67] Aristotle's text is given time later on.

[68] Dolar, *A Voice and Nothing More*, 24. Note the presupposed hierarchy here. Meaning said as if it were above the body from which it issues; ibid., 24. Poizat posited the 'significance' of coughing in terms of an unbearable silent voice in 'The Silence that Screams, The Other Silence'. He writes: 'Have you never noticed that no one ever coughs during the orchestra's fortissimi, only during pianissimi? For many spectators, coughing is not due to some chance conjuncture between a moment of silence and a tickling in the throat; more often than not, the larynx begins to tickle *because* there is silence.' See Poizat, *The Angel's Cry*, 89. Poizat's sentiment is echoed somewhat by a much-quoted line of Žižek: 'The true object voice is mute, "stuck in the throat," and what effectively reverberates is the void [...] "Why do we listen to music?": in order to avoid the horror of the encounter of the voice qua object. See, Žižek, "I Hear You with My Eyes", 93.

[69] Jacques Lacan, *The Seminar of Jacques Lacan: Book VIII Transference*, Trans. Cormac Gallagher. Accessed 19 January, 2019. https://www.valas.fr/IMG/pdf/THE-SEMINAR-OF-JACQUES-LACAN-VIII_le_transfert.pdf, 54.

'Pausaniou … pausamenou'.[70] He then asks 'Why would he have had a hiccup if there were no reason for it? I had no idea why he had a hiccup, but all the same encouraged by this little push.'[71] The answer Lacan suggests is that both Plato, voiced through Aristophanes, and Aristophanes are laughing at Pausanias. Lacan's evidence for this is that in the following sixteen lines Aristophanes repeats the word stop, or pause, a series of homophonies and isologies: 'eternally repeated *paus*'.[72] Dolar writes that Lacan:

> spoke in such a way that ultimately the entire interpretation depends on understanding this unintelligible voice, for which one can only propose the formula: *it means that it means.* This involuntary voice rising from the body's entrails can be read as Plato's version of mana: the condensation of a senseless sound and the elusive highest meaning, something which can ultimately decide the sense of the whole. This precultural, non-cultural voice can be seen as the zero-point of signification, the incidence of meaning, itself not meaning anything, the point around which other—meaningful—voices can be ordered, as if the hiccups stood at the very focus of the structure. The voice presents a short circuit between nature and culture, between physiology and structure; its vulgar nature is mysteriously transubstantiated into meaning *tout court.*

This is not the only instance of the sounds and noises of the body's entrails condensing into meaning. Catherine Millot, in *Life with Lacan*, tells of her visits to *La Vivarois* restaurant with Lacan. The chef, Peyrot, often came over their table to talk with her and Lacan. 'He always came over to chat with us, or rather with me, as chatter was not Lacan's forte.'[73] She writes of Lacan scribbling Borromean knots on a sheet of paper throughout dinner and responding to her questions with 'a yes or a no'.[74] Millot then recounts a conversation with a manageress at another restaurant. Upon mentioning Lacan, the woman told of how Peyrot 'was

[70] Ibid., 54; ('Pausanias paused (sorry about the pun—sophistic influence)' in Griffith's translation: Plato. *Symposium and Phaedrus.* Trans. Tom Griffith (New York, USA: Alfred A Knopf/Random House, 2000), 26.

[71] Lacan, *The Seminar of Jacques Lacan: Book VIII Transference*, 54.

[72] Ibid., 55.

[73] Catherine Millot, *Life with Lacan*, Trans. Andrew Brown (Cambridge, UK: Polity Press, 2018), 44.

[74] Ibid., 44.

convinced that the farts and burps which Lacan, as a free man, did not restrain in public, were meant to signal to Peyrot the syllables of his name!'[75]

Dolar closes 'The Linguistics of the Voice' by posing the ambiguities within the tensions he has presented thus far.

> If there is no linguistics of the voice, only the linguistics of the signifier, then the very notion of a linguistics of the non-voice would seem preposterous. Obviously all the non-voices, from coughing and hiccups to babbling, screaming, laughing, and singing, are not linguistic voices; they are not phonemes, yet they are not simply outside the linguistic structure: it is as if, by their very absence of articulation (or surplus-articulation in the case of singing), they were particularly apt to embody the structure as such, the structure at its minimal; or meaning as such, beyond the discernible meaning. If they are not submitted to phonology, they nevertheless embody its zero-point: the voice aiming at meaning, although neither the one nor the other can be articulated. So the paradoxical *facet* would be that there may be no linguistics of the voice, yet the non-voice which represents the voice untamed by structure is not external to linguistics. Neither is the object voice which we are pursuing.[76]

The passage is dissatisfying on a few levels. Firstly, it reveals the chapter to be a series of 'strawman arguments'. There is, of course, nothing wrong with this format or articulation—but are the proposed aspects of 'voice' set aside too quickly? Linguistics and phonology are set up and brushed aside, as are the emissions of the body such as coughs and hiccups. It is the sonic emissions of the body that are dealt with most unconvincingly. They are quickly plunged into the realm of the signifier and summarized as 'not simply outside the linguistic structure'. Is it too bold to suggest there is a sound of the body in voice that is not in support of any linguistic or significatory structure, as Barthes does in the oft-referenced 'The Grain of the Voice' essay: 'The 'grain' is the body in the voice'?[77] Dolar's claims that one can

> easily see that there is a whole "semiotics of coughing": one coughs while preparing to speak, one uses coughing as Jakobson's phatic communication, establishing a channel for communication proper; one can use coughing as bidding for time for re-flection, or as an ironic commentary which jeopardizes the sense of the utterance[78]

[75] Ibid., 45. 'Translator's note: '*Pet*' in French is 'fart'; '*rot*' is 'burp'.
[76] Dolar, *A Voice and Nothing More*, 32.
[77] Roland Barthes, *Image-Music-Text* (London: Fontana, 1977), 188.
[78] Dolar, *A Voice and Nothing More*, 24.

Such a statement, whilst no doubt true up to a point, and a helpful lead into the question of hiccups, glosses too readily over the body. Recall the analogy Dolar draws up with *The Matrix*. The scene—where Neo awakens from the virtual reality of the Matrix in a cell of machinic amniotic fluid—is one of striking corporeality rivalling David Cronenberg's body-horror scenes from the early works in his oeuvre. But such a striking presence of the body, those white limbs scrabbling about in pink gunk, is not mentioned. Confrontation with the physicality of voice, a physicality devoid of meaning, is neglected in much the same way albeit for the loaded faecal descriptor 'excrement of the signifier' (weighted with phobic aversion) that the signifying matrix cannot quite silence.[79]

Dolar's subsuming of the sonic emissions of the body in the signifying matrix may be a further symptom of his tendency to skirt the body. The most direct address of the relation of body to voice is located in a chapter titled 'The Linguistics of the Voice', whereby coughs and hiccups are couched as signifying, whereas the chapter 'The "Physics" of the Voice' focuses on the question of the acousmatic voice, where the source body is hidden.

There are two parallels worth posing. Is Dolar's accommodation of coughs and hiccups into the matrix of meaningful significance closer to Lacan's question of the Aristophanes' hiccups in Plato's *Symposium* or Peyrot's interpretation of Lacan's emissions? The former was given good reason to suppose significance (from his philosophical mentor Alexandre Kojève).[80] Additionally, the hiccups are within a narrative, Plato is not an inert Dictaphone, the presence of hiccups in the text, and their resonance with words and names, should not be dismissed as coincidence. Peyrot's interpretation, by contrast, is less convincing: the equivalence might well be a coincidence and any significance a pareidolic narcissistic fancy.[81] Is there not a difference between Lacan's non-verbal emissions during his seminars and his emissions at dinner? Sometimes the emissions of the body are just that, in voice there is sound without significance—not every part of it can be subsumed to meaning. Does Dolar's quick turn to couch hiccups and coughing as playing a part in semiotics bears similarity to Peyrot's

[79] Ibid., 20.

[80] Kojève was an extremely influential proponent of Hegel to French intellectual life. More specifically, it was he who introduced Lacan to Hegel. See Élisabeth Roudinesco, *Jacques Lacan*. Trans. Barbara Bray (New York, USA: Colombia University Press, 1997), 99.

[81] Pareidolia: perceiving meaning in random stimuli.

fanciful claim? The former proposes significance as a strategy to avoid the question of the non-meaning sounds of the body, whereas the latter is, one cannot help but feel, a register of a chef's narcissism. Either way, perhaps they both cook up significance where it may not be?

The French historian and psychoanalyst Élisabeth Roudinesco, in her biographical works on Lacan often references his voice. In *Lacan: In Spite of Everything*, she writes of his seminars as 'long running banquets' where 'the battles of Freudianism unfolded [...] via the magic of voice'.[82] She writes that Lacan was 'possessed of a veritable passion for orality' and that he

> spoke in a voice that was soft, booming or syncopated: a mixture of Sacha Guitry for the old France style of things and of Salvador Dali for the sense of modernity. He declaimed as he ate, devouring his favourite foods—truffles, asparagus, ortolans—and beings and things alike.[83]

The confluence of voice and eating, perhaps the most explicitly bodily thing one does in public, is apposite. On the point of Lacan's 'old style' we find in the large monograph, *Jacques Lacan*, a reference to psychologist Georges Dumas, who 'left a deep impression on Lacan' during his prentice years.[84] Roudinesco quotes Claude Lévi-Strauss' vivid description of the pedagogical manner:

> He never prepared them, trusting instead to the physical spell he knew he could cast over his audience by the *mobility of his mouth*, twisted into a perpetually changing smile. And especially by his voice—at the same time husky and melodious, a real siren's voice, with strange inflections recalling not only his native Languedoc but also, even more strikingly, certain *ancient modes of the music* of spoken French. So voice and face, though appealing to two different senses, both conjured up the same rustic but incisive style, the style of the fourteenth-century humanists, the physicians and philosophers whose race he seemed to perpetuate *in body* and mind.[85]

Drawing a lineage of Lacan's vocal and verbal idiosyncrasies, as appealing as it may be, is not an avenue that furthers discussion about the body

[82] Élisabeth Roudinesco, *Lacan: In Spite of Everything*, Trans. Gregory Elliot (London, UK: Verso, 2014), 63.

[83] Ibid., 59.

[84] Ibid., 21.

[85] Ibid., 21. Emphasis added. The corporeal contagion of voice, the figure of the siren, will be explored in 'Insidious'.

in voice or voice's relationships to meaning in terms of the question of object *a*. Alice Lagaay's observations of Lacan's speeches, however, do assist in the formulation of the presupposed significance in the non-linguistic emissions of the body. In 'Between Sound and Silence: Voice in the History of Psychoanalysis', she writes that Lacan was given to 'disturbances of voice'.[86]

> Michel de Certeau, who attended Lacan's seminar, recounts how such sounds as coughing, throat clearing, mumbling, the chewing of words and sighing—in short, an array of disturbances of the voice—constantly accompanied Lacan's practice of talking or holding speeches, as if what he said was always on the brink of dissolving, of retreating or regressing, into a kind of incomprehensible physicality. And whilst being clearly audible to the assembled listeners, these "scars of phonation", which would not so much interrupt as constitute the master's speech, remained totally incomprehensible with regard to their reference or meaning. (Certeau, 2002, p. 243)[87]

Disturbances from, rather than of, might be more apt. 'Scars of phonation' implies some damage of the voicing body being wrought on the ideal of a smooth communicative flow of meaning. Lagaay's spotlight on de Certeau's comments is salient on two levels. Firstly, there is the register of corporeality, and 'incomprehensible physicality' and its resonance with 'libidinal corporeality'—the scene of Lacan's coughing, mumbling and sighing may be interpreted as an example of the problematic relationship between the signifier and the body, whereby despite an organism being put to language an excess, recalcitrant to meaning, persists—***and speaks***, albeit not words. Secondly, alluded to via italicization in the previous line, this remainder of the speaking act is assumed as harbouring a mythical significance, 'speaking' an unsaid meaning beyond the horizon of the symbolic. To phrase it another way, we could say it is the physical remainder; an incarnation of what is unsaid gets stuck in the throat.

[86] Lagaay notes: 'The pivotal role of voice in Lacan's teachings takes on a peculiarly existential dimension, however, in the light of the fact that in the final stages of his life, Lacan suffered severe aphasia. Thus, the twenty-sixth seminar of 1978–1979 remains "silent", as by then Lacan had practically lost the ability to talk at all.'

[87] Alice Lagaay, "Between Sound and Silence: Voice in the History of Psychoanalysis," *E-pisteme* Vol. 1, (2008): 57 accessed 30 July 2017. http://research.ncl.ac.uk/e-pisteme/issues/issue01/contents/e-pisteme%20Vol.%201(1)%20%20Alice%20Lagaay%20(Full%20Text).pdf.

Returning to Lacan's graph of desire II: voice runs out, after the signifying operation. Structurally it is the resultant of the signifying operation and speaking. Would Lacan have coughed, cleared his throat, mumbled and sighed were it not for the task of speaking? Take the particularly phagous phrase 'chewing of the words'. The nonsensical sound of gnawing, whilst by no means linguistic or understandable for a particular significance, is a result of having words to voice. The chewing of words is entangled with the body's articulation of meaning: it is an excess that falls short of sensible execution, a non-signifying excess of the body.[88] The phagous phrase of de Certeau also evokes a physicality that strikes significance with two preliminary drives. Firstly, the oral drive's partial object, the nipple and the object *a* of taking in nothing. Secondly, the anal drive's partial object, scybalum and object *a* giving nothing bear a notable equivalence to 'words' that are *stuck* in the throat or, as Lagaay terms it chewed, neither swallowed nor spoken.

The immediate retort is that such moments are vocal, heard, whereas object *a* voice is repeatedly iterated as silent, aphonic. When Dolar and Žižek say stuck in the throat they mean mute.[89] There is, however, a case for demurring on taking an either/or position. Lacan, in his commentary sandwiching the completed graph of desire, writes:

> The very delimitation of the 'erogenous zone' that the drive isolates from the metabolism of the function (the act of devouring concerns other organs than the mouth—ask one of Pavlov's dogs) is the result of a cut (*coupure*) expressed in the anatomical mark (*trait*) of a margin or border—lips, 'the enclosure of the teeth', the rim of the anus, the tip of the penis, the vagina, the slit formed by the eyelids, even the horn-shaped aperture of the ear (I am avoiding embryological details here). Respiratory erogeneity has been little studied, but it is obviously through the spasm that it comes into play.[90]

It is here where the completed graph is shown. Voice remains in the same position in the second iteration of the graph presented previously. Lacan's comments, however, about the delimitation of the erogenous zone and the cut, whilst not immediately helpful for understanding voice, warrant some dismantling and application. If object *a* is the remainder

[88] There is potential for an onomatopoeic reinterpretation of Lacan's great concept *nom* du père.

[89] Dolar, *A Voice and Nothing More*, 69.

[90] Jacques Lacan, *Écrits: A Selection*. Trans. and Ed. Alan Sheridan. (London: Routledge, 1989), 240.

recalcitrant to the signifying operation and—in terms of the invocatory drive that results in the excrescence of the voice—sound is the partial object, then is the cut that isolates the metabolism of invocation the delimitation between speech and sound? Sound is the arbitrary locus of the invocatory drive (like the nipple is the partial object of the oral drive)—and voice is its resultant remainder beyond the signifying matrix. Might we suppose, then, that the interruptions of voice, those physical emissions that mire the invocative flow, are object *a*?

For the affirmative it can be said that such emissions of the speaking body are heard as registering some occluded meaning and significance. The mumbles, sighs and coughs (or hiccups) are taken, as de Certeau takes them to be, as references to a meaning beyond comprehension. The peculiar sounds take up some meaning beyond meaning, stand in place as a 'zero-point: the voice aiming at meaning'.[91] Lacan's comment about the significance of respiratory erogeneity, the spasm, resonates with his reading of Aristophanes hiccups in *Symposium*. There is a certain significance of the body in each case. In support of any acoustic prospect of object *a* we might notice the oddly porous categorical sweep Lacan takes below the graph. He says, that 'the cut is no less obviously present in the object described by analytic theory: the mamilla, faeces, the phallus (imaginary object), the urinary flow. (An unthinkable list, if one adds, as I do, the phoneme, the gaze, the voice—the nothing.)' [92] Lacan's array of added object *a* run from the phoneme through to 'the nothing'; there is a tension here. A phoneme is distinct, tangible, a thing of physical traits and difference; it is the part of voice 'the signifier has seized': phonemes sound.[93] The nothing, however, is precisely that. Might the question of object *a* voice be better thought of not as necessarily silent or tangibly audible phenomena but rather a corporeal presence—sonic or not?

Aphonic Voice

A chronological note regarding Lacan's seminars from 1978, in *The Cambridge Companion to Lacan,* states that after a 'minor car accident, Lacan appears tired and is often silent for long periods of time even in his seminars, in which discourse tends to be replaced by mute demonstrations

[91] Dolar, *A Voice and Nothing More*, 32.
[92] Lacan, *Écrits: A Selection*, 241.
[93] Dolar, *A Voice and Nothing More*, 19.

of new twists on Borromean knots.'[94] Millot, in *Life with Lacan*, writes that by this time (around the time he drew a big sigh and left his dinner with Roman Polanski) he 'was becoming more and more silent.'[95] She writes that in his last seminars 'the exhibition of chains and knots increasingly took over from speech.'[96] Lagaay too highlights the existential significance voice in absentia held in Lacan's final seminars. Unlike the 'disturbances of voice,' explored in the previous section, she writes of a voice that is deafening by its absence, a voided sonority.

> The pivotal role of voice in Lacan's teachings takes on a peculiarly existential dimension, however, in the light of the fact that in the final stages of his life, Lacan suffered severe aphasia. Thus, the twenty-sixth seminar of 1978–1979 remains "silent", as by then Lacan had practically lost the ability to talk at all.[97]

The biographical placement of a silent voice in Lacan's work strikes congruity with the Slovenian's refrain of 'the object voice' being inaudible and stuck in the throat. The prospect of the 'pregnant silence', to employ the well-worn term, resonates with Vanheule's comment that echoes the structural context of voice established thus far as beyond significance: that 'irrespective of how much signifying articulation takes place, something remains unsaid. There is no final signifier that can hook up the true signification of speech.'[98] There is a case for drawing up a continuum here that admits some liminal interzone between sound, the partial object and the silent object *a* voice. Might one draw an extrapolation, from the small disturbances of voice to the long silences employed with Borromean knots to the absolute absence of Lacan, departing with a screaming—'more *Écris* than *écrits*!'—silence?[99] One way into this prospect is to consider the problem of silence. Silence is heard, but it is not sound. Here the prospect of disturbances and omissions, onomatopoeic or void, unfolds as possible points on a vector that charts the object *a*.

[94] Jean-Michel Rabaté, *The Cambridge Companion to Lacan* (Cambridge, UK: Cambridge University Press, 2003), xxvii. He crashed into a crash barrier after missing his exit with Pierre Soury. See Millot, *Life with Lacan*, 112.

[95] Millot, *Life with Lacan*, 109.

[96] Ibid., 113.

[97] Lagaay, "Between Sound and Silence: Voice in the History of Psychoanalysis", 58.

[98] Vanheule, *The Subject of Psychosis: A Lacanian Perspective*, 130–131.

[99] Lagaay, "Between Sound and Silence: Voice in the History of Psychoanalysis", 58.

Miller suggests that any question of the relationship a subject, that is of the signifier, has to object *a*, that is recalcitrant to expression and/or accommodation in the signifying matrix, presents a tension. Indeed, the question of the subject's phenomenal or experiential relationship to object *a* is fraught with structural preventatives for anecdotal elaboration. Miller suggests that the subject's relation to object *a* is regarded to be a 'matricial' antinomy.[100] He asks how there can be a relation between the

> object that is not a signifier, and a subject defined, on the contrary, as what is supposed by the structure of language, that is, as subject of the signifier? This is a matricial problem in Lacan's teaching: he toiled for many years to match up these two requirements that may seem animated by an antinomy.[101]

The voice and the gaze, the two object *a* added as super-structural additions to the Freudian drives and their 'corresponding' partial objects by Lacan, do not share the same physicality of developmental stages. Lacan was explicit in developmental stages not being accounted for in his schemes. Vanheule writes of how in elaborating his ideas on object *a* Lacan 'didn't adhere to a developmental psychological perspective'.[102] He writes of how Lacan believed 'that, in the process that gives rise to the object *a*, the dialectical transition should be studied. Speculation about associated interpersonal and developmental dynamics is deemed irrelevant.'[103] Vanheule goes on to cite Lacan's reaction to a guest lecture by Piera Aulagnier in 1962 that explored the relation to the partial object to normality, neurosis, perversion and psychosis. Vanheule writes:

> Aulagnier argued that an individual's relation to partial objects reflects a past history, which can best be framed in terms of interactional dynamics between

[100] Note the maternal genesis of the word Matricial from Old French matrice ("pregnant animal"), from Latin mātrīx ("dam, womb"), from māter ("mother"). The significance of drawing attention to the confluence of Lacan's matricial paradox in terms of the mother will be elaborated later via Tomatis' theories concerning the intrauterine voice and its implications for a psychoanalytic reading. Whereas much is said of the voice of the Father, we shall explore how the horrors of the object *a* voice can be formulated through a maternal contextualization.

[101] Jacques-Alain Miller, 'Jacques Lacan and the Voice', *The Later Lacan: An Introduction (SUNY series in Psychoanalysis and Culture)*, Voruz and Wolf, eds (Albany, New York, USA: State University of New York Press, 2007), 138.

[102] Vanheule, *The Subject of Psychosis: A Lacanian Perspective*, 127.

[103] Ibid., 127.

a child and its parents. Both in his direct comments on Aulagnier's lecture and in the later seminars, Lacan does not follow her developmental logic. Instead, he focuses on the logical status of the object and on the dialectical structure in which it can be situated, not on presumed causal mechanisms.[104]

Considering this fealty to the logic, arithmetic and topology of Lacan's scheme of dialectical transition, the Scopic/Image/Gaze and Invocative/Sound/Voice structuration might be taken as standing in contrapposto to the developmental and historical foundations of Anal/Faeces/Withholding and Oral/Nipple/Not-Taking dynamics of Freud's foundational structure (or at least regarded as a significant departure). Whereas there are resolutely physical Oral and Anal stages in development, there are no strictly delineated material scopic or invocative stages. Given this, why does Lacan place gaze and voice in the same array as object *a* that result from the Oral and Anal stages? For Miller the answer is one of necessity; regard the adjective, emphasis added, that Miller opts for to evoke the ethereal nature of voice:

What put Lacan on to this lengthening of the Freudian list with the objects voice and gaze? The answer is simple: it is clinical experience. It is not, in the case of the object voice, a meditation on the subject's monologue with himself in his solitude. It is a clinical experience in which gaze and voice manifest themselves in separate forms, clearly characterized by their exteriority with regard to the subject. (...) it is from the phenomena of mental automatism—so named since Clérambault, whom Lacan acknowledged as his only master in psychiatry—that Lacan extracted the object voice. Here one speaks of voices, although these voices are all *immaterial*—they are nevertheless perfectly real to the subject. They are even what he cannot doubt, despite the fact that nobody can record them.[105]

Notice how the placement of voice in the Lacanian schema emerges as one that is experience albeit non-phenomenal or, to phrase it another way, something that is heard that does not sound.

Bogdan Wolf, writing in *Lacanian Coordinates: From the Logic of the Signifier to the Paradoxes of Guilt*, also explores voice within the guise of the late Lacanian object *a*. It is here where the structural and experiential alterity of the unsounding voice qua object *a* is directly addressed. Wolf,

[104] Ibid., 128.
[105] Jacques-Alain Miller, 'Jacques Lacan and the Voice', 140, emphasis added.

following Miller, writes of a voice as one that may be silent and unrecordable and separate from both signifier and signified.[106] But to be clear it is not the voice of or from the Other, it *is* Other:

> Lacan does not tell us much about the voice. He mentions it twice or thrice in *Seminar XI* (1977) but we do not hear of it more than that. For Lacan the voice is an object in the economy of desire. He marked it with the letter "*a*", the object *a*, to designate its separateness and antinomy from other elements like the signifier and the signified. This is the novelty. Lacan's voice is not a substance or a materiality in the sense in which language and the unconscious are. The voice is aphonic and does not belong to the order of material sonority. (…) In psychosis the voice can be invasive and persecutory as it does not support the belief of serving as a message to/from the Other but presents itself *as* the Other. Lacanian voice in the strict sense of the voice object is therefore not the voice in speech and does not belong to speaking.[107]

Wolf's movement to silence here is pertinent. Following the early Christian theologian and philosopher Saint Augustine of Hippo's conception of voice Wolf refers to Gregorian chants. Specifically, he writes of a voice residing in the silence between the chants—there is some parity here with Lacan's own pauses and long silences.

The chants are the sonic call for the response of the Other (God, in this theological sense). For Augustine, in *Confessions*, repeatedly 'expresses a desire to listen to the voice of the Other', this voice of the Other comes from God. It is an inaudible voice of the Other that floods the silence between the chants.[108] This sentiment is analogous to Miller's closing remarks in 'Jacques Lacan and the Voice' whereby the voice is adorned with a horror: 'voice as such emerges each time the signifier breaks down, and rejoins this object in horror […] the voice inhabits language, it haunts it. It is enough to speak for the menace to emerge that what cannot be said.'[109] Wolf's explication of this object *a* voice is framed, and emerges, from the theological.

[106] Recall the previous comment concerning Adrian Lyne's *Jacob's Ladder* (1990) there is an impressive evocation of the Other's speech whereby "dream on" evokes an aural hallucination. The voice of the Other, erupting, into the protagonist's experience.

[107] Bogdan Wolf, *Lacanian Coordinates: From the Logic of the Signifier to the Paradoxes of Guilt and Desire* (London, UK: Karnac Books, 2015), 93.

[108] Ibid., 93.

[109] Jacques-Alain Miller, 'Jacques Lacan and the Voice', 145.

Do Gregorian chants confront object *a*—the horror of silence? Might the chants be regarded as a precursor to the array of methods Miller proposes 'silence' the object *a* voice? Miller writes: 'if we organize symposiums, if we chat, if we sing and listen to singers, if we play music and listen to it, Lacan's thesis implies that it is in order to silence what warrants to be called the voice as object little *a*.'[110]

Consider Lacan's following comment on voice as

> petit *a* as fallen from the Other, we can exhaust its structural function only by bringing our inquiry to bear on what the Other is as a subject, for voice is the product and object fallen from the organ of speech, and the Other is the site where "it"—ça—speaks.[111]

So far, in exploring these Lacanian threads of object *a* voice, we've moved from coughs and hiccups to silences and noted how each plays a part in how the Other speaks. The Other may not necessarily speak as a sound, but it is heard. In these turns, is there not a certain sense of horror?

Object *a* voice manifests as a vertiginous rupture, a perceived lacuna or, to embed a flourish aping the prose of the horror writer Thomas Ligotti, a tear in the fragile gauze, the veil, of the world. The silence of God's deafening voice in the space between chants is one that evokes a world beyond present materiality and sonority. The topology of a modified Klein bottle may be utilized at this juncture.[112] Contemplate a Klein bottle with a hole in the middle, so that one side is faced with its other side, no longer obfuscated by its topological structure but facing the unknown part of its own innate structure. Might we place object *a* voice in this locale, structurally integral to one side, and manifesting as experience contingent on the structure? Lacan, rather than using a Klein bottle to illustrate this concept, used the example of a darning egg.

A darning egg is a small, egg-shaped and egg-sized object, perhaps made of wood, porcelain or stone used for repairing holes in fabric. The egg can be pressed into the heel of a sock (e.g.), poking and protruding through the offending hole of wear, so that the fabric can be sewn up (upon repair covering the darning egg). Lacan, as shall be examined

[110] Ibid., 145.
[111] Lacan, *Television: A Challenge to the Psychoanalytical Establishment*, 87.
[112] They make terrible carafes, better employed for illustrating concepts.

shortly, invokes the concept of the darning egg as something that presses, stretches and protrudes through the fabric of the subject.

Before appreciating these select moments of Lacan's teaching, a particular anecdote of his does warrant consideration. Lacan, in 'On a Question Preliminary to Any Possible Treatment of Psychosis' in *Écrits: A Selection*, tells of a young woman persecuted by her neighbours; the woman had left her husband and in-laws to pursue a character her mother was disapproving of.[113] The woman had told Lacan of how, when walking down a corridor, a neighbour called after her: 'Sow!'[114] Lacan asked the woman what she had said before this event. The woman admitted muttering, perhaps not even speaking audibly, 'I've just been to the pork butcher's....'[115] Lacan postulates that this episode is indicative of the woman's yearn to be fragmented. She is a 'prisoner of the dual relationship', but this drive to be in two places at once, this torsional drive, fails to explain the bizarre consistency, the seemingly illogical, irrational, thread of import—the inexplicable consistency between the offensive remark of the neighbour and the connection it has to the inaudible comment of the subject.[116]

Is this where object *a* voice lurks? As the bump, the darning egg, pressing into and rupturing the subject. Voice here is of the Other; it manifests as disparate utterances: on the one hand the verbal hallucination of a patient suffering from fears of persecution and on the other as her 'precognition' phrase moments beforehand. The signifying chain is broken for the subject, but a voice (not the specific word 'Sow!' but a consistent voice of a suidaen, piggy, swinish, theme behind the two parts of language experienced in the hallway: on the one hand vivisection and butchery, and on the other the frank announcement of 'Sow!') protrudes through.

A crucial import, as Miller identifies, is that, for the subject, the two experienced sentiments of voice, regardless of the physics of sound waves, cannot be accommodated by the subject. In terms of the 'Sow!' anecdote we can say that a fragment of the signifying chain is broken off, broken from the subject's 'grasp'. The persecuted woman cannot cognize the theme of pigs in these two moments. Thus, the signifying sequence's

[113] Jacques Lacan, *Écrits: A Selection*. Translated and Edited by Alan Sheridan. (London: Tavistock/Routledge, 1977), 201.

[114] *Sow* meaning female pig.

[115] Lacan, *Écrits: A Selection.*, 201.

[116] Ibid., 202.

continuity is disrupted: the subject's cosy symbolic fabric is snagged and pulled as a consequence of deviated *percipiens*.[117] Voice, then, appears in the form of the Other—or, to put it alternatively, where object *a* voice 'resonates':

> In this respect, what Lacan calls *voice* is an effect of the foreclosure of the signifier that is not reducible, as the vulgate would have it, to the famous foreclosure of the Name-of-the-Father. Insofar as a piece of signifying chain—broken because of what we call for now the libidinal charge—cannot be assumed by the subject, it passes in the real and is assigned to the Other. The voice appears in its dimension of object when it is the Other's voice.[118]

But to recall the mantra echoing around this voice in terms of the graph of desire, this voice of the Other, the object *a* voice (for *autre*, as mentioned previously, means other), is resolutely the outcome of the signifying operation (a signifying operation that is not afforded within the subject). Thus, the strange limb of voice, that Dolar quips, 'does it not know that it is dead' is absolutely a post-signifying operation, for it is not harboured within the signified *percipiens* of the subject. Here, we have a striking horrific alterity, vox-exo.[119] It resounds from the void/voice of the Other: 'the voice is the part of the signifying chain that the subject cannot assume as 'I' and which is subjectively assigned to the Other.'[120]

Miller is quick to pre-empt any misreading. He asks: 'But, after all, "sow" is also a word, a signifier that produces an effect of signification that we call an insult. So are we still properly in the register of the signifier and the signified?'[121] On one level, yes—'Sow!' is, of course, a word, an avatar, a sign with a corresponding meaning behind it. But this anecdote is not about a woman who wishes to call herself a pig and cannot (and hallucinates the insult in the form of a voice of the Other). No, the sign, the word that a voice of the Other arrives cloaked in, is unimportant for psychoanalysis. What is important is how that object *a* 're-calibrates' the chain of signification (in terms of the subject's perception). The object *a*

[117] Jacques Lacan. *The Seminar of Jacques Lacan: Book XI The Four Fundamental Concepts of Psychoanalysis.* Translated by Alan Sheridan, Edited by Jacques-Alain Miller (New York, USA: W.W. Norton and Company, 1998), 258.

[118] Jacques-Alain Miller, 'Jacques Lacan and the Voice', 144.

[119] Dolar, *A Voice and Nothing More*, 35.

[120] Jacques-Alain Miller, 'Jacques Lacan and the Voice', 144.

[121] Ibid.

reveals the drive to be a fragmented body only through the juxtaposition of the butchering comment and its unaccommodated phantom 'voice' that runs out into the Other (the object *a*). Object *a* voice may arrive in the costume of signifying words, but as Miller writes: 'in words that only slightly shift those that you have so far accepted, it contains a charge of jouissance that cannot be integrated in the signifying chain. (…) In this respect, the voice comes in the place of what is properly unspeakable about the subject, what Lacan called the subject's "surplus enjoyment".'[122]

This is why object *a* voice is an ineradicable excess, as Dolar terms it, a libidinal (or jouissance) excess that cannot be assumed within the signifying realm of the subject but, instead, runs out and sounds from the void of the Other. It may echo back in the form of an arbitrary word, but it is the Other's *voice*. 'In this respect, the voice is precisely that which cannot be said,' thought, uttered, comprehended or broached by the subject whose signifying chains 'lie' in relation to an unspeakable object.[123]

By this stage we see how silence, meaning, speech and acoustics have dissolved in terms of the question of object *a* voice. Object *a* may arrive dressed in such terms, in the guise such as *percipiens* of the subject but is by no means exclusive to any, nor reducible in such modes. There is, however, one facet that persists: the body. The corporeality of the scenario is unavoidable. The 'yearn to be fragmented' in this example—that on one level rests on a dialectical transition of meaning and significance for a subject (the *percipiens* voice of the Other)—locates the body of the subject to be at stake of vivisection. Vox-exo, a horrifying alterity, 'speaks' to the body from which it sounds in.

Synthesis: Object Horror (Demon Voices)

In 'From Interpretation to the Transference' in *The Four Fundamental Concepts of Psychoanalysis* Lacan speaks of the verbal hallucination (which is what the 'Sow!' anecdote in *The Écrits* concerns) as an instance of the object *a*. Miller suggests this to be a 'confrontation' (he uses the term twice) with the work of Maurice Merleau-Ponty, in particular his focus on the phenomenological status of motor-verbal hallucinations in

[122] Ibid., 144–145.
[123] Ibid., 145.

Phenomenology of Perception.[124] Vanheule, by contrast, suggests that Lacan takes up Merleau-Ponty's work, that it was a 'crucial source of inspiration for Lacan'.[125] Vanheule draws parallels between Lacan's rejections of both intellectualist and empiricist theories of hallucinations and Merleau-Ponty's work in *Phenomenology of Perception.* After detailing Merleau-Ponty's arguments he writes that Lacan 'takes up Merleau-Ponty's critique of empiricist and intellectualist theories of hallucination'. A summary of this 'take-up', or 'confrontation', is that verbal hallucinations cannot be accommodated by either intellectualist or empiricist theory. An empiricist approach does not address how the deaf can hear voices.[126] An intellectualist approach does not address how a subject's beliefs can create erroneous percepta that the subject disbelieves and regards as hallucinations.[127] Vanheule's claims that 'Lacan rarely cited this work, but clearly borrowed from Merleau-Ponty's critique of empiricist and intellectualist theories of hallucinations' is sustained and evidenced.[128] Whether this turn in Lacan's work is more a 'borrowing' or 'take-up' rather than a 'confrontation' is not crucial to understanding object *a* voice. Let's not pursue the intricacies and parallels in Merleau-Ponty's work and Lacan's. Let us, instead, return to Lacan's 'From Interpretation to the Transference', for it is here where some likeness between Lacan's conceptualization of the object *a* and recent philosophies on the question of horror can be graphed.

Late in the talk Lacan, using his example of the darning egg, posits a psychoanalyst-as-darner metaphor:

> It is a question of the privileged object, discovered by analysis, of that object whose very reality is purely topological, of that object around which the

[124] Ibid., 140; Maurice Merleau-Ponty, *Phenomenology of Perception.* Translated by Colin Smith. (London/New York: Routledge, 2005), 389–402.

[125] Vanheule, *The Subject of Psychosis: A Lacanian Perspective,* 82.

[126] 'Lacan considered the empiricist focus on sensorial processes as simply irrelevant. According to him the sensorial quality of hallucinations simply doesn't matter. Congenitally profoundly deaf people, who by definition have never processed auditory sensorial information, can indeed experience auditory verbal hallucinations. This would not be possible if a prerequisite for verbal hallucinations is an active auditory register, which is not the case in deaf people. Lacan rules this out and concludes that the act of hearing should not be understood in terms of the sensory registers involved, but in terms of a meaning-generating process.' Ibid., 84.

[127] Ibid., 83.

[128] Ibid., 82.

drives moves, of that object that rises like a *bump*, like the wooden darning egg in the material which, in analysis, you are darning—the *objet a*.[129]

This sense of something incurring, partially protruding 'like a bump', and warping the chain—might one say the integrity?—of signification for the subject resonates with Thacker's proposal of the horror of philosophy in *In the Dust of This Planet: Horror of Philosophy Vol. 1*.[130]

On many levels the Lacanian object *a* runs close to, in its structural role and position, the enigmatic thing of horror in Thacker's text.[131] Thacker's work does not explicitly align with the lineage of psychoanalysis, nor any specificities of Lacanian thought (generally Thacker's work is couched in the shadow of pessimist and nihilist philosophies). Lacan's name does not appear in the three volumes of *Horror of Philosophy*.[132] Voice features briefly, although it is only directly addressed once, in Thacker's first chapter, his opening gambit, 'Three Quaestio on Demonology'.[133] Here, the few references Thacker makes to voice place it as the partial register, evocation and symptom of horror. As the title divulges, Thacker's focus in this chapter concerns the figure of the demon (his later writings move to questions of the environmental, ecological and cosmological). Voice haunts the examples of possession and demonological presence he provides to detail this preliminary stage of his argument.

Thacker writes: 'the only real indication we have of this multitude of demons is the enigmatic resounding of the word "Legion." In a philosophical sense, that the demons choose to present themselves via voice and sound—at once present and absent—is noteworthy.'[134] This is the only time Thacker is explicit about the significance of voice in *Horror of Philosophy*. This brief acknowledgement of the presence and significance of

[129] Jacques Lacan. *The Seminar of Jacques Lacan: Book XI The Four Fundamental Concepts of Psychoanalysis*. Translated by Alan Sheridan, Edited by Jacques-Alain Miller (New York, USA: W.W. Norton and Company, 1998), 257—emphasis added, the horror of things that go *bump* in the night.

[130] Eugene Thacker, *In the Dust of This Planet: Horror of Philosophy Vol. 1*. (Winchester, UK: Zero Books, 2011).

[131] Thacker's work has influenced, or at least overlaps thematically with others, notably Dylan Trigg and Ben Woodward.

[132] His contemporary, Georges Bataille, features heavily.

[133] Ibid., 10–48.

[134] Ibid., 28.

voice within his preliminary moves for his conceptualization of horror warrants more than a note.

Voice is not a focus in Thacker's 'Three Quaestio on Demonology' chapter, yet it cannot escape notice that the examples he cites pivot around voices and sounds. In an inverse way, one can see in Lacan's work and his later commentators that although horror is by no means a claimed focus or theme in texts that explicitly address voice, there tends to be a refrain of horror terminology and/or themes. Miller, in 'Jacques Lacan and the Voice', concludes (explicitly referencing not only the horror of voice but also the theme of hauntings) that the emergence or sounding of such an object *a* is steeped in horror. He writes: 'If there is the voice, it is due to the fact that the signifier revolves around the unspeakable object. And the voice as such emerges each time the signifier breaks down, and rejoins this object *in horror*. (...) the voice inhabits language, it haunts it.'[135] Such a comment falls into the tendency for horror, hauntings and vocabularies of Gothic and post-Gothic narratives to be employed when discussing voice in Lacan's work. We have already seen this tendency in lines from Lacan, Dolar, Žižek, Lagaay and Vanheule, amongst others.

At the beginning of *In the Dust of This Planet: Horror of Philosophy Vol. 1* Thacker outlines how horror falls within a penumbral and mysterious realm between the subjective world and the objective world. He posits that horror is a nebulous zone between the *world-for-us* and the *world-in-itself*. Thacker writes that the world-for-us 'is the world that we, as human beings, interpret and give meaning to, the world that we relate to or feel alienated from, the world that we are at once a part of and that is also separate from the human'.[136] Thacker then goes on to concisely delineate the opposite aspect, the 'phantom objectivity' of world-in-itself:

> The world-in-itself is a paradoxical concept; the moment we think it and attempt to act on it, it ceases to be the world-in-itself and becomes the world-for-us. (...) Even though there is something out there that is not the world-for-us, and even though we can name it the world-in-itself, this latter constitutes a horizon for thought, always receding just beyond the bounds of intelligibility.[137]

[135] Voruz and Wolf, eds. *The Later Lacan: An Introduction (SUNY series in Psychoanalysis and Culture)*, 145.

[136] Thacker, *In the Dust of This Planet: Horror of Philosophy Vol.* 1, 4.

[137] Ibid., 6; 5.

The horrifying and penumbral world that lies between these two poles of thought is the *world-without-us*. Thacker writes that 'the world-without-us allows us to think the world-in-itself, without getting caught up in a vicious circle of logical paradox.'[138] Thacker's horror dynamic and his exploration of a penumbral interzone between these two poles of thought are dialectical insofar as thought strives to think the unthinkable only to, at the very point of such a thought, fold back, solidify and return to be precisely that: the thinkable *world-for-us*. As soon as the *world-in-itself* is thought it ceases to be the *world-in-itself* and becomes the *world-for-us*. The Klein bottle or Mobius strip, or even a glass sphere one might hold and twist in one's hand (like M.C. Escher's famous lithograph), is an illuminating visual for such a concept. Such objects evoke the hidden, illusive or illusory that presents an epistemological wavering, oscillating or vacillating: a crisis of at-once emergence and concealment: a *shimmering*.

Thacker, in outlining the shadowy or enigmatic nature of the *world-without-us*, writes that it 'is in the very fissures, lapses, or lacunae' in the *world-for-us* and the *world-in-itself*. This is an important subtlety. The *world-without-us* is more of a paradoxical negative in the world we know. The horrifying *world-without-us* 'is, in the words of dark mysticism, the "dark intelligible abyss" that is paradoxically manifest' as both *world-for-us* and *world-in-itself*.[139] The horrifying nature of the *world-without-us* is the paradoxical incursion of the unknown into the known. It might also be thought of as an epistemological crisis: to know one does not know. It is to be confronted and confounded by unknown thought, something alien to us, at once uncanny and Otherly: something of radical alterity. For Thacker it is this unwanted confrontation, this paradoxical moment of having to think the unthinkable, that is horrific—the confrontation of a philosophical lacuna. Genre horror, for Thacker, concerns itself with horrific confrontations with the unknown, when the *world-in-itself* somehow makes itself paradoxically present, albeit liminal and speculative, in the *world-for-us*. Genre horror is not just about thrills and scares; it is also a philosophical dilemma:

> Horror is not simply about fear, but instead about the enigmatic thought of the unknown. As H.P. Lovecraft famously noted, "the oldest and strongest emotion of mankind is fear, and the oldest and strongest kind of fear is of

[138] Ibid., 5.
[139] Ibid., 8.

> the unknown." Horror is about the paradoxical thought of the unthinkable. In so far as it deals with the limit of thought encapsulated in the phrase of the world-without-us, horror is "philosophical." (…) *"horror" is a non-philosophical attempt to think about the world-without-us philosophically.* (…) genre horror (…) takes aim at the presuppositions of philosophical inquiry—that the world is always the world-for-us—and makes of those blind spots its central concern.[140]

Genre horror, then, in evoking the creeping horror that the *world-for-us* is not all there is, must somehow allude to an unknown otherness. Story craft is very much about alluding, hinting and leaving clues for something else. In horror this something else tends to have a particularly unthinkable or 'unnatural' bent. It must provide strategies and narrative that conjure up a sense of the something lurking in shadows, in the lacunae. It must imply there is something not of this *world-for-us*.

Lacan's concept of the bump: the object *a* pushing against the subject's world's integrity, causing a rupture in the gauze of the subjectivity can be paralleled, or overlaid, with Thacker's concept of the *world-in-itself*, partially rupturing into the *world-for-us*. Lacan's conception of object *a* being things that move like a bump, beneath the signifying chain, distorting, perhaps manifesting as gazes or voices of the Other (disrupting the integrity of the subjective weave) could be interpreted and thought of as shadows and echoes of the world-in-itself. Except, these manifestations, these Lacanian bumps, are not bumps of cosmological infinity or ecological catastrophe incurring into our world; they are psychological. Thacker, in the 'Clouds of Unknowing' preface claims the aim of his book 'is to explore the relationship between philosophy and horror, through this motif of the "unthinkable world"'.[141] Might such a project be repurposed for the unthinkable subject—the unthinkable us? Might Thacker's thought be applied to gaining some sensation of the shimmering horrors of the object *a* voice?

In terms of voice, then, the in-itself that intrudes and manifests as an objet petit *a* might be an aural hallucination such as 'Sow!' This voice is not the cold world-out-there that Thacker posits as the realm of empirical science (environmental catastrophe, astrological physics, xenomorphs and extremophiles: things that confound our expectations of the world and

[140] Ibid., 8–9.
[141] Ibid., 1.

what life is) but something all the more horrifying. It could be said that it is the foreign part of one's being, one's alien side piercing through the weave of subjectivity. Lacan's example of an aural hallucination (a voice such as 'Sow!') is a horrific incursion. It is the 'encounter with the filth that may support him': a remnant of our drives, an excess, a vomit of the unconscious, that returns as the Other but was nevertheless our lacuna—the blind spot of our being.[142] This encounter with an unknown part of self, voiced in the macabre ventriloquism of the Other, still lurks in the same epistemological lacuna as the edges of science that Thacker writes of in *In the Dust of This Planet: Horror of Philosophy Vol. 1*– albeit with a more psychological, cloacal, horror.[143]

The most immediate method of drawing out the structural affinity between Lacan's object *a* and the horror of Thacker's dialectic along vectors of voice and horror is by way of the figure of the demon: the voice(s) of demon(s).

In 'From Interpretation to the Transference' Lacan provides a psychoanalytic reframing of Socrates' demon's voice: 'Take Socrates (…) at every moment, there is the demonic voice. Could one maintain that the voice that guides Socrates is not Socrates himself?'[144] Lacan's interpretation of Socrates' demonic voice strikes a chord with Thacker's exploration of demons: as strange objects masquerading as supernatural and/or Other. Thacker does mention Socrates' demon (*daimonion*). He couches it in terms of agency and free will. Thacker writes that Socrates' demons

> prevent him from taking the wrong course of action, he is invoking this more elemental meaning of the demon. The Greek demon is, in a sense, very much in keeping with the classical themes of human free will and destiny vis-à-vis the will of gods.[145]

[142] Jacques Lacan, *The Seminar of Jacques Lacan: Book XI The Four Fundamental Concepts of Psychoanalysis.* Trans. Alan Sheridan, Ed. Jacques-Alain Miller (New York, USA: W.W. Norton and Company, 1998), 258.

[143] Term employed to underscore what one cannot know of oneself with a physicality that evokes the drives. Cloacal, as well as opening towards other species, is a nod to the American horror author Thomas Ligotti.

[144] Lacan, *The Seminar of Jacques Lacan: Book XI The Four Fundamental Concepts of Psychoanalysis*, 258.

[145] Thacker, *In the Dust of This Planet: Horror of Philosophy Vol. 1*, 23.

There is scant horror in Socrates' demon; it is more of a guardian, a guiding force, not 'a malevolent figure' as Thacker notes. But it is manifest as a voice, an aural hallucination, *vox-exo*. Here is a structural similarity between the Greek *daimonion* and an aural hallucination such as 'Sow!' One's drives are the conjurer of such voices, in the case of the latter it is the drive to be fragmented, butchered and distributed. Lacan's suggestion that Socrates' guiding voice is 'himself' further supports the proposition that it is, like 'Sow!', a voice resultant from the subject's drive yet manifesting qua demonic Other. Of course, the perceived nature and intent of this Other voice is vastly different. One is benevolent, whereas the other is persecutory and derogatory.

The figure of the demon in Thacker's chapter, as an avatar for the unthinkable or unknowable, accommodates less benevolent voices. He writes of Freud's 1923 article 'A Neurosis of Demonical Possession in the Seventeenth Century'. Freud's study is pitched as demonical possession being recast from a folk-theistic paradigm to a clinical, medical and psychoanalytic framework: a shift from the theistic outside to the working of the unconscious. Thacker recounts:

> Christoph Haitzmann, a young painter who, in or around 1677, sees a priest, complaining of convulsions, hallucinations, and a sense of persecution. Aside from being an artist, the priest find nothing wrong with Haitzmann—except of course that he may be in consort with the devil.[146]

Thacker then provides Freud's remark that the demon is a 'father-substitute', 'a replacement for Haitzmann's mourned loss, as well as a crisis brought about by the absence the father as a figure of authority.' He then notes that the demon, in Freud's recasting, is taken to be an 'externalized projection, and the so-called possession really a form of therapeutic purging for Haitzmann'.[147]

This turn in Thacker's work, although he spends less than a page on the matter, is as close as he strays to exploring aural hallucinations and/or object *a* voice. As Freud's text tells us, the Devil was manifested physically in Haitzmann's case; he asked him questions, prompted him and proposed pacts, whilst also appearing in striking crimson anthropic form (shown in

[146] Ibid., 24.
[147] Ibid., 24.

the artist's painting).[148] Freud's recasting of Haitzmann's demonological possession is argued by Thacker to be indicative of the shift from medieval demon to the modern demon, after the classical Socratic benevolent demon.[149] Thacker delineates his demonological chronology:

> The demon historically passes through various phases: there is the classical demon, which is elemental, and at once a help and a hindrance ("*the demon beside me…*"); there is the Medieval demon, a super-natural and intermediary being that is a tempter ("*demons surround me…*"); a modern demon, rendered both natural and scientific through psychoanalysis, and internalized within the machinations of the unconscious ("*I am a demon to myself…*").[150]

This psychoanalytical figure of a demon, qua voice of the Other, is one way into *Vox-Exo*, insofar as serving as a concept for considering the horrors of object *a* voice. The demon voices the cloacal recesses of the unconscious: voice resonates along the drive vectors one is subject to. When Thacker writes: 'the demon often inhabits the edges of the human understanding of the world,' we can think of this 'human understanding' as subjectivity, as Thacker's briefly acknowledged internalization of the unknown—the voice of the demon is resultant of the machinations of the unconscious.[151] It is a voice that sounds out this unknown being felt in the subject—the horror of the object *a*. Ergo, Freud's analysis of Haitzmann, is what Lacan might refer to as the darning the horrors object *a* present to the subject. The placement of object *a* lurks within a lacuna—in psychoanalytical terms in the dark recesses of unconscious machinations or, to parse it out in Medieval terms, in a dangerous beyond within a world one does not fathom. In each case, it remains 'by definition, a limit; it designates both that which we stand in relation to and that which remains forever inaccessible to us. This limit is the unknown, and the unknown, as genre horror reminds us, is often a source of fear or dread.'[152]

Dylan Trigg's *The Thing: A Phenomenology of Horror*, was published three years after Thacker's first Volume of *Horror of Philosophy*. This small

[148] Sigmund Freud, *Complete Works*, Ed. Ivan Smith (2010). Accessed Jan, 10, 2019. https://www.valas.fr/IMG/pdf/Freud_Complete_Works.pdf. 3997–4027.

[149] Economically, as the painter entered into a pact with Satan.

[150] Thacker, *In the Dust of This Planet: Horror of Philosophy Vol. 1*, 25.

[151] Ibid., 25.

[152] Ibid., 26–27.

book, unsurprisingly given the title, leans heavily on the work on Merleau-Ponty. *Phenomenology of Perception* is referenced many times along with other works (there are ten listed in the bibliography). Lacan also features, although he does not receive sustained commentary. Nonetheless, Chapter 4, the 'The Flesh of the Thing', opens with a quote from Lacan's *The Ethics of Psychoanalysis*: 'The existence of the void at the centre of that reality called the Thing.'[153] Lacan's line here, standing on a plinth, no doubt informed the book's title. Lacan's thought from this work is picked up again in part VIII of the Conclusion, where Trigg, impressing the centrality of the body in this phenomenology of horror, uses Lacan's line of horrendous discovery of the 'secretory glands *par excellence*, the flesh from which everything exudes, at the very heart of the mystery [...] the final revelation *you are this—You are this, which is so far from you, this which is the ultimate formlessness*.'[154] Such a line evokes the void at the centre of subjectivity with the vivid corporeality.

Voice is mentioned briefly in Trigg's *The Thing: A Phenomenology of Horror*. Like Thacker it is introduced near the beginning of the book and not revisited. Trigg opens his thesis by providing an example of an empirical paradox. He recounts how a meteor, ALH84001, was found in Antarctica. This lump of 'rock', he declares, is one of the oldest pieces of the universe. Like the statute of Memnon or the statuettes of Silenus there is a voice concealed inside such hard material permanence.[155] Trigg writes of how within its 'grey core, fossilized organisms attesting to the existence of extraterrestrial life on ancient Mars have been found'.[156] He proposes that such a discovery prompts several questions. Life, any life, on earth, we suppose at present, started 3.5 billion years ago, '1 billion years after the existence of ALH84001'.[157] After a brief exploration of the possibilities of panspermia and various confounding extremophiles found on earth in recent years he writes:

[153] Dylan Trigg, *The Thing: A Phenomenology of Horror*. (Winchester, UK: Zero Books, 2014), 103.

[154] Ibid., 138.

[155] Mladen Dolar "The Voice and the Stone: From Hegel to Beckett" *Theory@Buffalo*, Issue 12. Ed. Gorlick, N and Kerr, L.R. 2008; Adriana Cavarero, *For More Than One Voice: Toward a Philosophy of Vocal Expression*, trans. Paul A. Kottman (Stanford, California: Stanford University Press, 2005), 71.

[156] Trigg, *The Thing: A Phenomenology of Horror*, 15.

[157] Ibid., 16.

> The questions of what life is and where it can be found, therefore, risk falling into circularity, in which both questions simply reinstate what we already know about the structure of life. Can thinking breach the limits of its own history in order to contend with the alterity of the alien? Or will we remain locked in a narcissistic vision of the cosmos, in which the alien is nothing more than a doppelganger of our own memories?
>
> To phrase these thoughts in the language of psychoanalysis, we might ask: is ALH84001 an object to be understood in astro-biological terms or is it a marker of a different kind, one that reveals the traces of our unconscious long before ALH84001 was "discovered" in the Antarctica?[158]

If the matter found in ALH84001 is, indeed, life, then our parameters of thinking about life and where it can be found can plunge into a vicious circularity: where life starts and what life *is* need to be rethought. Trigg's consideration of ALH84001 then shifts into a question of voice, not only positing the 'rock' as an object that transforms our understanding of the universe and confounds established scientific thought, but also one of oppression. Such a move, whilst running analogous with a *vox-exo* conceptualization of demon voice, also echoes the oppressive nature of this voice from the Other, this voice from outside our subjectivity. Trigg's move to voice here results in a conceptualization of a lump of rock that is conceptually harmonious with the 'Sow!' example of Lacan's and Thacker's presentation of Haitzmann and other demon voices. Trigg branches into a vocabulary steeped in psychoanalysis; he references not just oppression and voice but invokes the narcissism of subjectivity.

Trigg, by way of an anomalous meteor, couches an other-worldly voice (that is ultimately one's own) to be integral to the narcissism of subjectivity: 'The cosmos is transformed into a site of oppression (…) thereby forcing a confrontation with the limits of narcissism. Out there, in the silence without a witness, there is nothing. Nothing, that is, except your *own voice*.'[159]

Although Trigg's conclusion to the passage does not dwell much further on the voice, and Trigg is not referencing Lacan here, its conceptual similarity to the object *a* is conspicuous. Trigg even, after presenting a question of the world beyond our own, asks which avenue leads to such a discovery: 'science or the unconscious?'[160] He then unpacks the question:

[158] Ibid., 19.
[159] Ibid., 20.
[160] Ibid., 20.

> to what extent does ALH84001 mark a reality anterior to human experience? With Pascal, there is nausea in the silence of the cosmos—an endless night of anxiety and insomnia, in which something opposed to the subject remains as that: a *remainder*. The intervention of ALH84001 allows Mars to speak to us. The red planet has been terraformed, not through machines but through its symbolic appropriation as a planet that speaks to the Earth by echoing the materiality of its voice back to our planet.[161]

Such a passage is, indeed, saturated with psychoanalytical concepts and terms such as anxiety, insomnia, the symbolic. There are two particular references worth holding in mind. Firstly, that Trigg opts to refer to this horrifying prospect of confounding the subject's epistemological integrity as voice resonates with the Lacanian concept of the object *a* voice, the voice of the Other. Such a parallel is plain enough. Yet the most obvious resonance is the italicized word in the middle of the passage after the thumping colon: a *remainder,* the term used a dozen or more times by Dolar in *A Voice and Nothing More*.[162]

Unknown Horrors

Dolar, as has been referenced already, in 'The "Physics" of the Voice' refers to the etymological lineage of the term 'acousmatic'. Although lengthy, and much of the text proposes points that shall not be pursued, it is worthwhile stating them in full before departure.

> Chion borrowed the word "acousmatic" from Pierre Schaeffer and his famous *Traité des objets musicaux* (published in 1966, the same year as Lacan's *Écrits*). The word has a precise technical meaning: according to Larousse, "acousmatic" describes "the noise which we hear without seeing what is causing it." And it gives its philosophical origin: "The Acousmatics were Pythagoras' disciples who, concealed by a curtain, followed his teaching for five years without being able to see him." Larousse follows Diogenes Laertius (VIII, 10): "[His pupils] were silent for the period of five years and only listened to the speeches with- out seeing Pythagoras, until they proved themselves worthy of it." The Teacher, the Master behind a curtain, proffering his teaching from there without being seen: no doubt a stroke of genius which stands at the very origin of philosophy—Pythagoras was allegedly the

[161] Ibid., 20.

[162] Dolar, *A Voice and Nothing More*, 19, 20, 36, 38, 49, 54, 55, 63, 80.

> first to describe himself as a "philosopher," and also the first to found a philosophical school. The advantage of this mechanism was obvious: the students, the followers, were confined to "their Master's voice," not distracted by his looks or quirks of behavior, by visual forms, the spectacle of presentation, the theatrical effects which always pertain to lecturing; they had to concentrate merely on the voice and the meaning emanating from it. It appears that at its origin philosophy depends on a theatrical coup de force: there is the simple minimal device which defines the theatre, the curtain which serves as a screen, but a curtain not to be raised, not for many years—philosophy appears as the art of an actor behind the curtain.[163]

This passage, whilst touching upon Schaeffer's reanimation of the term and acknowledging Chion's film theory uptake of the concept (which focused more precisely on the question of an acousmatic voice), makes a few moves. Such moves by Dolar have already been alluded to. Nonetheless, it is worth taking stock of them here because it is precisely these moves that will *not* be taken. Dolar's invocation of acousmatic is a method of flight from the body, whereas in this book the prospect of an acousmatic voice will serve as a return to the body, in particular to the foetal or infant body. True to the book's title, *A Voice and Nothing More*, Dolar immediately takes the question of the acousmatic as the body being unseen. A question of audition that does not address the body. But which body? Surely, the body that does not see the voicer's body warrants some attention? This is one turn of sleight of hand in the passage: to take as a given the prospect of the acousmatic voice as one of no bodies, when in fact, it cannot be denied, it concerns two—one present, the other sensible.

The magician then provides a veiled admittance. To conceal and hide the body, to speak from behind a curtain is praised as 'a stroke of genius' worked at the inception of philosophy. Detractors of Lacan (particularly those who reduce this thought to opacity and mysticism) might smirk knowingly here and mistake such a comment as satisfying validation: that a notable disciple of Lacan considers philosophy to be at root a job of obfuscation. Yet the closing line is ambiguous: not only is there the seemingly tenuous insistence that philosophy 'appears' but additionally that it only does so as an actor. 'I'm going to tell you a lie, but I don't believe it myself!' is a possible import.[164]

[163] Dolar, *A Voice and Nothing More*, 61.

[164] To give credit, for one cannot always tell the whole story.

There is a confession embedded: the line detailing the advantage of speaking from behind a curtain. It is posited that a concealed body does not *distract*: idiosyncrasies, ticks or habits of the labour of speaking would not detract from the pure voice of reason, from the words carried in sonority. The scene of the corpus, once veiled, is no longer liable to distract, nor detract, from argument. Might such a passage be taken as a veiled declaration that 'no body's going to get in the way of my argument'?

Let's pursue a different tangent and return to the body, both the body that hears and the question of a body in an acousmatic voice. If one hears a voice but cannot see the body, then 'what body does such a voice come from?' Such a question confronts a lack of knowledge—an epistemological lacuna. On some level the acousmatic always refers to a philosophical horror; it confounds the listener with a disjunct between sense and world.

The British musician, author and professor of audio culture and improvisation David Toop, in the introduction to his book *Sinister Resonance: The Mediumship of the Listener*, confronts precisely this question.[165] Toop asks: 'Am I hearing things? Is anybody there? I began a new phase by asking such hypothetical questions.' [166] Toop immediately connects such questions to emotions of terror, fear and horror. He also wraps the emotive question up with experiences from infancy: 'Why, for example, are the frequent modalities of sound—from silence to noise—associated so frequently with disquiet, uncertainty and fear, with childhood terrors and *a horror of the unknown*.'[167]

Toop moves through horrors of the unknown in his preliminary questions. To begin, Toop confronts the ontological and phenomenological horror of doubting one's senses; he asks if the sound is real or a figment of his imagination: *Am I hearing things*? This question is then quickly met with another question, but rather than emerging from self-doubt and a distrust of sensory faculties, it is epistemological in essence: *Is anybody there*? What is there? What is making that sound? In each turn horror weighs heavy—for either by psychological, introspective doubt or outward listening there is a confrontation with the unknown. There is a parallel with Thacker's conception of horror and the structural location of the object *a*. Toop, in asking such questions of the sounds he hears and

[165] David Toop, *Sinister Resonance: The Mediumship of the Listener* (London, UK/New York, USA: Continuum, 2010).

[166] Ibid., x.

[167] Ibid., x, emphasis added.

confessing the doubts and horrors they bring, is articulating an experience not dissimilar in description nor structure of a subject confronted with the horrors of object *a*.

Part of the horror evoked by acousmatic voice emerges from the experience of asking what sounds mean. We have all come from a world without meaningful sounds to a world where every sound has a cause. Our early uterine experience is filled with sounds that have no cause; we inhabit (one likes to think) a blissfully simple sonic world, listening but not fearing a cause or source. Foeti are not versed in the visible or tactile correlates of sound. However, upon birth we are plunged into a kaleidoscopic world of vision, sound, touch and smell—it is here we learn that things, tactile, visible, aromatic things, make sounds. Small children spend a lot of time banging these things, fascinated by the sounds that these new sources can make. Toop touches on just this point: 'Four and a half months after conception we begin to hear. This is the first of our senses to function: hearing dominates amniotic life and yet after birth its importance is overtaken by seeing.'[168] It is this passage, from a sonic world of causeless sound to a world of multiple senses where sound now has causes, consequences, sources and origins, that Toop highlights as being key for Walter Murch, the revolutionary sound designer for films such as *The Conversation, THX-1138, American Graffiti* and *Apocalypse Now*. Murch wrote of this paradox of hearing, how all-encompassing audition comes to be overtaken by the other senses shortly after birth.

> 'The reasons, no doubt, go far back into our evolutionary past,' he wrote in an essay called 'Sound Design: The Dancing Shadow', 'but I suspect it has something to do with the child's discovery of causality. Sound, which had been absolute and causeless in the womb, becomes something understood to happen as a result of. The enjoyment a child takes in banging things together is the enjoyment of this discovery: first there is no sound, and then—bang!—there is.' If Murch is right, then sound without apparent source will always return us at some unconscious level to our pre-birth state, but with added anxiety and awareness, of knowing that sounds should have a cause. It they lack a cause, then our need is to invent one.[169]

Toop then traces this anxiety of sound back to our early beginnings in a cacophonous uterine world of causeless sounds and draws attention to

[168] Ibid., ix.
[169] Ibid., ix.

Freud's closing comments in 'The Uncanny': 'As for silence, solitude and darkness, all we can say is that these are factors connected with infantile anxiety, something that most of us never wholly overcome.'[170] Toop states that:

> Freud's description of the uncanny as eerie or frightening, the unhomely sensations arising from that which is unfamiliar and uncertain, particularly when they are once familiar feelings that have become secret or repressed, extended to the uncanny nature of silence and darkness. Inconclusively [...] he attributed this to infantile anxieties that none of us fully overcome. Such fears may be childish, but they are rooted in very deep memories of unknown sounds and eerie silences overheard in the dark. Perhaps this returns us again to the womb, floating in the darkness, eavesdropping on mysterious sounds from the unknown world outside. These anxieties are not easily overcome, so when a writer or director needs to evoke atmospheres, administer shocks or summon the uncanny, sound is powerful in its capacity to disturb, to unsettle and install dread.[171]

The acousmatic, the bump in the night and its concomitant horrors, is a philosophical flashback (or *knockback*) to an at once familiar and strange experience—a sonic déjà vu. The epistemological status of acousmatic sound is foreign to the adult yet also familiar from experience in utero and infancy. It is a time machine back to a stage when everything was acousmatic; sounds had 'no causes'. Acousmatic sound is uncanny on two levels. Firstly, 'we never wholly overcome the acousmatic experience.' We do still hear acousmatic voices and sounds—most of which we have yoked to familiarity, rubbish bins clattering, foxes screeching, railway lines chinging or cars whooshing. Yet every now and then there might be a sound we cannot quite *place*. It is at such a moment that we plunged back into a visual-sonic experience akin to our pre-natal existence. Secondly, post-infancy, when we experience the acousmatic sound, we are confronted with a deficit. We hear an acousmatic sound but *should* be able to fathom its cause, its place; we should be able to see it. We, as Toop describes in his line concerning the terrors of childhood, become fearful, exposed and anxious that something sounds or speaks or grunts that we *ought to be able* to see and locate but cannot.

[170] Sigmund Freud, *The Uncanny*, Trans. David McLintock. (London, UK: Penguin Books, 2003), 159.

[171] Toop, *Sinister Resonance: The Mediumship of the Listener*, xiv.

The acousmatic—as it is experienced in adult life as horrific or eerie, or uncanny—is such because of its tie to our universal uterine experience that has since become 'secret or repressed'. Post-infancy acousmatic sound is uncanny on one level and horrific on another. In terms of the uncanny it is a return to a once familiar now repressed experiential status. In terms of horror, it is an encounter with a crisis of experiential consolidation—an epistemological chasm, a void.

Consider the initial trauma of the infant, the small body, coming from a uterine world of darkness, a world where everything was acousmatic and sounds just sounded without origin or source. The trauma of the infant is its birth, that universal step from womb to world. Perhaps, our first trauma is the initial navigation from a merely sonic world to a world of many senses, a world where sounds must be matched with and correlated to sights, touches and smells.

Otto Rank, one of Freud's students, argues the trauma of birth has fundamental significance. In *The Trauma of Birth* (1924) Rank proposes that prior to the Oedipal stage the trauma of birth (experiencing female genitalia before repression and subsequently wishing to return to the womb) is relevant for almost all future neuroses, phobias and sexual proclivities in both genders. [172] Understandably, Freud distanced himself from Rank's work. Rank's 'all roads lead back to trauma of birth' and how 'all behaviors are essentially returns to the womb' logics usurp the significance of Freud's Oedipal stage. Rank's thought is, perhaps in retrospect, a touch unsubtle and overambitious in its universal application of the birth trauma. Nonetheless, consideration of his theory is a useful way to articulate the relation between experiencing acousmatic sound and horror.

In the preface Rank writes that 'we are led to recognize in the birth trauma the ultimate biological basis of the psychical.'[173] Rank's position vacillates between arguing that he builds on Freud's work to arguing for the (contra-Freud) universal centrality of the birth trauma. In seeking to establish a biological foundation of the unconscious Rank, perhaps because of the original and universal nature of birth, often slips into suggesting that the birth trauma is the biological basis of *the* unconscious. This slip is evidenced in the following passage:

[172] Otto Rank, *The Trauma of Birth* (Connecticut, USA: Martino Publishing, 2010).
[173] Ibid., xiii.

> If it has thus become possible to give a biological basis to the Unconscious, that is, to the psychical proper, discovered and investigated by Freud, then a second purpose of this work is to arrange synthetically, in its wide connection with the mechanics of the Unconscious thus founded, the *whole psychical development* of man as shown from the analytically recognized importance of the birth trauma and in the continuing attempts to overcome it.[174]

> *The analysis finally turns out to be a belated accomplishment of the incompleted mastery of the birth trauma.* [Rank's emphasis] [...] it is possible, however, that I may be driving back the Ego of the patient to earlier and yet earlier libido positions, so that finally it would not be surprising if, in the *terminal stage of analysis*, the *last flight of libido* were to the intrauterine stage. One might even hold that this would be the *final result* in the case of very prolonged analyses.[175]

Throughout *The Trauma of Birth* Rank seeks to establish his thesis (the significance of the birth trauma) with the architectures of Freud that focus on later traumas (such as the castration complex, penis envy). At each turn, Rank suggests the birth trauma is more primary than the subsequent complexes he seeks to prefix the birth trauma to. Rank's thesis is by no means incompatible with Freud.[176] Nor is it the sole key to Freud's observations and structures.

In the opening pages of 'Infantile Anxiety' Rank describes how the birth trauma is evoked by the infant's bed. When children are left alone in a dark room—such as their bedroom at night—they are returned to the sensorial context of the womb albeit 'with the important difference that the child is now consciously separated from the mother, whose womb is only "symbolically" replaced by the dark room or warm bed'.[177] Rank then suggests anxieties concerning closed spaces and/or darkness are manifestations of anxiety from birth.[178] An import to impress is that the context of acousmatic voices—the dark room—is steeped in histories of corporeal trauma.

[174] Ibid., xiv, emphasis added.

[175] Ibid., 5, emphasis added.

[176] It could be argued that the trauma of birth is merely a part of a continuum that spans from before and after both birth and death—but this is a concept for another time.

[177] Ibid., 11–12.

[178] A fear of darkness or claustrophobia being a conscious level manifestation of unconscious anxiety for traumatic birth: 'not again!'

At the same time, the yearn to return to the womb is manifested via partial and symbolic avatars (this extends through all modes of intellect and pleasure, according to Rank). Note the perhaps too broad a brush stroke in the following: 'it is easy to realize *how every infantile utterance of anxiety or fear is really a partial disposal of the birth anxiety.* [...] just as the anxiety at birth forms the basis of every anxiety or fear, so *every pleasure has as its aim the re-establishment of the intrauterine primal pleasure.*'[179] One might hesitate to echo the sentiment that *every* articulation of fear or anxiety is related to birth trauma. Let's be optimistic! There is a lifetime's opportunity for new traumatizing experiences. Likewise, to suggest that *every* pleasure is connected to returning to an intrauterine pleasure negates the plethora of pleasures the changing body navigates once born. Rank's proposal, however, is significant for the following question. What significance does the acousmatic voice hold in terms of trauma? Particularly in terms of the passage from a world of absolute acousmatic experience to one of occasional acousmatic experience amidst a kaleidoscope of other senses?

Rank writes of the popular children's game 'Hide and Seek', the game where children hide in enclosed, concealed and often dark spaces, whilst a chosen seeker strives to locate and uncover them. Such games, Rank proposes, serve more than mere distraction and folly.[180] He argues that games such as 'Hide and Seek', and other uncovering-covering-based games, are symptomatic of the birth trauma. He likens the games to neurotic symptoms, albeit with pleasurable outcomes for the child. In the following passage Rank explains how the mastery of the horrors and traumas of birth in the safe 'unreality' of symbolic play are not only cathartic but pleasurable too:

> It should be noticed, moreover, that every playful use of the tragic primal motive, which occurs with the consciousness of unreality, works in a pleasurable way in that it advantageously denies the reality of any trauma. Examples of this are the typical children's *games* from earliest "hiding" (hide-and-seek) to the games from of swinging, trains, dolls and doctor, which, moreover, as Freud very soon recognized, contain the same elements as the corresponding neurotic symptoms, only with positive pleasurable signs. The game of hiding (also conjuring), which children tirelessly repeat, represents

[179] Ibid., 17, original emphasis.

[180] Why does the act of hiding in 'Hide and Seek' always elicit giggles? The voice erupting as a give-away?

> the situation of separation (and of finding again) as not of a serious kind; the rhythmic games of movement (swinging, hopping, etc) simply repeat the rhythm felt in the embryonic state. This rhythm shows, in the neurotic symptom of dizziness, the other side of the Janus head. Soon the child's every game will somehow be subordinated to the viewpoint of its unreality. And Psychoanalysis has been able to show how, from the child's game, the higher and the highest pleasure-giving unrealities, namely phantasy and art, emerge. Even in the highest forms of the Greek tragedies, we are in a position to *enjoy anxiety* and *horror* because we abreact these primal affects, in the meaning of Aristotle's catharsis, just as the child now works off the separation from the mother, originally full of dread, in its game of willing concealment, which can easily and often be broken off and repeated at the child's pleasure.[181]

The initial trauma of birth, following Rank, is overcome by revisiting the trauma repeatedly, playing it out, re-living it through the symbolic, and such a cathartic repetition also affords pleasure. It is here where Rank's thesis of 1924 displays greatest fidelity to Freud's famous essay of 1920: *Beyond the Pleasure Principle.* In terms of Rank's structuration there is the body, subjected to trauma (the passage from an acousmatic world to a poly-sensory world), which is then *played out* as catharsis: games that pivot on seen and unseen modalities. In terms of Freud, as shall be detailed, we have catharses pitched as symbolic mastery—notably, the mastery in this case is executed via voice and language, as well as the seen and unseen.

Rank's notion of hiding and seeking being a catharsis of an unconscious trauma (the birth trauma) through repetitious and symbolic play is strikingly analogous to Freud's famous case of his grandson Ernst cited in *Beyond the Pleasure Principle.* In *Beyond the Pleasure Principle* Freud recounts the time he stayed with a mother and child in their home for a few weeks.[182] During this time Freud became puzzled by a game Ernst used to play. Ernst was essentially a well-behaved child who had, at eighteen months, not yet acquired language. Nonetheless, he knew which rooms and objects were off limits and could make himself understood using arbitrary noises to his mother and the maidservant.[183] The infant was accepting of his mother's disappearance and return and accepted her com-

[181] Ibid., 22–23, original emphasis.

[182] Sigmund Freud, *Beyond the Pleasure Principle* (Connecticut, USA: Martino Publishing, 2009), 11.

[183] Ibid., 11.

ings and goings without protest: 'above all he never cried when his mother went out and left him for hours.'[184]

Freud observed how the child 'evinced the troublesome habit of flinging into the corner of the room or under the bed all the little things he could lay his hands on, so that to gather up his toys was no light task.'[185] The boy would make a sound, 'an expression of interest and gratification'[186] (o-o-o-oh) that his mother understood to mean go away (*fort*). Freud comments that the child was using his toys and flinging them out of sight to 'play 'being gone' (*fortsein*) with them'.[187] Freud recounts the scene of the child 'playing' with the spool of thread:

> The child had a wooden reel with a piece of string wound round it. It never occurred to him, for example, to drag this after him on the floor and so to play horse and cart with it, but he kept throwing it with considerable skill, held by the string, over the side of his little draped cot, so that the reel disappeared into it, then said his significant 'o-o-o-oh' and drew the reel by the string out of the cot again, greeting its reappearance with a joyful '*Da*' (there). This was therefor the complete game, disappearance and return, [...] the greater pleasure unquestionably attached to the second act.[188]

For Freud this is the infant's mastery and playing out of his abandonment by his mother. On one level the child accepted his mother's frequent comings and goings. But on another level trauma lurked. Mastery, the playing out, of the trauma in the symbolic thus afforded great pleasure: o-o-o-oh. Freud writes how the

> meaning of the game was then not far to seek. It was connected with the child's remarkable cultural achievement—the forgoing of the satisfaction of an instinct—as the result of which he could let his mother go away without making any fuss. He made it right with himself, so to speak, by dramatizing the same disappearance and return with the objects he had at hand.[189]

[184] Ibid., 12.
[185] Ibid., 12.
[186] Ibid., 12.
[187] Ibid., 12.
[188] Ibid., 12–13.
[189] Ibid., 13.

Freud then goes on to ask how this accords to the pleasure principle: where is the pleasure for little Hans repeatedly re-enacting the traumatic disappearance of the mother who raised and nourished him?

The key thesis of *Beyond the Pleasure Principle* is that pleasure is not the main driver of our actions—there are other forces at play that do not necessarily lead to pleasure. Another question one could ask is why is pleasure yoked so tightly to a re-enactment of the opposite of pleasure (pain of separation, trauma, anxiety etc.). What benefit does re-enactment of a traumatic event hold for organisms that, supposedly, pursue pleasure? In the case of Ernst in *Beyond the Pleasure Principle*, the drive that overrides the organism's seeking of pleasure is the 'power' instinct:

> [Ernst] was in the first place passive, was overtaken by the experience, but now brings himself in as playing an active part, by repeating the experience as a game in spite of its unpleasing nature. This effort might be ascribed to the impulse to obtain mastery of a situation (the 'power' instinct, which remains independent of the question of the whether the recollection was a pleasant on or not.[190]

It is no great leap to synthesize Freud's reading of Ernst's Fort-Da game with Rank's sentiments concerning hide and seek. Such a synthesis, indeed its possibility, ought to be read qua register and demonstration of Rank's debt to Freud and his operation within a resolutely Freudian schema.

The trauma of moving from acousmatic womb to the multisensory world, the trauma of consolidating visual and tactile sources for sounds, is akin to the departure of the mother in Freud's great essay. A consistency across both contexts is the organism's departure from the mother's body. Rank's example is the departure from the womb at birth. Freud's case concerns a departure from the breast. In each case a small body is distanced from body that is the source of pleasure and nourishment. Hide and seek and Ernst's spool play can be framed as part of a continuum of cathartic symbolic plays that impose mastery over a traumatic orphaning from the body of the mother providing pleasure and nourishment.

Behaviours displayed in the shift from acousmatic to a multisensory world can be interpreted in a similar manner. The body's emersion into a world where sounds have causes, textures and visual correlates, is re-enacted with drums, xylophones or other toys. By banging a drum

[190] Ibid., 14.

children bring themselves into playing an active part in the new world of sounds that have tactile and visual causes. By exploring the causality of sound, banishing the acousmatic, discovering the sound source, children master their trauma and new station in the multisensory world. As small children bang drums their eyes track the sound to its source. Such an exercise affords the pleasure and gleeful fascination of mastery.

Every now and then, as Toop elucidates so well, an acousmatic sound presents itself, and we must return to the sonic-to-cause 'fort-da!' exercise ourselves. One might begin asking: Am I hearing things? Is anybody there? What is there? What is making that sound? Such questions, the fossils of a body's experience, are imbued with the prospect of the unknown—horror. This quick excursion through the work of Rank and Freud by no means addresses every import of the texts. But it has demonstrated a response to Dolar's pitch of the acousmatic question. The question of the acousmatic, when broached with recourse to psychoanalysis' foundational texts, is not a question of no body, but rather a question of jettisoned bodies, lost bodies, needing bodies, bodies subjected to trauma and horrors.

Freud's Vacuum

Freud's first paper was titled *On Aphasia* (1891). On a biographical level the paper's title may be read as ominous prophesy, an eerie spectre of his loss of the ability to speak, due to mouth cancer. This first paper concerns the loss of speech, but it is not a lack of speech that is notable in Freud's work; it is a lack of voice. Freud neglected voice, and privileged speech and language. One might say he heard the words but was deaf to voice.

Perhaps deaf is not the perfect adjective. Dolar, in 'Freud's Voices', notes that Freud proclaimed to be 'recalcitrant to music'.[191] In the same passage he presents a note by Freud explaining how he could not enjoy music because he could not 'understand' music. Yet, as Dolar notes, and even a light skim through biographical texts show, Freud was an opera fan.[192] His writings are peppered with references to opera and song; he would hum his favourite Don Giovanni arias to his dog.[193] Dolar

[191] Dolar, *A Voice and Nothing More*, 128.

[192] As one suspects Dolar to be too. His previous book in English is *Opera's Second Death*.

[193] Ibid., 128. Voice alone—semantic articulation omitted in favour of a vague vibratory melodic impression.

speculates that Freud's overt references to not understanding nor enjoying music might be a denegation. He asks: 'Doth he protest too much?'[194]

Dolar presents a passage from 'The Moses of Michaelangelo' (1914), where Freud writes that arts such as literature and sculpture do 'exercise a powerful effect' on him. Such an effect is, Freud claims, concomitant with contemplation and understanding. For Freud, the powerful effect occurs 'when I have been contemplating such things, to spend a long time before them trying to apprehend them in my own way, i.e., to explain to myself what their effect is due to.'[195] For Freud, conscious understanding, reasoning and appreciation are prerequisites for pleasure, it seems. In the following line, Freud's reasoning is that music does not afford pleasure precisely because it cannot be sufficiently analysed. He writes that whenever he cannot explain to himself what the effect is due to 'as for instance in music, I am almost incapable of obtaining any pleasure. Some rationalistic, or perhaps analytic, turn of mind in me rebels against being moved by a thing without knowing why I am thus affected and what it is that affects me' (PFL 14, p. 253).[196]

Dolar asks if there is not an 'anguish, or even panic, in front of something which threatens to enthrall him, flood him, make him lose his analytic stance and distance?'[197] Aversion can certainly be an interpretation of the phrase 'rebels against being moved'. Dolar's observation is that there is a paradox in this quotation from Freud: 'he is susceptible to literature and sculpture, but he can maintain his distance and analyze how they work; while music does not touch him, but also does not allow for a distance—should he surrender to its charm, it would engulf him like a black hole.'[198] It is peculiar the insistence that the experience a powerful and pleasurable effect is concomitant on understanding. Especially in terms of musical appreciation, can't the opposite be true? Isn't one enthralled by what one doesn't understand, thing that might be described as '*wonder*ful'?

Despite the origin of Freud's peculiar stance on understanding and enjoying music, Dolar then moves to suggest that Freud's deafness to the aesthetics of music, his refusal and/or inability to hear music as an object of veneration, allows Freud to listen to voices in a different register to the

[194] Ibid., 128.
[195] Ibid., 128.
[196] Ibid., 128.
[197] Ibid., 128–129.
[198] Ibid., 129.

Italian solider. He is deaf, 'immune' to the aesthetics of voice, the seductive Sirens' song.[199] Dolar writes that Freud's 'immunity to its aesthetics and its seductive Sirens' song has its counterpart in a great susceptibility for listening to voices in another register, and for hearing the voice precisely where the friend of the Italian opera is hearing-impaired.'[200] We can take this sentiment of Dolar's in terms of the binary he set up at the beginning of the book: meaning and aesthetics. If Freud is recalcitrant to musical affect, then perhaps he has a rationalistic, knowledge seeking, analytical ear? But this is not Dolar's take.

Dolar speculates how—and notes the embedded caveat of reticence—coming to 'terms with the voice *may* lie at the bottom of the basic insights of psychoanalysis'.[201] Dolar posits that voice is a discriminating factor. To begin, the 'voice' of the unconscious is described in textual terms—voice is presupposed as metaphysical, not acoustic or bodily. Dolar then moves to the question of drives and suggests 'their remarkable feature is that they are silent, stumm, mute, says Freud.'[202] Finally, Dolar arrives at the physical aperture, the mouth 'eating or speaking, that Deleuze dwelled on 'insistently'.[203] Notice, how even in this brief concession to the body, the word choice immediately muffles any sonority—if not chewing, then it must be articulating meaningful sounds. So, the import from the text goes.

Dolar's chapter is divided into three of Freud's voices: 'The voice as an excess, the voice as a reverberation, and the voice as silence.'[204] The excess concerns the click, an aural hallucination of a woman with persecution anxieties and a fear of being photographed whilst conducing an affair. The click is interpreted by Freud as a knock or beat of the clitoris; the case resonates with the scene of Nathaniel's love in E.T.A. Hoffmann's *Der Sandmann* that Dolar explores in 'At First Sight': man's view of woman as a mechanistic and logical automaton. Dolar comments: 'Freud rather enacts the role assigned to him by the feminist critique—the role of someone who imposes his own male fantasies about feminine sexuality on the hapless woman, so that he may be unwittingly providing an answer to another question, namely, "What makes men tick?" '[205] Dolar's treatment

[199] Ibid., 129.
[200] Ibid., 129.
[201] Ibid., 129, emphasis added.
[202] Ibid., 130.
[203] Ibid., 130.
[204] Ibid., 129.
[205] Ibid., 132.

of the click raises two questions. The click is couched as an accidental *noise* that is a marker of an excess not accommodated by language for the subject. Dolar, after detailing the significance of infants overhearing parental intercourse and fearing their own accidental noises might give them away, suggests that:

> The situation of the patient would thus be a displaced reenactment of a paradigmatic fantasy which is constructed entirely around the kernel of the voice, the grain of an inexplicable noise, a mysterious sound, which can appear even with the tiniest click. At the origin of fantasy there is a traumatic kernel materialized by the voice, the noise—we should allow full latitude here to a sonority not pertaining to language.[206]

Yet, is accidental noise voice? Is a rumbling stomach, a cracking ankle, a sneeze or cough voice? Secondly, is the onomatopoeia *click* that Dolar plumps for to indicate a 'full latitude to a sonority not pertaining to language' plausible? To re-phrase, is there any other onomatopoeic term that mimics absolute minimalism of sonorous content with the same brevity and neat concision as *click*? Click is a very unnoisy, very neat, very polite choice.

The sub-section '*Lalangue*', corresponding to the sign-posted 'voice as reverberation', commences in a similarly problematic methodology. The acoustic nature of voice is lost in din or words: Dolar's unfurling of 'the voice in the formations of the unconscious' takes up the Freudian impress of the significance of slips of the tongue—homonymy. To hear words, as sounding like other words, although it takes some listening to the voice to hear these doppelgängers returns voice to a servant of meaning (albeit plural meanings of interpretation).[207] Dolar's opting to explore the 'raw material' of words, their unconscious processes treated as 'sonic objects', their particular 'sonority, resonance, echoes, consonances, reverberations, contaminations' seemingly testifies to a confrontation with the acoustic. But it is ultimately an elliptical return to word that affords scant time to the acoustic component of voice other than its role in delivering meanings for the listener. Dolar strafes from any sustained address of the acoustic and corporeal facets of voice to pursue at length words and meanings.

[206] Ibid., 133.
[207] Ibid., 148.

This slippage is embedded within one of the most provoking insights of the book. Dolar, after examining by way of Jakobson and Lewis Carroll, writes of how the necessary sonic carrier of speech unavoidably results in an excess: 'irrelevant surplus' sounds, a 'frivolous addition [...] like a bodily parasite on a bodiless creature.'[208] Dolar then moves to make a distinction between hearing and listening:

> It is here that we can draw a provisional demarcation line between hearing and listening, and between meaning and sense. To be brief: hearing is after meaning, the signification which can be linguistically spelled out; *listening is, rather, being on the lookout for sense, something that announces itself in the voice beyond meaning*. We could say that hearing is entwined with understanding—hence the French double meaning (*double entendre!*) of *entendre, entendement*, being both hearing and understanding, intellect—that is, reducing the heard to the meaningful, reducing the audible to the intelligible; while listening implies an opening toward a sense which is undecidable, precarious, elusive, and which sticks to the voice. Sense [...] also alludes to the other use of sense: that of the five senses, of the sensual (to say nothing of the sensitive and the sensible). The equivoque of sense and sense (the sense of hearing) is, I suppose, structural; it is already encapsulated in the "sound and sense" formula, which could also be read as "sense and sense".[209]

It is here where Dolar's lapse back to meaning and the signifier is evinced. Listening is to look (the ocularcentrism of the phrase not to go unnoticed) *for* sense, for something that makes sense, beyond meaning.

John Mowitt, in chapter one, 'Facing the Radio', of *Radio: Essays in Bad Reception*, writes, reflecting his book's title, that Dolar's book 'avoids wrestling with precisely the acoustic character of the voice within which the voice as object is said to resonate'.[210] Mowitt's case for this claim is that Dolar's

> effortless gliding from voice to music, a gliding rendered in an arresting formulation late in the text: "What Freud and Kafka have in common ... is their claim that they are both completely unmusical—which made them particularly susceptible to the dimension of the voice"[211]

208 Ibid., 147.

209 Ibid., 148, emphasis added.

210 John Mowitt, *Radio: Essays in Bad Reception* (Berkeley, California, USA: University of California Press, 2011), 26–27.

211 Ibid., 27.

Mowitt's criticism here is that rather than face the voice, Dolar instead recedes into music—the aesthetic veneration he (Dolar) claims obfuscates the 'object voice'. Mowitt suggests that Dolar's logic here is one of inverse proportion—'The less you know about the music, the more you clearly don't know you know about the voice, and vice versa.'[212] Mowitt's highlight of Dolar's tendency to recede into the music that obfuscates voice to expedite a flight from (or circumvent any appraisal of) the acoustic character of the void voice resonates from is the counterpoint to the symptoms of Dolar's examination of Freud presented here. Presented here is the evidence file for Dolar's reticence to tackle this acoustic character manifesting as recourse to hearing meanings, words and semantics. Dolar's preliminary claim, articulated via the joke about Italian soldiers, is that there is a voice for meaning, the command obfuscates the voice, and the voice of beauty, a fetish object:

> I will try to argue that apart from those two widespread uses of the voice—the voice as the vehicle of meaning; the voice as the source of aesthetic admiration—there is a third level: an object voice which does not go up in smoke in the conveyance of meaning, and does not solidify in an object of fetish reverence, but an object which functions as a blind spot in the call and as a disturbance of aesthetic appreciation. One shows fidelity to the first by running to attack; one shows fidelity to the second by running to the opera. As for fidelity to the third, one has to turn to psychoanalysis. Army, opera, psychoanalysis?[213]

Upon proceeding to psychoanalysis Dolar is either hearing (or being on the *lookout*) for sense that might mean something and heeding the commands of meaning like a good soldier *or* fetishizing the aesthetics of the voice like the opera-loving Italian soldiers. 'Freud's Voices' is a particular example of this methodological limbo. The text is initiated by querying Freud's 'recalcitrance to music', a lack of fidelity to voice as a fetishistic object of reverence, but no sooner than such an idiosyncrasy been established, the course of arguing for voice is articulated via a sustained fidelity to meaning. Dolar's flexibility should be applauded, for it seems he can run to both the opera and attack. Dolar's trajectory in 'Freud's Voices', as well as succumbing to the bifurcation he wishes to overcome, resonates too well with how voice is treated by Freud—aphonic, yet *hyperphasic*.

[212] Ibid., 27.

[213] Dolar, *A Voice and Nothing More*, 4.

Beyond *Beyond the Pleasure Principle*

Let's listen closer to voice in Freud's work and focus on two examples in *Beyond the Pleasure Principle;* the 'Fort-da!' scene of his grandson Ernst and the interpretation and analysis of Torquato Tasso's romantic epic, *Gerusalemme Liberata* (1581).[214] The following examination of the Ernst scene—how Freud pitches an anecdotal or diegetic narrative of voice—is poised with a criticality partly stemming from Alice Lagaay's essay 'Between Sound and Silence: Voice in the History of Psychoanalysis' and Luce Irigaray's 'The Gesture in Psychoanalysis'. The reading of Freud's take-up of a scene from *Gerusalemme Liberata* utilizes Cathy Caruth's chapter 'The Wound and the Voice' in *Unclaimed Experience: Trauma, Narrative and History*. These re-readings of Freud's narratives allow an explication of how, to employ Lagaay's terms, voice emerges through any film of language or fetish reverence to be '*symptom* of, and [...] *gateway* to, [an] unconscious' trauma.[215] But before considering two moments of voice within *Beyond the Pleasure Principle* the broad problematic of voice in Freud's work ought to be afforded further remarks.

Voice often plays a key role in Freud's theses, yet he seldom goes as far as to directly discuss or explore the significance of voice in and of itself—either in psychoanalysis generally or in the illustrative narratives referenced. That is to say, voice, as a carrier of language, or as a phonic interruption of making sense, is considered qua voice subject to language, but the question of voice, especially in relation to audition and the body, is given scant attention. Freud's works are a cacophony of 'voices', but they are badly speaking voices, talking voices, meaningful voices. Freud, it seems, heard voice as speech. As we explored in the previous section, the audition, and the question, of voice is quickly subsumed to a focus on meanings.

A silent voice haunts Freud and psychoanalysis on a number of levels: biographical, practical, metaphorical and theoretical. Voice is present in an

[214] Freud, *Beyond the Pleasure Principle*, 23–24.

[215] Alice Lagaay, "Between Sound and Silence: Voice in the History of Psychoanalysis". *E-pisteme* Vol. 1, 2008. 53–62. ISSN 1756-8226. Accessed 30 July 2017. http://research.ncl.ac.uk/e-pisteme/issues/issue01/contents/episteme%20Vol.%201(1)%20%20Alice%20Lagaay%20(Full%20Text).pdf 54.

array of instances and anecdotes Freud developed his theories from.[216] Voice is there but does not take centre stage. Lagaay, in the aforementioned essay, writes of the 'banal' observation that psychoanalysis would later be referred to as 'the talking cure'.[217] That the voice is referenced, glossed and de-aestheticized, in a term that privileges language is apt. Nonetheless, despite this strange torsion of voice into talk, voices are no doubt threaded through the life and works of the Father (to use the term pointedly for the problematic of gender in this field) of psychoanalysis. There is a history of vocal contradiction, stemming from the man who listened to voices and opera, hummed to Jofi, his Chow Chow dog, yet dismissed, by varying degrees of convincement, any enjoyment of voice and music. Voice, contra speech, in Freud is rarely discussed explicitly, rarely announced as a case in point, but always resonates behind the text, in his case studies and examples as well as in his biographical life. The lurking centrality of voice in Freud's work should not be overlooked. Lagaay writes:

> Although in the actual writings of Sigmund Freud explicit references to voice are but few and far between, it is evident that Freud was in fact a uniquely attentive listener to voices and that voice played a central role at the scene of the birth of psychoanalysis, that is, at the time of Freud's collaboration with Josef Breuer on the treatment of hysterical patients (Freud, 1990). Voice is and always has been relevant to psychoanalysis not only in the rather banal sense that psychoanalysis first emerged as a "talking cure", as a practice, that is, that relies heavily on the spoken word; but more profoundly insofar as the voice, and in particular certain disturbances of the voice, from stammering and tongue-clicking, to unintelligible clackings, splutterings and groaning, or to the phenomenon of aphonia or total speech loss, came to be seen by Freud as manifestations of unconscious conflicts and tensions which it was the purpose of psychoanalysis to release. At the origin of psychoanalytic practice the voice appears therefore both as a material support for the *symptom* of, and as a *gateway* to, the unconscious.[218]

[216] In *The Uncanny*, he discusses the short story 'The Sandman' by E.T.A. Hoffmann. He notes the terror that strikes the story's protagonist Nathaniel when eavesdropping in his father's study when he hears the acousmatic (source unseen) voice of Coppelius, the Sandman: 'Hearing Coppelius shout 'Eyes here! Eyes here!' the little eavesdropper lets out a scream'. Again, a voice—and a notably acousmatic voice—is central to Freud's exemplary material, but not directly examined.

[217] The self-effacement in this observation is heavy—the term itself recalls a famous treatise on voice that Dolar, in his Jacques Vs. Jacques argument, does not serve well.

[218] Lagaay, "Between Sound and Silence: Voice in the History of Psychoanalysis", 54.

A voice, and not speech, being the symptom of and a gateway to unconscious trauma is evident, but not explicitly referenced, in two instances in Freud's writings. Both signal a trauma wrought upon and sounded out by the subject. One could say that voice in these instances is a horrific regurgitation of trauma, a horrifying return of terrors and discomforts previously unknowingly ingested.

A close scrutiny of two examples within *Beyond the Pleasure Principle* re-read in sonority with an analysis of Irigaray's support the claim that Freud's treatment of voice was more a treatment of speech, of hearing meaning, listening and being on the lookout for meanings. Freud, it can be said in the following examples, only had ears for the command—the film of signifiers, language and meaning that Dolar claims to veil the 'object voice'. This tendency is firstly evidenced via the reading of Ernst's vocalizations as verbalizations—a Freudian vacuum whereby voice is silenced and meanings flower. This is not a distinction Irigaray claims to make, but her text does, in considering the significance of the mouth's gesture in the scene, presuppose this striking difference by way of detailing the sounds the small boy's body made.

In the famous recounting of Ernst's repetitious act of 'Fort-da' in *Beyond the Pleasure Principle* voice is placed in a narrative of sounding a trauma from within a *supposedly* speaking subject. 'Fort-da' is a game that Ernst played when his mother was absent—exorcising, so the famous argument goes, the trauma of abandonment, in particular the mouth from the breast (this distinctly oral facet is precisely the facet Irigaray's text underscores). The game involved throwing a reel of cotton to and fro and voicing '*Fort*' (far away/gone/go away but vocalized as o-o-o-oh) and retrieving the reel by its string and saying *da*.[219]

Freud's claim here is that a cathartic playing out of the trauma in the symbolic realm (his diegetic mastery of trauma manifest in repetition) is exercised through vocalization of signifying sounds. Note, in this translation, the fill '*so to speak*': 'he made it right with himself, so to speak, by dramatising the same disappearance and return with the objects he had at hand.'[220] One could edit the line, to provide a choice concatenation, to read: *to speak made it right.*

[219] Sigmund Freud, *Beyond the Pleasure Principle*, (Connecticut, USA: Martino Publishing, 2009), 12–14.

[220] Ibid., 13.

Freud argues the meaning of this game was the child's 'cultural achievement'.[221] The child dramatized his estrangement from the breast, mastering the experience within a narrated game. Ernst was, in the first place, a passive subject, 'overtaken by the experience, but now brings himself in as playing an active part, by repeating the experience as a game in spite of its unpleasing nature.'[222]

Freud writes that Ernst, upon receiving the reel, 'accompanied this by an expression of interest and gratification, emitting a loud long-drawn-out 'o-o-o-oh' ' and even goes as far as to provide an onomatopoeia of the boy's vocalization.[223] But this is quickly glossed as a signifying sound 'which in the judgement of the mother (one that coincided with my own) was not an interjection but meant 'go away' (*fort*)'.[224] This slippage, the torsion of voice into a signifying utterance, is perhaps symptomatic of how Freud's fidelity errs on the side of the word, not the aesthetic nature of voice. Dolar's representation of Freud's writing about his anhedonic ear is worth recalling. Consider this line hinting at an aversion to music: 'Some rationalistic, or perhaps analytic, turn of mind in me rebels against being moved by a thing without knowing why I am thus affected and what it is that affects me.' Might this be doctored, then, too: 'Some rationalistic, or perhaps analytic, turn of mind in me rebels against *voice*'?[225]

Irigaray examines the significance of how Ernst *vocalized* (not spoke) these 'words' in 'The Gesture in Psychoanalysis'. Ernst, according to Freud, does not say 'Fort' but vocalizes an 'o-o-o-oh' sound.[226] Irigaray writes:

> The child throws the reel away from him, hides it, and then draws it back towards him, saying *0-0-0-0* and *da*, meaning, according to Freud *fort-da*. He throws it away from him over the side of the cot, where it is hidden from him, then pulls it towards him, back from behind the cot, so that he can see it. *Fort* means far away [*veut dire loin*], *da* means near [*veut dire pres*). In the economy of consonants and vowels, *fort* (or *0-0-0-0* as it in his discontinuous signal) plays on the far-and-near: it is articulated by the mouth's forming a little triangle, a triangle formed by lips and tongue: the *0* is inside it, but cannot be swallowed. The far away is not introjected; it describes, in the mouth above all, a determinate space, a frame, framing, as it were, a space of

[221] Ibid., 13.
[222] Ibid., 13.
[223] Ibid., 12.
[224] Ibid., 12.
[225] Dolar, *A Voice and Nothing More*, 128.
[226] Freud, *Beyond the Pleasure Principle*, 12.

> departure and return, coming to a halt with the *t*, if the word is *fort*, or with the discontinuity of the sound if it is the *0-0-0-0*. Whereas the *da* can be swallowed, a sharp, dry mouthful, thus inverting the fort, unless it [*da*] stays in the back of the palate. So, everything also happens in the mouth, between the lips, the tongue, the palate, the teeth, the larynx, which may be confused with the oesophagus, both of which may in turn be confused with the pharynx, and so on. *Da* is not sung, in any case, it is swallowed. Near, it is introjected; far, it can be mastered: it stays in the mouth like a sweet difficult to suck, or else becomes a discontinuous signal, difficult to transform into a melody.[227]

In this rich passage Irigaray draws out a schism within the repetition of mastery played out via a diegetic scene for the subject (the 'Fort-Da!' reel game). There is *Fort*, meaning 'away', and *Da*, meaning 'there' or 'nearby'. The latter is speech, whereas the former is voice. The two are quite different. Hence inverted commas must frame the plural term 'words'. There is not more than one word here.

Ernst's narration, his repetitious diegetic mastery, contains a schism. *Da*, meaning 'near', is introjected, swallowed. It is mastered, articulated. More plainly, it is a word. *Da* is speaking. It is spoken. *Fort*, however, is remarkably distinct from *Da*. *Fort* was never spoken. It was not a word, but a type of sound emitted through Ernst, a voice: 'o-o-o-oh'. Irigaray describes *fort* as a discontinuous signal; it is sung, vocalized, describing it as difficult to suck, staying in the mouth.[228] It is apt to recall the inedibility of voice, wrought by the denaturalized and signifying mouth, that Dolar describes (referencing Lacan in the final line):

> By speech mouth is denaturalized, diverted from its natural function, seized by the signifier (...). The Freudian name for this deterritorialization is the drive (...). Eating can never be the same once the mouth has been deterritorialized—it is seized by the drive, it turns around a new object which emerged in this operation, it keeps circumventing, circling around this eternally elusive object. Speech, in this denaturalizing function, is then subjected to a secondary territorialization, as it were: it acquires a second nature with its anchorage in meaning. (...) But this secondary nature can never quite succeed, and the bit that eludes it can be pinned down as the element of the voice, this pure alterity of what is said. This is the common ground it

[227] Luce Irigaray, "The gesture in psychoanalysis" in *Between Feminism & Psychoanalysis*, ed. Teresa Brennan, trans. Elizabeth Gould (Abingdon, UK, New York, USA: Routledge, 1989) 130–131.

[228] Freud, *Beyond the Pleasure Principle*, 12.

> shares with food, that in food which precisely escapes eating, the bone that gets stuck in the gullet.[229]

A phōnē stuck in the gullet.

Note the narrative location of Ernst's voice (contra his linguistic articulation), its context, within Freud's anecdote. Voice, the discontinuous 'o-o-o-oh' that plays a role in the repetition and mastery of abandonment, sounds in the place of far away, or gone. In the regurgitated diegetic limbo of attachment and detachment, suckling and isolation, a voiced 'o-o-o-oh' emits at the traumatizing side of the play: when the breast is gone and pleasure is no more. The far-away/gone facet of both the root experience and the diegetic mastery and re-enactment is the kernel of the child's trauma. Conversely, the here, *da*, is said at the point of a gratifying instance of comfort. *Da* is said as a marker of being reunited with the source of pleasure and nourishment. A non-signifying voice *sounds* in place, in the moment within a sequence, albeit diegetic, of the organism's trauma, whereas the spoken word, by contrast, is *said* in place of the mollifying act of resolution. Voice sounds in the instance of trauma for the subject—it sounds from and for the body's trauma.

Irigaray's oral and vocal focused reading of this scene is important, for not only does it develop a sustained terrain of equivoque concerning voicing, speaking and eating but it also points to the difference of Ernst's two vocalizations: one is said and the other is voiced. The text also draws out the sexual differences not accommodated by the text that takes the boy as a universal given: 'Ernst is a boy.'[230] Taking this profound difference between speech and voice in hand, lightly and without dwelling on it as is done so here, Irigaray's argument turns to the gestures of the body that are significant (our focus is slightly different, for voice is the main question at stake). To indulge in a heretical sentiment, wasn't Freud—well wasn't he a bit quick in taking up and agreeing with the judgement of the mother? Was it too quick—or *hyperphasic*?—to hear the discontinuous sound as a meaningful signal? Was the hasty interpretation of 'o-o-o-oh' as a symbolic word (fort) a case of Freud being on the lookout for sense but being deaf to voice?

Later in *Beyond the Pleasure Principle*, in explicating how persons repeat, unwittingly and unconsciously the same fate, Freud references a particularly tragic scene within *Gerusalemme Liberata* (1581), the epic

[229] Dolar, *A Voice and Nothing More*, 186–187.

[230] Irigaray, "The gesture in psychoanalysis", 132.

poem by Torquato Tasso.[231] Although Freud's point in this turn is, again, not explicitly concerned with voice, it does, once again, take centre stage in the moment within the diegesis he describes. It is a significant and pivotal point in the narrative of Tasso's poem.[232] Freud does refer to the voice, before explicating how the preceding action is an instance of repetition.

A brief synopsis of the scene is prudent (Freud provides a cursory outline in the text). Tancred, the hero of the poem, accidentally kills his love (Clorinda) in battle. After this tragedy he wanders into a dense forest. Freud recounts: 'The hero, Tancred, has unwittingly slain Clorinda, the maiden he loved, who fought with him disguised in the armour of an enemy knight. After her burial he penetrates the mysterious enchanted wood, the bane of the army of the crusaders.'[233] Once in the wood, Tancred lashes out at a tree, he hews it down with his sword, 'but from the gash in the trunk blood streams forth and the voice of Clorinda whose soul is imprisoned in the tree cries out to him in reproach that he has once more wrought a baleful deed on his beloved.'[234] A translation of the scene in question, by Max Wickert, is presented below:

> Crazed and distraught, he see before him stand,
> his wounded love, in tears, at whose appeals
> he cannot bear to see that quick blood flow
> or hear that languid sufferer's sighs of woe.[235]

Voice, here, cries out at the nexus of violence and trauma being repeated, and it sounds the horrors inflicted upon a body. This is one facet of Freud's argumentative drive the comparative literature scholar, Cathy Caruth, examines in the introductory chapter 'The Wound and the Voice' in *Unclaimed Experience: Trauma, Narrative and History*. Voice cries out from the wound, at once signalling and being resultant of repetition yet also retroactively confirming the act as repetition to its executor. Caruth writes:

[231] Freud, *Beyond the Pleasure Principle*, 23–24.
[232] Torquato Tasso, *The Liberation of Jerusalem (Oxford World Classics)*. Trans. Max Wickert. (Oxford, UK: The Oxford University Press, 2009), 247–248.
[233] Freud, *Beyond the Pleasure Principle*, 23–24.
[234] Ibid., 23–24.
[235] Tasso, *The Liberation of Jerusalem*, 248.

> For what seems to me particularly striking in the example of Tasso is not just the unconscious act of the infliction of an injury and inadvertent and unwished-for repetition, but the moving and sorrowful voice that cries out, a voice that is paradoxically released through the wound. Tancred does not only repeat his act, but, in repeating it he for the first time hears a voice that cries out to him to see what he has done. The voice of his beloved addresses him and, in this address, bears witness to the past he has unwittingly repeated. Tancred's story thus represents traumatic experience not only as the enigma of a human agent's repeated and unknowing acts but also as the enigma of the otherness of a human voice that cries out from the wound, a voice that witnesses a truth that Tancred himself cannot know.[236]

Freud's focus on the scene is Tancred's repetition of the tragic act. Caruth's focus concerns the locus of trauma: the wound and voice that signal trauma. Caruth is clear to indicate the voice emerges from a body subjected to violence. Clorinda (manifested in arboreous form) is a voice of otherness, an enigmatic voice. This voice from the wound, if we take a Freudian line concerning the voice heard by Tancred, is a voice of psychic tragedy, the repetitious act. Taking the voice of Clorinda, having more sensitivity to where the voice comes from akin to Caruth's take, there is an exogenous and supernatural voice sounding out violence and trauma.

There is a significant horror of otherness, of deafening alterity, in each instance. For Tancred, voice sounds out the unconscious drive to repeat, the compelling force beyond his conscious love for his Clorinda. In this moment voice confronts Tancred with his terrible repetition, in a sense announcing his repeated trauma to him. Structurally analogous to the case of little Ernst, it is a point of non-verbal vocalization resounding from *and for* trauma.

Voice is symptomatic not just of a moment of trauma but re-emerges and erupts from a historic trauma not yet accommodated by the subject. Voice in these contexts is symptomatic of and a gateway to a past trauma. Voice resounds in the context of repetition; it also sounds in the moment of a body in stress, either by the abandonment of pleasure or by the infliction of violence upon it. Voice emerges from the horrors of striking alterity, voicing either the repetitive bind of the subject or the barbarity of external violence for the organism. Vox-Exo, *a* horror.

[236] Cathy Caruth, *Unclaimed Experience: Trauma, Narrative, and History*, (Baltimore, Maryland, USA: Johns Hopkins University Press, 2016), 2–3.

Violence

> Phonology kills the voice, it stabs it with the signifying dagger, it does away with its living presence, with its flesh and blood. (Mladen Dolar[1])

Army, Opera, Flesh?

In the introduction of *A Voice and Nothing More* Dolar recounts an old joke about Italian soldiers.[2] It draws up a binary he utilizes throughout the book to approach the 'object voice': namely, language and aesthetics. The joke goes like this: An army commander cries 'Soldiers, attack!' No one moves. He commands again 'Soldiers, attack!' As before, no one moves. Thirdly, he cries 'Soldiers, attack!' 'At which point there is a response, a tiny voice rising from the trenches, saying appreciatively "*Che bella voce*!" "What a beautiful voice!"'[3]

The joke pivots on the stereotype of an Italian: they are opera lovers, not soldiers. It allows Dolar to demonstrate the dual nature of voice; there is a voice for language—orders and commands—but there is also a beautiful voice, an object to be appreciated in aesthetic, not semantic, terms.

[1] Dolar, *A Voice and Nothing More*, 19.
[2] Ibid., 4.
[3] Ibid., 3.

T. Adams, *Horrors of* a *Voice (object* a*)*,
https://doi.org/10.1007/978-3-031-62050-8_3

Dolar suggests the joke illustrates a double obfuscation of voice: on the one hand there is the wilful ignorance of the meaning (the words) that commonly obfuscate voice in terms of speech and command (one listens to the meaning of the words not the sound), yet on the other hand there is the reduction of the voice into a fetishized object of beauty, and this too obfuscates 'the object voice'.

Speaking and meaning conceal voice insofar as the meaning voice carries is attended to over voice. In the joke, the soldiers do not attend to meaning over voice: Dolar suggests the soldiers pull the trick of selective hearing and quips that one might doubt an alternative command announcing an afternoon off to pursue the 'beautiful girls' of the town would be ignored.[4] However, when the soldiers avoid the command, the call to action, and instead focus on voice as an object of beauty they fall into another level of obfuscation: 'the aesthetic concentration on the voice loses the voice precisely by turning it into a fetish object.'[5]

The implication behind this move, argued by way of a binary of two obfuscating tenors (meaning and aesthetics), is that there is a voice irreducible to both meaning and aesthetics: there is a voice apart from aesthetics and a voice apart from language and meaning. Voice may be thought of in aesthetic terms; it may be heard, perceived and listened to, as a sonic object of beauty. It may also be thought of as the sonic carrier of language, the ethereal material of words, its lilt and intonation, tone and timbre, might suffuse additional meaningfulness into words, into speech. Yet, either way it cannot be thought solely in such terms. Voice might partly constitute speech but is not reducible to language. It might be an object of aesthetic appreciation—but it cannot be wholly reduced to aesthetics either.

But if, to follow Dolar, voice is irreducible to both language and aesthetics, what, then, is the nature of this remaining facet of voice and how, in what terms, can one being thinking through this nature of voice? Dolar suggests that to attend to voice apart from meaning and apart from aesthetics one must turn to psychoanalysis and contemplate the 'object voice':

> which does not go up in smoke in the conveyance of meaning, and does not solidify in an object of fetish reverence, but an object which functions as a blind spot in the call and as a disturbance of aesthetic appreciation. One

[4] Ibid., 4.
[5] Ibid., 4.

> shows fidelity to the first by running to attack; one shows fidelity to the second by running to the opera. As for fidelity to the third, one has to turn to psychoanalysis. Army, opera, psychoanalysis?[6]

That there is a voice irreducible to meaning and aesthetics feels right, sure there is more to voice than way it says or how it sounds; this is the wonder of voice. But, is the turn to psychoanalysis not a little hasty? Perhaps before turning to psychoanalysis, one should consider the body and ask what voice means for (or against) the corpus that voices. In terms of meaning one should ask what is required of a body to put itself at the service of meaning, to be set to the task of voicing an impersonal and generalized language. In terms of aesthetics and beauty, what is required of the body to voice an object of beauty? What undertaking, pathos, suffering or sacrifice is required of the body to sound so beautifully?

Voice is intrinsically about the body as it is subjected to language or manifested via aesthetics. To return to Dolar's opening binary of meaning and aesthetics, in each instance there is always a body giving voice. Weather one heeds the meaning of the words and understands the command, or if one is an opera lover enthralled by the beautiful voice—'*Che bella voce*!'—there is body giving voice.

To turn to the body is, of course, recourse to a more empirical framework. This sounds plain enough, for the body is material, flesh, cartilage, bone and other substances. However, to attend to the question of the body in voice is not a radical departure from psychoanalysis. In many senses, one may claim it is indeed a return to psychoanalysis! Freud's methodology, was often clinical first, theoretical later and followed a trajectory of addressing and exhausting biological (empirical) avenues of enquiry first before any leap into the metaphysical or psychological. So, it is with a fealty to Freud that the ineradicable ambiguity of the 'object voice' is explored firstly in biological and evolutionary terms before any excursion into the metaphysical and psychoanalytical.[7] To counterpoise the moves here with Dolar's opening gambit we can say that whereas Dolar's opening trajectory is Language-Aesthetics-Psychoanalysis, to turn quickly to psychoanalysis, the task here is to turn to the living tissues, the flesh, cartilage and bone of the voicer. Contra to a

[6] Ibid., 4.
[7] Ibid., 56.

Language-Aesthetics-Psychoanalysis modality we shall follow a line of Language-Aesthetics-Body.

Voice in terms of body can be considered by way of some very basic questions. Where does voice come from? *How* does it come? How is it produced, and what is vocalization? What do bodies undergo when producing voice? And if voice is, in the first instance, in the service of language or aesthetics, then what does this mean for the body that produces voice? It is in asking these sorts of questions where we alight at a juncture of trauma, pain, violence and malady, where corporeal horrors abound.

Exquisite Delicacy and Barbarism

Voice has no particular organ of its own. This is one characteristic of voice explored by writer, journalist and sociologist Anne Karpf in *The Human Voice: A Story of Remarkable Talent*. She writes: '[I]t isn't produced by any single organ; rather many different body parts combine into a sequence or chain.'[8] It does not emanate from or reference any specific body part. The French otolaryngologist, Alfred A. Tomatis, makes a similar observation: 'We were given a digestive apparatus and a respiratory apparatus, but no specific oral-language apparatus.'[9] Karpf spends nearly two pages exploring how voice is produced by a plethora of parts and processes that have a more crucial primary purpose. The book's second chapter, 'How the Voice Achieves Its Range and Power', surfs heavily on Tomatis' research, particularly in terms of his wont of positioning voice as a uniquely human quirk of biological utilization against the grain of evolutionary and survivalist utility. Karpf quotes Tomatis before adding her own commentary:

> The ability to cry, to call out, to listen, to wilfully make sounds for one's own benefit as one's own audience and window on life is one of the most extraordinary humanizing mechanisms ever observed in the evolution of language.
>
> For the production of the human voice is not just a story of physics, biology, and neuroscience, but also a linguistic, phonetic and acoustic event that consists of three parts. Beginning by conceptualising a preverbal message,

[8] Anne Karpf, *The Human Voice: A Story of Remarkable Talent* (London, UK: Bloomsbury, 2007), 22.

[9] Alfred Tomatis, *The Ear and Language* (Ontario, Canada: Moulin Publishing, 1996), 59.

we then encode it in grammar and phonetics, only lastly articulating it through the co-ordination of muscles that leads to speech.[10]

The subtext of this passage is language. Both Tomatis and Karpf glide from talking about voice to talking about language, meaning, words and communication. The implicit argument about voice in their texts, their presupposition, is that voice is the body subjected to language. It is a common sleight of text; a discussion about voice results in a discussion of speech.

In the following section of Karpf's chapter, the production of voice is afforded greater focus. Even in this turn, the acute conception of voice as the sounding of a body subjected to voicing language is no less diffused. One symptom of this presupposition evident in the text is that, when referencing Tomatis, Karpf sometimes substitutes 'voice' for 'speech'. Despite these slips, the detailing of what a body undertakes when voicing (be it speech or not) are posed impressively by Karpf's use of Tomatis' research and writings. Following passage details an array of body parts and functions co-opted from their primary functions for voice:

> The voice is produced, as Tomatis noted, by a system *designed* biologically not for speech but for eating and breathing. Indeed, practically every one of the vocal organs—lungs, trachea, larynx (and vocal folds), pharynx, nose, jaw, and mouth (including the soft palette, hard palette, teeth, tongue, and lips)—is an impressive multi-tasker, carrying out some other crucial job in the body in addition to producing sounds.
>
> For example, although the larynx is also known as the voice-box, its chief function has nothing to do with the voice: it's to act as a sphincter to prevent anything but air entering the lungs. Alexander Graham Bell called the larynx 'the guardhouse of the lungs'. (…) As for the mouth itself, this serves the triple purpose of breathing, chewing, and speaking. The tongue in particular, as Aristotle observed, 'is used both for tasting and articulating.'[11]

In relying on Tomatis, Karpf's text imports an anthropocentric and theological shade. Firstly, there is the glaring retrofit of attribution in the term 'designed'. Evolution is, of course, not design unless one holds a particular theological position—nature doesn't plan. Secondly, and as exemplified by the book's title (*The Human Voice: A Story of Remarkable*

[10] Karpf, *The Human Voice: A Story of Remarkable Talent*, 22.
[11] Karpf, *The Human Voice: A Story of Remarkable Talent*, 23. Emphasis added.

Talent), these uses of the body, seconded in service of voice and/or language, are shaded with a distinct anthropocentricism, imparting the notion that vocal language is uniquely human. Such a bold segregation from other animals is not necessarily justified. Many animals use their mouths, throats, larynx and lungs for calling when they could just as well be eating.[12] Many mammals also employ parts and functions of their bodies, parts used for crucial life support, nourishment and breathing, for the service of vocalization.[13] However, calling and vocalizing alone are not necessarily language—such sounds *might* not be emissions of generalized semiotics with particular and specific meanings. Nonetheless, the too quick move, of anthropocentricizing discussions of voice, is symptomatic of not only voice's entanglement with producing speech but also its assumed status as evidence of anthropic accomplishments. Although translation is a difficult task, we are not the only animals to vocalize for communicative purposes.

The question of language-based communication between mammals is a contested issue and perhaps tells us more about ourselves than our cohabiters. Do whales have a generalized communicative language, an array of semiotic sonic emissions, or is it merely communicative sound? Our hesitancy to ascribe language to animals other than ourselves and to too readily reduce the communicative methods of other animals to mere sound and song exclusive of meaning is registered in the terms 'whale*song*' and 'bird*song*'. Rather than listening to the voice of non-human animals with the awe and openness that such a voice might and could be another's language, we domesticate a sound of unthinkable possibilities into 'song'—sounding beautiful but necessarily saying anything. Don Ihde, the North American postphenomenologist and philosopher of science and technology, illustrates this tendency in *Listening and Voice: Phenomenolgies of Sound*. He writes:

> Perception steeped in language poses a problem for us that we may not even recognize. For it is a perception that is always too quick to make familiar the most strange and other that we come upon in the world. (…) we give it a

[12] Benjamin D. Charlton, "Why female deer like a stag to be a big noise in the forest," University of Sussex, June 6 2007, accessed April 12, 2017, http://www.sussex.ac.uk/newsandevents/pressrelease/media/media625.html.

[13] Stefan M Brudzynski ed. *Mammalian Vocalization: An Integrative Neuroscience Approach (Handbook of Behavioral Neuroscience)* (USA: Academic Press, 2010).

name, domesticating it into our constant interpretation that centers us in the world.

I experienced such a novel event when I first heard the recorded sounds of a humpback whale. For the first moment the marvelous range and pattern of the whale voice presented the unique, never-before-heard. But too soon I began to bring this "song" into the familiarity, first of metaphor, then of name. I analogized the whale's voice such that its low notes were "like" those of a bellowing bull, its high notes "like" the shrill of a bird, and so on. This had also already been done in that the dust cover of the record proclaimed it as "whalesongs." In so doing the strangeness becomes domesticated. (…)

What does the whale do? Does he sing like a bird, or like the old operatic whale, sing of Figaro? Or does he speak the voices of language and communicate with his kind? Or all of these? There remains an essential mystery to the voice of the whale, a mystery that we have not yet fully entered, but that we might forget if we simply allow the whale's voice to be domesticated as singing.[14]

Let's continue to consider mammalian vocalization but move inland. In *Grooming, Gossip and the Evolution of Language* Robin Dunbar, the British anthropologist and evolutionary psychologist, details examples of apes utilizing generalized vocal sounds to transmit information about specific things.[15] He writes, in 'First Words', about the findings of Dorothy Cheney and Robert Seyfarth, whose studies show that the vocalizations of vervet monkeys do convey specific meanings to others. Vervet monkeys' 'calls refer to specific types of predator, and the hearer knows from the auditory information alone which type of predator the caller is describing.'[16] Dunbar acknowledges one 'can already see many hallmarks of human speech in the Old World monkeys.'[17] He illustrates how gelada exhibit the conversational patterns of call and response characteristic that human speech also has.[18]

Dunbar's argument in 'First Words' has two implications. It is not merely that many animals might be using basic forms of language ('In the

[14] Don Ihde, *Listening and Voice: Phenomenologies of Sound, Second Edition*, (New York, USA: State University of New York Press, 2007), 186–187.

[15] Robin Dunbar, *Grooming, Gossip and the Evolution of Language* (London, UK: Faber & Faber, 1996), 140.

[16] Dunbar, *Grooming, Gossip and the Evolution of Language*, 140.

[17] Ibid., 141.

[18] Ibid., 140–141.

vervet's calls we have an archetypal proto-language.'[19]) but also that much of our own, supposedly uniquely human ways of using language and vocalizing are less to do with highly complex transmissions of information (language) and more to do with facilitating social interaction. Group cohesion and emotional bonds are important, and as Dunbar points out via citing the trajectory of human relationships, after all words are exhausted we revert to the 'crude hormonal tricks' of mutual mauling, direct stimulation and grooming.[20] Dunbar's thesis in this step of his book is that language served to facilitate older manifestations of relationships, forms that elicit hormonal changes (dance, grooming, song, etc.) more than words ever could do. Although a fascinating and persuasive argument about the genesis of human language, it is perhaps not entirely surprising—how often do words fall short when a touch, a look, a move 'say' much more than the words? This very line is symptomatic of the privilege of language over the primacy of other communicative behaviours. How does one talk about what one cannot say?

The consistency between Tomatis, Karpf and Dunbar is that vocalization is a highly complex orchestration of a series of component corporeal parts. This facet of voice, be it from a bipedal being or not, stands. The purpose (language or not) of such virtuosic corporeal control might be discussed, and the reasons for how and why it came about may be argued and contested. So too might the question of if other animals vocalize for the purpose of proto-languages or not. But regardless, voice, be it for language or not, by humans or not, is a peculiarly skilful endeavour that co-opts myriad body parts and various functions.

The Italian philosopher and feminist thinker, Adriana Cavarero, highlights this aspect of vocalization in *For More Than One Voice: Toward a Philosophy of Vocal Expression*. She writes, 'lips, mouth, palate, tongue, teeth, (…) larynx, nasal cavities, lungs, diaphragm—come together for acoustic purposes.'[21] Michel Chion, the French sound theorist and composer, also notes in *The Voice in Cinema*, following in much the same anthropocentric vein as Tomatis: 'it paradoxically appears that the human body does not have a specific organ for phonation.'[22]

[19] Ibid., 141.

[20] Dunbar, *Grooming, Gossip and the Evolution of Language*, 148.

[21] Adriana Cavarero, *For More Than One Voice: Toward a Philosophy of Vocal Expression*, Translated by Paul A. Kottman (Stanford, California: Stanford University Press, 2005), 65.

[22] Michel Chion, *The Voice in Cinema*, Translated by Claudia Gorbman (New York, USA: Columbia
University Press, 1999), 127.

Dunbar's breakdown of what vocalizing requires of the body is detailed in a similar vein but with sensitivity to the exquisite delicacy of vocalization. His emphasis on the precarious sequencing of bodily processes and components to produce voice highlights the degree to which vocal and/or semiotic sounds rely on fine motor control. A finely timed dance of the lips and teeth for consonant articulation working in unison with regulated breathing is a prerequisite for producing the desired sound. Dunbar writes, referring to speaking (but such observations are applicable to singing):

> Speaking requires very fine motor control of the lips, tongue, vocal chords and chest, all of which have to be integrated in just the right sequence to produce a particular sound. Just try saying the sound *a*: as in *hay*—normally produced with the corners of the mouth pulled right back so that the lips are narrowly parted—but with the lips rounded and pouted as they would be when producing the sound *oh*:. The result is recognizable as an *a*: sound, but only just; it comes out more like a strangled *oi*: than anything else. In addition to fine motor control, speech also requires precise control of breathing so that air is released from the lungs in just the right quantity and with just the right amount of force (think about the difference between explosive sounds like *b* or *p* and softer ones like *e* or *c*.)[23]

Dunbar's description references a number of crucial processes for vocalizing specific sounds, drawing special attention to the oral control required to make the sound *a*. It is worth pausing to consider just how delicate an operation vocalization is, just the slightest change can de-tune our vocalization and result in erroneous pronunciation or delivery. Illness, injury, age, psychological state and emotions can affect the delicate task of voice. Karpf writes of how it is not just the mouth, lips and larynx that contribute to voice but also most of the torso including the back.[24] She also mentions how maladies outside the torso zone can affect voice.[25] Changes to psychological states also affect voice. 'Tongue-twisters' like 'She Sells Sea Shells' test and reveal the limits of our vocal dexterity, control and accomplishment. Vocalization is an accomplished, virtuosic to borrow from music, motor control of the many body parts and processes. It is the ability to breathe, make sounds and modulate them into vowels with labial-

[23] Dunbar, *Grooming, Gossip and the Evolution of Language*, 133.
[24] Karpf, *The Human Voice: A Story of Remarkable Talent*, 23.
[25] Ibid., 23.

dental partitions (consonants) in service of communication, language or song—an exquisite but precarious *delicacy*, at once delicate and delightful.

An anecdote of Tomatis underscores just how finely tuned vocalization is, how it is motor-mastery first and foremost of the body that produces sound. He recounts a meeting with the Italian opera singer Beniamino Gigli and describes how the tenor, famed for his beautiful voice and vocal techniques, re-learned his vowels—notably in silence—by practising and controlling his mouth shape and movement. Gigli would stand in front of a mirror, listening to old recordings of himself and practise oral shapes and movements, miming along to the sound of his younger self to rediscover the acoustics of the vowels on record. This activity also alloyed his muscle memory and fine motor control with his ear:

> Having chosen what he considered to be his best recordings, he listened to them with headphones while looking in a mirror. He reshaped his vowels by listening. (…) He said: "By training in this way, I realized that I had started to open my sounds too much; I was off the track. After realizing that, I was happy just to make the vowel shapes in front of the mirror without singing. I exercised by simulating each aria in this way, in vocal silence, strictly observing the shape and size of the vowel."[26]

It is not just mouth shape, movement and timing that modulate voice. Breathing must be timed to deliver the right amount of exhaled force for the desired sound. There is, however, more to breathing and speech than this. Breathing falls in line with the rhythm of words and sentences we utter. Breath, arguably the most crucial of all vital activities that support our body, kowtows to the arbitrary whims and peculiarities of syntax within whichever language we happen to be speaking. The Canadian cognitive psychologist and linguist, Steven Pinker, comments on just such a phenomenon: 'Syntax overrides carbon dioxide: we suppress the delicately tuned feedback loop that controls our breathing rate to regulate oxygen intake, and instead we time our exhalations to the length of the phrase or sentence we intend to utter.'[27]

Dunbar, in the passage quoted above, doesn't mention the larynx. It is the larynx that 'sonicizes' breath. Upon exhalation, the 'vocal cords' within the larynx activate and begin to vibrate. When these 'vocal cords'

[26] Tomatis, *The Ear and the Voice*, 107.

[27] Steven Pinker, *The Language Instinct* (London, UK: Penguin Books, 1994), 164.

begin to vibrate they imbue exhaled air with sound. This sound then resonates and echoes through the remaining parts of the body that fall under the name 'the vocal tract'. The tongue, palate, teeth, lips, nasal cavities all fall under the territory of 'the vocal tract' and, through myriad corpo-acoustic interactions, modulate the sound of the sonicized exhaled air further. The single quotation marks used for 'vocal cords' denote the tenuous prescription of purpose. The primary function of the larynx is to preventing solids from entering the lungs. Its 'chief function has nothing to do with the voice: it's to act as a sphincter to prevent anything but air entering the lungs.'[28] The larynx is crucial for the prevention of choking; yet we also refer to it as our 'voice box'. Such relabelling is also evident in terms such as 'vocal-tract' and 'vocal-apparatus' that refer to a conglomeration of body parts that have more crucial primary purposes that maintain of life. When vocalizing these parts are momentarily co-opted and seconded in a virtuosic amalgamation.

It is this nature of voice that plunges questions such as 'where does voice come from?' into a doomed rhetoric. For voice is irreducible to the body: untraceable to any origin. It is a result of many parts and yet reducible to none. Did voice begin as the silent air amongst the rafters (the air before inhalation), or is that where it ended up fading away in inaudible harmonies and echoes after it has passed through momentarily co-opted functions of respiration and nourishment?

Voice haunts the body and contorts its functions and parts as it goes. Its modality bears a striking functional similarity to the demon in William Peter Blatty's *The Exorcist* (given an almost verbatim cinematic adaptation by William Friedkin).[29] It comes from an indiscernible place, a lacuna: an epistemological void. But in the moment of announcing itself, via voice, it contorts the body it passes through and emanates from before dispersing into the ether. There may not be the spectacle of twisted necks or 'spider-walking' downstairs, but the possession and co-opting of breath and body are necessary prerequisites for voice.

Every part of the body that contributes to voice has a more vital, more important, role. The lungs ought to take in oxygen and expel the used air with higher levels of carbon dioxide but instead their pneumatic rhythm is repurposed and contorted in the service of song or syntax; the apoplexy of

[28] Karpf, *The Human Voice: A Story of Remarkable Talent*, 23.

[29] *The Exorcist*, Directed by William Friedkin (USA: Warner Bros.; Hoya Productions, 1973), Digital File.

the straining singer is symptomatic of this need being neglected. Such strains of the body register how much the voice needs vital organs such as the lungs at the expense of breathing.

Simon Frith, in *Performing Rites: On the Value of Popular Music*, approaches voice under four headings: 'as *a musical instrument*; as *a body*; as *a person* and as *a character*.'[30] In terms of approaching voice as a body Frith describes the 'sheer physical pleasure of singing [...] through the exploration of physical sensations and muscular powers'.[31] After acknowledging that hovering over his approaches to voice is 'the question (Barthes's question) of music and sexuality: what makes a voice *sexy*?' he moves to describe Crash Test Dummies' hit "Mmm Mmm Mmm Mmm" and writes: 'no one doubted that a major reason for its success was the novelty of Brad Roberts' bass voice, his *swollen vowels, the noise rumbling back down his throat*.'[32] Frith's descriptions of Roberts' skilful use of voice as bodily musical instrument are curious; as well as musical pleasure do they not also evoke a scene of asphyxiation?[33]

The teeth, tongue and palate are important for nourishment; in speech they are requisitioned for the sonic acrobatics of sounding consonants and modulating vowels. Is it hyperbole to exclaim that 'all this talking is killing me!'? Voice is a *harm*ony of vital organs violently employed for an alien purpose. Contra the common vitalist framing, voice is the sound of a body being used for something other than functions that maintain life: the *automallum,* the self-harm, of expression.

Let's move away from the biological microcosm of vocalization and consider voice in evolutionary terms. Dunbar, in 'First Words', outlines some evolutionary facets of the gestural theory of language. In particular he examines the conditions for and developments of the left side of the

[30] Simon Frith, Performing Rites: On the Value of Popular Music, (Oxford, UK: Oxford University Press, 1996), 187, original emphasis.

[31] Ibid., 193.

[32] Ibid., 194, my emphasis.

[33] This description is one page after detailing the autoerotic pleasure ('physical sensations') of singing (there is, certainly in a Barthesian sense of the term, a distinctly erotic vocabulary). That Frith plumps to describe a highly successful vocal via the resolutely unmusical, amelodic, word of 'noise' raising a number of questions. This choice is also evident in the line preceding the sentiment of what makes a voice sexy where he writes of how 'Elvis Presley, for example, seemed to bask [...] in the sheer voluptuousness of his own vocal noise' (Ibid., 193). Where exactly, in terms of acts of erotic pleasure, is the difference between noise and song? Should one assume that bodies make noises but aesthetes make song? Does too much pleasure of/in the body in the latter mode relegate even Elvis' voice to the former?

brain (the part responsible for language and conceptualization) to become utilized for speech. He explains that monkeys, likes dogs, have scapula and chests better suited to walking on all fours. Apes, however, have scapula that allow the arms to be raised above the head, allowing for vertical climbing and breathing independent from arm movement. Dunbar notes that 'in addition to preparing the way for the evolution of bipedal walking in our ancestors (...) [this] also freed the breathing apparatus from the constrictions suffered by monkeys.'[34] The constrictions he talks of are that of many quadrupeds: when the body weight is over the arms and the scapula are on the side of the ribcage the chests ability to constrict and expand is constricted: 'as a result monkeys can breathe once, and once only, with each stride.'[35]

But derestricting the lungs, and increasing shoulder mobility (as well as better balance for bipedalism), was not the only gain from this evolution of scapulae positioning.[36] Arms were freed to practise aimed throwing. Dunbar writes that aimed 'throwing is clearly important for hunting, so one obvious conclusion is that language evolved on the back of throwing. The fine motor control needed for aimed throwing (...) provided us with the neural machinery for fine motor control of the organs of speech.'[37] We should, perhaps, correct 'organs of speech' to 'organs employed for speech purposes'. Nonetheless, the connection made here, between aimed throwing and the neural prerequisite for finely vocalized communication, is interesting, for not only does it place vocal speech in a continuum of human corporeal evolution, but it also alloys speaking to violence.

Dunbar's evidencing of this theorem turns to handedness. The majority of human animals throw right-handed. Because sensory and motor-control nerves switch sides from brain to body, it follows that motor control for the right side of the body is centred in the left cerebral hemisphere: the side concerned with language and conceptualization.

Eva Maria Eberl, writing in *Mammalian Vocalization: An Integrative Neuroscience Approach (Handbook of Behavioral Neuroscience)*, explores the neurobiological aspects of gesture and vocalization in primates. Section II.B in 'Control of gestures and vocalizations in primates' lists evidence

[34] Dunbar, *Grooming, Gossip and the Evolution of Language*, 134.
[35] Ibid., 133.
[36] Ibid., 134.
[37] Ibid., 134.

that it might not just be the majority of human animals, who are right-handed but apes too.

Eberl writes: 'Cortical control of gestures in great apes shows human-like asymmetric hemispheric specialisation. Several studies have reported population-level right-handedness for gorillas and chimpanzees.'[38] Chimpanzees tend to be more proficient with 'precision grip' tasks (using the thumb and index-finger) with the right hand.[39] Some studies have findings that point to a possible correlation between handedness and bipedalism: 'Hopkins (1993) observed chimpanzees (*Pan troglodytes*) and orang-utans (*Pongo pygmaeus*) displaying right-hand preference only when in the bipedal position, but not in the quadrupedal position.'[40] Eberl notes that there is a potential connection between handedness and bipedalism before exploring this correlation in terms of communication.

The import here is that not only does the move from quadrupedalism free up the lungs for vocalization. It also frees the arms, the tools of gesture, which are freed, in evolutionary terms, to specialize in fine-control motor-activity: the type needed for complex vocalizations. Eberl writes:

> Regarding communication, gorillas and chimpanzees preferentially use the right hand for intentional and referential gestures (Shafer, 1993, 1997). In gorillas, a left hemispheric bias for motor control during communicative actions has been suggested. In a pilot study, gorillas showed a bias toward using the right hand synchronous with mouth movements (Forrester, 2008). Hopkins and Cantero (2003) observed an increase in right-hand use in chimpanzees when gestures were accompanied by vocalization. This finding suggests that communicative gestures and vocalizations are both lateralized in the left hemisphere, and linked at some level.[41]

[38] Stefan, M. Brudzynski ed., *Mammalian Vocalization: An Integrative Neuroscience Approach (Handbook of Behavioral Neuroscience)* (USA: Academic Press, 2010), 471.

[39] Ibid.,.

[40] Ibid.,.

[41] Ibid. Dunbar's illustration of the connections between gesture and speech is in the service of detailing the gesture theory's shortcomings; the chapter then builds to propose that language emerged out of necessity for organizing social bonding activities such as grooming, dance and song—he is not proposing language emerged solely from hunting. It should be noted that a great deal of Eberl's research about the connections between gesture and vocalization (for the purpose of communication) is from studies conducted after the publication of Dunbar's *Grooming, Gossip and the Evolution of Language*. Noting the chronology of the texts deployed is as far as needed for the question of voice at hand, any further comment on the differing positions in the fields of evolutionary psychology and seams of cognitive science that focus on language development would be as presumptuous as it would superfluous.

Let's return to Dolar's retelling of the joke about Italian soldiers, particularly the instance of the commander shouting 'Soldiers, Attack!'[42] Such a moment is, perhaps coincidentally, a concise exemplification of the intrinsic violence in the body subjected to language. However, the violence here is not the violence of war, not of commanding young men to brutalize and kill other young men (and often others), but of the speaker. The call for violence is, in itself, in a corporeal microcosm, a call *of* violence. This is the immediate physical level of vocalizing as violence. On a much wider level, in terms of evolutionary biology and phylogenetics, the words 'Soldiers, Attack!' can be heard as a voiced zenith of violence in human animals. Might such orders of voice be understood as the evolutionary vocal extension of aimed throwing?

The placing of the vocal projectile within the continuum of human violence and warfare sits well in a number of histories. One such account is the human history of warfare delineated by the German philosopher Peter Sloterdijk in *Terror from the Air*.[43] What begins as handed organism-to-handed-organism combat, once the arms are free, then extends to the fine motor control of throwing.[44] The organized phalanx, whereby all soldiers operate a spear with their right arm and shield with their left, is the military correlate of writing with a pen or articulating speech: a corporeally asymmetric, aggressive, aimed, projected and finely controlled motor-neurological organization.

But we must be careful not to conflate the violence of speech with voice. The left-hemisphere of the brain required for speech doesn't have the same bearing on non-speech vocalizations. Stroke patients whose cerebral hemisphere is affected can often laugh but not speak.[45] Perhaps the closest one can dare to go, in terms of the violence of voice, is to suggest complex vocalization—and not exclusively speech—can be couched in a continuum of the human animals' arms- and ballistics-based conflict with themselves and other animals, but voice's relationship to this prospect is less clear. Complex vocalization, then, is the immaterial extension of an

[42] Dolar, *A Voice and Nothing More*, 4.

[43] Peter Sloterdijk, *Terror from the Air (Semiotext(e) Foreign Agents Series)*, Trans. Amy Patton and Steve Corcoran (Cambridge, Mass and London: MIT Press, 2009), 13–15.

[44] Dunbar, *Grooming, Gossip and the Evolution of Language*, 137. Dunbar comments that battle scars on fossilized trilobites from 250 million years ago and dolphin skeletons of 20 million years ago exhibited asymmetric attack marks.

[45] Sophie Scott, "The Science of Laughter" *BBC Health*, September 11, 2016 accessed 17 April 2017, http://www.bbc.co.uk/news/health-37311320.

evolutionary development inextricable from combat; it is a violent projectile. It shares much in common with the spear or sword, just as much as any pen.[46]

However, there is no classic heroic triumph in this violent modality of voice. It cares not for its vessel; there is no agency. The modality of expulsion muddies resonance with the spear, sword or pen: contra the traditional phallic figuring, complex vocalization masters those who wield it. Irreducible on a physical level, of no fixed origin or form: we have no vocal apparatus.[47] It interrupts, disrupts, the autonomic protocols of primary functions that support life.[48] There is no agency other than the voice's own life. One's micro-asphyxiation in the service of syntax is not mastery, just as bipedalism is no accomplishment.

Spinal Trauma and Throats Torn with the Talk Sickness

Biomechanically, the degree of vocal complexity human animals can achieve is largely due to the relatively low location of the larynx compared with other mammals. This lower larynx allows the tongue greater freedom of movement for modulating complex sound. In an interview Daniel Charles Barker, Professor of Anorganic Semiotics at Kingsport College (MVU Mass), gave to a member of the Cybernetic Culture Research Unit (CCRU) in 1998 he frames bipedalism and the resultant laryngeal droop as a persisting injurious trauma of evolution. For Barker, this evolutionary drop of the larynx is a register an evolution trauma—a phylogenetic spinal injury. In the 'Spinal-Catastrophism' section of the dialogue Barker, so the transcript reads, said: 'For humans there is a particular crisis of bipedal erect posture. I was increasingly aware that all my real problems were modalities of back-pain, or phylogenetic spinal injury.'[49]

With specificity to complex human vocalization as a result of bipedalism Barker summarized the confluence of factors that contribute to upright speech as 'Palate-Tectonics'. Barker, the reader is led to believe, describes

[46] 'The pen is mightier than the sword'—Edward Bulwer–Lytton.

[47] Cavarero, *For More Than One Voice: Toward a Philosophy of Vocal Expression*, 65; Chion, *The Voice in Cinema*, 127; Tomatis, *The Ear and Language*, 59; Karpf, *The Human Voice: A Story of Remarkable Talent*, 23; Connor, *Dumbstruck: A Cultural History of Ventriloquism*, 208.

[48] Pinker, *The Language Instinct*, 164.

[49] Nick Land, *Fanged Noumena: Collected Writings 1987–2007*, (Falmouth, UK: Urbanomic/Sequence Press, 2011), 500.

with a precision and vividness redolent of J.G. Ballard's early prose, how the contemporary anthropic vocal apparatus is: 'a crash-site, in which thoracic impulses collide with the roof of the mouth. The bipedal head becomes a virtual speech-impediment, a sub-cranial pneumatic pile-up, discharged as linguo-gestural development and cephalization take-off.'[50]

Barker's render of the physical site of speech and vocalization as a site of trauma, an evolutionary impediment, an injury, a thoracic-cranial head-smash, resonates with a sentiment William Burroughs, the North American Beat poet, visual artist and science fiction author, expressed circa 1961. In the first novel of *The Nova Trilogy*, *The Soft Machine*, Burroughs refers to the symptoms of the crash site as a talk sickness: 'sick apes spitting blood bubbling throats torn with the talk sickness. (…) we waded into the warm mud-water. Hair and ape flesh off in screaming strips. (…) when we came out of the mud we had names.'[51]

Most immediately the line draws the parallels of speech, talking and language with sickness (pre-echoing the famous sentiment from the second book in the trilogy, *The Ticket That Exploded*, that language is a (exogenous) virus from outer space). More brutally physical than the more notorious virological framing of language, the gory scene of bloodied and hurt apes with ruptured throats alloys physical damage to language acquisition. The image of wading through and out of warm mud evokes the classic gendered series of silhouettes that cartoon the evolution of human animal's ascent to bipedal posture.

Both Barker and Burroughs stress the traumatic and violent history of the emergence of voice and speech 'acquisition', couching it in a horror thematic of corporeal injury, a phylogenetic malady or curse. Complex vocalization, speech, names and signifiers are remixed and auditioned as the viral proliferation of the trauma from evolutionary happenstance. The human animal's claim to distinction (speech) is the result of disfigurement, a skull and throat *extrusion* wrought by gravity. Human voice, one might say, is the sound of a mammal's laryngeal adaptation to upright posture. Speech and complex vocalization are outcomes of the evolutionary glitch: the larynx drooping as a result of verticality, a quirk of phylogenetic development.

Albeit conveyed in a gore-horror tapestry, the Barker and Burroughs texts delineate the same narrative of voice as rigorous studies of drier tone.

[50] Ibid., 502.

[51] William Burroughs, *The Soft Machine* (London, UK: Fourth Estate, 2010), 127.

The American evolutionary biologist and cognitive scientist William Tecumseh Fitch writes of a number of differences between the adult human larynx and that of other mammals. His work touches on the developmental shift the laryngeal position is subject to in humans. Fitch's text underscores how the larynx has, *speaking* in phylogenetic terms, undergone a strange slip in human animals. He writes:

> (Á)natomical studies comparing the vocal tract morphology of humans with non-human mammals suggest that the human vocal tract is fundamentally different from that of all other mammals. In particular, the resting location of the standard mammal larynx is high in the throat, and typically engaged in the nasopharynx, allowing animals to swallow fluids and breathe simultaneously. This position, and ability, also typifies human newborns. In contrast, the resting position of the larynx in adult humans is much lower in the throat. While this makes it impossible for us to engage the larynx in the nasopharynx, and thus to breathe and swallow simultaneously, it does appear to make possible a wider variety of vocal tract shapes, and thus speech patterns, than would otherwise be unattainable. In particular, the "descent of the larynx" that occurs in human ontogeny, gives adults a vocal tract with a horizontal oral tube and a vertical pharyngeal one. This two-tube vocal tract allows the production of quantal vowels such as /i/, /a/ and /u/, that feature in the vowel systems of most human languages.[52]

Evolutionarily, phylogenetically and ontogenetically adult humans *stand apart* from all many other mammals. By contrast to primates, humans have greater vocalization abilities. The human's dropped larynx, allowing an extended vocal tract, enables more vowels and more ways to modulate and contort sounds than other mammals, but this comes with a cost. Whilst a lower larynx grants the ability, paired with fine motor control, to produce a plethora of complex vocalizations, it also brings another difference we hold compared to other mammals: a choke-risk.

Humans have a much higher risk of choking than other mammals. This is because the human pharynx is relatively long and our larynx is, comparatively, slung low in the neck. Other mammals, whose 'vocal-tract' is relatively much shorter, do not exist under the same choke hazard as humans.

[52] William Tecumseh Fitch "Comparative Vocal production in nonhuman mammals: Implications for the evolution of speech." In *The Evolutions of Language: Proceedings of the 3rd International Conference*, 102–103, 2000.

Karpf underscores this difference with conversational concision. She writes: 'Apes, dogs, and monkeys, on the other hand, have mouths and tongues that allow them to swallow food without the risk of blocking their larynx, and eat and drink while they breathe.'[53] The caveat of our ability for complex vocalizations is constant jeopardy. Karpf quips: 'this is the trade off: talking makes us breathe and eat less efficiently, and splutter when drunk. Though we can speak, we can also easily choke on our food. Apes do neither, which is why they don't need to learn the Heimlich manoeuver.'[54]

The adult human larynx lies in a position so low that choking is possible and a significant lethal risk. It is, according to the North American National Safety Council, the fourth-leading cause of unintentional injury death.[55] According to the British Office of National Statistics, there were 219, 185 and 220 deaths from the obstruction of the respiratory tract in the years 2014, 2015 and 2016, respectively.[56] The adult human larynx in particular rests in a lethal position but one that affords the finely control and modulation of vocalization to serve complex articulation of speech. Utterance is bittersweet; it has a tragic undertone: the cost of human speech is a lurking peril.

The human larynx did not drop as an evolutionary 'response' to the survivalist applications of clearer or more complex vocal communications. It is better thought of as a biological 'glitch'—to technologize the history—resulting from ascent to pi-pedal verticality. Fitch notes: 'As early humans gradually adopted an erect posture, it gradually brought the position of their head back and up so that it tipped back at the base of the skull, thus causing the neck to emerge and the larynx to descend.'[57] Our ancestors lunged and teetered around for some time with the choke-threat before waxing eloquently over supper. The cause of the laryngeal descent

[53] Karpf, *The Human Voice: A Story of Remarkable Talent*, 53.

[54] Ibid., 53.

[55] 'Choking Prevention and Rescue Tips', *National Safety Council*, accessed April 2, 2019, https://www.nsc.org/home-safety/safety-topics/choking-suffocation.

[56] 'Number of choking deaths by place of occurrence and age, registered in England and Wales, 2014 to 2016,' *Office for National Statistics*, accessed April 3, 2019, https://www.ons.gov.uk/peoplepopulationandcommunity/birthsdeathsandmarriages/deaths/adhocs-/007747numberofchokingdeathsbyplaceofoccurrenceandageregisteredinenglandan-dwales2014to2016.

[57] Fitch, "Comparative Vocal production in nonhuman mammals: Implications for the evolution of speech." In *The Evolutions of Language: Proceedings of the 3rd International Conference*, 102–103, 2000.

was not 'adaptive' evolution but more a co-incidental corporeal re-organization resultant from bipedal verticality. Contrary to any supposition of fate, anthropological superiority, evolutionary accomplishment of 'design', human voice is an abnormality. Such a prospect at once decentres the human animal from its narcissism and disavows the classic modality of its assumed uniqueness and difference over other organisms.

Let's move from an evolutionary perspective to a developmental consideration of the larynx's journey. Let's start by considering very early human vocalizations.

Healthy newborns cry at once. Clearing of fluid from the airways is necessary physical reflex for the first breath to be taken. Akin to a hiccup, sneeze or cough there is no intentional affect in this first cry; it is a physical process that happens to make a sound. The human animal's initial emission of sound after birth is instinctive and reflexive.

However, this first cry/breath is not necessarily the first time the organism has produced sound. Sound making predates birth. Producing sound, like hearing, may well first occur in the *acousmatic* intrauterine stage. Karpf lists a number of instances for noisy foeti. She writes, imposing a sense of self-conscious development, that the: 'human foetus may be practicing the use of its voice already in utero.'[58] Detailing *vagitus uterinus*, she cites an example from 1923 whereby a physician eavesdropped on an unborn child, listening through the mother's stomach wall. She describes how 'George Ryder, heard the sound of a baby crying after he had applied traction with forceps. Listening via stethoscope, his assistant and nurses said the sounds were 'high and squealing, much like the sound of a kitten.'[59]

Subsequent infant cries yield nourishment, comfort and care. Infant cries do not change for hunger or pain; initially the cry 'signals' distress only. Many things may cause distress, but the causes of distress do not illicit different types of cry. The simplicity of the infant's distress cry does not detract from its crucial validity regarding the genesis of cultivating a voice. Crucially, at each cry of distress an interaction (one hopes) follows.

Karpf, makes the persuasive argument that by the connection of a sonic reflexive reaction to distress yielding care the germ of communicative voice is inaugurated. Karpf's argument rests on the development of vocalization, from a prolonged vocal reflex to stress to an intermittent

[58] Karpf, *The Human Voice: A Story of Remarkable Talent*, 95.
[59] Ibid., 94–95.

vocal emission. She proposes that newborn's 'cries are desperate because they haven't yet realised that they'll produce a response.'[60] Around six to eight weeks later vocalization changes a prolonged cry to an intermittent, cry-pause-cry pattern. It is a vocalization pattern that, Karpf argues, affords a space to listen. She writes that six- to eight-week-old infants 'go quiet after a bout of crying, to listen for their parent's footsteps. If they don't hear them, they then resume crying. The cry is no longer simply a reflex—now it's begun to be one side of a conversation.'[61] The claim is that there is a distinct development from a sounding physical reflex to distress to an intentioned vocalization. This shift is summarized as a move from merely making sound to finding voice, a voice for someone. Voice, in this sense, is characterized negatively, by virtue of its pauses, its ceasing, its silence. Voice is ontologically defined as such by leaving space for hearing, listening for the care provider, and entering into 'dialogue' that necessitates pauses; taking turns: 'Within a couple of months of being born, babies leave a space for a response to their cry: they've learned the art of turn taking.'[62]

In the transition from reflexive cries of distress to signalling distress cries embedded within a turn taking matrix, an important shift happens. The new cry has an expectation; indeed it is a minimal mode of call, not merely a sonic emission of the body; but a cry *for*: a vocalization *for*. The minimal structures of verbal communication emerge as the infant human is distanced from the breast; quarantined off from pleasure and enters the house of language where sound is not merely a sound but a call, a voice. For the infant, finding voice stands in an inverse correlation to comfort and pleasure. The infant's voice emerges as pleasures and comforts recede.

The pause, the wait, the listening that floods the silences in the intermissions of the infant's cries shares a number of traits with the object *a* voice. It is emergent from a minimal ingress into language which presupposes a—one hopes benevolent—other. But it is not wholly language; a part remains in excess of language. It is in excess of sound too, for this negative ontology of voice rests on the pause, the mute anxious listening: it is silent, stuck in the throat. The dawn of voice is alloyed to the body of an organism undergoing physical distress. Voice is born upon entrance to what Lacan called 'the torture house of language'.

[60] Ibid., 99.
[61] Ibid., 99.
[62] Ibid., 99.

Let's return to the larynx and consider it in developmental terms. The position and functional capacity of infant larynx are different to adult larynx. Young infants cannot choke during ingestion; they can simultaneously ingest and breathe, yet some words are impossible to articulate and sound; the infant is biologically suited to nourishment and care. Adult humans, however, can choke, cannot simultaneously breath and ingest, yet can accomplish a complete articulation of the semiotic noises of their language. Infants' larynxes allow simultaneous breathing and swallowing but cannot produce a full range of sounds. The adult can produce a greater range of complex vocalizations, but they can choke, and there is the risk of inhaling foreign matter such as food.

Fitch touches on this aspect of the human's difference to other species when he writes: 'the resting location of the standard mammal larynx is high in the throat, and typically engaged in the nasopharynx, allowing animals to swallow fluids and breathe simultaneously. This position, and ability, also typifies human newborns.'[63] Karpf highlights that it is precisely this development of the laryngeal position that allows highly articulate vocal expressions. She writes that a 'child's growing mastery of the sounds of speech is partly the result of the gradual descent of its larynx and the root of its tongue during the first two to six years of its life.'[64]

Young children often have difficulty articulating certain words. Their tongue is clumsy and not under their full control. Anecdotally, 'yellow' can be a frustrating single word tongue-twister, perhaps mispronounced as 'lellulow' or 'yayolo'. The infant's tongue and larynx are still descending into positions that would afford the tongue the space for the dexterity required to master the full phonetic range of their native language.

At crawling stage human infants cannot vocalize with the same complexity as adults, but by the time they are teetering around, venturing intrepid and gaining distance from the source(s) of care, their larynxes are dropping, and the burden of language looms, begins to shadow their corpus like the creeping gloomy tentacles of an oak. The laryngeal development necessary for complex vocalizations human traces the infant's estrangement from the breast and its increasingly bipedal mobility. The

[63] Fitch, "Comparative Vocal production in nonhuman mammals: Implications for the evolution of speech." In *The Evolutions of Language: Proceedings of the 3rd International Conference*, 102–103, 2000.

[64] Ibid., 53.

necessary biological preliminaries for complex vocal communication have an inverse relationship to the infant's proximity to pleasure and sustenance.

Development of the larynx in infants is a physical microcosm of the evolutionary descent of the larynx. The evolution of the larynx in the human animal follows a similar path as the larynx development terms; the larynx's droop in the 'ascent of man' is played out in a shorter timeframe in the child's ascent to bipedalism from crawling to walking upright. As the individual acquires, or is acquired by, as they master, or is mastered by, language it re-postures from a supine state to quadrupedal movement to vertical bipedalism and the jeopardy of foreign objects obstructing our respiratory tract looms. As the human type emerged as an upright mammal, as it waded out the mud, a choke risk and language (names) burdened it. As the child raised itself to walk, as its 'vocal tract' developed, trading complex vocalization for safe nourishment, the prospects of choking and language cast their shadows.

The similar developmental and evolutionary journeys of the larynx hold three implications. Firstly they provide a distinctly corporeal illustration, or elaboration, of Lacan's notion of language as a 'torture house' (we'll dig into this in more detail shortly). The descent of the larynx, the dawn of complex vocalization and the looming of corporeal jeopardy—asphyxiation—draw out the 'torture house' of language insofar as language has consequences for the human animal's body: grave consequences. The birth of a speaking subject—in both developmental and evolutionary terms—is figured here as the human's ascent to verticality with the concomitant lowered laryngeal formation affording verbal dexterity and possible suffocation. Secondly, the move impresses how corporeal registers of Lacan's concepts—an appraisal of the body—are by no means incompatible with elucidating a Lacanian concept such as object *a* voice. A turn to the body can serve a purpose in exploring Lacan's concepts. Thirdly, in exploring the corporeality, the violence of voice and language, the *alterity* of voice emerges—its exogenous nature is uncovered.

It is apposite, albeit an abrupt shift from the preceding evolutionary and developmental disciplines, to turn to Lacan's 'words' now. Lacan, during the third year of his seminars, made a claim that has been taken up numerous times. The text at the front of *The Psychoses: The Seminar of Jacques Lacan Book III 1955–1956*, states that he gave 'a concise definition of psychoanalysis: 'Psychoanalysis should be the science of language inhabited by the subject. From a Freudian point of view man is the subject captured and tortured by language."[65] We will consider some elaborations on this line from Žižek and the Italian philosopher Lorenzo Magnani shortly. But first, let us think about the context of this line.

The seminar was given, at the *Société Française de Psychanalyse*, on the centenary of Freud's birthday, May 16, 1856, some seventeen years after his death in London at the outbreak of WWII. The talk was titled *An Address: Freud in the Century*. The presentation is a grand survey of Freud's work. The nuances of Lacan's take cannot all be accommodated here, but a few particular lines evoke heavily the notion of the tortured organism, the human animal subjected to a rational language that cares not for its pleasure or comfort, in Freud's work. Lacan said, summarizing the Father's underlying questions within his oeuvre, that what concerns Freudian anthropology is 'what possesses man and makes him, not the support of the irrational—Freudianism isn't a form of irrationalism, on the contrary—but the support of a form of reason of which he is *more victim than master* and by which he is *condemned* to advance.'[66]

Various thematic prerequisites of torture pepper this line: prerequisites of possession, ensnarement, constraint, victimization and subjection. In the following turn Lacan declares that this is the 'red thread that passes through all of Freud's work'.[67] He then elaborates the overriding question of Freud's work, declaring that he 'only ever asked himself one question' which is, 'how can this literal logos take hold of an animal who doesn't need it and doesn't care about it—since it doesn't concern his needs?'[68] Lacan, then moving to ask what Freud's philosophy was, returns the line quoted above that concludes that man is 'the subject captured and tortured by language.'

Such a verdict is supported in two ways. Firstly, by way of providing a different tone of translation of Freud's from a note the original German 1938 preface to *Moses and Monotheism* and secondly by uncovering a buried musical refrain in the Latin version of *Oedipus at Colonus*, dated 1388. Heidegger who had visited Lacan's home at Guitrancourt the previous year may be the influence behind the first strategy. Heidegger's return to teaching after the war was famed for its commentaries (over and above the

[65] Jacques Lacan, *The Psychoses: The Seminar of Jacques Lacan Book III 1955–1965*, Trans. Russell Grigg, Ed. Jacques-Alain Miller (London, UK: Routledge, 1993), 243.

[66] Ibid., 242, emphasis added.

[67] Ibid., 242.

[68] Ibid., 242.

French reception of his problematic and sympathetically glossed philosophies).[69] During the preceding year Lacan and Heidegger had spent time together, and Lacan, in the autumn of 1955, began work on a translation of 'Logos' (although not in this particular seminar, Heidegger's work is addressed and re-articulated a number of times in Lacan's seminars from this period). It was in this text that, Roudinesco writes, Heidegger maintained 'that the German language, being superior to all others, was the only one capable of rediscovering the original truth of the Greek tongue and thus providing the human race with a doctrine of salvation through which it could transform the world'.[70] Given his personal circumstances this raises an emboldened question mark over his political sympathies.

The note of Freud that Lacan re-translates focuses on a response to Bernard Shaw's line that '*that man would be capable of achieving something only if he could live to be three hundred years old*'.[71] Lacan, continuing to provide the translation he contests, states, '*I do not believe this prolongation of life would have any advantages unless*, as the translation goes, *the conditions of the future were totally transformed*.'[72] Lacan, then provides his own: 'In German, this has quite a different sense—*many other things would have to be profoundly altered, at the base, at the root, in the determinations of life*.'[73] Lacan suggests that this note, written in 1938 (one cannot today, thankfully, quite imagine the dire circumstances of the author—persecuted on a political and cellular level)—echoes a line of the chorus that accompanies Oedipus on approach to the wood of Colonus. Lacan says:

> I'm astonished that nobody—except for someone who rendered this into Latin reasonably well—has ever managed to translate properly the *mê phunai* that the chorus then utters. It's reduced to the value of a verse that says it's better *not to have been born*, whereas the sense is absolutely clear—the only way to overcome all this business of logos, the only way to be rid of it all, would be *not to have been born like this*. This is the very sense accompany-

[69] See Roudinesco's comment about Jean Beaufret's blinkered adoration in 'Tribute to Martin Heidegger' chapter of *Jacques Lacan*, Trans. Barbara Bray (New York, USA: Colombia University Press, 1997), 221–226 specifically.

[70] Roudinesco, *Jacques Lacan*, 226–227.

[71] Lacan, *The Psychoses: The Seminar of Jacques Lacan Book III 1955–1965*, 243.

[72] Ibid., 243.

[73] Ibid., 243.

ing the gesture of the old Freud, when he rejected with his hand any wish that his life be prolonged.[74]

Lacan's exhibition of linguistic prowess and sensitivity, the shades and leanings of translations, as well as the biographical context of all three thinkers mentioned are remarkable, but further commentary would be a digression. There are, however, a number of imports from this passage of Lacan that bear on the prospect of voice as violence upon the organism's body.

Žižek's commentary and take-up of Lacan's line 'the torture house of language' is useful here. Žižek drives at impressing Lacan's departure from Heidegger.[75] A similar sentiment is also present 'Why Lacan is not a Heideggerian.' In the essay 'Language, Violence and Non-Violence' (and elsewhere) he rearticulates Lacan's remark that the entire psychopathology 'deployed by Freud, from conversion-symptoms inscribed into the body up to total psychotic breakdowns, are scars of this permanent torture, so many signs of an original and irremediable gap between subject and language, so many signs that man cannot ever be at home in his own home.'[76] Žižek's commentary of difference is to claim it is precisely the 'dark torturing other side of our dwelling in language' that Heidegger ignores.[77]

Lacan's 'dark', nihilistic—'the only way to be rid of it all, would be *not to have been born like this*'—interpretation of Freud is precisely his departure from Heidegger and the pertinent facet for the question of the violence of voice.

The more directly torturous and corporeal gloss Žižek adds couches language as violence the subject is trapped in. Such a rendering is not unwarranted, despite the vivid horror the re-animation of Lacan's comment on Freud is by no means bombastic. For the biographical context of Freud's line Lacan is focusing on is one of a sick man, a man that no longer

[74] Ibid., 244.

[75] Slavoj Žižek, "Language, Violence and Non-Violence" *International Journal of Žižek Studies*, Vol. 2, No. 3 (2008): 4.

[76] Žižek, "Language, Violence and Non-Violence", 4. Also see Žižek, *Trouble in Paradise: From the End of History to the End of Capitalism* (London, UK: Allen Lane, 2014), 171–172 and 'Preface to the New Edition: Why Lacan is not a Heideggerian' in *The Ticklish Subject: The Absent Centre of Political Ontology* (London, UK: Verso, 2008) vii–xxi.

[77] Ibid., 4.

wished for life but 'rejected with his hand any wish that his life be prolonged.'

In the voluminous *Less Than Nothing: Hegel and the Shadow of Dialectical Materialism* Žižek states that the 'torture house of language' is a persistent addition Lacan adds over the German's motif of language qua house of being:

> Throughout his work, Lacan varies Heidegger's motif of language as the house of being: language is not man's creation and instrument, it is man who 'dwells' in language: 'Psychoanalysis should be the science of language inhabited by the subject' Lacan's 'paranoid' twist, his additional Freudian turn of the screw, comes with his characterization of this house as a torture-house: 'In the light of the Freudian experience, man is a subject caught in and tortured by language.'[78]

Žižek, in the above passages, is not strictly writing about a form of physical suffering and torture, but the passages are laced with violence. Language is spoken of qua violence upon the organism. In a further text of Žižek, where most of the above lines precede, a distinctly corporeal consequence of the torture house is described. The following text is lifted from the preface, titled 'Why Lacan Is Not a Heideggerian' in the new edition of *The Ticklish Subject: The Absent Centre of Political Ontology*.

> Thus when Lacan implies that Heidegger misses a crucial dimension of subjectivity, his point is not a silly humanist argument to the effect that Heidegger overly 'passivizes' man, turning him into an instrument of the revelation of Being, and thus ignoring human creativity. Lacan's point, rather, is that Heidegger misses the properly traumatic impact of the very 'passivity' of being caught in language, the tension between the human animal and language: there is a 'subject' because the human animal does not 'fit' language; the Lacanian 'subject' is the tortured, mutilated, subject.[79]

A version of this parsing elsewhere is employed to illustrate the concept's significance in literal mutilations of the body. In *e-flux journal* the paragraph ends with: 'The most elementary dimension of the subject is

[78] Slavoj Žižek, *Less Than Nothing: Hegel and the Shadow of Dialectical Materialism* (London, UK: Verso, 2012), 870.

[79] Žižek,,'Preface to the New Edition: Why Lacan is not a Heideggerian,' *The Ticklish Subject: The Absent Centre of Political Ontology* (London, UK: Verso, 2008) vii–xxi.

not activity, but passivity, enduring. This is how Lacan locates rituals of initiation that perform a violent cut onto the body, mutilating it.'[80]

This physical torture of the human animal trapped in language is then extrapolated on to body as a scene of violence, damage and mutilation. Following the last line, Žižek claims 'This is how Lacan locates rituals of initiation that require the violent cutting and mutilation of the body' and evidences the comment with Lacan's words from 1959.

> The rituals of initiation assume the form of the changing of form of these desires, of conferring on them in this way a function through which the subject's being identifies itself or announces itself as such, through which the subject, if one can put it this way, fully becomes a man, but also a woman. The *mutilation* serves here to orientate desire, enabling it to assume precisely this function of index, of something which is realised and which can only articulate itself, express itself, in a *symbolic beyond*, a beyond which is the one we today call being, a realisation of being in the subject. (Jacques Lacan, *Le désir et son interprétation*, 20th May 1959[81])

It is this second line, particularly the incorporation of the question of desire and articulation, that strikes pertinence with the proposition of there being an intrinsic corporeal horror in the relation of voice and body explored thus far.

Returning to the infant's pause, specifically the reflex of distress muted to accommodate a listening of the other, is this not a mutilation of the body's reflex in service of the symbolic? What orientation does this obliteration of the cry *of*, to be replaced with a cry *for*—for an invocation—serve?

In this sense might we regard the voice of the infant as a voice vivisected with anxious bouts of listening, as voice after the signification complex proper: that is to say, a voice after language that emerges resultant but nonetheless irreducible to the signifying operation. Furthermore, consider the silence that intermittently cloaks the cry, is this not the terrible deafening silence of object *a* voice, a voice of the other, that the organism's early phenomenological and ontological development unfolds in relation to?

This application of Lacan's thought and Žižek's commentary is immediate and local in its interpretation of voice's significance for the body. The

[80] See https://www.e-flux.com/journal/32/68252/hegel-versus-heidegger/.
[81] Ibid.

take rests on the vocabulary employed by each which evoke the corporeal horror of torture and mutilation.

This immediate and local application to the germinal moments of vocalization finds resonance in a passage from Italian philosopher Lorenzo Magnani. This particular section is a direct commentary on both Lacan and Žižek's description of language. Notably, language as a torture and mutilation the subject is ensnared within—'Lacan's paranoid twist'—is emphasized in particularly physical terms.

In *Understanding Violence: The Intertwining of Moral and Religious Violence: A Philosophical Stance*, he writes, quoting the same lines of text from Žižek and Lacan consecutively:

> [A]cknowledging Lacan's ideas, Žižek tells us that it is man that 'dwells' in language in a sort of constitutive passivity, and not language that dwells in humans: 'man is a subject caught and tortured in language', language is the 'big Other', and, again, human animal does not 'fit' language: [...]
>
> An eloquent explanation of this kind of violent effect of language, which constitutively affects the individual psyche, is illustrated by the case of mutilations, where parts and/or aspects of the real body suffer—so to say—from the 'signifier' effected by the language activity. The semiotic pressure established by language constrains the body.[82]

In Magnani's implementation of Žižek's writing on Lacan's 'torture house of language', the 'paranoid twist' that departs from Heidegger, the physical constraint, suffering—the brutalizing facet of language—is drawn out. The real body suffers as emersion in the symbolic constrains and binds the body. Recall the imposition of speech on rhythms of autonomic respiration; the constraints of language imposed on breathing are a low-level asphyxiation: semiotic strangulation. On this level, the coming of voice as concomitant with entrance into the symbolic imposes suffering on the body.

On a wider level, the developmental and evolutionary trajectory of the corporeal formulation (the ascent to bipedalism) necessary for complex vocalization can be framed as the human animal's mutilation in phylogenetic and evolutionary terms, a history of becoming trapped in the torture

[82] Lorenzo Magnani, *Understanding Violence, The Intertwining of Morality, Religion and Violence: A Philosophical Stance* (Berlin–Heidelberg, Germany: Springer–Verlag, 2011), 51.

house of language. The gendered series of silhouettes that depict the ascent of man in evolutionary terms (but which also reflect developmental progress) is the scene of a gradual accommodation in the torture house of language. The human animal's voice rests as an outcome of entrance into the symbolic. Emerging voice and standing up right lie in a continuum of corporeal horror and violence wrought from without: *vox-exo*.

Ch*a*nges

Dreadful Symptoms: *Corpaural* Sleuthing

If the object *a* voice is a point of alterity and corporeal trauma—*vox-exo*—might it also be a locus of transformation: a change wrought from within and without? Rather than pursuing a Freudian presupposition of voice—to be a barometer of changes within the subject insofar as it delivers verbal language—timbre, tone, texture, volume and acoustics shall be listened to over and above the words such characteristics may articulate. This *stethoscopic* logic seeks to listen for transformations, mutations, variations and shifts from or to states the listener (or indeed the voicer) may not know.[1] We can do this by considering some diegetic examples from genre horror. Each concerns a moment of horror, often at the affective zenith of the narrative. In each case the stability of the human subject is in crisis, signalled as precarious by an inhuman voice.

But before exploring inhuman voices of transformation, we should consider how we attend to voice, how we presuppose its 'tells'. Karpf, in the opening chapter, 'What the Voice Can Tell Us', in *The Human Voice: A Story of Remarkable Talent*, writes:

[1] 'Stetho*scope*' has an ill-fitting ocularcentric etymology: from the Greek *stēthos* 'breast' + *skopein* 'look at'—yet, there is no looking involved.

T. Adams, *Horrors of* a *Voice (object* a*)*,
https://doi.org/10.1007/978-3-031-62050-8_4

> [t]he voice is a stethoscope, and transmits information not only about anatomical abnormalities but even illnesses. Our risk of coronary heart disease can be predicted, it's been claimed, on the basis of voice characteristics like volume and speed alone. Doctors have even maintained that picking up on changes to the sound of the voice can be life-saving in cases of throat cancer and people contemplating suicide.[2]

She then details an analysis of Joseph Hazelwood, the captain of the Exxon Valdez oil tanker that, in 1989, ran aground and caused a catastrophic oil spill in the Gulf of Alaska. Hazelwood was accused of being intoxicated with alcohol at the time of the incident. He was acquitted in 1990. Karpf writes of how analysis of tapes of his voice from the day before the disaster and the day of revealed he 'didn't only misarticulate words [...] at one point he called his ship 'Ekshon Valdez'—but also took 50 per cent longer to say its name at the time of the accident than the day before.'[3] Karpf, in the following passage, reels off further bio-acoustic reductions and mentions a 'drowsiness-predictor for pilots and air-traffic controllers based entirely on readings from their voice'.[4]

Listening for what voice may divulge of the voicer, *corpaural sleuthing*, operates on a number of levels. Taking Karpf's examples in turn, voice is presupposed to be a register for respiratory, oesophageal-cellular, psychological, neuro-chemical and fatigue-based alterations of the vocalizing human. One aspect of vocalization that lends itself to the presupposition of voice as sensitive register is its modality of production from and through the human body: its exquisite delicacy.[5]

Karpf writes that, due to having not a dedicated voice apparatus, many disparate body parts come together for voice.[6] Voice requires an orchestration of multiple body parts that culminate in a *harm*ony. The symphony, however, is easily disrupted; it is fragile: *unsound*. The harmony of voice is a distinctly sequential and temporal process; it is a 'sequence or chain'.[7] It is with such complexity—corporeal, sequential and temporal—where such delicacy and precarity come. Such complexities of production contribute

[2] Karpf, *The Human Voice: A Story of Remarkable Talent*, 10.

[3] Ibid., 10.

[4] Ibid., 10.

[5] Detailed in 'Violence', voice production requires the co-opting of an array of physical components and protocols.

[6] Ibid., 22.

[7] Ibid., 22.

to the capriciousness and sensitivity of voice, its easily affected nature. Voice qua 'canary in the cave' is, then, taken to be a delicate and sensitive barometer for physical, neurological or psychological variations.

Karpf, in 'How Our Emotions Shape the Sounds We Make (and Other People Hear Them)', describes how 'a group of aphasics listened to a speech being made by President Reagan, the so-called Great Communicator, they fell about laughing because they detected his histrionics and false cadences.'[8] Karpf goes on to quote from the anecdote (from Oliver Sacks' *The Man Who Mistook His Wife for a Hat*): 'They have an infallible ear for every vocal nuance, the tone, the rhythm, the cadences, the music, the subtlest modulations, inflections, intonations, which can give—or remove—verisimilitude to or from a man's voice'. Karpf provides a further line from Sacks which, running a sensorial balance sheet logic (a deficit in one sense being offset by additional sensorial abilities), suggests ' 'Something has gone ... it is true, but something has come, in its stead, has been immensely enhanced.'[9] The sentiments resonate with the preliminary aspect of Dolar's opening proposition in *A Voice and Nothing More*, that meaning, language and words obfuscate voice. Karpf's presentation is not critical; she reserves that for an endnote whereby she references a study that points to how aphasics' ability to pick up on non-semantic information was contingent to observations of facial expression.[10]

Karpf, in the following paragraph, begins with a somewhat tempered proposition that runs the same methodological sequence of Dolar (meaning, aesthetics, psychoanalysis) within the question of voice. The implication of Karpf's sentiment is that we may all be like aphasics are proposed to be: we might not take a person's word; we might listen out for what a voice conveys; and by doing so we make inferences concerning the voicer's psyche. She writes (invoking psychoanalysis):

> Potentially we each possess the skills of an aphasic. Most of us have an intuitive, post-Freudian sense of the intimate relationship between voice and psyche, embodied in words like tongue-tied, stiff-upper-lip, or lump-in-the-throat. At some level we're aware that the voice acts as an exquisite psychic

[8] Karpf, *The Human Voice: A Story of Remarkable Talent*, 134.
[9] Ibid., 134.
[10] Ibid., 328, note 6.

barometer, sensitive to micro-shifts in feelings, registering what words try and conceal.[11]

Karpf's line, however, bleeds out of the very focus it attests to. The question of voice quickly becomes a question of the execution of speech. The proposition that voice is a psychic barometer, that it may divulge some meaning not stated in speech, turns into a barometer that divulges by virtue of *how* speech is delivered, how words are vocalized. Voice, in this turn, is only attended to—is only heard—in terms of verbal delivery.

'Tongue-tied' and 'lump-in-the-throat' are the inability of the voicer to articulate speech, the inability to verbalize words. Such lay terms refer to momentary aphasia, the impairment of the production of speech. The terms Karpf lists as symptoms of voice are more verbal disturbances not vocal disturbances.

As has been touched on already by way of Alice Lagaay's essay "Between Sound and Silence: Voice in the History of Psychoanalysis", the disturbances of voice and speech, the aberration of normalized standards or verbalizing meaning such as 'tongue-clicking, to unintelligible clackings, splutterings' were 'seen by Freud as manifestations of unconscious conflicts and tensions'.[12]

The underlying question in Karpf's presentation of the aphasics study and the following invocation of psychoanalysis fold into manifesting an ear that, a la Freud, is attuned to speech but not voice: a question of how voice delivers or gets in the way of speech. The implicit ableism of hearkening 'deviations', hearing the 'disturbances', from an expected standard of articulation and verbal aptitude has a strict ear, an ear that does listen to verbal execution but does not listen to voice, a *hyperphasic* ear attuned to words yet neglectful of the sounds of vocalization beyond verbalization.

Karpf's chapter does move to provide an array of examples of how corporeal changes (stemming from an emotional state) can modulate voice, not just the vocalization of language. The examples are antithetical to Karpf's previous articulation of 'voice' as a psychic barometer. Whereas previously Karpf wrote of voice in terms of how it fell short of serving language, or failed to produce language (in the lay terms of 'lump-in-the-throat' or 'tongue-tied') these later examples focus on acoustical changes

[11] Ibid., 134.
[12] Lagaay, "Between Sound and Silence: Voice in the History of Psychoanalysis", 54.

without recourse to how they stand in service or disruption of verbalization.

By proposing examples of how emotional or psychological states modulate voice—not words—Karpf reinstates the causal thread of voice as a gateway to the unconscious without succumbing to *hyperphasia* (ears for speech alone). Voice, in these examples, is pitched as pertinent to psychological states on the basis of acoustic properties, not its adherence to an ideal execution of words. The move draws inferences concerning psychological states and changes based on acoustic vocal qualities.

Karpf's exploration of the ways voice betrays psychological states soon turns to focus on the body. She writes:

> When we're stressed or excited [...] our laryngeal muscles tense up, making the vocal folds tauter, so that the speaker has to produce more pressure to force the air through. The vocal musculature is a highly sensitive instrument. [...] Emotional states like deception, conflict and anxiety can change breathing, which in turn influences subglottal pressure and so impacts voice. [...] Simply remembering an emotion—a happy event, the shock of an accident—affects the movement of the diaphragm. [...] Changes in facial expression also affect the pharyngeal muscles. In a grimace, the corners of the mouth are turned down, the vocal tract shortened and its walls tensed. This helps make the voice higher, more nasal, and narrower. When a person is apprehensive or fearful, their voice 'shrinks' as the mucous membranes become dry.[13]

Many of the above examples are related to the affects of negative valence: stress, conflict, anxiety, shock and fear.[14] Such endogenous modulators of voice operate by corporeal proxy: a sounding body. As

[13] Karpf, *The Human Voice: A Story of Remarkable Talent*, 134–135.

[14] Emotions connected to aversive stimuli (e.g. fear, horror or panic) elicit the sympathetic nervous system, the 'fight or flight' response, whereby our heartbeat increases, our pupils dilate and our bodies become primed for escaping or defeating evolutionarily familiar dangers. A common example of voice reflecting our fear-modulated brains and bodies is nervous public speaker. In evolutionary terms standing in front of a large crowd focusing on us is dangerous, and our nerves have not evolved to differentiate between the eyes of hostile groups and earnestly expectant attendees of colloquium, wedding or business conference. Nervousness, essentially a fear of the group's gaze, is conspicuously noticeable in speakers; the voice is the give-away. The voice quivers, or consonants are stuttered or sentences rushed. Breathing whilst talking suddenly seems difficult; we might even speak in a slightly higher pitch than usual as our corporeal tenseness affects the vocal chords. Nonetheless, at root it is the physiological changes of fear that manifest themselves in our changing voice.

psychological changes bring physical variations voice is affected in turn. Voice, then, is taken as a holistic register that sounds out how neurological and/or psychological states impact the body.

Voice also betrays corporeal changes autonomous from emotions and conscious anxieties. As Karpf details by way of the accusations levelled at the captain of the Exxon Valdez oil tanker, changes to the body that are not only psychological (in this case neuro-chemical) can affect voice. A virus causing blocked sinuses or a sore throat is akin to a hangover, in this sense. A physical symptom of an exogenous agent is sounded out: voice might develop a nasal inflection if we are congested or deliver a hoarse timbre or uncharacteristic baritone if the throat is inflamed and sore. We might not *sound ourselves*.[15]

One can consider voices in genre horror sounding out profound corporeal change along similar lines. Rather than voice modulations being employed to evoke the psychobiological nuances of fear, horror, sadness or panic, the significance is extended to dramatic fantasy. Voice is posed as conveying a profound corporeal change, a change of body, perhaps from one type of being to another. Voice, in such diegetic contexts, is not evoking a change of a body such as fearful trembling, a spasm of grief or a hoarseness wrought from illness but reflect a body's transformation from 'natural' state to supernatural state, e.g. the transformation from human to werewolf. This vocal hint at an ontological transformation—a change in being—and a concomitant and ominous change in body as well as personality, is often preliminary to the more visual and corporeal transformation. In genre horror vocal change is frequently the primary flag that a human is changing into something else, something horrific.

Following Thacker's concept of horror—being confronted with a lacuna of knowledge: being aware of an epistemological deficit—voice hints that something is afoot: but what, we do not know.[16] In the examples

[15] Theresa May, the UK Prime Minister at the time of writing, when speaking to Parliament on May 13, 2019, said, 'I may not have my own voice but I do understand the voice of the country.' This is not the first time her voice has been dramatically affected. At the 2017 Conservative Party conference she croaked through her speech until a coughing fit halted proceedings altogether. After a tentative rally of applause and support the Chancellor of the Exchequer, Philip Hammond, delivered a 'cough sweet' to the PM. In a pleasing synergy of presentation materials, the F of the slogan 'Building a Country that Works for Everyone' on the blue board behind the PM then succumbed to gravity. This is a twofold example of *physics* impeding communicative lucidity.

[16] Thacker, *In the Dust of This Planet: Horror of Philosophy Vol. 1.*, 4–9.

explored next it is voice that announces a change to *something unknown*. In each case, the viewer knows the voicer is changing into *some*thing; the voice sounds out flux but nothing more. It is this question—'what type of thing?'—that follows the philosophical nature of horror Thacker sets out in *In the Dust of This Planet: Horror of Philosophy Vol. 1*. Voice of change in genre horror, be it of endogenous or exogenous impetus, confronts the viewer with a lacuna; it alludes to a physical or psychological change the viewer cannot begin to fathom. The following examples all pivot around voice sounding out a change from human form into fantastic, horrific or supernatural forms.

Thriller: Parallel Thrills

Michael Jackson's *Thriller* (1982), directed by John Landis, contains an instance of horrific corporeal transformation.[17] Much has been said about the video's influence, its massive cultural reach and its various accolades within the entertainment industry. It won two Grammy awards, and four MTV awards, including, in 1999, being number one in the *Greatest Music Videos of All Time*. It sold over nine million copies of the VHS reproduction.[18] The eponymous record, Kobena Mercer writes, 'sold over 35 million copies worldwide and is said to be the biggest selling LP in the history of pop'.[19] Some might say more.[20]

Much has also been said about the horror themes within the thirteen-minute video. The centrepiece zombie dance is, now, much copied, mimicked and parodied. The voice of veteran horror-film actor Vincent Price is notable for delivering a monologue, a rap, during the video and song. Price also provides his infamously sardonic cauldron-gargle cackle, precisely at the moment when Jackson breaks the fourth wall and grins

[17] *Thriller*, Directed by John Landis (USA: Optimum Productions, 1982), Digital File.

[18] "Michael Jackson's Thriller," *Wikipedia*, accessed March 4, 2019, https://en.wikipedia.org/wiki/Michael_Jackson%27s_Thriller_(music_video).

[19] Kobena Mercer, "Monster Metaphors: Notes on Michael Jackson's *Thriller*" in *Sound and Vision: The Music Video Reader*, eds Simon Frith, Andrew Goodwin and Lawrence Grossberg (London, UK: Routledge, 1993), 93. A prescient line –Jackson's Janus face and his double life, and this reading of schizophrenic Thriller qua eroticism and horror have taken on an uncomfortable new level significance since the original draft of this chapter. See *Leaving Neverland* HBO/Channel 4 2019. Dir. Dan Reed.

[20] "Did Thriller Really Sell a Hundred Million Copies?'," *New Yorker*, accessed April 2, 2019, https://www.newyorker.com/culture/culture-desk/did-thriller-really-sell-a-hundred-million-copies.

directly at the viewer at the end of the video. Margo Jefferson, in *On Michael Jackson*, writes that the piece is: 'a short masterpiece, a perfectly thought through and executed horror tale. It is the tale of the double, the man with two selves and two souls, like Dr. Jekyll and Mr. Hyde, like Poe's William Wilson or Dorian Gray and his portrait. The everyday man and his uncanny double.'[21]

Two selves and the change from one to *an other*. Transformation: a marked change in form, nature or appearance from one thing to another. But in witnessing transformation, in that penumbral interzone of flux, isn't the question always: to *what*?[22]

Thriller is a pop music video allegory concerning doubles, things being within, of one being two, a person being more than they seem (or *seam*). On a number of levels, it invites interpretation as an exercise in toying with the notion of authenticity.[23]

Because the person(s) in the video are multiple, and hold significance on different levels, a pluralistic mode of engagement is apt to explore Michael, 'Michael' and Michael Jackson. Readings of a subject/protagonist within a scene that segue into ruminations on the private individual performing the role can provide a productive parallax view. Similarly, the protagonist is taken in relation to a public persona (and the received composite of bilateral significance and inter-relations between these 'characters'). These strafing engagements, capricious approaches, befit the nexus of the subject(s): the chimerical Michael/Michael Jackson.[24]

Simon Frith's fourfold approach to voice in *Performing Rites* 'as *a musical instrument*; as *a body*; as *a person*; and as *a character*' is one way of affording such pluralism. Consideration(s) of Michael Jackson is nearly always plural and multi-levelled. One may consider Michael Jackson, performing 'Michael' to allude to the former. When we consider Michael

[21] Margo Jefferson, *On Michael Jackson* (New York, USA. Vintage Books/Random House, 2007), 15.

[22] The question resonates with biographical parallel of Jackson's transformation into a liminal and unique figure of vague race and gender. An excellent account of this transformation is Jefferson's chapter "Alone of All His Race, Alone of All Her Sex" in *On Michael Jackson*.

[23] Released in 1982, one cannot help but recall the spectre of Ted Bundy (the 'charming' serial killer who shoplifted in a suit and predated his victims with his arm in a cast, the ruse of vulnerability, a wolf in sheep's clothing).

[24] Articulated in terms of an alternate vector, the modality encompasses a sequence of levels for a multifaceted focus to be rendered and re-rendered: unpacking a Matryoshka subject/object.

Jackson's work, we are considering a performer performing a song and routine. Following Frith's sense, we can consider the multitude of Michaels and Michael Jacksons as instruments, bodies, persons (and personas) and characters.

Frith also, in *Performing Rites*, writes of tension; of excess inherent in performance, between what is meant (the score, the routine) and what is read (how we perceive the performance).[25] One of the most successful performers in music history warrants an analysis that is not limited to score and routine but also considers its execution (performance) and the relations of these aspects in terms of biographical and cultural context. That is to say, why sing and dance that, this way, now, then, given what's happened?[26]

The title, as Kobena Mercer highlights in 'Monster Metaphors: Notes on Michael Jackson's *Thriller*', is utilized in the chorus for Janus-meaning ambiguity. Mercer writes: 'The lyrics evoke allusions and references to the cinematic genre of horror films, but only to play on the meaning of the word "thriller".'[27] To begin, Mercer recounts the lyrics, that weave the story of 'viewing some ... gruesome horror movies with a lady friend'.[28]

> It's close to midnight and something evil's lurking from the dark ... You try to scream, but terror takes the sound before you make it You start to freeze, as horror looks you right between your eyes You're paralyzed.[29]

For Mercer, these verses are in the first person but consistently refer to 'you'. 'Who is this "you" being addressed?' he asks, rhetorically, before suggesting the pun within the title is revealed in the 'semantic turnaround of the third verse and chorus'.[30]

[25] Frith, *Performing Rites: On the Value of Popular Music*, 1996, 206.

[26] This strategy also considers, and takes as a given, persona in a similar manner as Philip Auslander takes up Frith's model: 'Following Simon Frith, I see a performer in popular music as defined by three layers: the real person (the performer as human being), the performance persona (the performer's self-presentation), and the character (a figure portrayed in the song text)).' (Auslander, *Performing Glam Rock: Gender and Theatricality in Popular Music*, 2006, 4).

[27] Mercer, "Monster Metaphors: Notes on Michael Jackson's *Thriller*", 38.

[28] Ibid., 38.

[29] Ibid., 38.

[30] Ibid., 38.

> Now is the time for you and I to cuddle close together
> All thru' the night, I'll save you from the terror on the screen
> I'll make you see that [Chorus]
> This is thriller, thriller-night, 'cause I could thrill you more
> than any ghost would dare to try
> Girl, this is thriller, thriller-night … So let me hold you close and a killer, thriller, tonight.[31]

Thriller plays on a '*double entendre* of the meaning of "thrill" '.[32] In addition to the semantic pun, the word-play, of *thrill's* neutral valence (thrills might be pleasurable *or* scary) there is an additional sonic facet to consider in the sense of a homophonic play. Was this double meaning of 'thriller-night' a machismo brag of 'thrill-*her*' night?

Margo Jefferson, in *On Michael Jackson*, draws attention to the strong themes of the macabre and freakish spectacles that resonated so profoundly with Jackson in later life.[33] Jefferson mentions some of the 'disciplinary' tactics Jackson's father used on Michael and his siblings. She then references the figure of a German chapbook character from the early sixteenth century; *Till Enulenspiegel* (scatological pranks where his pedagogical methodology of correcting vices). Jefferson suggests there was a 'freaky *Till Enulenspiegel* quality to some of the abuse.'[34] She writes of how Jackson's father

> put on ghoulish masks and scared his children awake, tapping on their bedroom window, pretending to break in and standing over their beds, waiting for them to wake up screaming. This adds a new dimension to the monsters in the haunted mansion of *Thriller*.[35]

Later in the book, in the chapter 'Home'—a pointed oxymoron for a touring family —Jefferson describes members of the Jackson family in turn.[36] She briefly references the older brothers' recreational activities, activities that occurred in close proximity to Michael in the various hotels and motels they stayed at during their *Jackson* 5 years. Jefferson

[31] Ibid., 39.

[32] Ibid., 39.

[33] See 'Freaks' chapter in Margo Jefferson, *On Michael Jackson* (New York, USA. Vintage Books/Random House, 2007), 3–27.

[34] Ibid., 34.

[35] Jefferson, *On Michael Jackson*, 34.

[36] Ibid., 28–52.

catalogues, her brevity evoking glib sibling cruelty, a couple of the brother's nicknames for their younger brother: 'They had the usual sibling ways of getting back at Michael. Cruel nicknames ("Liver Lips" and "Big Nose"), the light bullying all older children have at their command, plus the right to set the general pace of daily life.'[37] On this last point of elder privilege, she expands: 'This was especially true when it came to sex: Jackie, Tito and Jermaine flirted and fucked to their heart's content in plain sight of Michael.'[38]

Perhaps such experiences, the father's abuse and the brother's conduct of sex, were not 'in plain sight'. Perhaps such experiences were close enough to be audible (and olfactory) in the shared rooms each night during tours, but not necessarily *in sight*. In this sense the sounds of bodies—the neutral valence of thrill—opens speculation.[39]

Were the vocal registers of thrill heard with an incorrectly assumed negative valence in the small hours? *Are they hurting her/him*? In this sense, one wonders about the genesis of the term 'thriller night'. Taking the homophonic possibility of the term, thrill-her: perhaps young Michael did not experience this promise/or experience of thrill in the same way as his brother's might've employed the term? One speculates if young undercover Michael perceived the brothers' thrills and their father's nocturnal thrilling in equally negative valence. Considering a likely biographical genesis of the Janus-sensed *Thriller*, the play between terror, horror and sexual frisson is all the more troubling, in light of this early possibility of *acousmatic* horror.[40]

Mercer argues that this tension, between the two types of thrill, is conjured in the demarcations of voice that Roland Barthes detailed in his 'The Grain of the Voice'.[41] Mercer writes:

[37] Ibid., 48.

[38] Ibid., 48.

[39] This acousmatic stem of speculation is one avenue of fantasy Jean Laplanche and Jean-Bertrand Pontalis explore in "Fantasy and the Origins of Sexuality" in *Formations of Fantasy*, ed. Victor Burgin Victor; James Donald & Cora Kaplan (London/New York: Routledge, 1986), 5–34.

[40] Note at this juncture (before the discussion of jouissance) Poizat's description of Lulu's cry in Alban Berg's *Lulu*. 'the jouissance felt as tearful and trembling joy at the sound of beauty is overturned as well, and topples into the shudders and tears of pure horror.' (Poizat, *The Angel's Cry*, 205)

[41] Roland Barthes, *Image-Music-Text* (London: Fontana, 1977), 179–189.

> sexuality is perhaps *the* central preoccupation of the soul tradition. But [...] the power of soul as a cultural form to express sexuality does not so much lie in the literal meanings of the words but in the passion of the singer's voice and vocal performance. The explicit meanings of the lyrics are in this sense secondary to the sensual resonance of the individual character of the voice, its "grain." [...] the "grain" of the voice encodes the contradictions of sexual relationships, their pleasures and pain [...] In "Thriller" it is the grain of Jackson's voice that expresses and plays with this sexual subtext and it is this dimension that transgresses the denotation of the lyrics and escapes analytic reduction.[42]

Mercer's reading of Jackson's *Thriller* follows a demarcation Barthes appropriated from Julia Kristeva (and in turn Šaumjan Soboleva) and applied to song: the *pheno-song* and the *geno-song*, positing the concept of 'grain' as characteristic of the latter.[43] Although Mercer does not directly reference these terms his reading is clearly working from the difference between the sensuousness of voice and the coded language level of the lyric. There is the word and how the word is said.

Barthes defines the pheno-song as language in the broadest sense. He writes that the pheno-song 'covers all the phenomena, all the features which belong to the structure of the language being sung, the rules of the genre, the coded form of the melisma, [...] in short, everything in the performance which is in the service of communication'.[44] The *geno-song* by contrast is that which cannot be reduced to language, cannot be coded. Two facets of geno-song should be considered. Firstly, it concerns the sonic characteristics of a singing voice. Secondly, the geno-song harbours the 'grain' of voice. It is this 'grain' that Barthes argues to register the corporeal, sensual, *jouissance* and frisson of voice's relation to the body from which it issues. Barthes writes:

> The geno-song is the volume of the singing and speaking voice, the space where significations germinate 'from within language and its very materiality'; it forms a signifying play having nothing to do with communication, representation (of feelings), expression; it is that apex (or that depth) of

[42] Mercer, "Monster Metaphors: Notes on Michael Jackson's *Thriller*", 39.

[43] Itself borrowed from Šaumjan Soboleva. See Johanne Prud'homme and Lyne Légaré, "Semanalysis. Engendering the Formula,", *Signo: Theoretical Semiotics on the Web*, accessed April 10, 2019,
http://www.signosemio.com/kristeva/semanalysis.asp.

[44] Barthes, *Image-Music-Text*, 182.

> production where the melody really works at the language—not at what it says, but the voluptuousness of its sounds-signifiers.[45]

Barthes provides two illustrative examples of the difference between the grainy geno-song and the coded phenol-song: consecutively Charles Panzéra, the Swiss operatic and concert baritone (whom he favours), and Dietrich Fischer-Dieskau, the German baritone and conductor. When writing of Fischer-Dieskau, Barthes, in all but word, frames his voice as perfect but boring and lacking any sense of the corporeal. He writes that Fischer-Dieskau is

> assuredly an artist beyond reproach: everything in the (semantic and lyrical) structure is respected and yet nothing seduces, nothing sways us to *jouissance*. His art is inordinately expressive [...] and hence never exceeds culture: here it is the soul which accompanies the song, ***not the body***.[46]

Barthes diagnoses Fischer-Dieskau's anodyne inoffensiveness as symptomatic of the tyrannical privileging of respiration in singing pedagogy: 'the whole of musical pedagogy teaches not the culture of the 'grain' of the voice but the emotive modes of its delivery—the myth of respiration.'[47] What follows is a lament of perfect singing that lacks grain. It is a passionate turn with a whiff of 'writer's Beaujolais' whereby he errs towards the casual side of argument.[48] The passage contains an abrupt leap, almost non sequitur, disparaging the organs of respiration before succumbing to a phallocentric conceptualization of the pleasures of the body:

> How many singing teachers have we not heard prophesying that the art of vocal music rested entirely on the mastery, the correct discipline of breathing! [...] The lung, a stupid organ (lights for cats!), swells but gets no erection; it is in the throat, place where the phonic metal hardens and is segmented, in the mask that *significance* explodes, bringing not the soul but *jouissance*. With FD, I seem only to hear the lungs, never the tongue, the glottis, the teeth, the mucous membranes, the nose.[49]

[45] Ibid., 182.
[46] Ibid., 183, second emphasis added.
[47] Ibid., 183.
[48] Roland Barthes, *Mythologies* (New York: The Noonday Press, 1991), 58–59.
[49] Barthes, *Image-Music-Text*, 183.

On Charles Panzéra, he writes (one can see in this passage Panzéra's term 'patinated'—Barthes' word choice, 'grain', is perhaps a register of his admiration and fealty to the baritone's approach to singing):

> Panzera's art, on the contrary, was in the letters, not in the bellows. [...] With regard to the consonants, too readily thought to constitute the very armature of our language [...] and always prescribed as needing to be 'articulated', detached, emphasized in order to fulfill the clarity of meaning, Panzera recommended that in many cases they be *patinated*, given the wear of a language that had been living, functioning, and working for ages past.[50]

Mercer's description of how it is Jackson's voice evoking the thrills of *Thriller*, in thematic juxtaposition to the lyrics, clearly plays on Barthes' uptake of the Soboleva/Kristeva demarcation. It also runs Barthes' embedded parallel of thrills implicit in the term *jouissance*. Mercer's line—'the "grain" of the voice encodes the contradictions of sexual relationships, their pleasures and pain'—locates the ambiguous and/or vacillating valence of *thrill* in a similar sense as Barthes' jouissance in the grain of Jackson's voice.[51]

Mercer's diaphonic proposal that the grain of Jackson's voice evokes the sexual thrill in contradistinction to the horror themes of the lyrics not only carries over Barthes partitioning of song along the Soboleva/Kristeva differentiation of geno-text (the realm of grain) and pheno-text. Mercer's argument also takes up Barthes' emphasis on the sensual/corporeal relations grain evokes in voice. The sense of corporeal relation, sensuous, yet phantom in its quasi-tactile nature, is maintained in Mercer's reading of Jackson's voice. Barthes writes: 'The 'grain' is the body in the voice as it sings, [...] I am determined to listen to my relation with the body of the *man or woman singing* or playing and relation is erotic'.[52] Similarly Mercer pitches voice, qua medium for corporeal seduction and interaction, in terms of Jackson's infectious rhythmic funk. More specifically, the relation of bodies is levelled in terms of an incitement of dance, the compelling of the body. Mercer firstly frames dance with an erotic prospect. He writes of

[50] Ibid., 184.

[51] Mercer, "Monster Metaphors: Notes on Michael Jackson's *Thriller*", 39.

[52] Barthes, *Image-Music-Text*, 188, emphasis added in order to underscore a resonance with Jefferson's exploration of Jackson's liminal and paradoxical performances of gender(s). See Jefferson's chapter "Alone of All His Race, Alone of All Her Sex" in *On Michael Jackson*, 79–105.

dance as a 'cultural form and erotic ritual, [...] a mode of decoding the sound and meaning generated in the music.'[53] After priming the reader with the erotic prospect of dance Mercer then couches Jackson's soulful voice in *Thriller* as an 'incitement of the listener to dance, to become an active participant in the texture of voice, words and rhythm, soul music is not merely "about" sexuality, but is itself a musical means for the eroticization of the body'.[54]

Mercer's text effectively rearticulates Barthes' corporeal and erotic articulation of grain to draw out not just the ambiguous valence manifest in the voice/lyric dynamic of *Thriller* but also the libidinal infectiousness of a voice affecting the listener's body. Barthes writes: 'I can hear with certainty—the certainty of the body, of *thrill*.'[55] Mercer's application of the intrinsic *thrill* of grain—the frisson of erotic corporeal relation—works well to articulate the affective potency of Jackson's voice and addresses his idiosyncratic and rhythmic dynamicism. Mercer's contribution, his reading of *Thriller* as libidinous seduction and horror, is pertinent in the present context of narratives concerning Jackson. Listening to *Thriller* now and sensing these schizophrenic modalities of grain, its funk-laden eroticism will forever be alloyed to horror.

"Get Away!"

After a caveat establishing that Michael Jackson "in no way endorses a belief in the occult" we see the gore-blood font of the title, *Thriller*, shimmering against black. We hear breathing. Slow wispy breaths; are these Michael's? *When was the last time you heard the intimacy of respiration, in the dark, without the seeing a face?* These are heavy breaths. Exhaustion. What cause? Exertion? Haste? From passion or fear?

The breathing stops and the *slasher*-font title fades.[56] We hear the *ribbit* of amphibian serenade, the din of telegramming cicadas and stridulating crickets. We are in the country: *oppressive nature.* A car rolls past trees in the dark of night, and twigs snap underneath tyres. Its engine splutters and cuts out. Michael and *his girl* are in the car. Picking up the thread of reading *Thriller* as a dialectic horror-romance. Mercer writes:

[53] Mercer, "Monster Metaphors: Notes on Michael Jackson's *Thriller*", 39.
[54] Ibid., 39.
[55] Barthes, *Image-Music-Text*, 188, emphasis added.
[56] Reminiscent of Tobe Hooper's *The Texas Chainsaw Massacre* (1974).

> In the opening sequence equilibrium is established and then disrupted. The dialogue and exchange of glances between Michael and "the girl" (as male and female protagonists of the story) establish a "romance" as the narrative pretext. The girl's look at Michael as the car stops hints at a question, answered by bemused incredulity on his face. Did he stop the car on purpose? Was it a romantic ruse, to lure her into a trap? The girl's coquettish response to Michael's defence ("Honestly, we're out of gas") lingers sensually on the syllables, "*So* ... what are we going to do now?" Her question, and his smile in return, hint at and exacerbate the underlying erotic tension of romantic intrigue between the two characters.[57]

This moment has the sex-death *thrill* dyad of teen horror: teenagers venture away from the suburbs (rural locales, Hollywood would have us fear, are chock-full of lethal threats—either maniac yokels or supernatural beings), on an odyssey of sexual awakening, a covert quest for romantic experience.[58] The 'girl' (played by Ola Ray) when she asks Michael '*So* ... what are we going to do now?' is not only asking Michael a question—she's also asking, almost on the viewer's behalf, to resolve the erotic tension of the narrative pretext.

Reid Kane, in 'The King of Pop's Two Bodies, or Thriller as Allegory', writes that the scene 'stages a paradigmatic display of heteronormative sexual virility, in which the varsity-jacket sporting boy with car "runs out of gas", an idiomatic attempt at seduction.'[59] After 'the girl's' question the scene cuts, and we see feet clicking against a pavement.[60] The girl's legs walk alongside Michael's, his Blue Jeans rolled to display ice-white sports socks and those shiny black *Bass Weejuns* slip-ons. The scene is theatrical

[57] Mercer, "Monster Metaphors: Notes on Michael Jackson's *Thriller*", 42.

[58] Sex is the premise that leads to death, a demise. A petite-mort becomes mort proper, usually in the form of overblown heteronormative and phallonarcissistic brutality—a chase, some ravaging, a painful penetration. *Texas Chainsaw Massacre* is just as much about middle-class townies experiencing the thrill of the local boys one summer as it is an exercise in re-hashing the back-water deprivations and depravations of Ed Gein.

[59] Reid Kane, 'The King of Pop's two bodies, or Thriller as allegory,' *The Resistible Demise of*

Michael Jackson, ed. Mark Fisher, 233–243 (Winchester, UK: Zero Books, 2009), 237.

[60] Michael's a minimal impression of a male protagonist, video-tape-thin. The girl is just as wilfully depthless. Mercer writes: 'Michael's dialogue gives a minimal "character" to his role as the boyfriend: he appears to be a somewhat shy, very proper and polite "boy next door." The girl, on the other hand, is not so much a character as the "girlfriend" type.'

Americana—a sort of *horromance*.[61] As the camera pans up, we see their 1950s' get-up, a normative burlesque pairing of cheerleader and top jock.

This opening segment is, according to director John Landis, partially based on the 1957 film *I Was a Teenage Werewolf*.[62] Mercer writes 'their clothes—a pastiche fifties retro style—connote youthful innocence, the couple as archetypal teen lovers.'[63] Jefferson too notes the loaded retro costumes:

> *Thriller* begins as Michael, wearing red leather, walks along a deserted street with a fresh faced, pony-tailed girl in a felt skirt, white blouse and saddle shoes. They are 1950s vintage teenagers. (We rarely saw such Negro boys and girls next door in the 1950s.)[64]

Returning to the diegesis, it is clear the car has run out of fuel. 'I'm sorry I didn't believe you.' The girl says (it *wasn't* a ruse). 'Can I ask you something?' Asks Michael in his boyishly smooth lilt. They are alone, just dark trees and foliage foley. Jefferson offers commentary:

> "You know I like you," he tells her, shyly but winningly. "And I like you," she says eagerly. "Will you be my girl?" he asks. "Oh, yes," she answers. But there's something he wants to say to her. A shadow crosses his face. "You know I'm not like the other guys," he says, to which she responds, "I know. That's why I like you."[65]

With starched formality Michael asks: 'I was wondering if … you would be my girl.'[66] She is delighted. 'Oh, Michael', she sighs and they embrace. Michael, then, presents her with a ring. 'It's beautiful.' She says, holding

[61] A mix of whole-milk-Spielbergesque nostalgia fused with George Lucas' *American Graffiti*—all cars, girls (objects without names) and school-sport backdrops.

[62] John Landis, "John Landis on the making of Michael Jackson's Thriller: 'I was adamant he couldn't look too hideous'," *The Guardian*, August 31, 2017, accessed March 20, 2019 https://www.theguardian.com/film/2017/aug/31/john-landis-on-the-making-of-michael-jacksons-thriller-i-was-adamant-he-couldnt-look-too-hideous.

[63] Mercer, "Monster Metaphors: Notes on Michael Jackson's *Thriller*", 42.

[64] Jefferson, *On Michael Jackson*, 15.

[65] Ibid., 15–16.

[66] Invoking 'the theme of possession'. See Reid Kane, "The King of Pop's two bodies, or Thriller as allegory' in *The Resistible Demise of Michael Jackson*, edited by Mark Fisher, 233–243 (Winchester, UK: Zero Books, 2009), 237.

her hand up to admire the forged material symbolizing ownership. 'Now it's official,' smiles Michael.

Michael, however, has one more thing to say, something difficult to say: a confession. He looks up timidly. 'A shadow crosses his face. "You know I'm not like other guys," he says, to which she responds, "I know, that's why I like you."'[67] Michael, now serious and unsmiling goes on: 'no, I mean I'm different.'[68] His girl, now confused, asks him what he is talking about before an array of horror tropes are unleashed. A flute solo, in an eerie, suspended or diminished sounding scale, evoking confusion or ominous uncertainty, flutters and twists. Dark clouds part to reveal a full moon.

Michael looks scared, he bends double holding his stomach as if in pain. His face is hidden from view. He gives a slight yelp before folding over, out of shot. His girl asks: 'Are you alright?' We hear a strange croaking, a deep whine or growl. *What is happening to Michael?* He is obviously in pain; something has suddenly brought this on. The deep guttural noises imply a drastic physical change or awful symptom is underway. But what? Moments later, our questions are answered. Michael looks up at his girl and barks 'get away!' Jefferson writes of this as 'The defacement.'[69]

It is a strange, horrifying voice, an inhuman voice. It sounds as if it comes from two places at once, its resonance artificial. There is an odd dissonance, a gravelly metallic quality to the words. It sounds quite unlike the Michael we knew from the beginning of the video. His soft, boyish voice is coarsened, deepened and pained. It is a voice with over-drive added (and *just what drive* might that be?), distorted and crackly: *bristling with noise*. This voice hits the viewer before Jackson's appearance sinks in.[70] His eyes are yellow, bright yellow like cat's eyes, and his teeth are now pointed. The T of 'Get Away!' reveals two rows of vicious-looking incisors. Michael is transforming: a 'grotesque metamorphosis'.[71] Jefferson writes that Michael 'turns from a beautiful young man into a hairy, red-eyed werewolf.'[72]

[67] Jefferson, *On Michael Jackson*, 16.

[68] *Of course* Michael is 'not like other guys' the scene is eerily close to biographical parallel. The superstar Michael adored, loved and categorically not like other guys. Allegedly, when Michael presented the video to his family his brothers fell about laughing at this line. Michael told them to 'shut up'.

[69] Jefferson, *On Michael Jackson*, 16.

[70] In cinema physics are backwards, sound is faster, more immediate than screen.

[71] Kane, "The King of Pop's two bodies, or Thriller as allegory", 237.

[72] Jefferson, *On Michael Jackson*, 16.

The moment is similar to the transformation scenes in John Landis' *An American Werewolf in London* (1981). The depiction of hair and nail growth, excruciatingly extending limbs, protruding bones, is achieved by the same make-up team and follows a similar cinematography. Rick Baker's transformative make-up effects are effectively transposed from the werewolf transformation scenes in *An American Werewolf in London* onto Michael in *Thriller* (only this time the transformation is to a type of "Werecat").[73] Why is Michael's voice so striking when 'he' says 'Get away!' in this opening hypo-diegetic sequence?

In *An American Werewolf in London* a transforming body is depicted and the character, David Kessler played by David Naughton, vocalizes. But this voice does not elicit quite the same horror as Michael's 'Get away!'[74] There are a few differences between Michael's transformation and that of David Kessler. Michael's transformation occurs just moments into *Thriller*, in the hypo-diegetic film-within-a-film opening sequence. It's a prelude of sorts. The scene of 'Get away!' is revealed to be a hammed-up 1950s' B-movie horror film Michael and his girl watch in a cinema. In the 1950s' B-movie scene, it is not certain what makes the '50s Michael 'not like other guys' or why he folds double when a shadow falls across his face. When Michael looks up and barks 'Get away!' it is the first time the viewer can perceive (see *and* hear) that a profound physical change is at hand. David Kessler's transformation in *An American Werewolf in London* occurs, by contrast, almost an hour into the film, whereby the viewer knows exactly what sort of change is coming. Secondly, in *An American Werewolf in London*, the visual clues of lycanthropic metamorphosis are delivered well before any vocalization can signal the horrific change. The voice that sounds from Kessler comes *after* the body undergoes great change. We see his hand growing, his body elongating, this back sprout thick black hairs; we see his teeth change and his posture revert to quadrupedalism, all before Kessler's voice sounds different to its usual tone.

The 'Get away!' moment in *Thriller* is quite different. It has horrific impact because it announces change but does not confirm what change is meant. The guttural 'Get away!' that vents from the body of Michael is the

[73] John Landis, "John Landis on the making of Michael Jackson's Thriller: 'I was adamant he couldn't look too hideous.'"

[74] Anecdotal accounts from viewers suggest that it is the moment when Michael suddenly looks up and growls 'Get away!' as the most terrifying and horrific moment in the video. See "Michael Jackson, "Thriller"," *1980s Music Video Closet*, accessed March 19, 2019, https://videoclosetblog.wordpress.com/michael-jackson-thriller/.

first clue that a corporeal change is imminent (in tandem with his yellow eyes and sharp teeth). It is a liminal voice, a sound of change but not a voice resultant from a completed change. Kessler's voice, in structural contrast, limps behind the spectacle of make-up and prophetic effects, all of which imply a transformation the viewer not just understands but *expects*. The vocalization from the almost completed lycanthropic transformation of Kessler is an affirming return to cohesion: a werewolf that looks *and* sounds like one. Once the prosthetic special effects have established Kessler's change into a werewolf in visual terms the vocal component sounds out in resolve: he looks like a dog, and, now, sounds like one too. In sounding body terms Michael's transformation is an inversion of Kessler. A voice that does not sound like Michael arrives first, along with minimal clues (just the teeth and eyes) that a change is looming.

A further difference is that this moment of voice in *Thriller* is also a command/warning. 'Get away!' is speech albeit voiced in a guttural and harsh tone one might not expect from the boyish teen in the varsity jacket. This additional difference invites an uncomfortable import. From Aristotle to Lacan, language is presupposed as exclusively human. Whales and birds may have 'song' but only humans speak, only humans, so the fallacy goes, apply vocalization to language. Thus, when Michael seems to growl 'Get away!' a tension opens up. A split nature is evoked. Due to the utterance of a human language one takes Michael to on some level *still* be the same human being who *honestly ran out of gas* (the caring human, now concerned for 'his girl'). The command frames the figure of Michael as not completely 'dehumanized' beyond the horizon of human (in this case American-English) language. This is, however, voiced in a voice that is radically different from the young man we've witnessed for a few seconds of dialogue previously. Thus, voice and its words sound out in a striking lycanthropic contrapposto: a dissonance of species, a question of being, opens up in this voice. The utterance is a schizo-voice: voicing the anthropic concern of the human-teen in, and through, an 'inhuman' phonic *palette*.

The following moments in *Thriller* show Michael's transformation into a fully transitioned werecat; Rick Baker's elaborate make-up artistry is the spectacle here. These are much the same as the bulk of the werewolf transformation scenes in *An American Werewolf in London*.

Reid Kane writes of how once Michael has finished transforming '[t]he creature corners the girl, pinning her down, overwhelming her with masculine/animal sexual virility run amok.'[75] Note the forward slash in Kane's comment—suggesting the video's depiction of physical dominance and predatory devouring as either/or human male sexuality and animal.[76]

Mercer writes that, 'werewolf mythology—lycanthropy—concerns the representation of male sexuality as "naturally" predatory, bestial, aggressive, violent—in a word, "monstrous".'[77] He notes that the werecat 'chases her, pins her down', in an act of physical dominance. Mercer continues:

> the monster's dominant position and the supine position of the victim suggests rape, fusing the underlying sexual relation of romance with terror and violence. As the monster, Michael transformation might suggest that beneath the boy-next-door image there is a "real" man waiting to break out, a man whose masculinity is measured by a rapacious sexual appetite, "hungry like the wolf."[78]

The werecat scene is notably a hypo-diegesis. After were-Michael *gets* 'his girl' we cut to see Michael and another girl watching the scene in a cinema. This story within a story, film-within-a-film, narrative location of a super-masculinized teen (to horrific supernatural proportions) could be interpreted as Jackson's expression of discomfort and cynicism for his revamped macho and adult persona.

Epic records were pushing to portray Jackson as a 'red-blooded' young man. In the main sequence his red leather jacket, designed by Deborah Landis, was designed to make him appear more 'virile'.[79] The deep red trousers and V-shaped jacket of the main sequence are so overblown that Michael appears like a caricature of heteronormative masculinity. Was this short hypo-diegesis within *Thriller* Jackson's part-veiled critique of a record company wishing to portray him as a safely marketable sexually normative adult male? Landis said 'The reality is, it was a vanity video. Everything that happened on 'Thriller' happened because Michael wanted

[75] Reid Kane, "The King of Pop's two bodies, or Thriller as allegory' in *The Resistible Demise of* Michael Jackson, 237.

[76] *Gorgeous* can be taken in a similar double meaning as *thrill*. To gorge.

[77] Mercer, "Monster Metaphors: Notes on Michael Jackson's *Thriller*", 46.

[78] Ibid.,. 46.

[79] His deep red trousers and V-shaped jacket of the main sequence are so overblown that Michael appears more like a camp and caricaturesque representation of heteronormative masculinity. Perhaps that was his critical intention.

to turn into a monster.'[80] It is as if he is performing the absurdity of his new image. *So you want me to be virile and red-blooded huh?*

Michael's transformation can be regarded as metaphor for puberty and awakened sexual desire. The growth of hair, whiskers and fur where there was none before. The sudden change in temperament from an innocent and polite young man to one of violent impulse and predatory aggression. The corporeal transformations of puberty are caricatured, in *Thriller*, as B-movie body-horror tropes. The werecat has a larger head, longer fingers, bigger arms, feet and hands. Landis, commenting on the popular tendency to couch puberty in terms of supernatural transformation, said that in adolescence 'youngsters begin to grow hair in unexpected places and parts of their anatomy swell and grow (…) Everyone experiences these physical transformations in their bodies and new, unfamiliar, sexual thoughts in their minds. No wonder we readily accept the concept of a literal metamorphosis.'[81]

For the child-superstar that did not want to grow up, the soul superstar who wanted to remain a boy forever in a Never-Neverland, the effects of puberty are aptly couched in the vocabulary of horror.

A parallel between the absurd transformation from boy to werecat within the horror-film hypo-diegesis and the ultra-macho crimson leather wardrobe of the main cinema date/zombie narrative leads to a pointed question: which is the more horrific depiction of imposed maturity? The date/zombie sequence is an extended metaphor for the enforced dressing up and posturing as a virile young normative male: doing the moves but 'dead inside'. The werecat hypo-diegesis, by contrast, might well be an elaborate metaphor of how Jackson regarded growing up. This latter prospect is a change of the body; the former is merely a change of wardrobe. One can always disrobe off set, whereas the body, as biographical details sadly evidence, is not so easily shed. To re-purpose Landis' comment: "Thriller' happened because Michael wanted to turn into a monster'[82]: *because he didn't want to turn into a monster.*

The change of voice that sounds the words 'Get away!' may be read as conveying corporeal horror of puberty. In this sense the scene is pubescent

[80] "12 Thrilling Facts about Michael Jackson's Thriller," *Rolling Stone*, accessed March 3, 2019, https://www.rollingstone.com/music/news/12-thrilling-facts-about-michael-jacksons-thriller-20131029.

[81] Ibid.

[82] Ibid.

male voice transformation writ large in the tropes of 1950s' B-movie horror. It reanimates, within a horror-genre narrative and pretext, sudden changes of voice resultant from the increase in vocal tract length that occurs at the onset of puberty in humans. This voice change (sometimes referred to as voice mutation or voice break) results in approximately an octave drop in vocal tone for adult male humans.[83]

In *Foundations of Voice Studies: An Interdisciplinary Approach to Voice Production and Perception* Kreiman and Siditis detail this pubescent 'mutation'. They write that males:

> undergo voice mutation ("change in voice") as a result of laryngeal growth. Although mutation is highly variable and can last up to three years (…), the process usually begins between ages 11 and 14, and lasts between eight and 26 months (with an average duration of about 18 months). During this time, the angle of the male thyroid cartilage decreases to about 70-85 degrees. (The angle remains fairly constant in females throughout life (…)) This narrowing, combined with the disproportionate growth in the membranous part of the vocal folds, results in the protrusion of the apex of the cartilage, called the thyroid notch of "Adam's apple." (…) The bulk of the thyroarytenoid muscle also increases, and the vocal folds thicken and change shape as a result. (…) This causes important changes in *how* the vocal folds vibrate.[84]

Kreiman and Siditis then detail how these changes, in turn, alter the sound of voice.[85] Physical changes manifest through a voice of 'greater overall amplitude' and 'richer harmonic structure'.[86] They also describe how '[r]apid change in the size and configuration of the vocal folds also causes pitch breaks (sudden, unwanted shifts between modal and falsetto phonation) in male voices as males learn new muscular patterns to control the new shape of the vocal folds.'[87] Note that such sudden and unwanted shifts of voice sound out a lack of control and mastery over voice. This aspect of voice change resonates with a typical horror thematic: the dispossession of the subject wrought by exogenous possession: puberty qua

[83] Jody Kreiman and Siditis, Diana, *Foundations of Voice Studies: An Interdisciplinary Approach to Voice Production and Perception* (Chichester, UK: Wiley-Blackwell, 2013), 114.

[84] Ibid., 114–115.

[85] Alter—from Medieval Latin *alterare* ("to make other").

[86] Kreiman and Siditis, *Foundations of Voice Studies: An Interdisciplinary Approach to Voice Production and Perception*, 115.

[87] Ibid., 115.

curse. The body transformed and possessed by a foreign and unfamiliar force affects the human's mastery of voice.

One can sympathize with the anxiety and horror this sudden and unwanted lack of control might yield for a person such as Jackson. Jackson was originally a child singer, and his body changed remarkably in the period between early Jackson 5 recordings and the *Thriller* LP, by which time he was twenty-four. It is not too much of a claim to suggest that up to this point much of his success and identity rested on his mastery of his body, in terms of either vocal accomplishment or dance. Michael Jackson was *Michael Jackson* because of this corporeal mastery.

The horror of puberty possessing the corpus, affecting vocal tract cartilage, creating strange new growths, is re-enacted in 'Get away!' as a supernatural and lycanthropic force. The Kreiman and Siditis passage is peppered with terms that would not be out of place in the margins of a horror movie script. The throat and its cartilage are written about in terms of 'mutation', 'disproportionate growth' and 'protrusion'.

When Michael looks up and reveals his teeth and yellow eyes, when he snarls 'Get away!' in a noise-laden metallic rasp, was this how Michael feared his voice might sound once puberty had transformed him from a boy? Referring, once again to Director John Landis' remark that *Thriller* happened 'because Michael wanted to turn into a monster', we can regard *Thriller* as not only a vanity project about mainstream depictions of a public adult persona and physical horror trope expressions of puberty but as a candid autobiographical expression of the dread and horror of pubescent voice mutation.

There is a further biographical parallel to consider. Gratis of an iTunes-fickle sonic survey of Jackson's later hits, the horrifying moment of 'Get away!' is eerily prescient. *It is not unlike Michael's future voice.* 'Get away!', viewed today, is a horrifying vocal premonition, a phonic-spectre.[88]

Thriller harbours a horrifying kernel of the changes ahead. Listening to the *Thriller* album, Jackson's voice is mostly disco-synth smooth. Even on "Beat It", the most aggressive expression of machismo on *Thriller*, Jackson's voice is smoothly sonorous and tuneful. It seldom breaks into

[88] Colin Davis "Hauntology, Spectres and Phantoms" in *French Studies*, Volume 59, Issue 3, 1 July 2005, Pages 373–379—I use spectre pointedly here as precursor, a spectre as being futural, in contradistinction to a phantom—a misleading figure from the past. To summarize the distinction briefly and disregard a plethora of imports—phantoms are liars from the past, whereas spectres are figures of foreboding.

the strained rasp and growl of his later sound. *Bad* (1987) contains a radically different voice. Listen to the gasps, rasps or yelps on a track such as "Another Part of Me" (from *Bad*) or the rabid gnashing, gibbering and clucking backing track on "Smooth Criminal" (also *Bad*). The soulfulness of Jackson's early voice is melded to asignifying 'animalistic' vocal tics: snaps, barks and bites that erupt spasmodically between more soulful lines. By 1992's *Dangerous* Jackson would be more Werecat than the soul-cat of his earlier recordings. Tracks such as 'Jam', 'Why You Wanna Trip On Me' and 'Black or White' contain barely any of the boyishly smooth vocal tones of his earlier voice, the voice of *Off The Wall* and *Thriller* (1979 and 1982 respectively). In the albums that followed *Thriller*, when Jackson is not barking words in raspy rhythmic spasms of staccato glossolalia, he howls anguished lines, strained gravely and hoarse, more like the pained vocal tear of Cobain's raw baritone than the voice of the smooth young man from The Jackson 5.

The moment in *Thriller* when Michael growls 'Get away!' is a horrifying precursor of what had yet to come on a number of levels: massive physical changes, increasingly reclusive, a voice hoarsened and prone to break out in unrepressed gnashes of fervid aggression and bubbling predation.[89] This brief moment in the 1950s' horror-spoof hypo-diegesis at the beginning of *Thriller*, despite being theatrical and synthetic, is much closer to the future Jackson than the 'virile' red leather jacket of the main narrative. It vocalizes not just Jackson's anxieties about adulthood but sounds out his future voice with uncanny accuracy: a vocal spectre, a horrifying omen, that at once disrupts the viewer's epistemological security of the body on screen and registers unfathomable corporeal changes.

Biographical prescience aside, it is worth returning to a comparison of this horrifying vocal moment with the '*Che Bella Voce!*' joke Dolar utilizes in his introduction in *A Voice and Nothing More*. This liminal verbal torsion between lycanthropic voice and human language returns us once more to the two obfuscatory modes of voice that Dolar claims obfuscate 'the object voice'.

Dolar's approach takes this binary as an either/or premise (e.g. the Italian soldiers in the introductory '*Che Bella Voce!*' joke hear voice but seem deaf to the command).[90] But is it not the case that the affective and

[89] As noted previously, see, with trepidation, *Leaving Neverland* HBO/Channel 42,019. Dir. Dan Reed.

[90] Dolar, *A Voice and Nothing More*, 3.

distinctly corporeal essence of this verbal growl lies in a voice that resists to be taken in either signifying or aesthetic registers but oscillates between? In this tension between articulated speech—the meaning of which is over-coded with voice—and a voice not of the young man on screen (but is, nonetheless, in service of his sentiment) a chasm, a lacuna, opens. An irresolvable question, a dissonance, arrives. Perhaps it is in the opening up of this penumbra where a horror of object *a* voice emerges?

Of course, unlike the Italian soldiers the viewer does not hear a voice of beauty, but its timbre and sonic character are highly affective (albeit in negative valence). Yet, there is a command, an instruction of 'Get Away!' This is the torsion of the scene that evokes horror: not the grain of the voice, not the sound or sense of the body, nor the words it carries but a voice of mercurial body beyond each.

After presenting the '*Che Bella Voce!*' joke, Dolar ventures to use a passage from Walter Benjamin's 'Theses on the Philosophy of History'. More specifically, Dolar uses Benjamin's account of an automaton chess player created by Wolfgang von Kempelen (later taken over and toured by Johann Nepomuk Maelzel) as a prolegomenon. This passage is a little jump, there is a break in the text from the preceding '*Che Bella Voce!*' example that sets meaning and aesthetics as antithetical foci that obfuscate 'the object voice'. This subsequent section, concerning the chess player, does not address beauty or language. Dolar provides details about the origins of this chess automaton.[91] Its history, although fascinating, does not need to be recounted here. Benjamin's text describes the puppet 'in Turkish attire' whereby 'a little hunchback who was an expert chess player' pulled the strings.[92] He then writes of a 'philosophical counterpart to this puppetry': 'The puppet called "historiographical materialism" is to win all the time.'[93] Dolar declares that the main focus of Benjamin's text, 'historical materialism and theology', be left aside.[94] He then asks a question that lies at the heart of the instance of horror when 'Michael' snarls 'Get Away!': 'Who is literally pulling the strings?'[95]

[91] Dolar, *A Voice and Nothing More*, 6–7. Dolar has a tendency to focus on automaton. See his use of the figure of Olimpia (an automaton from E.T.A Hoffmann's *The Sandman* in Mladen Dolar. "At First Sight" in *Gaze and Voice as Love Objects*, eds Renata Salecl and Slavoj Žižek (Durham and London, UK: Duke University Press, 1996), 144.

[92] Ibid., 5.

[93] Ibid., 5.

[94] Ibid., 5.

[95] Ibid., 5.

Dolar, some pages later, suggests the point of the story is how the chess automaton was presented. The attraction was part of a double bill. Kempelen presented his speaking machine as an introductory spectacle to the chess player. Dolar writes that 'the sequence of the two is crucial.'[96] He elaborates:

> The difference between the two was ostentatious and didactic: first of all, the chess automaton was constructed in such a way as to appear as human like as possible—it made the pretense of being engrossed in deep thought, it rolled its eyes, and so on—while the speaking machine was as mechanical as possible: it did not try to hide its mechanical nature; on the contrary, it exhibited it conspicuously. Its main attraction was the enigma of how something so utterly non-human could produce human effects. The anthropomorphic thinking machine was counter balanced by the non-anthropomorphic speaking machine.[97]

Dolar then continues to explicate the significance of how the speaking machine and chess player were presented. He argues it was the voice machine that was the necessary prerequisite for the chess player to appear as a thinking chess machine: 'The first machine was the secret of the second, and the second, the anthropomorphic puppet, had to enlist the services of the first if it was to win.'[98] Dolar's argument then abruptly brings in Lacan's line: 'there is a cause only in something that doesn't work' (from *The Four Fundamental Concepts of Psycho-Analysis*). He then explains:

> The cause appears only at the point of a hitch in causality, a limp, a troubled causality—and this is precisely where Lacan situated the object, the object-cause. But this can perhaps also be seen as the lever of thought, as opposed to the anthropomorphic masquerade of thinking.[99]

As Mowitt notes in other turns, Dolar's tone has tentativeness: *can perhaps also*. Dolar, then, provides the following conclusion:

[96] Ibid., 8.
[97] Ibid., 8–9.
[98] Ibid., 10.
[99] Ibid., 10–11.

> [w]e could bend or transform Benjamin's thesis: *if the puppet called historical materialism is to win, it should enlist the services of the voice.* Hence the need for a theory of voice, the object voice, the voice as one of the paramount "embodiments" of what Lacan called *object petit a.*[100]

Dolar's contribution, at this introductory stage, is clearly marked by the difference in phraseology. He declares: 'the object voice' contra *objet petit a*. Further still, note that the text winces and holds at length the term that evokes the corporeal: 'embodiments'.

Yet, it is in the register of the body that the scene of the two machines is significant. The speaking machine's 'uncanniness', as Dolar terms it, stems from the production of a 'uniquely human' voice via mechanical means.[101] Michael's hoarse bark of 'Get Away!' within *Thriller* is the opposite of the speaking machine: the body looks human, but the voice is a radical departure from the voice associated with the adolescent boy on screen (and Jackson more generally). Michael's 'defacement', as Jefferson terms it, is an inversion of the trajectory of the introduction of the speaking machine serving as a primer before the chess automaton. In *Thriller* it is radical voice that masks the body it erupts from: the body is reduced to a horrific mask by the voice. Dolar describes the sequence of the speaking machine before the chess automaton as a weak teleology whereby the 'former made the latter plausible'.[102] In terms of 'Get Away!' it can be said that voice renders the body on screen implausible, a mere mask of something unknown. The scene is an antithesis to the wonderment of the automaton whereby voice reduces the corpus to horrific façade, one liable to monstrous change. Whereas Dolar suggests that voice may act as the lever of thought—'as opposed to the anthropomorphic masquerade'—might it not also act as provocation of horror unthinkable?

Inhuman Noise and Interspecies Grain in *Black or White*

In 'Glove, socks, zombies, puppets: The unheimlich maneuvers and undead metonyms of Michael Jackson' Sam Davies writes: 'Jackson's voice, with its constant appeal to the unspeakable, its recourse to a

[100] Ibid., 11. Original emphasis.
[101] Ibid., 7.
[102] Ibid., 9.

spasmodic, tic-like, wordless vocabulary, carries the virus which disperses him in inhuman parts.'[103] The line highlights Jackson's frequent recourse from language: his voice's recession into an unspeakable modality of ticks, shrieks, hiccups and clucks. This observation echoes Barthes' partitioning of song in terms of granular (patinated) geno-song and coded expression of the pheno-song. Secondly, this departure from language is couched as animal, a departure from 'the human'. Davies' line draws up a voice departing from language to be a departure from the human.

The notion of animals as being outside the privileges and torments of language is an anthropocentric position (one that runs from Aristotle to Lacan). That said, the suggestion of Jackson's voice as a gateway to an inhuman presence resonates with multiple facets of his oeuvre. Jackson campaigned (in dance and song) against any normative notion of 'the human'. This project frequently manifested as Jackson transforming into other people, animals, werewolves, zombies and invisibility. Taking each theatrical transmutation in turn, one can regard a continuum of flight from the normative human singular: a flight from species, to fantasy, to plurality to ethereality. In terms of instances of morphing into other animals there is an interspecies transcendence. There is a departure from the natural in changes into supernatural figures, such as werewolves/werecats and zombies. Lastly, there is the existential symptom of neurotic want of invisibility: emancipation not just from various forms but also from flesh and blood—the wholesale escape from materiality. In each case, as evidenced by a number of texts, a question of gender, either as an aestheticization, subversion, melding or amalgamation takes place. However, over and above the question of gender is a question of body. Reformulating the phrase connoting fame and infamy, *not just anybody*, Jackson's repeated transformations, reinventions, inhabitations and flights to and from various forms may be read as a claim for *any body* and, equally, *no body.*

Mercer quotes the audience reaction to early footage of Jackson's performance on a 1983 TV special celebrating Motown's twenty-fifth anniversary. The text reads:

> The audience almost visibly tensed as Michael's voice … took complete control, attacking the songs with that increased repertoire of whoops, hiccups

[103] Sam Davies, "Glove, socks, zombies, puppets: The unheimlich maneuvers and undead metonyms of Michael Jackson", *The Resistible Demise of Michael Jackson*, ed. Mark Fisher (Winchester, UK: Zero Books, 2009), 229.

and gasps, with which he punctuates the lyric to such stylish, relaxing effect. And then he danced. The cocky strut of a super confident child had been replaced by a lithe, menacing grace, and his impossibly lean frame, still boyishly gangly, when galvanized by music, assumed a hypnotic, androgynous sexuality.[104]

In the video promo for *Beat It* (1983), Jackson wore a hyper-masculinized wide-shouldered red leather Jacket. The jacket would also feature in *Thriller* (1984). It was designed to evoke the grown-up Michael, to impress the image of Michael as a virile young man.[105] In retrospect the aesthetic looks overcooked, tipping tragically and with pointed critical force into camp.[106] This doomed vein of performing motifs of Western masculinity carried through into the dance routine of *Beat It* whereby Jackson 'disarms the street gangs with his superior charm as he leads an all-male cast through a choreographic sequence that synthesizes the cinematic imagery of *The Warriors* and *West Side Story*'.[107]

Jackson's performance of normative masculine sexuality not just extends beyond the supposed notions of what a young black heterosexual male should be by blurring the borders of high camp, rock glamour and

[104] Mercer, "Monster Metaphors: Notes on Michael Jackson's *Thriller*", 49. This image, of the spasmodic granulated voice and coming from an agile and lissome body, immediately evokes a feline silhouette. There is a history of black performers courting and re-appropriating colonial Western notions of the primitive through the figure of the cat. Maria J Guzman, in her influential thesis "Grace Jones in One Man Show: Music and Culture", in exploring Grace Jones' re-appropriation of the tropes of primitivism and androgyny draws out precisely this appropriation operating in an interspecies modality. Guzman writes of how the 'primitivist symbol of black female sexuality, the wild cat (…) has been used to symbolize black women in art and theatre since the early twentieth century.' Maria, J. Guzman "Grace Jones in One Man Show: Music and Culture" (MA. College of Fine Arts of Ohio University, 2007), 29. Placing Jackson in this continuum is not quite right, for he does not slot into such a lineage for a number of reasons. Firstly, the examples Guzman employs are female and embedded in the history of 'popular images and stereotypes about the black female body, at once desirable and unsettling.' Ibid.,. 25.

[105] Lauren Goode. "Deborah Landis, Designer of the Red Jacket Michael Jackson Wore in "Thriller"". *The Wall Street Journal*. June 30, 2009. https://blogs.wsj.com/speakeasy/2009/06/30/deborah-landis-designer-of-the-red-jacket-michael-jackson-wore-in-thriller/.

[106] An image that would be reprised in *Bad*. The opening lyric is 'your butt is mine.' The character role of this opening lyric within the dance-street-gang confrontation was offered to Prince. In an Interview with comedian Chris Rock, he explains his reasons for declining the role here: https://www.youtube.com/watch?v=KqVqXynZC2M.

[107] Mercer, "Monster Metaphors: Notes on Michael Jackson's *Thriller*", 49.

traditional machismo tropes, but pushed the enacted paradox into different species. In an earlier video for a single off the *Thriller* record, *Billie Jean* (1983), when performing in the guise of a solitary, brooding, predatory and powerful young man Jackson's figure slips into feline form.

Jefferson notes how Jackson's play with Western gender normativity was not just notably non-binary but always exercised (or exorcised?) through the voice and body. She writes:

> Michael Jackson has been a sexual impersonator since age five. As a child, he played adolescents and men. Once he became a man, he played up, down and around masculine sexuality. The real erotic power was always in the rhythms of his voice and body.[108]

Jefferson's final line in the above comment echoes the Panzéra-Barthes granular trajectory of voice-body-eroticism. A choreographic and vocal example of this erotic power manifesting as physical and vocal impersonations is evident in *Black or White*.[109]

Taking up Jefferson's option for the charged term 'power' it cannot escape comment that *Black or White* dramatizes the destructive potential of sounds in physical terms.[110] In the musicless street scene, the figure of Jackson on his knees ripping his shirt off cries out (the vocal over-coded with a ripped shriek of a feline vocalization), and the neon *Royal Arms Hotel* sign behind him begins to spark before falling from the building front.[111]

[108] Jefferson, *On Michael Jackson*, 100.

[109] As music videos go, it is the ur-form of corporate indulgence and excess overriding thematic consistency and narrative coherence that typified Jackson's later work and wont of portraying a global trans age-gender-sex-ethnicity-species messiah figure.

[110] Macaulay Culkin, in an opening skit of playing up the Spinal Tap idiom 'up to eleven'. After being told to turn his music down, wheels guitar amps into the living room and, upon striking an overdriven power chord, blows his father (played by George Wendt) through the suburban roof of the family home into space.

[111] This musicless/scoreless scene, read in Frith's terms, smacks of confession. Frith writes of the score/routine as a safety net for embarrassment of 'performer and audience alike. It is this safety net which the performance artist abandons, and one can therefore conclude that the essence of performance art is, in the end, embarrassment, a constant sense of the inappropriate' (Frith, *Performing Rites*, 1996 206). Whether this is a moment of media performance art or not cannot be broached here. What is certain is that there is a strong sense of embarrassment, of inappropriateness, of awkwardness about the scene.

The video's performance section contains people of varying ethnicities morphing into one another in sequence, all the time miming along to Jackson's voice: a cinematic ventriloquism of Jackson singing through all the ethnicities and cultures of the world. This narrative of Jackson as a post-gender, post-race chameleon—Jackson qua messianic T-1000 pop-superstar—is then revealed as a 'soundstage all along'.[112] The video then segues into a further narrative after the song has finished. The camera pans back, and on the studio floor a panther growls and prowls out of the studio, down noir-moonlit metal stairs. The large cat is CGI stretched, ripped up from quadrupedalism into an Astaire-gangster version of Michael Jackson.[113] David Stubbs, in 'The "King" is dead; long live everything else', describes the scene as a

> deserted, smoky street set that reminds of a cross between something from *The Terminator* and *Singin' In The Rain* (...) he (...) undertakes his entire repertoire of tense, angular robo-moves like they were a set of karate exercises, grabbing constantly at his crotch as if afraid that that's the next thing part of him that's going to drop off.[114]

It is in this scene, a marked tonal departure from the rest of the video, where the 'scandalous' crotch grab dance routine is performed.[115] Time changes everything. Not dissimilar from the ultra-macho silhouette and virility-signalling hue of the *Thriller* red leather jacket, there is something amiss, something off, awry. It is not the presentation of normative

[112] "On A Soundstage All Along," *TV Tropes*, accessed September 10, 2018 http://tvtropes.org/pmwiki/pmwiki.php/Main/OnASoundstageAllAlong.

[113] This is not the only time Jackson has transformed into or from a cat. He does in *Billy Jean* and, as we shall examine in detail, in the John Landis *Thriller* video.

[114] David Stubbs. "The "King" is dead; long live everything else" in *The Resistible Demise of Michael Jackson*, ed. Mark Fisher (Winchester, UK: Zero Books, 2009), 76.

[115] Jefferson describes the paradox of Jackson's crotch clutching as 'at once desperate and abstract.' Jefferson, *On Michael Jackson*, 102.

masculinity but more of a statement of masculinity.[116] Is it a question of misarticulated claim or performative parody of masculinity or a deft accomplishment of both? The street scene is liminal on a number of levels. It is the torsion of two facets, an interzone: a 'cross between something'.[117]

Cracks: Stubbs writes that the sequence 'comes across like an immaculately set and choreographed psychotic episode, conceived and executed at Jackson's behest'.[118] The scene is filled with anger, frustration and directionless imploding altruism (hate), a sort of aggressive messianic love (born from torment?): 'there's an undercurrent of implacable, inordinate and inappropriate rage inherent in late Michael Jackson.'[119] The sequence

[116] Both the crotch grab and the jacket *lie* in a catalogue of actions and performances that seek to affirm masculinity via performative re-appropriations and co-optings of the tropes of masculinity. One questions if such moments are Jackson's misguided and absurd claims made in earnest under the pressure of the recording industry or knowing parodies. Jefferson writes that 'It is as if he were telling us, "Fine, you need to know I'm a man, a black man? Here's my dick: I'll thrust my dick at you! Isn't this what a black man's supposed to do? But I'm Michael Jackson, so just look but you can't touch." It wasn't real, it was symbolic. Not a penis but a phallus.' Jefferson, *On Michael Jackson*, 102. Ibid., 102. This note of Jefferson's is one of a few comments she makes about the paradox of his dance, or what I'd refer to as postural antinomies. There is the crotch grab—at once insisting on a male appendage but also covering, concealing and denying and touch. Then there is the *Billy Jean* crouch—crouched down, hiding, diminishing in stature—but on tiptoes. There is the classic 'arms out chorus stance', all rock ballad torso, microphone in hand, head up but with funky-chicken legs—all knock-knee'd and pigeon-toed. In the 1983 of Billie Jean performance he works wields these antimonies like a magician. All half-mime tricks (one white glove) half singer-dancer (gold microphone and sparkly socks). We see him throw dice, he takes an invisible comb out of his pocket, slick's his hair 1950s' style and replaces the imaginary prop. To do away with his trilby hat, the real prop he'd hide his doe-eyes under in later years vampiric mystique, he fakes the crowd. He snaps right, head jutting rightwards, arm held out the trilby presented to the right of the stage before snapping his right wrist, the hat flies across his body into the audience his left, he duped half the crowd, misdirection, a magician—body motion antinomies.

[117] David Stubbs, "The "King" is dead; long live everything else" in *The Resistible Demise of Michael Jackson*, 76. The sequence is steeped in flux, a penumbral indeterminacy. The only conviction is for its lack—the figure of Jackson qua schizophrenic, vacillating from grimace and grin.

[118] Stubbs, "The "King" is dead; long live everything else", 76.

[119] Ibid. Additionally, note the Jekyll and Hyde flips of intonation running through his lines. One moment a caramel-lux soul note the next a gnashing frustrated rasp. In the chorus of *Black or White* the word 'black' is spat, expelled, in throaty hoarseness (a precursor to the disjointed pneumatic rage of *Scream* (1995) or the syncopated vampire hush-gasps of *Blood on the Dance Floor* (1997)), whereas the concluding word, 'white', is markedly smoother, close to Jackson's affected child-tone talk voice, with a sumptuous vibrato overlaid.

finishes when, after smashing a glass bottle, a car's windows and panes of glass on adjacent buildings, Jackson drops to his knees, rips his vest, crouches over, puts two hands on the floor and melts back into a panther.

Stubbs' comment 'inappropriate rage' resonates with not only Frith's discussion of inappropriateness and embarrassment in performance but also his suggestion that as well as a performance involving a *double enactment* of star personality and song personality there is a second 'complication' of 'the site of desire—as a body, and as a person'.[120] Frith notes that just as 'discussions of voice and body are haunted by questions of sexuality. So are discussions of the body as body.'[121] Thus, although the following comment does commence with a concern for singing, the sentiment, as Frith notes, goes for the body too. Frith writes:

> Singing, as an organization of vocal gestures, means enacting the protagonist in the song (the right emotions for the part), enacting the part of the star (the moves in keeping with the image), *and* giving some intimation of a real material being—a physical body producing a physical sound; sweat produced by real work; a physicality that *overflows* the formal constraints of the performance.[122]

Could it not be posited that the undercurrent of inordinate and inappropriate rage that Stubbs observes is, in this particular scene, overflowing? Isn't this a scene whereby the site of desire, the body and its physicality, are foregrounded, over and above the '*double enactment*' of performance?

Consider the role of voice within this routine. The spectacle of violence and the sexualized dance routine distract from voice within the video. At the start of the sequence, we hear Jackson's gibbering rasping staccato scatting along with his tapping and shuffling footwork (an onomatopoeic Street-Fighter killer-combo phonic-percussive counter-score). At the end of the sequence, as he drops to his knees, his screams, one is led to believe, explode the neon *Royal Arms Hotel* sign, sparks fly. As he continues to scream the luminous tubes come loose and the sign falls to the floor. It is implied that Jackson's voice, his phonic wrath, had destructive force.

But is it Jackson's (human) voice? Between the less rage-drenched intro of his characteristic erratic/erotic popping, locking and taut-tap-dancing

[120] Frith, *Performing Rites*, 212.
[121] Ibid., 212–213.
[122] Ibid., original emphasis.

mechanism—replete with a spat-whisper staccato adlib—and the raging finale of smashing, shouting and screaming through the set, another voice is heard.[123] Stubbs notes that the scene is not accompanied by music; the only 'soundtrack' is a dual vocalization of Jackson and a grating feline yowl. Stubbs describes these sounds as 'treated growls [...] half-panther, half-human'.[124] The scene sounds the dual voice of both of Jackson's corporeal visual iterations: one human, one panther. Jackson's voice is overlaid with feline sounding growls, the sort of ripping snarl a panther might make. The street sequence is wordless but contains a cacophony of vocalizations, human and not.

At the beginning of the sequence we see a domestic cat jump from a dustbin. It emits the classic back-alley stretched and torsional meow (another noir-trope). As Jackson's popping and locking routine intensifies he emits his first demi-feline snarl: a metallic rasping drawl. He then makes the first crotch grab of the section. On top of a car, crowbarring through the windscreen, he emits a second *pantheresque* yowl. A second later, after the close-up of a suggestive index finger crotch caress, he emits another torn snarl. After throwing a dustbin through a window he then stands atop a vent, à la Marilyn Monroe in *The Seven Year Itch*, and his shirt rises up and he strikes a number of poses.[125] Jackson then pluralizes in a visual-vertigo of infinite refrain; his voice is partly wind howl partly panther yowl. The steam clears, and he runs and spins before dropping to his knees. He rips open his shirt and vest; the ripping sounds are once more overlaid with the sound of a pained cat, an animal noise.

The scene is Astaire-noir horror: quintessential Jackson. It carries through the genre-horror themes of *Thriller*, with the following two—candidly titled in retrospect—albums *Bad* and *Dangerous*.[126] The half pan-

[123] The tap-scatting tracking/puppeteering Jackson's physical movements.

[124] Stubbs. "The "King" is dead; long live everything else", 76.

[125] K of Skirt substituted for H. Skirt-to-shirt.

[126] These two subsequent albums introduced a gangster sensibility to Jackson's performances, lurking predation rehearsed and replayed. By the release of *Black or White* Jackson's eyes were often hid behind a trilby hat in his performances. Pale, thinner, hiding in the shadows (biographically, choreographically and figuratively) he resembles a number of horror protagonists. Here, in human form in the street scene, wearing dark trousers and a shirt, he resembles a resurrected Eric Draven (*The Crow*, 1994) after ransacking a prohibition-era film's wardrobe (*Smooth Criminal* is essentially Marvel Comics villain *Morbius the Vampire* doing *Bugsy Malone*). In this context, that the other form Jackson adopts in the scene is that of a panther—an apex predator defined by its melanism—strikes as being one of hitherto overlooked significance.

ther, half Jackson vocal may be auditioned as interspecies noise, a noise that evokes horror. In introducing a voice *which is not one*, *a* voice that is at once human and non-human, horror is evoked. A vocalization carrying noise of an unknown other inaugurates the epistemological crisis that defines, following Thacker, horror. In particular, this noise of an other is a plural corporeal noise: the grain of bodies.

Barthes, in 'The Grain of the Voice', references 'noise' in a discussion comparing two sung deaths: that of Mélisande in Debussy's *Pelléas et Mélisande* and of Boris Godunov's death in Mussorgsky's eponymous opera. For Barthes neither death-song is erotic. Each, he argues, is prosaic and standardized. Nonetheless, it is at this juncture he brings in the concept of noise. Barthes laments that Mélisande 'dies prosodically'.[127] He writes:

> Mélisande dies *without any noise* (understanding the term in its cybernetic sense): nothing occurs to interfere with the signifier and there is no compulsion to redundance; simply, the production of a music-language with the function of preventing the singer from being expressive.[128]

Barthes' complains about the death of Boris in Mussorgsky's opera: is that it is '*expressive* or, if preferred, *hysterical*; it is overloaded with historical, affective contents.'[129]

Barthes' noise is corporeal interference, the body interfering with the production of voice. Barthes writes: 'The 'grain' is the body in the voice as it sings, the hand as it writes, the limb as it performs.'[130] In each case it is the corporeal interfering with the mode of producing a performance; in terms of voice it is the voicer's body adding additional sound over articulation. Barthes' specific examples are Panzéra's body interfering with the production of sung words (most notably consonants) and Wanda Landowska's harpsichord playing that 'comes from her inner body and not from the petty digital scramble of so many harpsichordists'.[131]

[127] Barthes, *Image-Music-Text*, 187.

[128] Ibid., 187.

[129] Ibid., 186. One wonders of the dismay Barthes might feel where he to hear the clichéd phonic platitudes of television talent show singing—the standardized guttural retching to 'punk-up' covers, the overblown breathiness of faux intimate ballads or the blue-eyed-soul post-Winehouse tendency of evoke pathos with a vocal-fry affectation.

[130] Barthes, *Image-Music-Text*, 188.

[131] Ibid., 189.

Barthes' epistemological certainty is striking; there is a surety in his sensing the body via the additional noise it adds to musical expression. He writes: 'I know at once which part of the body is playing—if it is muscled like a dancer's calves, the clutch of the finger-tips (...) or if, on the contrary, it is the only erotic part of a pianist's body, the pad of the fingers whose 'grain' is so rarely heard.'[132] Barthes then suggests that the long-playing record has flattened these corporeal frissons into pheno-text perfection (like Fischer Dieskau). Grain, for Barthes, is by no means exclusive to voice; it extends to all forms of music. But one thing is sure: the body from which 'grain' issues is heard or felt in distinctly corporeal terms.

The British music journalist, critic and author Simon Reynolds, in the essay 'Noise' in *Audio Culture: Readings in Modern Music*, describes the connection between noise and horror, effectively taking up the notion of Barthes' grain/noise and arguing it to be a locus of horror. Reynolds claims noise and horror are both defined by a departure from meaning, that it is from such congruence that noise is horrific. Noise, Reynolds argues, insofar as it is an unmeaning sound, is alloyed to horror. He writes:

> Noise is about fascination, the antithesis of meaning. If music is a language, communicating moods and feelings, then noise is like an eruption within the material out of which language is shaped. We are arrested, fascinated, by a convulsion of sound to which we are unable to assign meaning. We are mesmerized by the materiality of music. This is why noise and horror go hand in hand—because madness and violence are senseless and arbitrary (...) and the only response is wordless—to scream.[133]

Later in the essay he couches the concept of noise as breakages in the voices of singers. Reynolds makes explicit reference to Jackson, before invoking Barthes' formulation of grain in terms of 'genotext over phenotext'. He writes:

> noise occurs in moments, tiny breakages and stresses dispersed all over the surface of music, all kinds of music. Maybe we should listen out for the noise in the voices of [...] Prince, Michael Jackson—the way they chew and twist language not for any decipherable, expressive reason [...], but for the gratuitous voluptuousness of the utterance itself. In their voices, you can hear a

[132] Ibid., 189.

[133] Simon Reynolds, "Noise", *Audio Culture: Readings in Modern Music*, eds Christopher Cox and Daniel Warner (New York/London: Bloomsbury Academic, 2007), 57.

> surplus of form over content, of genotext over phenotext, semiotic over symbolic, Barthes's "grain" (the resistance of the body to the voice) over technique.[134]

The argument, that Jackson's voice *had grain*, is persuasive. However, consider the word, *grain*, qua *jouissance* as a further register of Jackson's erotic horror. Grain, like the double reading of '*Thriller*', the word itself may be heard as an inadvertent portmanteau of 'grown', 'groan' and 'pain'.[135] Reynolds' employment of the term comes in during a narrative that is about noise qua unknown interference. He writes of grain as an 'interference, *something* which blocks transmission (…) This dark, unimaginable matter of horror and sickness is a kind of cultural noise, causing a blockage and destabilization of the codes by which we make sense of the world.'[136]

Here, Reynolds' framing of grain as noise, which is an interference that wreaks epistemological destabilization, bringing horror, departs from Barthes' thesis. Barthes' conception of grain is something that re-establishes corporeal relations through voice and yields frisson, *jouissance* and eroticism. Barthes uses the term noise but as patina, something special or unique. There is no negative valence. In terms of Michael Jackson there are both. Jackson's staccato gnashing and scatting evoke the sense of the corporeal body, the groove and funk of his music that compels the body into animation. Mercer details the infectiousness of dance, the rhythmic dynamicism communicated (or felt) through Jackson's voice.

> While the "grain" of the voice encodes the contradictions of sexual relationships, their pleasures and pain, the insistence of the rhythm is an open invitation to the body to dance. Dance, as a cultural form and erotic ritual, is a mode of decoding the sound and meaning generated in the music. In its incitement of the listener to dance, to become an active participant in the texture of voice, words and rhythm, soul music is not merely "about" sexuality, but is itself a musical means for the eroticization of the body.[137]

Although this understanding of grain is closer to Barthes', it differs in one striking aspect: rhythm. Rhythm is absent in Barthes' essay.

[134] Ibid., 58.

[135] The groans that result from the pain of bring grown.

[136] Ibid., 55, emphasis added.

[137] Mercer, "Monster Metaphors: Notes on Michael Jackson's *Thriller*", 39.

Nonetheless, each text puts 'grain' in terms of erotic relation between bodies. Barthes' text does so in terms of sound texture and patina, whereas Mercer does so in terms of rhythm and movement. Each takes as a given a relation between bodies, known bodies.

Reynolds, by contrast, denies this epistemological-corporeal certainty. Instead he puts 'grain' in the context of *something* interfering. Reynolds' formulation of 'grain' is more appropriate for the instances in Jackson that explore transitions between species. The panther yowl layered atop his anguished screams in the *Black or White* street-rage segment certainly sound as interference, sound from elsewhere, and are notably lacking any rhythmic or funky eroticism. This animal noise-grain erupting into Jackson's voice is evident in another key music video, *Thriller*, where, again, Jackson transforms into a cat.[138]

In the *Black or White* street segment, noise—as the interference of unknown bodies—can be taken in a plural sense of noises. There is a double interference of a large cat's yowl over-coding Jackson's own modulated cries, and there is the mechanical gibbering of Jackson's scat, an oral percussive score amalgamated with his feet. To echo Barthes' deployment of noise as a cybernetic term, Jackson's pneumatic popping and locking appears as error: a robot going wrong before systemic psychotic breakdown. The scene follows a main sequence where a messianic Jackson morphs between multiple ethnicities and species, yet in the noir-lit street Jackson resembles a cyclone of post-*Korova* Astaire performance cues fused with a funky-chicken-*glitching*-strutting T–1000. Jackson's *in a funk*. Imploding frustration, charged repressed sexualities and interspecies ambiguity are voiced in terms of Michael's grain: a thematic *Neverland* of the groans of pain of being grown. Grain, here, qua horrific noise(s) strikes an unnerving relevance—as a voicing of *thrill*—at once *jouissance*, horror,

[138] There are three notable human-cat transformations in Jackson's oeuvre. Firstly, in *Billie Jean*, we see domestic cats transform into Tigers as they disappear and reappear behind dustbins. Later in the video, the private detective who had followed Michael (who vanished next to, one assumes, Billie Jean, and walks invisibly upon illuminating slabs) is arrested as the prowler reported by a woman in the basement flat. As he is being marched down the pavement he drops the tiger skin cloth Michael used to buff his white spats at the start of the video. Then a tiger, appearing out of nowhere, picks the cloth up. The imagery of domestic cat to Tiger mirrors The Jackson 5 child coming of age and emerging as a young man—but, as soon as he does, he changes into a predatory cat. Chronologically, *Thriller* is the next instance of interspecies transformation, followed by *Black or White*.

anguish, frustration, eroticism and violence. Jackson's grain is the interference of not just a body, but bodies.

Are we addressing object *a* voice in this reading? Might object *a* voice to manifest as sonorous multiplicities from within *and* without a body?

Late in Dolar's book (in 'Freud's Voices' chapter) Freud's 'A Case of Paranoia Running Counter to the Psychoanalytic Theory of the Disease' (1915) draws commentary. It concerns a young woman who, with the fear of being photographed during infidelities, hears 'a click' that interrupts proceedings. Dolar writes: 'The prospect of lovemaking was interrupted by a mysterious sound, a *noise*, a click, a knock, a beat, a tick.'[139] After articulating how this noise is a retroactive interpretation of paranoia he writes: 'The tiny *noise*, the inexplicable tick, is like a *grain* of desire, a small provocation which triggers off massive consequences. And to start with we could say: in the unconscious it doesn't only speak, it ticks, and perhaps there is no *ça parle* without a *ça cliquète*.'[140]

Dolar's stray into describing aural phenomena as grain and noise is apt beyond shared terminology. But isn't this parsing out of noise a little, well, neat? That the noise of the body and desire is presented in this turn of 'Freud's Voices' as a minimal sonic expression, an austere, neat and concise tick, or click, is a notable register of Dolar's recalcitrance to confront corporeality reflected—symptom—in sonorous terms. Nonetheless, the last line is pertinent: the unconscious does not *speak*. There are, it almost goes without saying, a lot of noises and sounds between a mere click and fully articulated speech. Might the grain of desire be more than just a click? Dolar suggests that the click evokes Freud's stereotypical primal fantasy of overhearing parental intercourse. Dolar then comments:

> The situation of the patient would thus be a displaced reenactment of a paradigmatic fantasy which is constructed entirely around the kernel of the voice, the grain of an inexplicable noise, a mysterious sound, which can appear even with the tiniest click. At the origin of fantasy there is a traumatic kernel materialized by the voice, the noise—we should allow full latitude here to a sonority not pertaining to language.[141]

Here, Dolar acquiesces or at least reads as if being open to the possibility of 'the object voice' in sonorities not in service of speech extending

[139] Dolar, *A Voice and Nothing More*, 131, emphasis added.
[140] Ibid., 131, emphasis added (first line).
[141] Ibid., 133.

beyond the minimalism and brevity of clicks, ticks and knocks. But he does not go further than this. Let's do so here with a drive to interpret the cacophony of inhuman growls, yowls and snarls in the wordless *Black or White* street scene.

The immediate take would be to hear such noises as the further register of Jackson's motel-room double valence *thrill*: a formative scene of horror whereby violence and libido reverberate.[142] Are these noises, of which the striking plurality adds weight to a biographical significance (brothers), a re-enactment?[143]

This mode of application is not quite right; we are comparing a subject's aural phenomenon (a hallucination, the click) to the highly developed group project of the music video. There are, nonetheless, a number of equivalences to be drawn out. Both are scenes of non-human noises sounding within and without a body ridden with desire. And it is in each, in this modality of non-human noises sounding from or through the desiring corpus, where horror emerges. Is it not the plurality of 'inhuman' voices sounded through Jackson that lends the scene its horror?

The click, in Freud's case, comes from within *and* without: it is not a clitoral beat as Freud suggested or the clock's 'ticking' as the subject supposed. Freud wrote that the subject 'heard a noise like a click or a beat.'[144] Is this line to be taken as meaning a series of clicks or the singular minimal instance of a click? Might a click, even with the singular determiner, also refer to a clicking of clicks? Object *a* voice here is one of pluralism, not 'the object voice' (singularly determined).

The yowls and torsional vocalizations of the street scene, and the gnashing rabid scatting and percussive breaths, are atomized. They are at once endogenous and exogenous vocal expressions. The cacophony can be read as symptomatic of desire's insidious diffusion beyond a singular body. Dolar, in the closing section before his treatment of '*the* click' (note his choice of the definitive singular), writes: the 'drives don't speak, although they make a lot of noise, they provide the clamour of life—but only the libido, Eros, whereas its counterpart, the mysterious death drive, keeps

[142] In continuation of this nocturnal rooting, the scene is a dream sequence departure from the main video thread.

[143] Resonating with Laplanche. '[T]hat seduction, or a traumatic sexual exposure of the child, is indeed at the bottom not only of all hysteria but also of any subject formation.'—Dolar, *A Voice and Nothing More*, 134.

[144] Freud, *Complete Works*, 3062.

silent, invisible and inaudible, albeit omnipresent.'[145] Is a clamour not an accumulation of noises, a panoply of sounds? The *Black or White* street scene is a scene of noisy drives as much as deathly silence; the misty and deserted moonlit street hosts a figure that is the locus and conduit of a plethora of noisy life. Jackson is a vessel for voices that extend beyond the human singular. Here is the horror of desire sounded as non-human plurality; object *a* voice from within and without: *vox-exo*.

To explicate why this pluralism of voice is horrific we can return once more to Barthes. Barthes' line that most succinctly defines the experience of grain is 'the 'grain' is the body in the voice as it sings, the hand as it writes, the limb as it performs. (…) I am determined to listen to my relation with the body of the man or woman singing or playing and that relation is erotic—but in no way subjective.'[146] Note the tonal shift that occurs when the first line is edited to reflect the pluralism of grain presented in this analysis of *Black or White* 'the bodies in the voices as they sing, the hands, the limbs'.[147] This is the horror of *Black or White*: granularities not grain. Over and above the liminal explication of frustration (in a *funk*), the violence and sexualized performativity, the grain(s) of Jackson's voice(s) is irreducible to a referent of any singular or fathomable body.[148] A voice of grains, patina from multiple bodies, noise from unknown: horrors of *vox-exo*: Jackson *qua* legion.[149]

[145] Ibid, 130.

[146] Barthes, *Image-Music-Text*, 183.

[147] Ibid., 183.

[148] Poizat's highlight of the heterogeneous character of Kundry in Wagner's *Parsifal* holds a similar sentiment. There are numerous points of equivalence. He writes: 'Wagner's letters to Mathilde Wesendonck indicate that this character, a synthesis of several female characters who appear in Wolfram's epic, represented an important breakthrough for him in the composition of the opera. But is Kundry truly *one* woman? She is first of all the Grail *messenger*: Kundry is an angel. But she is also the temptress, the sorceress, Klingsor's slave and accomplice: Kundry is a demon. She thus represents in its purest form that image of The Woman ever present in opera, the privileged medium of The Voice in its purest embodiment as object. It therefore comes as no surprise that her vocal score calls for cry, plaint, moan, and then the silence to which the entire third act confines her despite her continued presence on stage.' (Poizat, *The Angel's Cry*, 194.)

[149] This line added in 2019. It is difficult not to read the *Black or White* street scene as a confessional antithesis to the video's main theme of Jackson qua messianic man of all people. A theological reading is on the cards. Whereas much of the performance section sees Jackson in a white shirt at various locations around the world in the street scene Jackson is wearing Black.

*In*sidious

> Old English *slim* "slime," from Proto-Germanic **slimaz* (source also of Old Norse *slim*, Old Frisian *slym*, Dutch *slijm* "slime, phlegm," German Schleim "slime"), probably related to Old English *lim* "birdlime; sticky substance," from PIE root * *(s)lei-* "slimy, sticky, slippery" (source also of Sanskrit *linati* "sticks, stays, adheres to; slips into, disappears;" Russian *slimak* "snail;" Old Church Slavonic *slina* "spittle;" Old Irish *sligim* "to smear," *leinam* "I follow," literally "I stick to;" Welsh *llyfn* "smooth;" Greek *leimax* "snail," *limne* "marsh, pool, lake," *alinein* "to anoint, besmear;" Latin *limus* "slime, mud, mire," *linere* "to daub, besmear, rub out, erase"). As an insult to a person from mid-15c. *Slime-mold* is from 1880.[1]

Phlegmy, slippery, sticky, smeary, muddy, faecal. The etymology of slime oozes material indeterminacy and filth: filth that is expelled and *gets everywhere*, excessive and uncontainable: contagious. Dross, gunge and scum that sticks and smears. The Latin *limus* refers to mud, slime and muck. It also refers to faeces within the bowels, filth and pollution.[2] A plurality haunts the term. It never ends. There is always more. And it gets everywhere, from within and without. Slime shares a few qualities with voice.

[1] "Slime," *Etymology Online*, accessed June 2, 2018, https://www.etymonline.com/word/slime.

[2] "Limus,", *Wikipedia*, accessed June 2, 2018, https://en.wiktionary.org/wiki/limus.

T. Adams, *Horrors of* a *Voice (object* a*),*
https://doi.org/10.1007/978-3-031-62050-8_5

In slime there is also rampant vitality. The etymology is steeped in swampy gooey life: snails, marshes. This life is an excessive vitalism, an insidious life: a life that seeps, creeps and oozes. Just such a life repulses, it is a repugnant life that brings a nauseous shudder, a horror.

Voice is seldom described as slimy. A foreign force's modulation of voice, the symptoms of ill-health, a virus or malady is commonly described with a forceful insistence of solid presence—rough, grating, gravelly or cracked calcifies the sliminess of voice into a solidifying lexicon. There is, however, a particular archaic term that alludes to the slimy and viral nature of voice: Phlegmatic. '"Any trade doing here?" he asked *phlegmatically*,' to lift an example from Thomas Hardy's *The Mayor of Casterbridge*.[3] Merriam-Webster defines the term as '*resembling*, *consisting* of, or *producing* the humor phlegm'.[4] The following section details a series of connections, trails, smears and residues that contribute to the prospect that the term is unnervingly more apt than many other adjectival terms that seek to frame voice with a textured and determinable materiality. Voice, in its structural indeterminacy, its sliminess, is more phlegmatic than rough or gravelly. It seeps. It produces and proliferates, resounds and echoes. It infects like a virus or takes up residence like a parasite. Voice is a slimy phenomenon, more akin to a worm, a creepy-crawly, than anything solid or dry. Slimy phlegm is a symptom of another incorporeal life infecting and living in and through us. Voice, too, 'lives' *in and through* us.

In *Slime Dynamics* Ben Woodward explores the philosophical implications of slime.[5] This slim(y), garishly verdant paperback broadly follows a similar line of argument as the opening chapters of Thacker's *In the Dust of This Planet: Horror of Philosophy Vol. 1*.[6] Rather than focusing on demons, the foci are microbial, bacterial, viral and slimy. Slime, in a sense, is proposed to be a material that confounds—something of horrifying

[3] Thomas Hardy, *The Mayor of Casterbridge (Oxford World's Classics)*, (Oxford, UK: Oxford University Press, 2008), 7.

[4] "Phlegmatic," Merriam-Webster, accessed June 2, 2018, https://www.merriam-webster.com/dictionary/phlegmatic Emphasis added. Its alternate definition relates to the four humours of personality (a proto-psychology based on the equivalence of bodily fluids and personality). Phlegmatic, it should be noted, is distinctly sluggish, passive. Phlegmatic personality, stemming from Hippocrates' four elements and their temperaments, is connected with water.

[5] Ben Woodward, *Slime Dynamics* (Winchester, UK: Zero Books, 2012).

[6] Eugene Thacker, *In the Dust of this Planet: Horror of Philosophy Vol. 1.* (Winchester, UK: Zero

Books, 2011).

ontological instability. Woodward glosses slime, viruses, bacteria and parasites as concepts that invoke a destabilizing uncertainty, an epistemological precariousness, which feature in the turns of Thacker's conception of horror.

One cultural similarity between slime and voice is the genre horror trend of referencing a supernatural presence. Each tends to be presented within a similar narrative context. An acousmatic voice, heard without the body being seen, is a popular methodology of registering and evoking a supernatural presence. Slime is deployed in horror fiction and film in much the same fashion. It is often a register of an unthinkable entity—ghouls and other supernatural entities and/or forces sometimes leave a slimy trail: ectoplasm. Slimer in *Ghostbusters* (whilst perhaps not the ur-example) is an example of this in popular culture.[7]

Woodward begins 'The Nightmarish Microbial' chapter by way of Stephen Jay Gould's anti-anthropocentric remarks concerning how the human evolved from bacteria. Rather than privileging humans as the 'peak' of a linear and hierarchical evolutionary 'progression' Woodward echoes Gould's point that 'we are only an accidental outgrowth as a result of episodic and pointless addition.' The anthropocentric privileging of the human (a complex organism that itself categorizes others (including its own) based on arbitrarily perceived differences in form) is symptomatic of the fallacy that evolutionary progress is analogous to increasing biological complexity. Woodward, quoting Gould, writes: 'He goes on to say "Our impression that life evolves toward greater complexity is probably a bias inspired by parochial focus on ourselves, and consequent overattention to complexifying creatures, while we ignore just as many lineages adapting equally well by becoming simpler in form." '[8]

Delusions of anthropocentricism are not limited to evolutionary contexts. Such fallacies shade our understanding of what life is. Importantly, decentring the human and accepting the human's distinct lack of private definition—its entanglement with the world, negating the annexed throne of solo *man*—are potentialities wrought on us, absurd cephalized and bipedal mammals, *by* slime, viruses and parasites. In exploring these prospects, one arrives not just at unctuous and insidious parallels of proliferation in voice, viruses, parasites and slime but broaches the prospect of a

[7] *Ghostbusters*. Digital File. Directed by Ivan Reitman. USA: Colombia Pictures; Delphi Films; Black Rhino Productions, 1984.

[8] Woodward, *Slime Dynamics*, 14.

resolutely inhuman voice—or rather, to parse the thought with a hammy theatricality—a Lovecraftian shudder—the horrifying inhumanism of voice.

Woodward quotes Thacker some pages later: 'Microbes establish networks of infection within a body, and networks of contagion between bodies, and our modern transportation systems extend that connectivity across geopolitical borders.'[9] One can appreciate this line in terms of voice transmission, the plurality of voices being transmitted across those same borders by technology.

Woodward writes, following writings of Nick Land, Reza Negarestani and Eugene Thacker of a 'radical or epidemic openness'.[10] One import of his move through these thinkers' work is the horror of being confounded by forms of life that do not adhere to an anthropocentric presupposition of what life is. In a sense Woodward is posing the question of which terms we recognize and cognize as being 'life'. He writes of putrefaction and disease as forms of a rampant life, an excess of life that not only 'serve as an uncomfortable reminder of how tenuous our so-called dominion over nature turns out to be' but also negate what we understand death to be.[11] 'The microbial is not only a terrifying means of death (given its *invisible nature*) but also a killing of death itself, in the putrid obfuscation of contagion.'[12]

This Mobius nature of vitalism is something voice also harbours. In broad terms, is this not why voice is often posited as an eerie presence—a living death or a non-living emanation of the living? Dolar notes the Klein bottle resonance of voice—paradoxically at once vital and necrotic—in the aptly punctuated 'The "Physics" of the Voice' chapter in *A Voice and Nothing More*.[13] Dolar writes of how voice is the 'mere oscillation of air which keeps vanishing the moment it is produced, materiality at its most intangible and hence most tenacious form'.[14] Intangible and tenacious: are such adjectives not just as applicable to horrifying microbial life and virus (the stock of so much genre horror referenced in Woodward's book) as

[9] Ibid., 19.

[10] Ibid., 18.

[11] Ibid., 19.

[12] Ibid., 19, emphasis added. (Voice is also invisible regardless of coming from a live source or, aptly, from a dead, supernatural or recorded form. See Engh's reference to Edison's 'voices from the dead'.)

[13] Dolar, *A Voice and Nothing More*, 59.

[14] Ibid., 59.

voice? The fold of life into death is further underscored by Dolar when he invokes the Latin phrase *Verba volante, scripta manent* (spoken words fly away, written words remain)—reversed by Lacan to propose that voice remains and letters fly.[15] Dolar, however, seeks to open out a *vivre-mort* paradox within the kernel of voice. The move is subtle. He writes: 'The first obvious quality of voice is that it fades away the moment it is produced. *Verba volante, scripta manent:* Lacan reversed this classical proverb, since it is only the voice which remains there, on the spot where it was emitted and which it cannot leave,' but then, consecutively, he adds in the *vivre-mort* fold: 'where it is born and where it dies at the same moment.'[16]

The horror of something at once dead and alive—a living dead thing that infects and infiltrates the body through an orifice. Dolar, throughout *A Voice and Nothing More*, returns to this *vivre-mort* antinomy, this shudder-yielding indeterminacy of voice. It is close to a leitmotif in the writings of Dolar and Žižek. Žižek repeatedly couches voice as 'neither dead nor alive: its primordial phenomenological status is rather that of the living dead, of a spectral apparition that somehow survives its own death (…) the uncanny life of an undead monster.'[17] Dolar's question of voice—'does it not know that it is dead?'– is a further reformulation of the horror of not knowing if something is dead or alive.[18] Dolar's question rests on the living dead/undead presupposition, but it immediately leads to a further question: do dead things 'know' they are dead? The undead emerges at the point at which Dolar presupposes an ontological consideration for a non-living entity. Voice, virus, putrefaction, slime and microbial nightmares are a heterogeneous array of horrors that oscillate in the uncanny fold of being at once living and dead. They exist in the passage, the hyphen, of *vivre-mort.*

The uncertain ontological status of such horrors is symptomatic of an anthropocentric epistemology for contemplating life—life must be clearly delineated in physical form. It must be like us, with a clear border (and to

[15] Jacques Lacan, *The Seminar of Jacques Lacan: Book II The Ego in Freud's Theory and in the Technique of Psychoanalysis 1954–1955.* Trans. Sylvana Tomaselli, Ed. Jacques-Alain Miller (New York, USA: W.W. Norton and Company, 1991), 198.

[16] Dolar, *A Voice and Nothing More*, 59.

[17] Renata Salecl and Slavoj Žižek eds, *Gaze and Voice as Love Objects* (Durham and London, UK: Duke University Press. 1996), 103. This line is repeated and reused by Zizek in multiple texts and books.

[18] Dolar, *A Voice and Nothing More*, 35.

recall Woodward's use of Stephen Jay Gould, the more complicated the life form, the better). The intangibility and tenaciousness of voice confounds our expectations of clearly demarcated phenomena in much the same manner as the porous and insidious nature of viroid 'life'. The physics of voice have a notable similarity with microbial life, insects, worms and viruses. Both voice and viruses are physically vague in themselves *and* insidiously physical things in that they exist and move *in and through* us. Woodward writes of the tension of location and the deficit of clearly demarcated borders in viroid life:

> This horror is found in the physical framework of the virus itself. The curable/destructible confusion and the network obfuscation of virus transmission meet yet another ambiguity—one which is within the virus itself. Debate still continues over whether viruses are organic compounds (components of life) or forms of life themselves. (…) While viruses contain RNA or DNA they are not made of cells and replicate only by hijacking cells of organisms to spread themselves.
>
> Where the qualification of life may be difficult to place on the virus' squirmy chained body, the event of disease is, as Eugene Thacker points out, even more complex as it functions on the macro level as an assemblage of living forms such as the case of the Black Death, "bacillus-flea-rat-human".[19]

Viroid life cannot be grounded in terms of physics—it is not a body in space, it certainly moves through space, it has effects and consequences—it is irreducible to the anthropocentric view of what a living thing must be. Both voice and virus are irreconcilable with the human view of 'living things'.

Voice is horrifically viroid in its incorporeal insidiousness, its shiftiness. The literary scholar Steven Connor, in *Dumbstruck: A Cultural History of Ventriloquism*, opens the book with a now oft-quoted observation: 'voice comes and goes. For you, it comes from me. For me, it goes out from me.'[20] Such an observation, Connor's 'jump off' for his treatise on ventriloquism, is as much to do with the intangibility and tenaciousness of 'the "physics" of voice' as it is to do with voice's phenomenology being one of infectiousness and contagion. Not only does it seep, echo and bleed, sound *and* resound, amorphous and polymorphous— ethereal in its *myst*ery—through acoustic space in ways we cannot see, touch or fathom, it does so, akin to a virus or parasite, *in and through* us.

[19] Woodward, *Slime Dynamics*, 18.
[20] Connor, *Dumbstruck: A Cultural History of Ventriloquism*, 3.

Reverting to Žižek, once more, who pastes 'I hear myself speaking, yet what I hear is never fully myself but a parasite, a foreign body in my very heart. This stranger in myself acquires positive existence in different guises.'[21] Voice is, once again, formulated as a form of inhuman life that infects, like a virus or parasite, and 'lives' in an inhuman modality—provoking a shudder. This line, detailing the experience of a voice that comes and goes, is symptomatic of both the ontological crisis of voice and our anthropocentric epistemological approach to considering what life is and is not.

To worm, used as a verb, is 'to achieve something by insidious procedure (usually followed by *into*).'[22] The noun, worm, is defined as an 'insidiously tormenting or devouring force'.[23] In Merriam-Webster a horrific definition of the term 'wormlike' is provided: 'something that torments or devours from within.'[24] The figure of the worm has been used to describe the insidious nature of sound. Particularly 'catchy' songs, rhymes and jingles have been described as 'earworms': melodic voices that worm inside and get 'stuck in the head'. The etymology of the term 'earworm' is vermiculated with themes of infection and incursion.

A Merriam-Webster article about the etymology of the term 'earworm', 'The Wriggly History of 'Earworm': I just can't get you out of my head', states that 'earworm' is a *possible* calque of the German *Ohrwurm*. The article goes on to elaborate how the term has an etymological history tied to corporeal incursion—the entry of one small organism into another. In part it is related to earwigs that were believed to crawl into human ears.[25] According to the Merriam-Webster dictionary, the term—previously applied to a virulent pest that burrowed into the ears of corn—was subsequently applied to name the phenomena of INMI around the 'late 1950s and early 1960s'.[26] Jakubowski et al. write of how 'Involuntary musical

[21] Žižek, *Gaze and Voice as Love Objects*, 103. Certain texts of Žižek are repeated in multiple books and essays.

[22] "Worm," Dictionary.com, accessed April 6, 2018 http://www.dictionary.com/browse/wormlike.

[23] "Worm-like," The Free Dictionary, accessed 7 April, 2018, https://www.thefreedictionary.com/worm-like.

[24] "Wormlike," Merriam-Webster, accessed 6 April, 2018, https://www.merriam-webster.com/dictionary/wormlike.

[25] "The Wriggly History of 'Earworm': I just can't get you out of my head", *Merriam-Webster, Word History*. Accessed June 6, 2018. https://www.merriam-webster.com/words-at-play/earworm-meaning-origin.

[26] Ibid.

imagery (INMI, also known as "earworms") is the experience of a tune being spontaneously recalled and repeated within the mind.'[27]

Oliver Sacks, in 'Brainworms, Sticky Music and Catchy Tunes', in *Musicophilia: Tales of Music and the Brain*, notes in parentheses that 'One newsmagazine, in 1987, defined them, half facetiously, as "cognitively infectious musical agents".'[28] The chapter title references worms, also employs two adjectives. 'Sticky' evokes the putrid and slimy, whereas 'Catchy' is common parlance for contagiousness. The parenthesized definition Sacks provides is notable. Such a definition of INMI, as infectious *agents*, as beings with their own agency, runs along the vermiform themes, possibilities and incursions, of voice. Let's consider the anxiety of the ear, its vulnerability to an entity, an agency, of insidious coming and going.

There is an obvious entomological etymology at play within the term. *Earworm* refers to a non-human insect that was feared to worm, crawl or creep its way into the ears of those asleep (or of a plant organism's anthropomorphized 'ears' of corn). The Merriam-Webster article closes by citing the popular horror writer Stephen King, who, it argues, popularized the term that has been in English use since the 1980s. A biographical confession from an article of King is employed to open the article. It is lifted from 'Stephen King on songs that stick in your head', first published in *Entertainment Weekly*. King Writes:

> A couple of months ago, I woke up at three in the morning, thirsty as hell (probably because I'd donated blood the day before), and shambled into the bathroom for a glass of water. I was 20 percent awake at best. And as I turned on the faucet, I realized I was singing this: "They say a man should always dress/For the job he wants/So why'm I dressed up like a pirate/In this restaurant?"
>
> Dear God, I thought, I've been infected by an earworm.
>
> My friend the Longhair says that's what you call songs that burrow into your head and commence chewing your brains. The dreaded earworm can turn even a great song into something you'd run from, screaming at the top of your lungs. If only you could.[29]

[27] Jakubowski, K. and Finkel, S. and Stewart, L. and Müllensiefen, D. 'Dissecting an earworm: Melodic features and song popularity predict involuntary musical imagery.' *Psychology of Aesthetics, Creativity, and the Arts.* Vol 11 (2), May 2017, 122–135.

[28] Oliver Sacks, *Musicophilia: Tales of Music and the Brain* (New York/Toronto: Alfred A. Knopf, 2007), 41.

[29] King, Stephen. 'Stephen King on songs that stick in your head' *Entertainment Weekly.* April 17, 2009, accessed June 6, 2018. http://www.ew.com/article/2009/04/17/stephen-king-songs-stick-your-head/.

It is apt that Merriam-Webster points to one of the most successful horror writers of the twenty-first century to underscore the horrific nature of the sonic earworm. The (h)earworm, its infectiousness and contagion, its incursion into and penetration of the body, indeed its modality echoes its wormy etymology. The entomological etymology of common parlance for INMI is a series of prescient referents to the equivalence worms and worming agents have to the physics of audition. The ears are open orifices; one can close one's eyes—but not the ears.

The Canadian composer, writer and environmentalist R. Murray Schafer, arguably the progenitor of sound studies, writes '[the] sense of hearing cannot be closed off at will. There are no earlids. When we go to sleep, our perception of sound is the last door to close and is also the first to open when we awaken.'[30] This acute and succinct observation of Schafer nestles in the 'Ears and Clairaudience' section of the introduction to *The Soundscape: Our Sonic Environment and the Tuning of the World* (originally published in 1977). The argument in this turn is that clear and focused hearing is an accomplishment and not a given that much of the Western world (due to privileging the eye over the ear amidst a noisy industrialized environment) has, generally, lost some sensitivity and attentiveness of hearing that existed in older non-Western civilizations. The section finishes by citing the media theorist Marshall McLuhan and commenting on noise pollution. Schafer writes: 'The very emergence of noise pollution as a topic of public concern testifies to the fact that modern man is at last becoming concerned to *clean the sludge* out of his ears and regain the talent for clairaudience—*clean* hearing.'[31]

The over-exposure to sonic material—one might say, disparagingly, detritus—is noted with subjective tone by Sacks in the closing paragraph of 'Brainworms, Sticky Music and Catchy Tunes', his chapter on earworms. The passage moves from tut-tutting observations of the democratization and portability of listening practices to lamenting the contemporary prevalence of music being piped into public spaces before implying that we are swimming in seas of sonic effluvia where there is an omnipresence of catchy worms that arrive unbidden.[32] He writes:

[30] R. Murray Schafer, *The Soundscape: Our Sonic Environment and the Tuning of the World*, (Rochester, USA: Destiny Books, 1994), 11.

[31] Ibid., 11, emphasis added.

[32] I use the oceanic here as a slight presentiment for Sirens.

> Half of us are plugged into iPods, immersed in daylong concerts of our own choosing, virtually oblivious to the environment—and for those who are not plugged in, there is nonstop music, unavoidable and often of deafening intensity, in restaurants, bars, shops, and gyms. This barrage of music puts a certain strain on our exquisitely sensitive auditory systems, which cannot be overloaded without dire consequences. One such consequence is the ever-increasing prevalence of serious hearing loss, even among young people, and particularly among musicians. Another is the omnipresence of annoyingly catchy tunes, the brainworms that arrive unbidden and leave only in their own time—catchy tunes that may, in fact, be nothing more than advertisements for toothpaste but are, neurologically, completely irresistible.[33]

The vulnerability of the aural orifice is laid on heavily. Consider the vocabulary employed to propose the ear's always-open exposure to sounds. The ear is impuissant to *pollution*, to unwanted incursions that leave it dirtied and unclean (the vocabulary of McLuhan and Sacks veers towards the realm of slime and scum). There is also a distinct subtext of contagion, of unwanted exogenous sonic muck incurring, penetrating or creeping, into the ear. The question of audition is a question of the septic—of foulness getting in. The sentiment, in terms of the always-open ear and a fear of external filth incurring into us, unfolds in disconcerting synchrony with the definitions of the earworm. Earwigs, earworms, are carriers of filth that threaten to worm into the body through the ear. Likewise, sound, the noise pollution so prevalent in much of modern life, is conveyed in terms of filth: a noise that incurs unwanted into one's ears. *Ugh! It gets everywhere!*

Published two years before Schafer's *The Soundscape: Our Sonic Environment and the Tuning of the World*, Robert Erickson's *Sound Structure of Music* carries the same sentiment concerning the vulnerability of the gaping aural orifice. In the first chapter, Robert Erickson writes: 'We cannot close our ears; we have no ear lids. When a sound is loud enough, or especially meaningful—one's name, a baby's cry—one may react to it though asleep. Sounds that are unimportant to us are ignored, asleep or awake, even when quite loud.'[34] The passage harbours the anxiety of sounds that *creep* into the ear. Echoing the anxieties of nocturnal earwigs. It is, following Sacks, dreadful that the ear is subjected to a cacophony (the prefix of faecal denigration) of sonic effluvia, but it is dou-

[33] Sacks, *Musicophilia: Tales of Music and the Brain*, 48.

[34] Robert Erickson, *Sound Structure in Music* (California, USA: University of California Press, 1975), 1.

bly unsettling that, like the prospect of the nocturnal earwig, we may well not be, or *are not*, aware of their penetration. Erickson writes: 'Not that we do not hear them: we are always aware of the whole passing sound stream while selecting some sounds for focal attention.'[35] The insidious creeping nature of sound, analogous to the epistemological lacuna of horror, is an ever-present prospect—due to the structural openness of the ear, anything and everything can incur into us (awake or not).

Some of these sounds are warranted with conscious attention, some trouble because they cannot be placed. In a sense, some of the sonic effluvia that makes its way into our bodies and then to consciousness evokes horror because it signals something one does not know. Erickson continues: 'When we hear a strange sound—thinking "What was that?"—we focus upon it, listen carefully, wait for a repetition. We try to identify it. Once it has been identified we relax.'[36]

David Toop, in 'Chair Creaks, But No One Sits There' in *Sinister Resonance: The Mediumship of the Listener*, elaborates this anxiety. He opens the 'Floor Ee-Creaks' sub-section by recounting two occasions his home was invaded: burgled at night (a biographical and (un)homely metatext to the vulnerability of the ear—the 'last door to close', as Schafer terms it).[37] In addition to the staging of (h)ear-qua-house resonance, an ever-vulnerable opening, there is a nocturnal gothic horror staging that recalls Nietzsche's aphorism 250 from *Daybreak: Thoughts on the Prejudices of Morality*:

> *Night and music*—the ear, the organ of fear, could have evolved as greatly as it has only in the night and twilight of obscure caves and woods, in accordance with the mode of life of the age of timidity, that is to say the longest human age there has ever been: in bright daylight the ear is less necessary. This is how music acquired the character of an art of night and twilight.[38]

[35] Ibid.

[36] Ibid.

[37] Schafer, *The Soundscape: Our Sonic Environment and the Tuning of the World*, 11.

[38] Friedrich Nietzsche, *Daybreak: Thoughts on the Prejudices of Morality (Cambridge Texts in the History of Philosophy)* Eds. Maudemarie Clark and Brian Leiter (Cambridge, UK: Cambridge University Press, 1997), 253.

Toop's passage focuses on the nature of sounds that arrive when one is asleep or slumbering in liminal doze.[39] The second recollection of burglary by Toop highlights the question of what or how 'unheard' sounds might awaken. The sounds in this instance are not vocal; he is dealing with the domestic disturbances of locks being sprung open and creaking floorboards—nonetheless, each is a sonic register of a human-made sound incurring into the listener via the ear that, seemingly, fails to sleep and close like other senses. Voice, in *Sinister Resonance: The Mediumship of the Listener*, is a literary elephant in the room on two levels: diegetic and textual. For Toop's array of haunting and eerie sounds are overwhelmingly vocal. In the passage below, his first recourse to an example of night-sounds is that of a drunk human—a sounding body, perhaps loquacious or garrulous in their bacchanalian state. Like the sentiments of Schafer and Erickson detailed previously, the passage's somnolent pre-text evokes the nocturnal fear of the earwig and the human cephalic organization of senses in sleep: the shut eyes but always-open ears. This human cephalic structure can be squared with the break-in points of the home. Toop writes:

> I was woken during the night by a burglar who had sprung the lock on the front door and was at that moment stealing my wallet downstairs. Thought I had no consciousness of hearing a sound I knew there was an alien presence within the familiarity and security of my private place, my home. I walked to the top of the stairs, not knowing why, and saw a man run out of the front door. Some mystery surrounds the question of why we wake when we do, not always the noise of a drunk in the street or the breaking of a window. A terse passage of dialogue from Cormac McCarthy's novel, *The Crossing*, encapsulates this mystery:
>
> What woke you? he said
> You did.

[39] As we are in the domestic setting of dozes and thresholds (dreamland) it is worth recalling the 'dream of a burning child' Freud references in Chapter VII of *The Interpretation of Dreams*. A father naps after his child dies, leaving the dead body under watch of an old man. He dreams his child stands beside his bed, grabs his arm, and says 'Father, don't you see I'm burning.' The sleeping father awakens to find a bright glare coming from the next room where the corpse of his child is supposed to be under watch. The wrappings and one of the child's arms had been burnt, and were burning, by a fire ignited by a fallen candle. This dream story is already third hand, having been heard at a lecture by one of his patients and recounted to Freud. Freud's thesis frames the dream as wish fulfilment: that the child is alive, and 'traces' the phrase 'I'm burning' to a recent fever. It is worth noting that fire (as something permeating both dream and waking life in this anecdote) points to visual and olfactory interzone sensations, perhaps more than voice. See Freud, *The Interpretation of Dreams* Ed. Angela Richards, Trans. James Strachey (London, UK: Penguin Books 1991), 652–653.

I didn't make a sound.
I know it.[40]

Later in the section, Toop glides from detailing a house-door-room-cochlea continuum to propose that such a harbinger of 'threat, unease, disturbance, fear (…) enters in the way of an animal or *insect*: mouse, rat, spider, cockroach, fly, wasp, wood*worm* or the uncanny ticking of death-watch beetles.'[41]

The term earworm (the alloy of the aural orifice with worm in its multiple guises) registers the horror of incursion—of a grotesque exogenous thing entering the body: the penetrative ability of sound to be heard without consent (for hearing is less directional than vision, we cannot close our ears or hear-away).[42] As Toop underscores, via a distinctly horror-laden and ominous vocabulary, there is always the question of *what* gets in. Not only have we no agency over sonic incursion, but frequently unidentified foreign objects, when they do appear on the radar of consciousness, signal a horror—something unknown.

'Crazy'

Voice is a foreign object, sometimes identified, sometimes unidentified, by those whose ever open and vulnerable aural orifices it may creep into. *Vox-exo* qua 'insidiously tormenting or devouring force'.[43] Something that

[40] David Toop, *Sinister Resonance: The Mediumship of the Listener* (London, UK/New York, USA:
Continuum, 2010), 149.

[41] Ibid., 150, emphasis added.

[42] The pupil can be guarded, but the tympanic membrane is ever vulnerable (even in sleep). The openness of the ear, when applied to vision, takes the form of torture. When the eye is as overtly susceptible as the ear it is a scene of torture and horror. Alex, the narrator of British novelist's Anthony Burgess' famous *A Clockwork Orange*, complains when subjected to a form of cinematic aversion therapy for his anti-social and violent proclivities: 'One veshch I did not like, thcough, was when they put clips on the skin of my forehead, so that my top glazz-lids were pulled up and up and up and I could not shut my glazzies no matter how I tried.' See Anthony Burgess, *A Clockwork Orange* (London, UK: Penguin Books, 1972), 80–81. This complaint of Alex refers to the Ludovico aversion therapy he undergoes to curb his violent behaviour. The aural equivalent of Alex's retinal perma-sight is, according to Schafer, McLuhan and Erickson, the normalized 'din' and 'noise' of everyday exposure.

[43] "Worm," *The Free Dictionary by Farlex*, accessed June 6, 2018. https://www.thefreedictionary.com/worm-like.

'devours from within'.[44] With this penetrative modality of voice comes a risk of contagion.[45] The ability of a vocal earworm to infect the mind is a recurring theme in popular music. Such music is often described in folk parlance as containing an infectious or catchy ***hook:*** a distinctly phallic and aggressive term registering the penetrative nature of sound and voice. This section, after a brief framing of vocal contagion, will introduce a few examples of voracious popular music earworms—contagious melodic voices that stubbornly lodge in one's head.

Empirically observed examples of vocal contagion are found in affective empathy studies and/or emotional contagion studies. Many of these studies focus on voice as both the medium and evidence of emotional contagion. The mode of contagion proliferation is vocal-aural-vocal. Kari Weil in 'Empathy', in *The Edinburgh Companion to Animal Studies*, addresses empathy in terms of its general submission to the affective turn. A trend, somewhat bolstered by advances in neuroscience, which adds to the project of rendering previously human and sacred concepts (such as empathy) as pre-conscious affects akin to nervous reflexes the human shares with other animals. Weil provides a commentary on the Dutch primatologist and ethologist Frans De Waal's arguments in *The Bonobo and the Atheist.* She writes that 'De Waal argues that our capacity for empathy, and indeed for morality, is not what separates us from non-human animals, but rather is grounded in our biology and derived from our primate origins.'[46] Weil's continued commentary on how De Waal's work contributes to the decentring of the subject is worth following a little further. She writes:

> De Waal's work highlights the key role that empathy plays in the affective (or counter-linguistic) and ethical turns in critical theory (…) A return to

[44] "Wormlike," Merriam-Webster, accessed June 6, 2018, https://www.merriam-webster.com/dictionary/wormlike.

[45] The rapacious nature of voice, to be heard without consent, is registered in the various modes of Pan. Pan, the god of unrestrained sensuality and nature, is an emblem for transgressions from accepted forms of manifested desires, he is 'a god, half man, half beast, who rapes and ravishes men and women alike'. Although an earworm, with its potential to infiltrate bodies, is not specifically vocal (an earworm might be musical, a melody without voice) it is notable how many 'earworms' are musical voice and not just instrumental music. See David Toop, *Sinister Resonance: The Mediumship of the Listener* (London, UK/New York, USA: Continuum, 2010), 12.

[46] Kari Weil, "Empathy" in *The Edinburgh Companion to Animal Studies*, eds. Lynn Turner, Undine Sellbach and Ron Broglio (Edinburgh, UK: Edinburgh University Press, 2018), 127.

> the body and the pre-cognitive as the material ground of emotions, the affective turn often relies upon evidence from neuroscience. For example, mirror neurons, which make one imitate or feel the expressions seen on another, were first discovered in macaques. 'Putting it in neuroscience language, we activate neural representations of motor actions in our own brain similar to the ones we perceive or expect in the other. That we do so unconsciously has been tested with facial expressions on a computer screen.' Whereas science used to think of empathy as a cognitive skill, De Waal explains, we now know better: 'humans don't decide to be empathic; they just are.'[47]

This couching of empathy as non-conscious and neurobiologically based and not the result of human cognitive abilities eliminates empathy from the shrinking cart of sacrosanct human traits. Weil's thread leads to a dethroning of the traditional markers of what it is to be human that in turn leads one to appreciate that animals such as dogs may be better empathic readers than many human animals.

Within the eliminativist materialism project, affect and emotional contagion studies that pivot around voice are useful in approaching a conception of voice that lives in and through arbitrary bodies with open aural and oral orifices that serve its proliferation. Such studies underscore the inhuman affective contagion of voice. This contagion not only is symptomatic of the vulnerability of the ear to sound but also details how a voice lives on, and is sounded out, via the bodies it spreads through.

Social psychologist Daniel C. Batson writes of how, in 1976, Sagi and Hoffman 'presented one- to two-day-old infants either with tape-recorded sounds of another infant crying, with sounds of a synthetic nonhuman cry, or with no sounds. Those infants presented with another infant's cry cried significantly more than those presented with a synthetic cry or with silence.'[48] Batson presents this study as evidence of vocally induced and manifested empathy as pre-conscious and animal—he couches his argument in terms of an eliminativist materialism that poses the crying infant merely as a body responding with its own survivalist evolutionary proclivity. He likens the infants to tweeting birds in a nest, competing for the attention that comes with nourishment. Batson firstly poses that what look

[47] Weil, "Empathy", 127.

[48] Daniel. C. Batson "These Things Called Empathy: Eight Related but Distinct Phenomena" in *The Social Neuroscience of Empathy*. Eds. J. Decety and W. Ickes (Cambridge, MA: MIT Press, 2011) 6.

and sound like empathic vocal reactions may be in fact human evolutionary competitiveness: 'crying in response to another infant's cry may be a competitive response that increases the chances of getting food or comfort. (The infants in the Sagi and Hoffman study were tested 1 to 1-1/2 hours before feeding time.)'[49] Before reinterpreting the scenario in the figure of a different species, he asks the reader to 'imagine that we did a similar study using baby birds in a nest. We would not likely interpret the rapid spread of peeping and open-mouth straining once one baby bird starts peeping and straining as a rudimentary empathetic reaction.'[50]

Affective empathy studies such as these—and interpretations such as Batson's—that focus on voice as both medium and symptom of contagion lend an evidenced explication of voice as an inhuman mode of contagion: something autonomous from conscious thought and agency. Reframing the voice to be an inhuman contagion is not the drive of such studies nor the commentary from Weil, De Waal or Batson: they all have different main foci as well. Nonetheless, this emergent secondary import of such studies falls into a history of voice being detailed as a contagious agent. Particularly a type of voice wrapped up in the negation of traditional markers of the human: faculties of self-control, agency and conscious thought.

The Sagi and Hoffman study rests on a technological playback of voice. It shares these technics with popular music. From the dissemination of standardized notation (itself a subset of post-Gutenberg technology) to the mechanical developments of the phonograph and gramophone, to telegraphy and electromagnetic modes of transmission right up to the vinyl-tape-CD-MP3/internet/vinyl aural smorgasbord of contemporary music distribution, some form of technology has been a prerequisite that shapes, sounds and resounds popular music. The paradoxically named *micro*phone (for it results in the opposite) is a conspicuous visual motif of popular music talent shows, karaoke and stage performance promotion. The relationship of voice and technology is far too broad a theme to survey at this turn. Yet a brief consideration of how vocal earworms in popular music are sounded (in the widest sense) through a form of technology leads to an obvious analogy in terms of themes and questions of contagion, infection and proliferation.[51]

[49] Ibid., 6.

[50] Ibid., 6.

[51] The themes that emerge from this relationship are surveyed so rigorously, and by so many others, that it is close to a discipline in itself.

Technologically afforded dissemination of voice in popular music shares a similarity with how viroid life lives (and kills) through progressions in technological networks or commerce. The ontological parallels of voice and virus extend to the dissemination of each through technological networks and human information and commerce matrices. In terms of how a voice lives and infects, proliferates and spreads—through a global network of commerce, via differing technological advances of the ages, before finally passing into the head of a host body through an open orifice—there is little to distinguish it from a virus or bacterium that has lived vicariously through humans and other animals. Woodward, in *Slime Dynamics*, describes how '[t]he virus, the viroid, the deadly bacterium, all crept into center stage prior to the turn of the twentieth to twenty first century.'[52] He goes on to elaborate the equivalence: 'The vague swarming of the deadly microbial and subsequent paranoia emerged alongside the rise of a globalized and interconnected world, where proximity and speed elevated the potency and spread of contagion.'[53]

The spread of bacteria or transfer of viroid 'life' is structurally analogous to the dissemination of voice via phonographic and tele/cyber-phonographic methods. Similarly, the haunted record (phonographic phantom) and the supernatural presence registered via telephonic means are horror trope analogues to the structural equivalence of voice and virus.[54] Barbara Engh, in 'Adorno and the Sirens', in drawing up a history of gendered telephonic bodies, touches on precisely this technologically afforded contagion. She writes of Edison, 'raising the voices from the dead'.[55] Edison opened a gateway, a new space where voices might sound. However, as Engh notes, the new aural and vocal space did not usurp the written word as Edison imagined. Engh describes how Edison predicted that the phonograph would do more for the poor than the printing press, that it would 'replace the newspaper [and] eliminate the position of secretary-typist'.[56] Engh writes of how the most overlooked capacity of the machine would be the basis of its commercial viability: 'Although its

[52] Woodward, *Slime Dynamics*, 14.

[53] Ibid., 14.

[54] Jeffrey Sconce, *Haunted Media: Electronic Presence from Telegraphy to Television (Consoleing Passions)* (Durham and London, UK: Duke University Press, 2000), 81–91.

[55] Barbara Engh, 'Adorno and the Sirens' in Dunn, Leslie C. and Nancy A. Jones. *Embodied voices: Representing female vocality in western culture* (Cambridge, UK: Cambridge University Press, 1996), 124.

[56] Ibid., 124.

inventors had imagined that it would also record sound, the phonograph's commercial viability turned out to consist in its playback function, of mass-produced music. Capital prevailed in the form of the record industry, for as long as people produced their own recorded materials, the market for the phonograph was limited.'[57] There is, no doubt, a gloss to be made here concerning capital's genocide of folk-voice and common vocality. Disseminating technologies have, since the phonograph's commercial rise, usurped and eradicated local music and familiar music production and installed mass-marketed and produced vocals in their place.[58] There is a case here for couching the recording industry as a cyber-vocal manifestation of capital qua disease. Recalling Woodward's comments, the equivalence of popular music and technologically disseminated diseases is structurally plain, not least because of the global network culminating in an airborne interaction reliant on acoustic proximity. The popular music earworm is phonic equivalent of virus' insidiousness and proliferation through globalized interconnectedness and militarized bio-warfare.[59] Radio, television, CDs, mp3s and internet platforms disseminating popular music are, in a sense, new avenues that the viral voice may be spread through, in the same structural sense as increased air-travel and commercial global interconnectedness increasingly (occasionally alarmingly) disseminate viruses and species to new territories.[60]

[57] Ibid.

[58] Consider the top 40 acoustic presence in British soaps such as EastEnders.

[59] Engh, 'Adorno and the Sirens,' 124.

[60] Take Britney Spears' capitalist pop-triptych. "(You Drive Me) Crazy" (1999) is not just nominative register of the mental torment of earworms; the emphasis on drive also alludes to a loss of agency—the insidious voice that drives the listener. The song resonates with the modalities of *Ophiocordyceps unilateralis* and *Sacculina* parasites. "I'm a Slave 4 U" (2001), similarly, spells out being subject to an exogenous entity that takes up hose in one's body. "Toxic" (2004) registers sonic pollution, the sepsis of infection from an unwanted voice. The tracks hit status' perform, operate on and attest to the vocal spell of contagion. The chorus lyrics, a vocal INMI, an earworm, remain lodged in idling consciousness for days after initial audition after some unwitting chance encounter in an Augéan 'non-place' such as the consumerist temple of the shopping mall. Post-exposure it resonates within the body, an eternal tormenting incubation period stemming from an audition the host may not consciously register at the time of incursion/audition. A brief survey of pop song titles reveals a tendency to attest to the viral and infectious potential of melodic voice. 'Crazy' is a common word in pop song lyrics and one of the most frequently employed pop song titles. See "Most Popular Title for Top 40 Hits," *EveryHit*, accessed September 22, 2016, http://www.everyhit.com/populartitles.html.

Stewart et al.'s 'Dissecting an Earworm: Melodic Features and Song Popularity Predict Involuntary Musical Imagery' examines a pop song's capacity to project an earworm, an INMI, in a set of some 3000 participants.[61] The study was limited (in order to address recency and popularity factors) to songs that had been in the UK Singles chart (thus ruling out advertising jingles, classical music or children's songs). Of the 1558 charting songs mentioned, the most frequently mentioned, 33 times, was Lady Gaga's 'Bad Romance'. Kylie Minogue's 'Can't Get You Out of My Head' was the second most frequently mentioned charting pop song in the study—mentioned 24 times.[62] Studies such as these, whilst fascinating to a point, bring with them several presuppositions and impositions. Despite a number of such studies' declarations of how, where and why the data sets are considered and evaluated, the concluding remarks are easy to export into journalistic generalizations. One must only regard the findings as limited to the data set. A particular territory's popular music singles sales chart is subject to many factors of control, censorship and doctoring. Further to this, the fixation on melodies that adhere to Western standardized notation is a further paradigm that renders such findings to be acute and contextual rather than the objective sheen granted to them in common discussions. Infection does not heed borders, nationalities or standardization—to approach the subject of earworms and their capacity for sonic infection within such limits is problematic.

Woodward's observation regarding the globalization of infection as a result of increasingly interconnected commercial networks presupposes that contagion moves through non-human networks. Proliferation and contagion are not subject to anthropological structures, but will spread through networks of human making.[63] There are, of course, different strains and types of infection. Cholera, for example, is caused by several different bacteria (*Vibrio cholerae*). There is no 'Spanish Cholera'. To ask

[61] Note the parallel with entomological vivisection the title draws up.

[62] Stewart, L et al. "Dissecting an Earworm: Melodic Features and Song Popularity Predict Involuntary Musical Imagery" *Psychology of Aesthetics, Creativity and the Arts*. Vol. 11, No 2, (2017): 126. DOI: https://doi.org/10.1037/aca0000090. NB. Minogue's biggest hit registers the *in*sidious nature of catchy pop melodies—at once an industry insider's brag of the music 'going viral' and a sentiment of infatuation. "Kylie Minogue's Official Number 1 Singles' Sales Revealed!," *Official Charts*, accessed September 22, 2016, http://www.officialcharts.com/chart-news/kylie-minogue-s-official-number-1-singles-sales-revealed-__3849/.

[63] Woodward, *Slime Dynamics*, 14.

such a question is to narrow the scope of enquiry so that evaluations can adhere to a distinct set of presuppositions, a paradigmatic approach. The narrowing scope of such evaluation is exemplified by the following lines from Stewart et al. concerning an 'anomaly' in the melodic feature extraction stage of the study:

> The full melody line of each of the 202 songs (including all verses, repetitions, etc.) was also extracted for use in some of the subsequent analyses. During this process, it was noted that one INMI tune ("Funky Cold Medina") was comprised primarily of spoken words rather than a melody line. As such, this song and its matched non-INMI tune were excluded from subsequent analysis.[64]

Thus, because a reported earworm, an INMI, "Funky Cold Medina" did not match the musical paradigm the authors sought to work with, it was excluded from further consideration and evaluation. The reason for this elision is given ('spoken words rather than a melody line'), but the reason why this is a criterion for exclusion is not. Note that the track in question is a vocal track consisting of spoken words, a rap by Tone Loc with a minimal percussive backing track with electric guitar samples (perhaps a proto nu-metal hip-hop rock skeleton?). Why is a vocal rap with a percussive backing track *not* music? This presupposition may be due to the study being conducted according to a very Western notion of what music is, or it may be symptomatic of a lay-racist view that rap is not 'real' music. Whatever the presupposition is, it is difficult to read it as a register of anything other than prejudice—be it musicological, cultural, racial or otherwise. Or one might ask a simpler question to underscore this claim: *what*—other than musical stimuli—elicits INMI?

The elision of Tone Loc's rap from the study points firstly how elusive the properties of earworm are, the phenomena of IMNI, what makes a song catchy, is shrouded in more mystique than viruses, pathogens and bacteria whose material properties and protocols of proliferation and infection are better understood. Secondly, it points to the significance voice has for the question: earworms are often voiced, not merely musical, not merely speech, but a voiced manifestation of what Dolar considers to be the two obfuscatory modes of voice. Voice harbours a lacuna of

[64] Stewart, L et al. "Dissecting an Earworm: Melodic Features and Song Popularity Predict Involuntary Musical Imagery", 127.

contagious, possessive, influence over the human mind and body. Recalcitrant to reduction to musical or semantic terms, it is the portal from which voice may worm.

Parasites and Earworms

In William Burroughs' 1967 novel *The Ticket That Exploded*, he famously described the word as a virus. The description is potted with adjectival choices that evoke the word as not only something that invades and infects, but also something that makes one ill. He compares the word to a flu-virus. Reading the passage today, one cannot help but regard the passage as holding an eerie prescience for the human immunodeficiency virus (HIV, first clinically observed in 1981) that would be signalled, with striking symptomatic resonance, by flu-like symptoms. Burroughs writes, parsing the word as virus, drawing a parallel of its co-opting of the respiratory apparatus and underscoring its capacity to infect the brain: 'The word is now a virus. The flu virus may once have been a healthy living cell. It is now a parasite organism that invades and damages the lungs. The word may once have been a healthy living cell. It is now a parasitic organism that invades and damages the central nervous system.'[65]

Mark Twain's short story, *A Literary Nightmare* (1876), contains an example of a textual earworm, a voice of words that infects, like a language virus. Twain's story describes a contagious voice that never sounds but leaps from printed word to repetitious mental torment through the eye. Nonetheless, despite the voice being unsounding, its symptoms are distinctly corporeal and horrific. The short story, told in first person, details a rhyme that lodges within the narrator's consciousness after he reads it in a newspaper. Mark, the protagonist, in the first line, asks the reader (of male pronoun) to read the offending lines: 'Will the reader please to cast his eye over the following lines, and see if he can discover anything harmful in them?'[66] Then the 'jingling rhyme' is detailed in text. It goes like this:

> *"Conductor, when you receive a fare,*
> *Punch in the presence of the passenjare!*
> *A blue trip slip for an eight-cent fare,*

[65] William Burroughs, *The Ticket That Exploded* (London, UK: Penguin, 2014), 56.

[66] Mark Twain, *The Best Short Stories of Mark Twain (Modern Library Classics)* (New York, USA. Modern Library/Random House, 2004), 67.

A buff trip slip for a six-cent fare,
A pink trip slip for a three-cent fare,
Punch in the presence of the passenjare!
CHORUS
Punch, brothers! punch with care!
Punch in the presence of the passenjare!'"[67]

Every sound reminds him of the ditty. He tries to distract himself from the incessant earworm, he goes for a walk, but this doesn't dispel the parasitic rhyme. The narrator is a writer, just like Stephen King and his famous part-biographical scribe-grump Jack Torrance in *The Shining*.[68] The much-parodied repetition of 'All Work and No Play Makes Jack a Dull Boy' manic symptom in Kubrick's adaptation is not in the novel.[69] But there is a similarity, prompting one to contemplate the continuum of writers writing about writers' problems. Like Torrance (and one might quip writers generally—ed.), Mark is easily distracted. For when he goes to write he can only write out the tormenting lyrics. He is a vessel doomed to parrot and echo the contagious text.[70]

This is precisely what Sacks observes in Twain's short story; he writes of a narrator 'rendered helpless after encountering some "jingling rhymes" '.[71] He then quotes the passage that best deals the contagion and torment of the rhyme:

[67] Ibid., 67.

[68] Stephen King, *The Shining; Carrie; Misery: Three Novels in One Volume* (London, UK: Chancellor Press, 1992).

[69] *The Shining*. Digital File. Directed by Stanley Kubrick. UK/USA: Warner Brothers/ Hawk Films, 1980.

[70] This symptom, of course, resonates with Burrough's concept of language being a virus. It can, additionally, be read as a fantastic and exaggerated example of how filler words and ticks (the parallel with the small arachnid *parasitiforme* intended) plague one whose vocation is conducted in the medium of word (explored briefly in "Accelerations and speed limits: An essay on the vocal limits of semiocapitalism"). To embed a contemporary tick of irking semantic antinomy in Burroughs' line: 'Language is, *like-literally*, a virus.' From 'y'know', 'um', 'like-literally', to the managerial verbal-excess of pseudo-Deleuzian abstraction ('irregardless', 'moving forwards' 'scope', 'granularities') or, on campus, the halting baroque pedagogy of 'let us, then, now, unpack the problematic implicit in such a dialectic'. There is also, Freud's problematic tick thesis concerning feminine sexuality—the clitoris couched in horological synthesis.

[71] Sacks, *Musicophilia*, 43.

> They took instant and entire possession of me. All through breakfast they went waltzing through my brain .... I fought hard for an hour, but it was useless. My head kept humming .... I drifted downtown, and presently discovered that my feet were keeping time to that relentless jingle .... [I] jingled all through the evening, went to bed, rolled, tossed, and jingled all night long.[72]

Sometime later in the story Mark, looking ill, tired and vacant, meets a friend, Rev. Mr. —, for a walk. As they walk Rev. Mr. — talks constantly but Mark is plagued by the jingle and cannot concentrate on the conversation. The catchy jingle is so plaguing that he cannot listen or answer Rev. Mr. —. Instead, he just repeats the lyrics back, entranced, zombie-like, cursed. Here he passes the jingle on, it transfers, like the 'third type' of demon referenced by Thacker, 'the word-of-mouth among the people, which itself spreads like a disease.'[73] Mark murmurs the jingle absentmindedly before noticing that the curse has transferred:

> The Rev. Mr. — turned a lack-luster eye upon me, drew a deep sigh, and said, without animation, without apparent consciousness:
>
> "Punch, brothers, punch with care! Punch in the presence of the passenjare!"
>
> A pang shot through me as I said to myself, "Poor fellow, poor fellow! he has got it, now."[74]

The catchy jingle like viroid life that lives *through* a multitude of organisms (i.e. The Black Death 'bacillus-flea-rat-human') is manifested as, and via, an assemblage of bodies.[75] The jingle exists through Mark and The Rev. Mr. —. To parse it differently, it can be exorcised, expelled and passed on to another host. Much like parasites that move from one host to another, the insidious ditty can take up residence in another. The transfer (exorcism of one and infection for another) takes place via voice. The remainder of Twain's story details the woes of The Rev. Mr. — who, at a funeral speaking engagement, cannot speak but only mutter the lines of the jingle.

[72] Ibid.
[73] Thacker, *In the Dust of This Planet: Horror of Philosophy Vol. 1*, 28.
[74] Twain, *The Best Short Stories of Mark Twain (Modern Library Classics)*, 68–69.
[75] Woodward, *Slime Dynamics*, 18.

The reverend confides in Mark and resigns himself to a life of torment. 'Something tells me that my tongue is doomed to wag forever to the jigger of that remorseless jingle. There—there it is coming on me again: a blue trip slip for an eight-cent fare, a buff trip slip for a—'[76] Mark notes how Mr. —'s murmurings grew faint, and he sank into a peaceful trance, some respite from the jingly torment. Luckily for Mr. —, Mark (who one feels should take responsibility for his friend's suffering, it was, after all, a consequence of his own relief, inadvertently passing the jingle on) saves him from the asylum. Mark, we may assume, is now savvy to the jingle's modus operandi; it exists through transfer. It cannot be got rid of but can be passed on. Exorcism of the jingle is always a matter of contagion, of transmitting it to another host. Sacks details the passage of infection, moving through bodies and minds, succinctly: 'narrator meets an old friend, a pastor, and inadvertently "infects" him with the jingle; the pastor, in turn, inadvertently infects his entire congregation.'[77] Mark, the narrator, tells of how he

> took him [the Reverend] to a neighboring university and made him discharge the burden of his persecuting rhymes into the eager ears of the poor, unthinking students. How is it with them, now? The result is too sad to tell. Why did I write this article? It was for a worthy, even a noble, purpose. It was to warn you, reader, if you should came across those merciless rhymes, to avoid them—avoid them as you would a pestilence.[78]

By giving a lecture, the Reverend transferred the parasitic affliction to eagerly listening students.[79] Although much of the short tale describes the anguish and torment of the jingle, an explicit reference to the horror of voice's contagiousness is delivered in the closing line: the catchy, tormenting jingle is likened to pestilence. *Punch, Brothers! Punch* is more parasitic than viral, like both a virus and parasite it moves through an array of bodies; it lives a transitory life and only manifests as an aberration of an

[76] Twain, *The Best Short Stories of Mark Twain (Modern Library Classics)*, 71.

[77] Sacks, *Musicophilia*, 43.

[78] Twain, *The Best Short Stories of Mark Twain (Modern Library Classics)*, 71.

[79] Note the two forms of transfer. From Mark to Mr. — then from Mr. — to countless students are not quite the same as the original leap of contagion. Mark first reads the jingle on a page, the earworm leaps silently from print to mind—whereas the latter acts of contagion work along the medium of voice. Mark inadvertently passes the jingle on to Mr. — and he to his students by vocalizing it.

organism's functioning. It is this second aspect that leans closer to parasitism than a viral modality. *Punch, Brothers! Punch* has a vague agency—a way of compelling its host to proliferate its spread, a knack for infection—for moving from host to host.

The jingle shares this trait with several parasites. There is no need to exhaustively appraise the taxonomy, but one warrants mention. *Ophiocordyceps unilateralis* (sometimes referred to casually as the zombie fungus) is a type of parasitic fungus—an entomopathogen—that infects insects (hosts), in particular ants. Like, an earworm, *Ophiocordyceps unilateralis* takes over the body and 'mind' of the ant, compelling it to climb upwards, away from its nest, before irrupting from the host's head. The alteration, one might say possession or puppetry, of the ant's behaviour is advantageous for the parasite's procreation. In the case of *Ophiocordyceps unilateralis*, it is the more effective dispersal of its spores. Bekker et al. write:

> Fungal parasites within this genus alter the behavior of their ant hosts in ways that facilitate the dispersal of spores. Foraging ants presumably get infected when these spores attach to, and penetrate, their cuticle, after which their body is colonized, as has been shown for related fungal entomopathogens such as Metarhizium (Clarkson and Charnley 1996). After the colonization period, the ant abandons its normal activities and leaves the nest. Once outside, the infected ant climbs up the foliage where it latches onto vegetation (Andersen et al. 2009; Pontoppidan et al. 2009). Atrophy of the mandible muscles prevents the animals from falling as they (typically) die hanging upside down from a leaf or twig (Hughes et al. 2011a; C. de Bekker, L. Quevillon, P. B. Smith, K. Fleming, D. Gosh, A. D. Patterson, and D. P. Hughes, submitted for publication). After death, the fungus grows out of the cadaver. It uses its host as a carbon source and as a base for propagation and dissemination of spores (Andersen et al. 2009). The cycle ends with the production of a stroma (stalk) from which sexual spores are transmitted to new ants.[80]

The pathenogizing parasite that compels and takes possession—using the host body as a zombie puppet to maximize the effectiveness of its spread to other bodies—shares a modality with the pernicious *Punch,*

[80] Charissa de Bekker; Martha Merrow and David P. Hughes. "From Behavior to Mechanisms: An Integrative Approach to the Manipulation by a Parasitic Fungus (Ophiocordyceps unilateralis s.l.) of Its Host Ants (Camponotus spp.)" *Integrative and Comparative Biology*, Volume 54, Issue 2, 1 July 1st 2014, 166–176. Accessed July 19 2018. https://academic.oup.com/icb/article/54/2/166/2797855.

Brothers! Punch. Both pathogens compel the host corpus into an action that expedites its spread. The body, be it an ant, a human writer or reverend, inadvertently produces actions (movements or vocalizations—of which the latter is also the former) that facilitate the spread of infection to other hosts. In the case of *A Literary Nightmare* Mark, the narrator, cannot help but rehearse the dreadful jingle during conversation with the reverend. Once the reverend is infected, he does the same—but rather than pass to earworm from one to another he does so more like the proliferation of Ophiocordyceps Unilateralis—he speaks from a vantage point and spreads the jingle to a large group.

The Twain tale does not specify if the reverend was reading from a page during his lecture or not. But it is clear from the outset that Mark, the narrator, first read the jingle in a newspaper. An alternative term for page or paper is leaf. And it is from vantage of the leaf that both *Punch, Brothers! Punch* and *Ophiocordyceps unilateralis* hold maximum potential for a virulent infection of multiple bodies that become pathenogized hosts. Although Twain's tale is anecdotal and does not offer much context outside of the narrator's subjective experience—an inevitable symptom of first-person fiction—one wonders who else read the offending jingle in the newspaper Mark picked up. Newspapers, especially during the time of Twain's writing, were widely circulated and a dominant form of information dissemination. *Punch, Brothers! Punch* could be couched as a proto-viral, a precursor to the Internet meme (the Dawkinsian term itself alluding to proliferating procreation that moves through host bodies).

The parasite earworm, which leaps from the leaf to torment and compel the body and mind of the host(s), is reflected on a textual and meta-textual level. Firstly, the narrator asks the reader to read the infectious lines. 'Will the reader please to cast his eye over the following lines, and see if he can discover anything harmful in them?'[81] This re-voicing of the infecting rhyme brings the jingle too close to *phone*. It imposes the contagion from the diegesis on the reader before the narrator tells of the horrors it brings. Secondly, on a meta-textual level, the publishing history performs a pathogenic editorial symptom. The original title was *A Literary Nightmare*, and it was subsequently published in later volumes as *Punch, Brothers, Punch*—the story's title was replaced with the chorus line of the contagious rhyme featured within the diegesis. The change in the title of

[81] Mark Twain, *The Best Short Stories of Mark Twain (Modern Library Classics)* (New York, USA. Modern Library/Random House, 2004), 67.

the short story can be read as an editorial meta-text that performs the viral nature of the rhyme in print.

Let's now focus on some more pointed uses of pathogens. Eugene Thacker, in 'Cryptobiologies', writes of instances whereby disease and contagion are weaponized. He describes two methods of proto-biological warfare: 'Thucydides remarks that, during the Peloponnesian war, there were rumours of the wells being intentionally poisoned—a possible early example of biological warfare. The mediaeval practice of catapulting diseased and/or decaying cadavers of soldiers and animals would carry this further.'[82]

Horror writer Stephen King's domestic torment of his wife takes a mode of spreading infection, albeit of sonic medium and INMI symptom, the malicious infection of an earworm. King, with a gleeful undertone, tells of his strategy for maximizing the earworm's potential for infection. He would wait till she was engaged in errands before launching a sonic parasite through the home architecture. His earworm of choice for the cruel jape was the Latin infused *Mambo No 5* by Lou Bega.[83] King confesses: 'Concerning this last one, I want to share that my wife once informed me that she would disembowel me with her sharpest Ginsu knife if I played the extended version one more time. I waited until she was running errands, then played it ... not once but several times.'[84] King notes that 'Latin-tinged songs [...] scored high on the this-makes-me-crazy

[82] Eugene Thacker, "Cryptobiologies" *Artnodes*, Issue 6 (Barcelona, Spain: Universiat Oberta de Catalunya: 2006) Available at *Posthuman Destinies: Science, Culture and Integral Yoga*. Accessed July 192,018: http://www.sciy.org/?p=5631.

[83] I have conducted similar experiments during the writing of this text to similar effect. My father often hums the tunes from pop music he hears. He easily succumbs to a catchy earworm. Over summer I applied myself to maintaining Michael Jackson's *Bad* guitar riff as the earworm in my father. To begin, I'd make sure to play the riff loudly on my electric guitar whenever he came home from work. Or I might play it at a marginally lower volume while he napped downstairs. Often, if I noticed he was not humming the riff or was humming the melody of another pop song, perhaps something he heard on the radio, I'd go upstairs and play the riff again. Sure enough, this worked and to my quiet delight I'd catch him humming the Jackson hit melody later on in the day. There is satisfaction in applying the infectious nature of sound to loved ones: an indulgence in light melodic torment. Of all the riffs I know Jackson's *Bad* was most effective (perhaps due to how well known the song is) and an ideal melody to be rehearsed on a guitar with no other instrumental accompaniment available.

[84] Stephen King 'Stephen King on songs that stick in your head' *Entertainment Weekly*, April 17, 2009. Accessed June 6, 2018. http://www.ew.com/article/2009/04/17/stephen-king-songs-stick-your-head/.

meter.'[85] On the Stephen King forum there is an Earworm Friday topic thread.[86] There are a number of Latin-themed popular songs posted in the form of YouTube videos (although one cannot help but notice that the opening post of the thread is an embed of Kylie Minogue's aptly titled ode *to and for* cerebral infection: *Can't Get You Out of My Head*).

A weaponized Latin-themed earworm, the infectious, compelling and corrupting nature of song, is pushed to comedic exaggeration in the comedy-fantasy film *The Mask* (1994).[87] In this scene Stanley Ipkiss (played by Jim Carrey), wearing the Hulkesque pale-green ego-amplifying mask, is on the run from police. He exits a park and with CGI acme-style exaggeration hammers, chains, boards up and bolts the gates shut behind him only to turn around and see a mass of police cars and law enforcement officers lying in wait with guns and spotlights trained on him. Recalling *Ren & Stimpy* cartoons, his skull facia, eyes and tongue shoot from his mask projecting into the area of threat in horror: defacing panic. Ipkiss, The Mask, is cornered.

A police officer tells him through megaphone that 'it is all over,' and he is warned to put his hands over his head; non-compliance will result in open fire. Various gun-Foley sounds are heard, implying the lethal menace of phallocentric firearms being 'cocked' ready for discharge. But Ipkiss has an idea; his eyes narrow and he grinds his teeth (lesser hesitations outside of Hollywood fantasy have resulted in unarmed civilians being shot dead on the streets of North America). He clicks his fingers and says, 'hit it!' In addition to the spotlights trained on him others light up. Some percussive Latin music starts. Ipkiss is now Cuban Pete, a Cuban heeled, satin-shirted, maraca wielding Svengali. He begins to dance, with the knowing, cajoling, predation of a holiday resort entertainer. An infectious melody comes on. A 'cop'—gun raised and pointed at Ipkiss/Cuban Pete—begins to shrug his shoulders in time with the beat. As Cuban Pete sings, he shakes his hips, and more officers within the hoard begin to move in unison. Cuban Pete then throws his maracas away and provides a series of dance references, swinging around *Singing in the Rain* street furniture like parking meters, street lamps and seesawing a builder's trestle. Then after

[85] Ibid., no pagination.

[86] https://stephenking.com/xf/index.php?threads/earworm-friday.18984/.

[87] *The Mask*, directed by Chuck Russell (as Charles Russell), (USA: New Line Cinema; Dark Horse Entertainment, 1994), digital file. This wonderful film, starring Jim Carey, should be regarded as a prescient allegory for how we portray exaggerated and over-positive versions of ourselves on social media.

the second verse, Cuban Pete sings 'Chic-chic-ky-boom, Chic-chic-ky-boom, Chic-chic-ky-boom' (thrice, unlike previously). He then Merlin-waves his fingers at a police officer stoically pointing a gun at him; we hear a stardust sonic twinkle. A spell is cast.

The police officer starts singing. She sings, at first with confusion but then with zeal: 'He's a really modest guy, although he's the hottest guy, In Havana, in Havana.' The badge on her hat glints viridescent. Cuban Pete grabs the officer, and we see others singing along. Cuban Pete proceeds to invade the officer's personal space on top of a car: a Hollywood-musical dance sequence that at once depicts and makes light of sexual assault. He picks her up, she slaps his face twice, and rather than pursuing her further (a la Bond), he lets her go and she pirouettes into the arms of her law-enforcement colleagues. A conga line is then formed behind Cuban Pete. The scene is one of chaos and revelry. Cuban Pete departs before the two officers from the Park, Lt. Kellaway and Doyle, who have spent the scene scaling and climbing over the park walls, can break up the party.

Although fantastic, it is a succinct example of song's *disarming* infectiousness, its contagion, how it passes from one body to another and proliferates through a crowd. The police threat is neutralized by their compulsion to sing along with Cuban Pete. The Mask effectively utilizes the contagious nature of song for his own ends, stripping the police officers of agency, compelling them to sing and dance before making his escape.

Pawley and Müllensiefen, in a study of sing-along behaviours in pubs and clubs in the north of England, note how several evolutionary theories suggest music's development in humans may have been due to its capacity to aid 'social bonding and cohesion, and synchronizing group mood'.[88] Cuban Pete's exploitation of the social human animal via the medium of voice is an example of song's capacity to override political power structures. Cuban Pete slots into a continuum of disruptively infectious 'corrupting' song, a lineage Dolar draws up, from Chinese emperor Chun (c. 2200 BC) to Plato to the various theological containments of song's infectious power.[89]

[88] Alisun Pawley and Daniel Müllensiefen, 'The Science of Singing Along: A Quantitative Field Study on Sing-Along Behavior in the North of England', *Music Perception: An Interdisciplinary Journal.* Vol 30, No. 2 (2012): 129 doi: 10.1525/mp.2012.30.2.129.

[89] Dolar, *A Voice and Nothing More*, 43–47.

E.B. White's short story, *The Supremacy of Uruguay*, originally published in *The New Yorker*, on November 25, 1933, tells of a Uruguayan who notices the potent and insidious power of voice. In this case a tenor's croons are amplified and his voice ricochets and permeates deep into the urban space:

> A platform had been erected on the marquee of one of the theatres, and in an interval between speeches a cold young man in an overcoat was singing into a microphone, "Thanks," he crooned, "for all the lovely dee-light I found in your embrace ..." The inflection of the love words was that of a murmurous voice, but the volume of the amplified sound was enormous; it carried for blocks, deep into the ranks of the electorate.[90]

The description of how the tenor's amplified voice seeps and echoes into every nook and cranny of urban architecture is a further register of the sonic insidiousness of voice.[91] On the same page the narrator describes the voice as 'the great *slimy* sounds of the love embrace'.[92] Note that the narrator's chosen adjective to describe the insidious contagion of voice is slimy.

White details the enchantment that results of hearing voice. Voice, an invisible and powerful mode of twentieth-century propaganda, can brainwash, take over, enchant and unbalance individuals who happen to be within its sonic reach: 'The faces, the mask faces, the chill air, the advertising lights, the steam rising from the jumbo cup of A. & P. Coffee high over Forty-seventh Street, these added to his enchantment and his unbalance.'[93] The protagonist in White's story then exports this powerful brainwashing strategy to his homeland. His development is to augment the infectiousness of voice with military aviation:

[90] White, E. B. 'The Supremacy of Uruguay' in *Timeless Stories for Today and Tomorrow*, ed. Ray Bradbury (New York, USA: Bantam Books, 1952), 201.

[91] Unlike sights, the voice (and in particular the technologically amplified voice) incurs into the body uninvited by virtue of it expansiveness, autonomous from the constraints of lightness, darkness, being seen or shown. This, omnipresent and uninvited life of voice resounds in Calvino's short story, *A King Listens*. The King, installed and imprisoned on his throne in his palace-cum-cochlear, is the aural equivalent of Alex, in Burgess' *Clockwork Orange*. The King is helpless, ears always open, bombarded, plagued, with voices that slither and seep through the maze of his palace and kingdom to haunt, threaten and horrify him.

[92] White, 'The Supremacy of Uruguay', 201, emphasis added.

[93] Ibid.

> Ten months later he had perfected and turned over to his government a war machine unique in military history -a radio-controlled plane carrying an electric phonograph with a retractable streamlined horn. Casablanca had got hold of Uruguay's loudest tenor, and had recorded the bar of music he had heard in Times Square. (...) His theory was that a squadron of pilotless planes scattering this unendurable sound over foreign territories would immediately reduce the populace to insanity. Then Uruguay, at her leisure, could send in her armies, subdue the idiots, and annex the land.[94]

The canny Uruguayan's plan worked. Everyone who heard the tenor's voice is reduced to a state of voice-haunted zombie.

> The effect was as Casablanca had predicted. In forty-eight hours the peoples were hopelessly mad, ravaged by an ineradicable noise, ears shattered, minds unseated. No defense had been possible because the minute anyone came within range of the sound, he lost his sanity and, being daft, proved ineffectual in a military way. After the planes had passed over, life went on much as before, except that it was more secure, sanity being gone. No one could hear anything except the noise in his own head. At the actual moment when people had been smitten with the noise, there had been of course, some rather amusing incidents. A lady in West Philadelphia happened to be talking to her butcher on the phone. "Thanks," she had just said, "for taking back that tough steak yesterday. And thanks," she added, as the plane passed over, "for unforgettable nights I never can replace."[95]

The phonograph carrying drones of Uruguay unleashed madness on the world. As detailed above, those infected can only mindlessly parrot the lyrics. But there is a further analogy too that extend past the remit of vocalization: those tormented by the incessant vocal earworm cannot write either, albeit to scrawl out the vacuous lyrics of the tenor. In White's story the:

> 'Linotype operators in composing-rooms [were] chopped off in the middle of sentences, like the one who was setting a story about an admiral in San Pedro:
>
> I am tremendously grateful to all the ladies of San Pedro for the wonderful hospitality they have shown the men of the fleet during our recent

[94] Ibid., 202.
[95] Ibid., 202.

maneuvers and thanks for unforgettable nights I never can replace and thanks for unforgettable nights I nev-[96]

The voice's power to infiltrate and take over, to torment and render 'crazy', to plague the non-consenting listener is a register of its horrific contagious potency—in unwelcome incursion that erodes agency, the patrician reserve of mastery of one's body: self-control.

In an inversion of the traditional horror philosophy, we have seen in Thacker the infectious voice doesn't make the listener aware of a lack of knowledge but instead, and just as horrifically, surreptitiously erodes the subject's agency of mind and autonomy. Rather than being alerted to a lack of knowledge one is alerted to a lack of agency and control of one's faculties. Mind and body are plunged into a vicarious remove: self-doubt and distrust. The beguiling voice is the aural equivalent not of realizing there may be something one cannot see but realizing that what one sees cannot be trusted, horrific Cartesian scepticism. Voice's spell can yank the ontological rug out from under those exposed. Vocal contagion manifests in the role of the 'demon'.[97] The 'evil mind, who is all powerful and cunning'.[98]

Infectious vocal earworms are not always a case of listeners falling victim and becoming unwittingly enchanted and robbed of agency. The protagonist of Alfred Bester's *The Demolished Man*, Ben Reich, wilfully seeks out an infectious earworm. Set in the twenty-fourth century, Reich is the head of a vast business empire that spans the solar system (Monarch Utilities & Resources). Because of a paranoid misunderstanding Reich sees the elimination of D'Courtney as his only option and sets out kill him. However, in the twenty-fourth century, seventy years have passed since the last murder. The telepathic reading of minds 'peeping' is common practice. Espers, a supposedly superior people with the telepathic ability to deeply read minds, can even read the unconscious thoughts of others (whereas non-Esper 'peepers' can only discern the conscious thoughts of

[96] Ibid., 203.

[97] None of the versions I have access to use the anthropic term 'demon', but a wealth of later analyses frame Descartes move as such. Such framing is apt, for Descartes uses terms such as 'mind', 'energies' and 'cunning' to describe the force. He also (though there might be some difference in the original Latin from 1641) uses 'they' and 'their'. There is certainly an anthropomorphic narrative employed to express the sentiment of doubt and scepticism.

[98] René Descartes, *Meditations and Other Metaphysical Writings (Penguin Classics)* Trans. Desmond M Clarke (London, England: Penguin, 2000), 22.

another). Reich's pursuit of murdering D'Courtney without his intentions being detected by either Espers or Peepers is nigh impossible, particularly because both Reich and D'Courtney employ and are surrounded by Espers.

Reich's solution to this problem is to acquire a 'temporary mind block'.[99] He travels to *Psych-Songs Inc* on Melody Lane (leading one to believe the production of catchy advertising jingles is a large industry in this science fiction future world). *Psych Songs Inc.*'s work extends to ear-worms used for political repression; Bester writes that it was 'run by a clever young woman who had written some jingles for his sales division and some devastating strike-break songs for Propaganda back when Monarch needed everything to smash last year's labor fracas.'[100] Reich asks the 'clever young women', Duffy:

> "What's the most persistent tune you ever wrote?"
> "Persistent?"
> "You know what I mean. Like those advertising jingles you can't get out of your head."

[99] Alfred Bester, *The Demolished Man (SF Masterworks Series)* (London, UK: Gollancz, 1999), 29.

[100] Sacks, in 'Brainworms, Sticky Music and Catchy Tunes' in *Musicophilia*, briefly mentions Nicolas Slonimsky. '[A] composer and musicologist, was deliberately inventing musical forms or phrases that could hook the mind and force it to mimicry and repetition, as early as the 1920s.' (See Sacks, Musicophilia: Tales of Music and the Brain, 42.) Slonimsky's intention in his work cannot be gleaned from his introduction to *Thesaurus of Scales and Melodic Patterns*. (Nicolas Slonimsky, *Thesaurus of Scales and Melodic Patterns* (New York, USA: Schirmer Books, 1975). But it is notable, contra Stewart et al.'s study, that much of the book focuses on, in Tom Schnable's description, 'Indian scales, North African and African styles, Middle Eastern modes, and more.' (Tom Schnable, "Rhythm Planet: Coltrane, Nicolas Slonimsky, Modal Music and Trance". *KCRW*. June 15, 2011. Accessed 6 July 2018. http://blogs.kcrw.com/music/2011/06/coltrane-nicolas-slonimsky-modal-music-and-trance/.) Maria Konnikova, writing in *The New Yorker*, states that Slonimsky was a great influence on Frank Zappa and John Coltrane. (Maria Konnikova "Anatomy of an Earworm" *The New Yorker*, February 28, 2014. Accessed 6 June, 2018. https://www.newyorker.com/tech/elements/anatomy-of-an-earworm) Schnable's blog post, in expounding the trance like qualities of Coltrane's Slonimsky-informed improvisations, notably lapses into granting the music a possessive and infectious sonic agency. He writes, of Coltrane studying Slonimsky's patterns and modes and speculates that 'perhaps this was why Coltrane could make his soprano saxophone sound more like the Indian shehnai, the Indian oboe used by snake charmers to hypnotize cobras.' (Tom Schnable, "Rhythm Planet: Coltrane, Nicolas Slonimsky, Modal Music and Trance".) Like King's comment on Latin music, Cuban Pete and the omission of Tone Loc, there is distinctly colonial attitude.

(…) Duffy winced in recollection. "Hate to think of it even now. Guaranteed to obsess you for a month. It haunted me for a year."
"You're rocketting."
"Scout's honor, Mr. Reich. It was 'Tenser, Said The Tensor.' (…)
"Let's hear it."
"I couldn't do that to you."
"Come on, Duffy. I'm really curious."
"You'll regret it."[101]

Reich opts to infect himself with a vocal earworm, a jingle that would engulf his mind with its incessant repetition so that any peeper hoping to read his mind would perceive, 'peep', the catchy jingle rather than his murderous intent. The following passage describes how Duffy sings the earworm jingle, and it immediately resounds in Reich. The lines of the song also interrupt the text, evoking the contagious torment in the reader:

A tune of utter monotony filled the room with agonizing, unforgettable banality. It was the quintessence of every melodic cliché Reich had ever heard. No matter what melody you tried to remember, it invariably led down the path of familiarity to "Tenser, Said The Tensor." Then Duffy began to sing:

Eight, sir; seven, sir;
Six, sir; five, sir;
Four, sir; three, sir;
Two, sir; one!
Tenser, said the Tensor.
Tenser, said the Tensor.
Tension, apprehension,
And dissention have begun.

"You little devil!" Reich started to his feet, pounding his palms on his ears. "I'm accursed. How long is this affliction going to last?"
"Not more than a month."
As Reich had planned, the song established itself firmly in his mind and echoed again and again all the way down the street. *Tenser, said the Tensor. Tenser, said the Tensor. Tension, apprehension, and dissention have begun.* RIFF. A perfect mind-block for a non-Esper. What peeper could get past that? *Tension, apprehension, and dissention have begun.*[102]

[101] Bester, *The Demolished Man (SF Masterworks Series)*, 47–48.
[102] Ibid., 48–49.

Reich succumbs to the infectious ditty, not as an unwilling victim robbed of agency but as a shrewd conscious torment installed to obfuscate his homicidal endeavour. Reich's autoinfection with contagious tormenting voice is a case of cunning application. In this sci-fi narrative the melodic voice and the infectiousness of the earworm (INMI) to strip conscious lucidity from a human are taken as a given and used as a plot device. Bester's use of the earworm is not inventive; it is a slightly exaggerated description of advertising jingles.

These fictional examples of the insidiousness of voice all pertain to a voice's delivery of words. The lyrical earworm can be regarded as an inversion of Dolar's first claimed mode of obfuscation. Rather than language and meaning obfuscating voice, the lilt, rhythm and inflection of the lyrical delivery beguiles over semantic content. Yet INMI, lyrical rhyming jingles, earworms are not the reduction of voice to a fetish object, an object of aesthetic reverence. This penumbral position the earworm holds when considered in terms of the language/aesthetics binary Dolar draws up at the beginning of *A Voice and Nothing More* is not enough to declare the vocal earworm to be an object *a*. There are, however, a number of observations worth positing for their contribution to the re-contextualizing of the prospect of the object *a* voice in terms of audition, the body and horror.

The sequence of earworms presented here, as well as sharing a parasitic modality, all take the form of an exogenous voice that manifests as an aural hallucination, an internal resonance within a host body. Vocal earworms, and INMI, manifest in a similar form as the aural hallucinations that Lacan described. In the sense of internal resonance, one key characteristic earworms share with the genealogy of object *a* voice is its autonomy from sound. Both are voice aural phenomena but not limited to sonic modalities. The method of contagion may be via sound, but much of their manifestation is a silent sounding within a host body.

Earworms, by virtue of their status as aural mirages, manifest in a modality analogous to object *a* voice: as silent but nonetheless experienced: heard. A further equivalence to consider is the corporeal horror implicit in the earworm and object *a* voice. There is a torment, a horror, a stripping of agency in all cases here as well as a possession and compelling of the body that mimics the mode of viruses and parasites. All affect the body—the arbitrary vessel—they move, propagate, disseminate and sound within and through. The claim here is not that tormenting earworms are forms of object *a*, but that an appraisal of voice in the modality of such phenomenon leads to a conception of voice that shares many of the traits of the object *a* voice especially in terms of audition and the body. A claim that can be made subsequently to drawing up such equivalences is one of horror: that no sooner does one begin to approach a voice in the structural context of object *a* and consider its manifestation in terms of audition and corporeality, horror abounds.

Sirens' Spell

Spell, qua verb, refers to the array of letters that create words—their order. Spell, qua noun, is magical, powerful—it is a force, but not order. Like mist: mysterious; like voice: diffuse. Spells, particularly those from—note gender—women, mermaids, sirens and witches, have historically been framed as curses to be guarded against on a number of levels: physically, politically and legislatively.

There is a categorical shift at play in the preceding line. The move from spell to spells goes from a way something is done to a sense of force that is impossible to quantify or discern. It carries an ominous portent. In this shift there is a lurch from the known to the nebulous. Secondly, the guarding against spells is articulated in three terms—physical, political and legislatively—that bridge from the material prospect of spells to their immaterial incarnation. It is here where the voice as spell finds its parallel with the spectre of contagion horror: the plague. Let's consider how female voices *and* vocality are framed as a horrifying sonic force, a beguiling or enchanting spell, to be avoided or controlled like, with deliberate connotations of contagion, the plague.

In the introduction to *Embodied Voices: Representing Female Vocality in Western Culture* Leslie C. Dunn and Nancy A. Jones address the difference between voice and vocality. They write that the 'move from "voice" to "vocality" implies a shift from a concern with the phenomenological roots of voice to a conception to vocality as a cultural construct.'[103] They then note the important link of embodiment at play in and between the two terms:

[103] Leslie C. Dunn and Nancy A. Jones, "Introduction" in *Embodied voices: Representing female vocality in western culture*, ed. Leslie C. Dunn and Nancy A. Jones (Cambridge, UK: Cambridge University Press, 1996), 2.

> [b]y specifying female vocality, we also assert the centrality of gender in shaping that construction. Here our third term comes into play. As a material link between "inside" and "outside," self and other, the voice is, in Nelly Furman's words, "the locus of articulation of an individual's body to language and society." Since both language and society are structured by codes of sexual difference, both the body and its voice are inescapably gendered.[104]

Gender is not the only factor at play in the embodying between voice and vocality. Race, its vocality and embodiment, also plays a significant role.[105]

Returning to Dunn and Jones' introductory remarks, and the focus on female voice, vocality and embodiment, the following passage yokes the traditional framing of female voice as disorder, unbound nature and physical materiality. Although the authors are not deliberately intending to frame female voice as an object of horror there is a striking equivalence in terms of vocabulary and theme. The themes employed below are not what the authors posit female voice to be, but rather how normative and traditional framings of female voice—vocality— come with a palette of associations. Such associations, emphasized below, resonate with the thematic pitch of genre horror and contemporary theorizing of horror. Dunn and Jones write:

> The anchoring of the female voice in the female body confers upon it all the conventional associations of femininity with *nature and matter*, with emotion and *irrationality*. More concretely, it leads to associations of the female voice with bodily fluids (milk, menstrual blood) and the consequent devaluation of feminine utterance as *formless* and free-flowing babble, a sign of *uncontrolled* female *generativity*.[106]

We see in this passage the same thematic palette as Woodward and Thacker explore, albeit not along the lines of gender, in their work on horror and philosophy. In the above instance, female voice evokes an array of unthinkable excesses that run amok in genre horror—nature unbound,

[104] Ibid.

[105] For an excellent discussion (utilizing as an example a vocal coach's deeply bodied and clichéd comments about different voices) see Nina Sun Eidsheim's Ph.D. thesis, particularly the section "Performing Race: Shaping Vocal Racialized Timbre". Nina Sun Eidsheim, *Voice as a technology of selfhood: towards an analysis of racialized timbre and vocal performance* (Ph.D. UC San Diego, 2008), 205–209.

[106] Dunn and Jones, "Introduction", 3, emphasis added.

excessiveness, formless, unfathomable, material but not solid material, a rampant form of slippery life that does not adhere to traditional patrician rationalism.

The second line of the passage links to female sexuality. Again, couching this within the horror continuum, one cannot help but feel the shadow of Plato; chaste, in denial of the body, of impulse, and tactility. Dunn and Jones write that such associations 'further point to the identification of women's vocality with her sexuality: like the body from which it emanates, the female voice is construed as both a signifier of sexual otherness and a source of sexual power, an object at once of desire and fear.'[107] This last line in the paragraph ends with the dreaded noun so apt for horror, retroactively inscribing an allusion to the horror palette vocabulary framing female voice and vocality in the preceding line.

The equivalences between horror, voice and female vocality qua objects of desire/fear, objects that are 'natural', irrational, formless and uncontrolled, operate in terms of both voice and vocality. In terms of voice (the physics of voice and audition need not be rehashed too laboriously at this turn), sound is formless and uncontrolled; it is ethereal, radiates without light, it's insidious and penetrating. We've already considered the physical horrors of voice in term of such characteristics. Such horrors of emission and emersion (and the hope of controlling exposure) are a significant facet of the following maritime narrative. In terms of vocality, the following texts are examples of how gender and horror are coded onto the body and voice of the female figure within Western narratives. Following Dunn and Jones, gender is inscribed in the voice as it is heard. There is a conspicuous horror thematic in such symptoms of female vocality.

Consider Sirens, what Melissa Mia Hall introduces as a 'seductive icon of horror and the supernatural'.[108] This is indeed the figure Dunn and Jones move to discuss in the following paragraph of their introductory text:

> The archetypal figures of this seductive but dangerous vocality are the Sirens, whose song lures men to their destruction with a false promise of bliss. Yet Odysseus proves able to resist that lure, and in some versions of the story the Sirens must die when their vocal power is "mastered" by a greater masculine power. This narrative pattern (...) recurs throughout the history

[107] Ibid., 3

[108] Melissa Mia Hall, "The Siren" in *Icons of Horror and the Supernatural: An Encyclopedia of Our Worst Nightmares, Volumes 1 & 2.* Ed, S.T. Joshi (Westport, Connecticut, USA: Greenwood Press, 2007), 507.

of Western literary and musical traditions, producing a series of cultural icons that figure the mythic relationship between gender and vocality.[109]

The sirens introduced at this juncture highlight a narrative pattern. The seductiveness of the feminine voice is framed as an object of horror, a beguiling voice to fear and guard against. A thread emerges in the modality of its contagion. From sirens to birds to music there is a maelstrom (male-storm?) of framing voice as the corrupting figure of woman, and, ergo nature unbound.

The theme of unbound nature, the chaos of vitality, extends to the corporeal figuring of the Siren as an interspecies *being* at once feminine and avian. The physical figure of the siren is an amalgamation of woman and bird. Sirens were/are composite beings, accounts state various compositions: either female bodies with bird's heads or birds with the faces of women, sometimes sparrows sometimes swans.[110] The figure of horror that operates in a modality of contagious and excessive nature—voice—manifests as a penumbral silhouette that, in itself, embodies the confounding of *man's* ordered taxonomy and categorizing of nature. On another, more immediate level, the figural blur of woman and bird falls into a long continuum of engendering which places one gender in nature (which must be mastered) and the remainder as supposedly sage empiricist rational master.

The recurrent narrative pattern of the archetypal Sirens is one of at once seductive but dangerous female voice and vocality: beguiling but disordered excesses of nature. In this sense it is the tension between two spells, *one* verb, ordered and *correct(ed)*, the *other* a noun. The juxtaposition of these two different spells is the difference, the dichotomy, of the enchanting but dangerous generative magic of the natural world (which includes women) and the supposedly ordered state of men that regard themselves as separate masters of the world.

Let's turn now to the narrative of the Sirens in *The Odyssey*.[111] Odysseus, the eponymous hero of Homer's epic, is warned (by Circe) of the power of the Sirens' song:

[109] Dunn and Jones, "Introduction", 3.

[110] "Seirênas", *Suda Online: Byzantine Lexicography*, accessed December 8, 2018. http://www.stoa.org/sol-bin//search.pl?search_method=QUERY&login=&enlogin=&searchstr=sigma,280&field=adlerhw_gr&db=REAL.

[111] Samuel Butler's translation is the text employed here.

> 'and now pay attention to what I am about to tell you- heaven itself, indeed, will recall it to your recollection. First you will come to the Sirens who enchant all who come near them. If any one unwarily draws in too close and hears the singing of the Sirens, his wife and children will never welcome him home again, for they sit in a green field and warble him to death with the sweetness of their song. There is a great heap of dead men's bones lying all around, with the flesh still rotting off them. Therefore pass these Sirens by, and stop your men's ears with wax that none of them may hear; but if you like you can listen yourself, for you may get the men to bind you as you stand upright on a cross-piece half way up the mast, and they must lash the rope's ends to the mast itself, that you may have the pleasure of listening. If you beg and pray the men to unloose you, then they must bind you faster.[112]

Odysseus can listen provided he is incapacitated, provided there is no possibility of him acting upon the spellbinding voice(s) he hears. His crew must not listen, and they must bung their ears with wax to blot out the song. Here, the physicality of voice—its incurring, insidious characteristic—is writ large. Biological intrusion, the risk of contagion follows a trajectory that genre horror narratives would come to take up in terms of parasites, spores and viruses. The equivalence of Odysseus and his men with intrepid protagonists of biohazard sci-fi horror is the fear of other life breaching one's own physical limits. The wax the men bung their ears with is an aural analogue to a modern hazardous materials body suit. Because the Sirens' voices are autonomous from physical limits, like parasitic spores, bacteria and other figures of corporeal horror, precautions must be taken to ensure it to not incur into the body.

Let's visit the moment when Odysseus and his men venture into a territory within 'earshot' of the Sirens' voices:

> When we had got within earshot of the land, and the ship was going at a good rate, the Sirens saw that we were getting in shore and began with their singing.
>
> "'Come here,' they sang, 'renowned Ulysses, honour to the Achaean name, and listen to our two voices. No one ever sailed past us without staying to hear the enchanting sweetness of our song- and he who listens will go on his way not only charmed, but wiser, for we know all the ills that the gods

[112] Homer, *The Odyssey*, Trans. Samuel Butler, Eds. Timothy Power and Gregory Nagy (A.C. Fifield, London, 1900) Accessed December 18, 2018, http://www.perseus.tufts.edu/hopper/text?doc=urn:cts:greekLit:tlg0012.tlg002.perseus-eng2:1.1-1.1.

laid upon the Argives and Trojans before Troy, and can tell you everything that is going to happen over the whole world.'

"They sang these words most musically, and as I longed to hear them further I made by frowning to my men that they should set me free; but they quickened their stroke, and Eurylochus and Perimedes bound me with still stronger bonds till we had got out of hearing of the Sirens' voices. Then my men took the wax from their ears and unbound me.[113]

In Homer's text the Sirens are musical; they sing and call out to Odysseus. They beckon him and promise knowledge, enlightenment. The enchanting sweetness of the Sirens' voices is such that Odysseus loses himself, and he looks to his men in the hope that they will untie him from the boat mast. Upon hearing the Sirens' voices, bound to the mast, Odysseus' consistency dissolves, and he gives orders that contradict his previous commands. Eurylochus and Perimedes, deaf to the Sirens' song, ears bunged with wax, remember their leader's earlier instructions and act accordingly, fastening him tighter, ignoring the commands he gives whilst under the spell of the Sirens' voices. The aurally insulated crew preserve their faculties by virtue of not hearing the Siren's voices and succumbing to their spell.[114] When Odysseus is enchanted by the Sirens' song, the military order, the chain of command, is dissolved. Upon hearing, and enjoying, the Sirens' song his status within the ship is outside of the crew's military structure. The crew ignores his command, his voice, and treat him more as a captive, rather than their leader.

Sirens feature in more than one essay in Dunn and Jones' *Embodied Voices: Representing Female Vocality in Western Culture*. Charles Segal, the North American scholar of Greek and Latin literature, in "The Gorgon and the nightingale: the voice of female lament in and Pindar's Twelfth *Pythian Ode*", writes that in archaic and classical Greek literature the female voice serves two purposes. He argues that it is employed either to

[113] Ibid.

[114] This aural quarantine, as well as being a guard against corruption and spell, can be regarded as an archaic example of silencing female vocal agency (Odysseus's boat is a state vessel, military), one that continues today in large organizations, law, politics and media—to remove agency, to neutralize any power or effect, one simply needs to cease hearing, reporting, acknowledging.

'*embody* the beauty of song [...] and immortalize the deeds of men'[115] or to 'lament [...] expressing sorrow at death of *kings* and *heroes*'.[116] In this opening framing, these roles of female voice are pitched as either lending a body to aesthetic reverence or mourning and immortalizing the actions of men. Segal does not highlight this aspect (his focus is altogether more acute and concerns the subjects of the essay title); nonetheless, even this general remark of the female voice in Greek literature inadvertently sums up the patrician acoustics that female voice resounds or *echoes* in.[117]

Segal does, however, offer a more precise comment about the effects of female voice in these instances, one that evokes not only jeopardy, pestilence, rot and disorder (a series of registers for the horrors of nature unbound) but also magic and force. He writes how in both roles the female voice has a 'dangerous side and awakens ambivalence in the male-dominated society of early Greece, in part because women are associated with pollution, corruption, decay, and disorder. In its aural appeal and its power to dispel cares by its "charm," *thelxis*, the female voice also exercises magical power and seduction.'[118] Segal suggests that the 'songs of the Sirens and of Circe in the *Odyssey* are the earliest and most famous examples.'[119] He describes how the Sirens' song would lure Odysseus off course, noting that the only victims of the song are men. He also notes how Circe's beautiful song is used similarly to lure the companions of Odysseus before transforming them into animals. Moving from these examples Segal argues that, in terms of the epic narratives in Greek literature, 'the danger of the female voice is closely associated with its physicality' before referencing Odysseus' physical stopping of the sound penetrating the 'organs of hearing'.[120]

In the same collection, Linda Phyllis Austern's essay, '"No women are indeed": the boy actor as vocal seductress in late sixteenth—and early

[115] Charles Segal, "The Gorgon and the nightingale: the voice of female lament in and Pindar's Twelfth *Pythian Ode*" in *Embodied voices: Representing female vocality in western culture*, ed. Leslie C. Dunn and Nancy A. Jones (Cambridge, UK: Cambridge University Press, 1996), 17, emphasis added.

[116] Ibid., emphasis added.

[117] Like Echo, the nymph in love with Narcissus, whose voice was an echo of the male narcissist. Her voice was always of and for the self-obsessed male.

[118] Charles Segal, "The Gorgon and the nightingale: the voice of female lament and Pindar's Twelfth *Pythian Ode*", 17.

[119] Ibid., 18.

[120] Ibid., 18. Segal also notes that the effects of Circe's song are also neutralized by direct physical means.

seventeenth—century English drama' refers to the Sirens.[121] Austern, in addressing the narrative of feminine vocality, recourses to this early maritime example within Homer's *Odyssey*. She writes: 'by far the most prevalent, are the immoral stage sirens who use music as a means to pursue their own sexual pleasure, often to the utter destruction of men who become caught in their webs of enchantment.'[122]

Austern contextualizes this ur-example of female vocality, as a harbinger of both libido and death. She draws up the Siren voice, and its cultural legacy, to evoke at once libidinal frisson and the horrors of impending death. The Siren voice is framed as a Janus-natured *acoustral* jouissance.[123] After positing such a voice to embody and signal, like a spectre, at once libidinal frisson and impending death she posits how Sirens are the 'foremothers' of the 'stock archetype of English Renaissance fiction'. Austern describes the Siren's echo in English Renaissance fiction as an:

> absolutely deadly woman who is ruled by her insatiable sexual appetite and who attracts men through a glittering web of lies, deceit, and musical artifice [… whose] presentation ranges from the benign […] to the fatally attractive courtesans of Jacobean and Caroline drama whose glances are poison and whose voices are death.[124]

Once again, the Siren voice and its legacy and analogues are couched as at once enchanting, spellbinding, beguiling (to employ the vocabulary of intense love) whilst also bringing a risk, a morbid harmony (argued to be operative in such Siren vocality). The thread running through the Siren's episode in Homer's epic, and the observations brought forward by Segal and Austern, can be summarized as explicating the double meaning of *spells*. The fold of spell: spells of enchantment that are also spells of possession, contagion and infection.

David Toop, the British composer, musician and author, presents *The Voyage of Máel Dúin*, an ancient Irish text from approximately 700 AD, as

[121] Linda Phyllis Austern, ""No women are indeed": the boy actor as vocal seductress in late sixteenth- and early seventeenth-century English drama" in *Embodied voices: Representing female vocality in western culture*, ed. Leslie C. Dunn and Nancy A. Jones (Cambridge, UK: Cambridge University Press, 1996), 83–102.

[122] Ibid., 91.

[123] Is there an acoustic equivalent to spectre? Acoustral? The opposite of echo?

[124] Linda Phyllis Austern, ""No women are indeed": the boy actor as vocal seductress in late sixteenth- and early seventeenth- century English drama", 92–93.

an account that highlights the sinister nature of sound in *Sinister Resonance: The Mediumship of the Listener*. This is symptomatic of *Sinister Resonance*.[125] Toop's argument concerns sound, yet so many of his examples are voice based—a categorical specificity he does not acknowledge.

Nonetheless, this example he brings to light should be afforded some comments, for it sits within the continuum inaugurated by the stock archetype of the Sirens. Part of the narrative is very similar to Odysseus' brush with the Sirens in Homer's epic. Similarly, Máel Dúin and his men's confrontation with voice also runs along a thematic framework with analogues in Odysseus's voyage within earshot of the Sirens.[126] However, unlike the forewarned Odysseus, Maeldun and his men suffer the consequences of hearing the enchanting voices.

Toop does not provide the original text (written in Old Irish) but leaps to Tennyson's poem, *The Voyage of Maeldun* (1880).[127] He writes that Tennyson 'set off on his own romantic voyage' in comparison to earlier translators of the text Lady Gregory, P.W. Joyce and Whitley Stokes.[128] On Tennyson's version Toop comments that it is

> built upon the theme of hearing and sound. He wrote, for example, of the Silent Isle, a place of barkless dogs and songless larks where 'a silent ocean always broke on a silent shore.' Maeldune and his men abhor this paradise, quiet as death, where streams, waterfalls and birds may be viewed in all their beauty but not heard. Their voices, usually ***manly and warlike***, become 'thinner and fainter than any flittermouse-shriek'.[129]

It cannot escape comment that it is the absolute absence of sound being framed here as sinister. Taking a 'Dolarian' angle, the scene is ripe for

[125] David Toop, *Sinister Resonance: The Mediumship of the Listener* (London, UK/New York, USA:
Continuum, 2010).

[126] There is an oceanic thread. From Sirens in *The Odyssey*, to *The Voyage of Máel Dúin*, to John Donne's *Song* the figure of the mermaid emerges as seductive but dangerous and deceitful to men's salted ears.

[127] Alfred Tennyson, "The Voyage of Maeldune", *Words*, accessed December 14, 2018. https://www.telelib.com/authors/T/TennysonAlfred/verse/ballads/maeldune.html.

[128] Toop, *Sinister Resonance: The Mediumship of the Listener*, 20.

[129] Ibid., 20. Emphasis added. Note the imposed gendering on vocal qualities. The import is that a 'manly' voice is the opposite of the following adjectives. Toop continues: 'the heroes are flustered by feminization, this transposition into falsetto, hysteria and insubstantiality, this fade to grey.'

pitching as an example of the horrors of the inaudible 'object voice'. Not only would such a phrasing continue the muffling of voice in Dolar's project, but it would also further explicate the voided nature, the vacuum the 'object voice', we are told, 'resonates' in. A root, perhaps a key instigator of this tendency that is frequently cited, can be found in 'Jacques Lacan et la Voix' by Jacques-Alain Miller in *La voix* (1989, colloquium proceedings from January 1988). An English translation is not at present available; however, Miller's line: 'If we make music and listen to it,... it is in order to silence what deserves to be called the voice as the object *a*'[130] is present in a number of Dolar's texts.[131]

Toop provides a reading of another passage—The Isle of Shouting—that draws out two concepts of female vocality outlined by Linda Phyllis Austern. Toop privileges descriptive fervour over criticality, he writes: 'As for the isle of speaking or shouting birds, this was a seductive sound, according to Joyce. The question of what manner of beings might constitute such a spectral heterophonic choir motivates the sailors to row for many hours, from the faint edges of a sonic territory to its core.'[132] Toop's commentary on Joyce's translation presents the seductive, enchanting and magnetic (in the Homeric sense) characterization of Siren (female/avian) voices. The parallel with possession and spell is not a stretch. He then implies that the sailors discover the source of such song, *de-acousmatize* the voice heard at sea: 'Their curiosity satisfied, they sail on, as if merely perplexed.'[133] Before any further rumination, the Tennyson text concerning the scene should be presented. The fourth stanza details the Isle of Shouting:

> And we carne to the Isle of Shouting, we landed, a score of wild birds
> Cried from the topmost summit with human voices and words;
> Once in an hour they cried, and whenever their voices peal'd
> The steer fell down at the plow and the harvest died from the field,
> And the men dropt dead in the valleys and half of the cattle went lame,
> And the roof sank in on the hearth, and the dwelling broke into flame;

[130] Dolar, *A Voice and Nothing More*, 31.

[131] See also "The Object Voice" in *Gaze and Voice as Love Objects*, eds. Renata Salecl and Slavoj Žižek (Durham and London, UK: Duke University Press, 1996), 10. "The Linguistics of the Voice", *The Sound Studies Reader*, ed. Jonathan Sterne (Oxford, UK: Routledge, 2012), 551.

[132] Toop, *Sinister Resonance: The Mediumship of the Listener*, 21.

[133] Ibid., 21.

And the shouting of these wild birds ran into the hearts of my crew,
Till they shouted along with the shouting and seized one another and slew;
But I drew them the one from the other; I saw that we could not stay,
And we left the dead to the birds and we sail'd with our wounded away.[134]

Toop argues that Tennyson's translation, by contrast, emphasizes the physicality of voice. The corporeal effect of voice is amplified to destructive force. Toop writes that Tennyson's text amplifies 'the shouting of these wild birds to *weapons level*'.[135] The result of such vocal force upon the bodies within sonic reach is described to be one of apocalyptic levels. One recalls John Martin's 1853 painting 'The Great Day of His Wrath': 'men and cattle fall dead, buildings collapse and catch fire, crops wither.'[136] Toop then adds an additional nugget of commentary: the violence and destruction of the voices is implied to not only be a sonic and physical force but also an insidious and infectious spell that overcomes the men and compels them to chaotic barbarity towards one another. Toop opts to use the term 'inflamed', immediately evoking not only infection but carrying vaguely dermatological and symptomatic connotations. 'Maeldune's men are infected and inflamed by its destructive force. Shout leads to shout and before long they are seizing and slaying all over again.'[137]

As has been touched on already, in Tennyson's text the source of corrupting, violent and contagious voice is emitted from birds. Siren song is figured in an avian guise. Not dissimilar to the corrupting magic of the Homeric Sirens, the effect is one of chaos whereby all the aberrations to order and violence of nature take hold, possess and compel. Like the effect on Odysseus, one notable effect of such voice is military disorder—chaos spread to men. The crewmembers of Maeldun's boat become violent and attack each another. Compelled by the shrieks they lash and slay each other, intoxicated by voice they succumb to insensate butchery until Maeldun leads them off the isle.

Such a scene can be read in two ways. One option is to take the classical line of contagious feminine Siren voices, of which Austern delineates and criticizes. The birds of Tennyson's text and the dual species of Joyce's translation are avatars for an infectious feminine voice that only leads to

[134] Tennyson, "The Voyage of Maeldune".

[135] Toop, *Sinister Resonance: The Mediumship of the Listener*, 21, emphasis added. This is no slight; 'amplifying to weapons level' works well, of course, on more than one level.

[136] Ibid., 21.

[137] Ibid., 21.

violent horrors and corporeal destruction. Another option, whilst perhaps a touch glib, does underscore the vocality of such voice in narratives such as *The Voyage of Máel Dúin* and subsequent translations and iterations. One could add, and this is close to an antithesis of Toop's fantastic and vivid reading in *Sinister Resonance*, that the onus does not rest in voice but in men. Is it wrong to ask: does it only take birdsong to spark men into violence and disorder? Perhaps the answer to this question can be located within Tennyson's text. Might one read Maeldun's prudence as an affirmative to the posed question? By the ninth stanza Maeldun is canny to the risks of voices and intervenes before his men become spellbound:

> And we past to the Isle of Witches and heard their musical cry—
> 'Come to us, O come, come' in the stormy red of a sky
> Dashing the fires and the shadows of dawn on the beautiful shapes,
> For a wild witch naked as heaven stood on each of the loftiest capes,
> And a hundred ranged on the rock like white sea-birds in a row,
> And a hundred gamboll'd and pranced on the wrecks in the sand below,
> And a hundred splash'd from the ledges, and bosom'd the burst of the spray,
> But I knew we should fall on each other, and hastily sail'd away.[138]

In this scene voice is that of witches. The source of voice has reverted to a classic figure of vilified women. This matriarchal group follows the narrative mode of Homer's Sirens. Their voices call out to the sailors, tempting, luring and enchanting them. The scene has a distinct air of bacchanalia, revelry: the unchained enjoyment of pleasure (be it corporeal or sonic). There is, as in Odysseus' voyage past the sirens, a distinct gender dichotomy running along themes of contagious voice and corrupting song. Men are led astray from the prescribed grid of military order. Misconduct is resultant from enjoying a female voice.[139]

The horrors of a corrupting and infectious voice have, in this introduction of a distinct gender question, opened up a number of questions: a *Pandora's Box*, to continue the theme vilifying the female human. One key facet of the thread of this section is the conflation of the female body with nature in terms of voice. In a sense, birdsong, sirens, witches are all cursed with the same vocality; that is to say that the narratives surveyed thus far

[138] Tennyson, "The Voyage of Maeldune".

[139] The parasitic parallel is evident. A female voice strips men of their agency, much like the parasites such as *Sacculina carcini*, which 'take over' male host body and compel the corpus to female behaviour patterns.

all exhibit framings of voices, their contagion and horrors, steeped in misogyny and ornithophobia. The narratives all come from generally patrician cultures, a point that does not need labouring. Thus, the horrors are that of a particular subject: patrician horrors of the other cast as the unknown, the disordered, the corrupting and enchanting. The spells of voice explored here are not really spells, but they do spell out men's fears and horrors.

Sounds Like Us: Vivisection

The previous section spelled out the aspect of voice cast as horror: the sonorous, sensuous, enchanting voice of the other (which is not man). Such voices are explicitly sonorous, the physical contagion and force of voice is writ large, as is the melodious nature of beguiling spells. But the words have been given scant attention; it is almost as if the men of such tales hear voice but not speech. 'Come here' the Sirens sing in Homer's Odyssey; one wonders if these words were understood as a semantic performativity of the attraction of song, attesting to the irresistible draw of their chorus. But what else did the Sirens say? Did Odysseus hear the words or just the melodic enchantment of the song? The same question can be levelled at Maeldun's men on the Isle of Shouting. The corrupting physicality of voice is described, but what were the avian creatures shouting about?

Let's return to *Che Bella Voce!* In Dolar's binary formulation of a voice that delivers sonorous words there is a Mobius characteristic. We are led to believe that no sooner does one *hear* the words, there is, without doubt, a sonority one's ears fail to listen to. Conversely, should one, like the opera-loving Italian soldier, listen to the melodic nature of the voice, should one be attuned to its grain and timbre, then heeding the meaning of the words is neglected.

Of course, this formulation is by no means absolute; a voice may be sonorous without delivering any meaning, without being in the service of language. Similarly, words not require sound. The type you're reading now can serve as an example. But the formulation does serve to illustrate a vivisection that has haunted voice: how to hear the words of voice without risking submission to the insidious spell of sonority? Dolar's section 'A Brief Course in the History of Metaphysics' within his second chapter, 'The Metaphysics of the Voice', outlines this dynamic well. Indeed, one import of Dolar's survey is that the sonority of voice is consistently deemed as feminine, natural, sensuous, corrupting and contagious—something to be guarded against. The words, the meaning and language of voice are, by contrast, the concern of men. This line drawn through voice builds a partition whereby men are interested in words and others concern themselves with the rest of voice. Such a project finds a register in the sniggering emasculation of the Italian stereotype in the joke—they are not men, not soldiers but effeminate opera lovers.

Thus, language, logos and sense have been prized targets in an annexation of voice. These cherished objects need, the projects of which various men presuppose, the residue of voice to be sloughed off—voice must be muffled, its insidious, irksome, slime must be guarded against lest it taint metaphysical purity, ideal.

Voice, as an entanglement of words, meaning, language, sonority and sensuous melody, has posed a problematic morass for those who wish to pursue projects of division between man and non-man. One overarching symptom of such projects manifests as the simultaneous discredit or demonization of the corporeal and/or sensuous facets of voice and a privileging of language, meaning and thought. The vivisection of voice, the annexation of logos from phone, operates across and determines vectors of the political, species and gender. Central to these procedures on voice—of guarding meaning and thought against sonorous contagion or sensuous corruption —is the question of soul.

Both Plato's and Aristotle's works contain moves for the quest of delineating voice from word. We see, in each case, troubled inscriptions around the limits between voice and language. Such attempts are often played out in metaphysical, physical or zoological terms. In each case, and they are quite different cases, they share a similarity: the attempt to quarantine the insidious resonance of voice. Aristotle first.

Aristotle's formulation of voice, what voice is, deserves attention before any consideration how word was or is cleaved from voice. His moves pivot along presupposed differences between species, of the presence of soul, to a methodology of phonation before being pitched as political difference. To avoid mis-rendering Aristotelian voice, and its relation and context alongside the question of species and soul, some close readings of particular passages are required.

But before embarking on such a task the placement of his frankest statements regarding voice should be noted. A pertinent facet of the text hides in plain sight. The most direct addresses of voice, and its definition, are found in *De Anima*. One can suppose, even before reading the text, that the question of voice is intrinsically couched within the question of soul: that, by virtue of the question of voice being housed within a larger text concerning the question of soul, there is, for Aristotle, a strong connection, a contingency or even a causal relation between soul and voice. Indeed, there is on several levels: texturally, thematically and *physically*. It should be emphasized that this is not the soul as it is to be understood by today's terms. Soul, for Aristotle, is, in a sense, the *material* of meaning.

Stepping down a level, and getting into the text behind the title, the section within *De Anima* that focuses on voice is the second part of chapter 8, titled 'Hearing' (in Hugh Lawson-Tancred's translation) and concerns the nature of sound for the most part. In J.A. Smith's translation no title has be retroactively provided. However, the opening lines of each declare the fold at which voice (and what we might call soul) operates across today: hearing and sound.

In Lawson-Tancred's version the text commences thus: 'But now let us first determine about sound *and* hearing.'[140] Smith's version is less portentous. It begins: 'Now let us, to begin with, make certain distinctions about sound and hearing.'[141] Translation quibbles aside the context of Aristotle's distinctions of voice comes within a treatise on soul and meaning and *then* within a passage concerning both hearing and sound. To gloss over the text and suppose what voice is for Aristotle, resting only on its textual context, its reference within the book, within a chapter, before any thorough reading of the passage or its nuances, it could be supposed that voice is contingent to soul, audition and sound. This is not wrong, but it is not the whole story and does not quite get at some important nuances within the text.

Let's now turn to the passage of *De Anima* in question. In Hugh Lawson-Tancred's translation of Aristotle's *De Anima* there is the following line: 'Now voice is a kind of sound of an ensouled thing. For none of the things without soul gives voice, though some are said by analogy to give voice, such as the flute and the lyre and whatever other of the things without soul have the production of a sustained, varied and articulate sound.'[142] Notice that although inanimate musical objects are said to have what we might suppose is a soulful sounding sound, they do not quite

[140] Aristotle, *De Anima (On The Soul)* (London: Penguin, 1986), 176, emphasis added.

[141] Aristotle, *The Basic Works of Aristotle (Modern Library)*. Ed. Richard McKeon (New York, USA: The Modern Library, 2001), 570.

[142] Aristotle, *De Anima (On The Soul)* (London: Penguin, 1986), 178.

have voice because they do not have soul. This is a quite clear distinction the voice section of the chapter opens with: voice is contingent to soul, and soul is the preserve of the living. One wonders what Aristotle would think about antique musical instruments that contain a patina of acoustic properties difficult to replicate in other objects; we might assume that he'd discount any unique property of an object and instead suppose that such instruments are mere conduits for the vital soulful voice of the player. There is, even in this turn, a linearity of contingency that negates any plurality of soul and installs its determination within the body, an animated body: a body with soul.

Aristotle then makes a further division. Not all animals, for Aristotle, have soul. 'But many of the animals do not have voice, such as the bloodless ones and, of the ones with blood, the fish.'[143] In the following line Aristotle's example is the Achelous fish that make sounds with their gills 'or some other such part.' He proclaims the example fits his account, because gills do not contain the pneumatic mechanisms of other animals, such as land mammals, that breathe. Note that what is at stake in this turn is already absolutely vocalization. Aristotle is not answering a question of what sound a voice makes, but rather is focused on what biological process, and of what biology, constitute voice. Aristotle is not tackling a question of audition but one of vocalization. This is evident in the following line whereby the argument structure is laid out in syntax without committing to specificity (at least in this translation). He writes that 'everything gives sound by something striking and against something and *in* something, and as this last is air it is reasonable that only those things that admit air should give voice.'[144] Just because a fish makes a sound does not mean it has voice: the distinctions rests on whether or not air is taken in and out to strike against the soul.

The argument at this stage is a *striking physical* account of voice. Aristotle's definition of voice rests on air being breathed in and striking 'against something': an internal soul (more on the nature of this soul, for Aristotle, shortly). Marcello Zanatta, in his survey of Aristotle's references to voice, "Voice as Difference in Aristotelian Zoology", makes the same observation concerning the stark biological empiricism of the argument in this turn. He writes that Aristotle's conception of voice is 'developed both from the point of view of the emission process and of the bodily parts

[143] Ibid.

[144] Ibid., 178–179, emphasis added.

controlling this function'.[145] Later in the text, the crucial role of the soul's engagement within the process of vocalization is pronounced.

> It is then the striking of this inhaled air by the soul in these parts of the body against the so-called windpipe that is voice. For it is not every sound of an animal that is voice, as we have said (for it is possible even with the tongue just to make a some sound and to make a sound like coughing), rather it is necessary that that which strikes be ensouled and have a kind of imagination, as voice is a kind of sound *with meaning*, and not, like a cough, just of the in breathed air, though it is this that it strikes the air in the windpipe against the windpipe.[146]

This lurch from strict empiricism (vocalizing processes in different animals) to the theorizing of soul's necessity for voice is highlighted by Lawson-Tancred. In an endnote to his translation he writes 'In this curious passage, Nuyens, with some plausibility, detected one of the clearest traces of instrumentalist theory.'[147] Indeed, Aristotle's proto-instrumentalism, the leap from observation to theorizing—from biological prerequisites of vocalization to the supposed interaction of inhaled air with soul—does not go unmentioned by Zanatta either, who refers to the positing of voice's contingency to striking upon soul as being 'enunciated in a synthetic form'.[148]

But this is as far as Zanatta pursues the synthetic embedding of soul within the Aristotelian concept of voice. Instead, Zanatta draws up several instances in *De Anima* and *Historia Animalium*, where Aristotle, via empirical evidencing and without recourse to synthesizing theory, explores how different vocal apparatus may lead to different voices and for different ends of communicative efficacy.[149] Although the contingency of voice to soul is not Zanatta's core focus, his survey of Aristotle's comments concerning voice still reveals the presupposed causation of air striking soul leading to voice.

[145] Marcello Zanatta, "Voice as Difference in Aristotelian Zoology" *Journal of Ancient Philosophy*, Vol. 7, No.1 (2013): 3: https://doi.org/10.11606/issn.1981-9471.v7i1p1-18.

[146] Aristotle, *De Anima (On The Soul)* (London: Penguin, 1986), 179.

[147] Ibid., 240, note 60.

[148] Zanatta, "Voice as Difference in Aristotelian Zoology," 3.

[149] Zanatta, "Voice as Difference in Aristotelian Zoology," 5–6.

Zanatta references the passage from *De Anima* (quoted above) that juxtaposes ensouled animals with flute and lyre.[150] He writes that 'voice is peculiar to animals, in so far as it is linked to a certain activity of the soul.'[151] For the remainder of the text Zanatta refers to soul twice more. His declared focus is to explore a nuance in Aristotle's text that shows an anticipation of animal communication contra the traditional 'human language on the flat opposition between man and animal.'[152] There are three comments to be made here. Firstly, the distinction between a specifically gendered human and all other species, although not acknowledged nor commented on any further, does display a fealty to Aristotle's text. Zanatta does not provide any further commentary on this division that rests on not only species but gender too. Secondly, the presupposition—the implied given—that communication and language are the same thing is a deafening moot point. Thirdly, although the survey is persuasive in terms of analysing the varying formulations of vocalization and language across species, the synthetic kernel of soul within the process is not given the scrutiny that biological differences are. The closing line of the conclusion—'On the other hand, these analyses cast new light on the Aristotelian theory of language as such, in particular with respect to the relation between the activity of the soul and voice articulation.'—betrays a certain framing of soul, in particular a metaphysical framing of soul, at odds with its materiality of the time: *pneuma*.[153] Zanatta does not address the 'synthetic' role of soul in Aristotle's accounts of vocalization in various species and objects. This will be examined in the light of the Cavarero's commentary later; it not merely will reveal an anthropocentricism already evident in its embeddedness in phonation apparatus (that are distinguished by degrees of similarity to the human vocalization apparatus and protocols), but additionally leads to a patrician paradigm that does dichotomize, installs a 'flat opposition between *man* and animal'.[154] Or, to be more precise, '*man* and [other non-man] animals'.

Laid on top of Aristotle's synthetic necessity of soul for voice is a communicative hierarchy that privileges speech. Despite non-human animals having voice qua emitting sounds from a windpipe whereby air strikes the

[150] Aristotle, *De Anima (On The Soul)*, 178.
[151] Zanatta, "Voice as Difference in Aristotelian Zoology," 6.
[152] Ibid., 17.
[153] Ibid., 17; Which shall be explored later.
[154] Zanatta, "Voice as Difference in Aristotelian Zoology," 17.

soul, and despite some animals, heeding Zanatta's elucidation of some nuances in the texts, have communicative ability, there is, in other works by Aristotle, a hierarchy that places speech over voice (and voice over mere sound). Dolar surveys these instances in *A Voice and Nothing More*. In 'The Politics of Voice' he opens with a long passage from Aristotle's *Politics* (the following quotes are taken from the same edition Dolar employs). Aristotle's vivisection of voice, his cleaving of word from a natural and corrupting mess, is presented as operating along a distinction between man and animals:

> Now, that man is more of a political animal than bees or any other gregarious animals is evident. Nature, as we often say, makes nothing in vain, and man is the only animal whom she has endowed with the gift of speech. And whereas mere voice (*phone*) is but an indication of pleasure of pain, and is therefore found in other animals (for their nature attains to the perception of pleasure and pain and the intimation of them to one another, and no further), the power of speech is intended to set forth the expedient and inexpedient, and therefore likewise the just and unjust. And it is a characteristic of man that he alone has any sense of good and evil, of just and unjust, and the like, and an association of living beings who have this sense makes a family and a state.[155]

Here, we already sense the kernel of an implicit hierarchy. Voice is *mere* voice, despite being contingent to striking upon a soul, and not speech; it may evoke and affect the pleasure and pain of the soul but is no good for designating 'the expedient and inexpedient', which is to say, it is not practical, cannot be utilized for arguing and stating what is best, just or unjust. In this turn, voice might reflect the pain or pleasure of a certain toxic or sweet berry, but it cannot state 'the red ones are bad' or 'the blue ones are tasty.' Non-verbal vocalizations are often ambiguous; recall the classical sex-death dichotomy of Siren song (or thrills in *Thriller*) and consider moans and groans. Sensation may be 'signalled', but exactly what that sensation is can be mistaken or misinterpreted.

Animals have voice; they too can emit a sound when experiencing pleasure or pain. Voice is the emitting of sound with some *intentful* drive, an expression. Just as birds sing and dogs bark, humans cry in sadness, shriek

[155] Aristotle, *The Basic Works of Aristotle (Modern Library)*, Ed. Richard McKeon (New York, USA: The Modern Library, 2001), 1129. Cited in Dolar, *A Voice and Nothing More*, 105.

or laugh in excitement, hum in pleasure and scream in pain: this is voice; it does not have a strictly semantic meaning. For Aristotle, voice is intrinsically natural; it is 'just' a sonic expression of living beings, ensouled things: the sonic sound of in-breathed air striking against the soul within the windpipe. For Aristotle, voice is the vocal expression before language is added into it (as if Lacan's diagram were to be read right to left). Whereas speech is voice with meaning, speech is a sound that also signifies. Dogs bark, but they do not bark orders, meanings or words, like a military commander.[156]

Zanatta touches on this difference between immediate affectations of the soul, the direct expression of pleasure or pain (or horror) and more abstracted, expedient, speech. He quotes a passage from *De Interpreatione:*

> now spoken sound are symbols of affections in the soul, and written marks symbols of spoken sounds. And just as written marks are not the same for all men, neither are spoken sounds. But what these are in the first place signs of—affections of the soul—are the same for all; and what these affections are likenesses of—actual things—are also the same. (tr. Ackrill)[157]

Let's turn to Lacan. We can see in a few moments of his thought that the difference between symbols of an affectation of the soul and mere affectations of the soul is the difference that separates human animals from other animals.

Owen Hewitson, in his essay 'What Does Lacan Say About … The Signifier', draws out several instances that pitch humans as distinct from other animals by virtue of the exclusivity of the symbol. Firstly, he points to Seminar III, where Lacan utilizes the scene of Man Friday's footprint in Robinson Crusoe as a tool for explicating the trace, sign and signifier.

[156] Of course, we all know that in human social power relations the structure does not rest on the meaning of words but the context and act of vocalizing. The words are arbitrary—recall the Marching scenes in Kubrick's *Full Metal Jacket*, or think of sports chants, football songs, that stripped of collective vocalization, rhythm and context are innocuous and or absurd.

[157] Zanatta, "Voice as Difference in Aristotelian Zoology," 2. The E. M. Edghill translation (in the *Basic Works* Volume) reads: 'Spoken words are the symbols of mental experience and written words are the symbols of spoken words. Just as all men have not the same writing, so all men have not the same speech sounds, but the mental experiences, which these directly symbolize, are the same for all, as also are those things of which our experiences are the images.'—Aristotle, *The Basic Works of Aristotle (Modern Library)*, 40.

> Let's begin with the biological sign. In the very structure, in the morphology, of animals there is something that has this captivating value due to which its receiver, who sees the red of the robin redbreast for instance, and who is made for receiving it, undertakes a series of actions or henceforth unitary behaviour that links the bearer of this sign to its perceiver. Here you have what gives us a precise idea of what may be called natural meaning. Without otherwise seeking how this might take place in man, it is clear that by means of a series of transitions we can manage to purify, neurtralise, the natural sign.
>
> Then there is the trace, the footprint in the sand, the sign about which Robinson Crusoe makes no mistake. Here sign and object separate. The trace, in its negative aspect, draws the natural sign to a limit at which it becomes evanescent. The distinction between sign and object is quite clear here, since the trace is precisely what the object leaves behind once it has gone off somewhere else. Objectively there is no need for any subject to recognise a sign for it to be there—a trace exists even if there is nobody to look at it.
>
> When have we passed over into the order of the signifier? The signifier may extend over many of the elements within the domain of the sign. But the signifier is a sign that doesn't refer to any object, not even to one in the form of a trace, even though the trace nevertheless heralds the signifier's essential feature. It, too, is the sign of an absence. But insofar as it forms part of language, the signifier is a sign which refers to another sign, which is as such structured to signify the absence of another sign, in other words, to be opposed to it in a couple (Seminar III, p.167).[158]

Hewitson summarizes that firstly 'The sign is the equivalent to the code in the animal kingdom. It is a complete equivalence of thing and meaning that allows for no ambiguity.'[159] Secondly that 'The trace is the mark of an absence, a missing object like the foot in the sand of Man Friday.'[160] And thirdly that the 'signifier is a sign without any referent. It does not refer to anything, although it shares with the trace absence as its fundamental feature.'[161] Despite the location of voice in Lacan being post-signifier we can see in this turn, following Hewitson, a similarity concerning human speech and affective vocalization of other animals. There is an anthropo-

[158] Owen Hewitson, 'What Does Lacan Say About … The Signifier?' *LacanOnline.Com*, June 20, 2010. Accessed January 14, 2019. http://www.lacanonline.com/index/2010/06/what-does-lacan-say-about-the-signifier/.

[159] Ibid.

[160] Ibid.

[161] Ibid.

centric arrogance of assuming humans are the zenith of communicative beings that have broached a new paradigm of the signifier, the symbol without direct correlation, without strict referent, to its signified.[162]

Hewitson subsequently presents a very similar passage of Lacan's teachings from Seminar VI. In this seminar Lacan waxes on the subject of Man Friday's footprint in Daniel Defoe's *Robinson Crusoe* (1719). He frames the footprint as an effacement of the trace (this is Lacan's *pied*alogical formulation of the palimpsest signifier). Lacan 'writes':

> I spoke to you about Robinson Crusoe and about the footstep, the trace of Friday's footprint, and we dwelt a little while on the following: is this already the signifier, and I told you that the signifier begins, not with the trace, but with whatever effaces the trace, and it is not the effaced trace which constitutes the signifier, it is something which poses itself as being able to be effaced, which inaugurates the signifier. In other words, Robinson Crusoe effaces the trace of Friday's footprint, but what does he put in its place? If he wants to preserve the place of Friday's footprint, he needs at least a cross, namely a bar and another bar across it. This is the specific signifier. The specific signifier is something which presents itself as being itself able to be effaced and which subsists precisely in this operation of effacing as such. I mean that the effaced signifier already presents itself as such with the properties proper to the unsaid. In so far as I cancel the signifier with the bar, I perpetuate it as such indefinitely, I inaugurate the dimension of the signifier as such. Making a cross is properly speaking something that does not exist in any form of locating that is permitted in any way. You must not think that non-speaking beings, the animals, do not locate things, but they do not do it intentionally with something said, but with traces of traces.[163]

At this juncture the nuances between trace, sign and signifier do not need further comment. What warrants underscoring, however, is the striking similarity in the structure of language and species. Obviously, the final line contains the slippage of not just declaring animals as 'non-speaking' but the syntactical division 'the animals' that presupposes the author and

[162] See criticism of Lacan's anthropocentricism in Jacques Derrida's 'And Say the Animal Responded' in *The Animal That Therefore I Am (Perspectives in Continental Philosophy)*. Ed. Marie-Louise Mallet. Trans. David Wills (New York, USA: Fordham University Press, 2008), 119–140.

[163] Jacques Lacan, *The Seminar of Jacques Lacan: Book VI Desire and its Interpretation*. Trans. Cormac Gallagher. Accessed January 14, 2019. http://www.lacaninireland.com/web/wp-content/uploads/2010/06/THE-SEMINAR-OF-JACQUES-LACAN-VI.pdf.

his readers are not of the same category. Lacan rests the anthropocentric exclusivity of language on its signifying dimension: being divorced from that which it signifies. Both Aristotle and Lacan share an insistence on a series of partitions. Speech is a symbol or an affectation of a soul. The signifier is, too, symbolic, without specific referent; it concerns a constellation of generalizable and interchangeable signs. Aristotle and Lacan both emphasize the great importance between, for example's sake, the vocalization of pain and the spoken declaration of 'I am in pain.' The former is a firm referent in the malady affecting the vocalizer, whereas the latter is abstracted to a generalizable symbol. Yet, in each case, and despite the Lacanian location of voice as posthumous to the necrotic signifier, speech cannot quite be disengaged, cleaved or vivisected from voice. It is either a necessary phonological step (in Aristotle's formulation) or an unavoidable outcome of the signifying operation (for Lacan). Voice, insidious, ineradicable and irreducible *gets everywhere* like irksome slime.

The lofty enterprise of language (to delineate the just and unjust by way of symbols) must be protected from the voice. Across this division the metaphysical battlements of man and others are overlaid. This is precisely *the politics of voice* that Dolar examines in the chapter of the same name. On the same page as the Aristotle quote (presented above concerning the differences between man and bees and what is "expedient and inexpedient, and therefore likewise the just and unjust") Dolar adds commentary regarding Aristotle's voice.[164] He writes that:

> mere voice is what animals and men have in common, it is the animal part of man. It can indicate only pleasure and pain, experiences shared by both animals and humans. But speech, logos, does not merely indicate, it expresses or, better still, it manifests: it manifests the advantageous (useful) and the harmful, and consequently the just and the unjust, the good and the evil. If one receives a blow, one may well scream, that is, emit voice to vent one's pain, and that is what a horse or a dog would also do. But at the same time one can say: "I have been wronged" (harmed, ill-treated), and thereby the speech introduces the measure of right and wrong. It does not just give vent to feelings, it introduces a standard of judgement.[165]

[164] Dolar, *A Voice and Nothing More*, 105; the ambiguity of the literary term well intended here.

[165] Dolar, *A Voice and Nothing More*, 105–106.

The differences between speech and voice are glossed here with another dimension. It is not just a case of practical application (the expedient) or significatory difference from affect or impression (as in Lacan's comments) but one that is necessary for morals and judgements. For Aristotle, mere vocal expressions cannot navigate and communicate moral or political conundrums, but words and speech can. Animals may emit sonic expressions of their feelings, but they do not *communicate* what is right, just or expedient. Thus, without speech (a voice imbued with meaning, yoked to language, *logos*), without a sound signifying something, one is forever rendered apolitical and immoral. Speech is what builds cities and makes moral laws and honourable states, as the final line of the passage presented both here and in Dolar's chapter suggests: 'And it is a characteristic of man that he alone has any sense of good and evil, of just and unjust, and the like, and an association of living beings who have this sense makes a family and a state.'[166]

This is the dichotomy of voice and speech extrapolated into politics. *Phone* is distinct from *logos*. Sound is distinct from semantics and language. Music is apart from law and order. And it is precisely the exclusivity of man and language that sets this type of animal apart from all the chaos and din of other natures. The problem in all of this is guarding *logos* from the contagion of *phone*.

Bacchic Frenzy: Forgetting How to Walk and Speak

Such a polarizing formulation is by no means original to Aristotle. Aristotle's position can be regarded as an extension of Platonic logocentrism, the primacy of language, meaning and thought over sensuous sound, the body and voice. Plato (Aristotle's teacher) repeatedly displays an almost phobic aversion to voice and the possibilities of enjoying sound without strict meaning or language. Plato was not the first patriarchal figure to fear and actively repress the arousing and infectious potency of voice whilst insisting the word of law, the language of good sense and meaning, is followed without any sensuous or emotional distraction. Dolar references a very early instance of such a sentiment: 'Chinese emperor Chun (c. 2200 BC) offers the following simple precept: "Let the music

[166] Aristotle, *The Basic Works of Aristotle (Modern Library)*, Ed. Richard McKeon (New York, USA: The Modern Library, 2001), 1129. Cited in Dolar, *A Voice and Nothing More*, 105.

follow the sense of the words. Keep it simple and ingenuous. One must condemn pretentious music which is devoid of sense and effeminate." '[167] In this quote, and resonating with Zanatta's re-voice of Aristotle's sentiment, a 'flat opposition between *man* and animal' is drawn up.[168] A gendering division segregates meaning and language from sound and melody. Voice qua enjoyable sonic is feminine where voice yoked to the code of language and put to moral, just and expedient ends is masculine.

This is the binary at play in the narratives of Odysseus and the Sirens and Maeldun and his men visiting the islands of strange nonsensical sounds. But notice too, recalling the previous explorations of sound qua slime, the insidious horror of voice, how Dolar, in rearticulating Platonic logocentrism and its resultant binary of gender (the sensuous and the sensible), couches the sonic mode of voice, the voice unchained from language, in a vocabulary that evokes the fear and anxiety of the infectious, potent and contagious. Dolar writes:

> Music, and in particular the voice, should not stray away from words which endow it with sense; as soon as it departs from its textual anchorage, the voice becomes senseless and *threatening*—all the more so because of its seductive and *intoxicating powers*. Furthermore, the voice beyond sense is self evidently equated with femininity, whereas the text, the instance of signification, is in this simple paradigmatic opposition on the side of masculinity. (Some four thousand years later, Wagner will write in a famous letter to Liszt: "Die Musik ist ein Weib," music is a woman.) The voice beyond words is a senseless play of sensuality, it possesses a *dangerous force*, although in itself it is empty and frivolous.[169]

This senseless play of sensuality can be regarded as symptomatic of privileging one sense over another *sense*. In 'Freud's Voices' Dolar (in perhaps the most strikingly relevant passage for sound studies in the book) writes of the difference between hearing and listening (this latter very much analogous to Pierre Schaeffer's projects exploring sound in itself).[170] Permeating throughout Dolar's examples of musical voice juxtaposed with voice as a servant of meaningful language, the dichotomy of the

[167] Dolar, *A Voice and Nothing More*, 43.

[168] Zanatta, "Voice as Difference in Aristotelian Zoology," 17.

[169] Dolar, *A Voice and Nothing More*, 43, emphasis added.

[170] A bold claim, but the passage warrants great attention over the glibly misused object voice treatises that proliferate so much extant literature.

Italian soldiers casts its shadow. The politics of voice is to guard against the enjoyment of *che bella voce!*—to ensure the command is heard for practical, just and expedient ends. Dolar, just over 140 pages after recounting the Italian soldier joke on page 3, writes:

> [W]e can draw a provisional demarcation line between hearing and listening, and between meaning and sense. To be brief: hearing is after meaning, the signification which can be spelled out; listening is, rather, being on the lookout for sense, something that announces itself in the voice beyond meaning. We could say that hearing is entwined with understanding—hence the French double meaning (double entendre!) of *entendre, entendement*, being both hearing and understanding, intellect—that is, reducing the heard to the meaningful, reducing the audible to the intelligible; while listening implies an opening toward a sense which is undecidable, precarious, elusive, and which sticks to the voice. Sense (…) also alludes to the other use of sense: that of the five senses, of the sensual (to say nothing of the sensitive and sensible). The equivoque of sense and sense (sense of hearing) is, I suppose, structural; it is already encapsulated in the "sound and sense" formula, which could be read as "sense and sense".[171]

What follows is an example of guarding against one sense: seeking to protect meaningful sense from the infectious *jouissance* of sound. How to have patrician voice, used for conveying meaning, without risking the audience listening? How to ensure the voice is heard and heeded for expedient and just ends but not listened to, not sensed and enjoyed, like the Italian soldiers do.

Plato argues for the division between the signifying voice and non-signifying voice, and further impresses the division over politics, morals and genders. The non-signifying sound of voice is repeatedly framed as being corrupting, infectious, immoral and, above all, feminine. In *Symposium* Eryximachus, records Plato (Plato ventriloquizes, as we shall see, most frankly through others), draws the engendering lines of signifying and asignifying voice most plainly: speaking is for men of good standing, moral just men, whereas music and singing is for women. The two, he repeatedly suggests, should be partitioned for the benefit of the former: 'I've another suggestion to make. I don't think we need this flute girl who's just started playing. She can play for herself, or to the women

[171] Dolar, *A Voice and Nothing More*, 148.

upstairs, if she feels like it, but for this evening I suggest *we* stick to conversation.'[172]

In Plato's dialogue with Protagoras there is an eruption of the author's contempt for musical frivolity, his disdain for the supposed femininity of asignifying voice and its enjoyment. Most secondary sources of this text focus on the first half (his frank dismissals of both women and musical enjoyment); however, the continuum of speaking for men and voice and music for others continues into a diatribe against poetry also. By the end of the passage, Plato has not only posited that sober conversation alone is the proper conduct of men, educated and respectable men, but also that even the aesthetic pleasure of poetry is improper. Plato's fidelity to logos is strict and orthodox.[173]

> Conversation about poetry reminds me too much of the wine parties of second-rate and commonplace people. Such men, being too uneducated to entertain themselves as they drink by using their own voices and conversational resources, put up the price of female musicians, paying them well for the hire of an extraneous voice—that of the pipe—and find their entertainment in its warblings. But where the drinkers are men of worth and culture, you will find no girls piping or dancing or harping. They are quite capable of enjoying their own company without such frivolous nonsense, using their own voices in sober discussion and each taking his turn to speak or listen—even if the drinking is really heavy. In the same way gatherings like our own, if they consist of men such as most of us claim to be, call for no *extraneous voices*—not even poets.[174]

Much of the anxieties, the horrors, about voice untethered from language—or at least not in the service of language—concern the corrupting sensuous musicality of flutes or pipes and what potential aural aesthetic pleasure can do to men. To guard against such pernicious corrupting forces music should be subject to legislation; it should be controlled, and ordered—codified. For Plato the stakes of men being exposed to voice unleashed from codifying order could not be understated.

[172] Plato, *Symposium and Phaedrus*, Trans. Tom Griffith (New York, USA: Alfred A Knopf/ Random House, 2000), 13.

[173] What would Freud make of Plato's aural anxiety, his phobia of pleasure in voice?

[174] Plato, *The Collected Dialogues of Plato (Bollingen Series)*, trans. Lane Cooper, Ed. Edith Hamilton and Huntington Cairns (Princeton, New Jersey, USA: Princeton University Press, 1961), 340.

In *Republic*, Dolar quotes in 'The Metaphysics of Voice', any shift of musical mode must be scrutinized lest it ferments disorder.[175]

> A change to a new type of music is something to beware of as hazard to all our fortunes. For the modes of music are never disturbed without unsettling of the most fundamental political and social conventions .... It is here, then, I said, that our guardians must build their guardhouse and post of watch. It is certain he said, that this is the kind of lawlessness that easily insinuates itself unobserved. Yes, said I, because it is supposed to be only a form of play and to work no harm. Nor does it work any, he said, except that by gradual infiltration it softly overflows upon the characters and pursuits of men and from these issues forth grown greater to attack their business dealings, and from these relations it proceeds against the laws and the constitution with wanton license, Socrates, till finally it overthrows all things public and private.[176]

Republic is in the voice of Socrates, the narrator (although Plato's kin Thrasymachus, and Glaucon and Adeimantus, amongst a few others, also feature). This is, however, an instance of Plato ventriloquizing through others: in this case Adeimantus. It is by no means an isolated example of diegetic masquerading in place of earnest first-person committal. Curiously, Plato almost disowns, and holds at arm's length, some of his dearest thoughts.

Plato's sentiment here is expressed in a vocabulary that could well express the anxiety of infection. Could he not also be talking about a virus or a bacteria-based plague when he warns of what 'insinuates itself unobserved'? Voice, in this register for Plato, is the virus that corrupts the societal order: it is a case of precautions, guarding against the threat of voice. Plato's horror of voice is a horror of an assumed possibility. His horror and phobia of voice stems from his paradigmatic privileging, politicizing and engendering of voice and word, not—it should be highlighted—any recourse to empirical observation. In this sense Plato's conceptualization of voice, his demarcations of voice for man and any other animal, stands in

[175] Dolar, *A Voice and Nothing More*, 43–44.

[176] Plato, *The Collected Dialogues of Plato (Bollingen Series)*, 666. This is the same translation that Dolar employs in *A Voice and Nothing More*; it is much more concise than the Desmond Lee version for the focus at hand.

stark contrast to the biological argument and empiricism of his student, Aristotle.[177]

Plato's precautionary measures against voice without words for aesthetic pleasure, musical enjoyment, are most vigorously delineated in *Laws*. The control of music, enforcing its adherence to a code is part of the logocentric project we are partially charting in this question of voice. We see, in *Laws*, multiple instances of Plato arguing for sound to be ordered into meaning, for *phone* to yield to *logos*.

Laws is one of Plato's 'Socratic dialogues'; like *Republic*, philosophical and political questions and propositions are elucidated, demonstrated and argued via a fictional *parlé*; ventriloquized via diegetic figures. The premise of *Laws* is 'three elderly gentlemen' travelling from Crete to Mount Ida (Zeus' birthplace), during which they discuss laws and constitutions (this discussion takes up the first three books). The text presented below is from Book III. John M. Cooper notes, in a short introductory text in *Plato: Complete Works,* the 'all apparently fictional' men are named thus: 'Clinias from Crete, Megilus, a Spartan, and an unnamed Athenian'.[178] The words below are that of the unnamed Athenian. Could Plato's veil of anonymity be any less transparent? Is it not the same sentiment, albeit much more elaborated, as was expressed in *Republic*?

> Our music was formally divided into several kinds and patterns. One kind of song, which went by the name of a hymn, consisted of prayers to the gods; there was a second and contrasting kind which might well have been called a *lament; paeans* were a third kind, and there was a forth, the *dithyramb*, as it was called, dealing, if I am not mistaken, with the birth of Dionysus. (…) Now these and other types were definitely fixed, and it was not permissible to misuse one kind of melody for another. The competence to take cognizance of these rules, to pass verdicts in accord with them, and, in case of need, to penalize their infraction was not left, as it is today, to the catcalls and discordant outcries of the crowd, nor yet to the clapping of applauders; the educated made it their rule to hear the performances through in silence, and for the boys, their attendants, and the rabble at large, there was the discipline of the official's rod to enforce order. Thus the bulk of the popu-

[177] To make a contemporary cybernetic analogy Plato's horror of the virus is not dissimilar to the mediatized maelstrom of anxiety leading up to the 2000/Y2K computer malfunction.

[178] Plato, *Plato: Complete Works*, Ed. John M. Cooper (Indianapolis, Indiana, USA: Hackett Publishing Company, 1997), 1318. Again, the Lane Cooper translation Dolar uses 44–45, albeit a longer section here.

lace was content to submit to this strict control in such matters without venturing to pronounce judgment by its clamors.

Afterward, in course of time, an unmusical license set in with the appearance of poets who were men a native genius, but ignorant of what is right and legitimate in the realm of the Muses. Possessed by a frantic and unhallowed lust for pleasure, they contaminated laments with hymns and paeans with dithyrambs, actually imitated the strains of the flute on the harp, and created a universal confusion of forms. Thus their folly led them unintentionally to slander their profession by the assumption that in music there is no such thing as a right and a wrong, the right standard of judgment being the pleasure given to the hearer, be he high or low. By compositions of such a kind and discourse to the same effect, they naturally inspired the multitude with contempt of musical law, and a conceit of their own competence as judges. Thus our once silent audiences have found a voice, in the persuasion that they understand what is good and bad in art; the old "sovereignty of the best" in that sphere has given way to an evil "sovereignty of the audience." If the consequence had been even a democracy, no great harm would have been done, so long as the democracy was confined to art, and composed of free men. But, as things are with us, music has given occasion to a general conceit of universal knowledge and contempt for law, and liberty has followed in their train. Fear was cast out by confidence in supposed knowledge, and the loss of it gave birth to impudence. For to be unconcerned for the judgment of one's betters in the assurance which comes of a reckless excess of liberty is nothing in the world but reprehensible impudence. So the next stage of the journey toward liberty will be refusal to submit to magistrates, and on this will follow emancipation from the authority and correction of parents and elders; then, as the goal of the race is approached, comes the effort to escape obedience to the law, and, when that goal is all but reached, contempt for oaths, for the plighted word, and all religion. The spectacle of the Titanic nature of which our old legends speak is reenacted; man returns to the old condition of a hell of unending misery."[179]

A sneering judgement is threaded though the unnamed Athenian's derision of those who actively enjoy music and the emergence of the dithyramb (the anthem of Dionysus that shall be given consideration shortly). Like previous texts presented, in this call for control of music, rhythm, voice and poetry so as guard against the corrupting forces of sound (that run along gender vectors) a vocabulary of anxiety and contagion is

[179] Plato, *The Collected Dialogues of Plato (Bollingen Series)*, 1294–1295.

evident, as is a tone of repulsion.[180] The dithyrambs that imitate the flute are contaminations.

Trevor J. Saunders' translation has a satisfyingly blunter tone of derision and disdain, a touch more hand-wringing and hyperbole. Misuse is replaced with 'perverted' and 'catcalls' is followed by 'uncouth yelling'. But it is the lines concerning the poets that strikes the most familiar chord of an elder's stubborn dislike of new forms of vocal aesthetics: 'Gripped by a frenzied and excessive lust for pleasure, they jumbled together laments and hymns, mixed paeans and dithyrambs, and even imitated pipe tunes on the lyre.'[181]

Dithyrambs were choral poems connected to the worship of the birth of Dionysus.[182] The dithyramb, as the texts evidence, were regarded as a voice-based portal into a de-subjectifying state of Bacchic frenzy, associated with wine, libido expressed in terms of physical interactions: 'springtime want'.[183] The unnamed Athenian in *Laws*, in Book II, during a dialogue with Clinias, touches on Dionysian revelry: 'There is a little-known current of story and tradition which says that Dionysus was robbed of his wits by his stepmother Hera, and that he gets his revenge by stimulating us to Bacchic frenzies and all the mad dancing that results; and this was precisely the reason why he made us a present of wine.'[184] Nietzsche, in 'The Dionysian World View', provides a sense of the aesthetic and human interactions associated with songs and festivities stemming from Dionysian worship:

> Dionysiac art, by contrast, is based on play with intoxication, with the state of ecstasy. There are two principal forces which bring naive, natural man to the self-oblivion of intense intoxication: the drive of spring and narcotic drink. Their effects are symbolized in the figure of Dionysos. In both states the principium individuationis is disrupted, subjectivity dis-appears entirely before the erupting force of the general element in human life, indeed of the general element in nature. Not only do the festivals of Dionysos forge a bond between human beings, they also reconcile human beings and nature. Freely the earth brings its gifts, the fiercest beasts approach one another in peace; the flower-decked chariot of Dionysos is drawn by panthers and tigers. All the caste-like divisions which necessity and arbitrary power have

[180] There is also a conspicuous contempt for other social classes.

[181] Plato, *Plato: Complete Works*, 1389.

[182] Ibid., 517, note 16.

[183] Not dissimilar to the jolly Pagan revelry that contemporary outdoor music festivals promise.

[184] Plato, *Plato: Complete Works*, 1362.

established between men disappear; the slave is a free-man, the aristocrat and the man of lowly birth unite in the same Bacchic choruses. In ever-swelling bands the gospel of universal harmony' rolls on from place to place; as they sing and dance, human beings express their membership of a higher, more ideal community; they have *forgotten how to walk and speak*."[185]

The prevalence of alcohol, the giddy swirl of dance and intoxication looms heavy. Several other facets deserve mention: disrupted individualities, de-subjectification, a return to the *mass* of chaotic nature. Just, expedient, moral and political divisions are dissolved (Plato wincing here) in the deliquescence of social hierarchies. Most pertinent for the theme of this chapter, though, is, again, the spectre of contagion in the last line. Ever-swelling choruses roll from place to place: there is a sense of proliferation, of some other agency yielding raucous murmuration in human bodies. A possessive and parasitic theme is threaded through the description. Not only are human beings de-subjectified and de-politicized but like a host riddled with a pathogenic parasite, they lose the traits commonly ascribed as the privilege of the human animal—bipedal walking and speech. The pleasure elicited from unrestricted, asignifying, voice is, according to Plato, dangerous and infectious, because (like the parasites *Ophiocordyceps unilateralis* and *Sacculina*) it insidiously strips and overtakes cognitive (reasoning for expedient ends) agency. The Bacchic choruses dethrone man to a position of animality; man is reduced to an animal that does not speak for the expedient or just, but most certainly sings.[186]

Plato's particular anxiety of the contagious and corrupting forces of the Dionysian dithyramb echoes in contemporary authorities: during a review contemplating the closure of London's *Fabric* nightclub the committee chair asked if lowering the BPM of music played inside the establishment would impact drug use.[187] A common practice at contemporary music festivals, when crowds rush forward, risking and/or crushing spectators in front, is for the music act to cease playing and request calm, withholding their performance until safer levels of crowd movement are re-established.

[185] Friedrich Nietzsche, *The Birth of Tragedy And Other Writings (Cambridge Texts in the History of Philosophy)*, Ed. Raymoud Geuss and Ronald Speirs, Trans. Ronald Speirs (Cambridge, UK: Cambridge University Press, 2007), 120. Emphasis added.

[186] To tow the gendering sewn by Plato and Aristotle.

[187] Christopher Hooton, 'Fabric review board actually considered lowering BPMs to get the kids off drugs,' *Independent*, Sept 7, 2016, https://www.independent.co.uk/arts-entertainment/music/news/fabric-review-board-actually-considered-lowering-bpms-to-get-the-kids-off-drugs-a7229511.html. See also 2019 commentaries concerning Drill music in relation to violence.

Section 63 of the *Criminal Justice and Public Order Act 1994* contains a similar presupposition of the relationship music and social order.[188]

As Socrates, speaking in *Republic*, Plato's distinctly ocularcentric solution to the dangers of voice is to keep watch (rather than *listen, or hearken*) and ensure that these intoxicating and corrupting sounds of voice and music adhere to order. Dolar rehearses Plato's anxiety of musical freedom: it 'should be treated with the greatest philosophical concern and the utmost vigilance (…) any license invariably produces general decadence; it undermines the social fabric, its laws and mores, and threatens the very ontological order.'[189]

Decadence, chaos, the abandonment to baser passions and the dissolution of social and moral orders begin with music and voices not yoked and shackled to a signifying code, to order and meaning. It is, for Plato, a question of rightness, and to be 'right' is to be moral and just. Thus, to be right, moral and just sound must signify, phone must signify; it must refer

[188] 'Powers to remove persons attending or preparing for a rave.

This section applies to a gathering on land in the open air of [F120] or more persons (whether or not trespassers) at which amplified music is played during the night (with or without intermissions) and is such as, by reason of its loudness and duration and the time at which it is played, is likely to cause serious distress to the inhabitants of the locality; and for this purpose—

(a) such a gathering continues during intermissions in the music and, where the gathering extends over several days, throughout the period during which amplified music is played at night (with or without intermissions); and

(b) "music" includes sounds wholly or predominantly characterised by the emission of a succession of repetitive beats.

This section also applies to a gathering if—

(a) it is a gathering on land of 20 or more persons who are trespassing on the land; and

(b) it would be a gathering of a kind mentioned in subsection (1) above if it took place on land in the open air.]

(2) If, as respects any land F3 …, a police officer of at least the rank of superintendent reasonably believes that—

(a) two or more persons are making preparations for the holding there of a gathering to which this section applies,

(b) ten or more persons are waiting for such a gathering to begin there, or

(c) ten or more persons are attending such a gathering which is in progress". Emphasis Added.

Autechre's subversive response in the liner notes to *Anti* warrants note: "Warning. Lost and Djarum contain repetitive beats. We advise you not to play these tracks if the Criminal Justice Bill becomes law. Flutter has been programmed in such a way that no bars contain identical beats and can therefore be played under the proposed new law. However, we advise DJs to have a lawyer and a musicologist present at all times to confirm the non-repetitive nature of the music in the event of police harassment.'

[189] Dolar, *A Voice and Nothing More*, 44.

to logos. Sound and voice cannot just be enjoyed and experienced for their own sake but must refer to a code or meaning: this is being just. Music and voice for pleasure are, for Plato, resolutely *not right*. Dolar presents the following text from *Laws II* in parentheses: ' It is commonly said that the standard of rightness in music is its pleasure-giving effect. That, however, is an intolerable sentiment; in fact, tis a piece of flat blasphemy.'[190] Similar to the debilitating effects that uncontrolled and intoxicating sounds had on Maeldun's men (and Odysseus), and like the Dionysian possession of forgetting *how to walk and speak*" music and song can render even the strongest warrior ineffective.[191] As Plato, in *The Republic*, frets:

> Now when a man abandons himself to music, to play upon him and pour into his soul as it were through the funnel of his ears those sweet, soft, and dirgelike airs ... and gives his entire time to the warblings and blandishments of song, the first result is that the principle of high spirit, if he had it, is softened like iron and is made useful instead of useless and brittle. But when he continues the practice without remission and is spellbound, the effect begins to be that he melts and liquefies till he completely dissolves away his spirit, cuts out as it were the very sinews of his soul and makes of himself a "feeble warrior".[192]

Even the man of strongest and most virtuous body and soul can be corrupted and incapacitated by the infectiousness of voice, song and music. Plato's prescription, Dolar presents, is that 'music and the rhythm must follow the speech' (Plato 1978, Republic III, 398d, 400d). For the core of the danger is the voice that sets itself loose from the word, the voice beyond logos, the lawless voice.'.[193]

Concerns over the contagion of the Dionysian dithyramb have already been touched on. But this was not the only musical mode regarded to warrant caution and state control. Dolar recounts, it is not just singing voice that must be yoked to the signifying shackles or 'just' and 'right' word and meaning: various musical modes are considered too; some with

[190] Ibid., 44–45.

[191] Friedrich Nietzsche, *The Birth of Tragedy And Other Writings (Cambridge Texts in the History of Philosophy)*, 120. Emphasis added.

[192] Plato, *The Collected Dialogues of Plato (Bollingen Series)*, 655. Quoted in Dolar, *A Voice and Nothing More*, 47.

[193] Dolar, *A Voice and Nothing More*, 45.

contempt, others with grudging acceptance. The Lydian mode is supposedly mollifying, "dirgelike" and induces laxity, thus these 'are useless even to women who are to make the best of themselves, let alone to men'.[194] The Dorian and Phrygian modes are the concessions, by virtue of being, supposedly, more suited to men and warrior sorts.

In each turn, musical modes and enjoyment of voice apart from word are framed as a problem to be guarded against. Contagious affects, insidious potentials to possess and rob the human animal of expedient traits that supposedly distinguish it from others are threats, must be warded off and quarantined by the good men of the state who fear that the aesthetic pleasure and jouissance of voice is a gateway to horrors, a 'hell of unending misery'.[195]

Flauting Sense

A conspicuous theme in this narrative is the flute. Like Odysseus' men who protect against sensing voice by bunging their ears with wax this instrument has been repeatedly muted lest it corrupts men. The sensual (insensible) sound of the flute, sonicizing breath through its structure, is a leitmotif of sonic contagion and potential corruption. Those who seek to banish its sound, guarding meaningful sense from sensual sensing, have demonized the flute.

Demonization is not hyperbole. Pan the libidinal: erotic and joyous flautist (substituted by Ovid for Marsyas) is the aesthetic root of Judeo-Christian depictions of the Devil. Like pictorial representations of the Devil, Pan is also depicted or described as having the hindquarters and horns of a goat. The flute playing of Pan/Marsyas is frequently framed as a corrupting force, an unregulated force that threatens order, compliance and civil obedience. The figure of Pan also signifies untamed nature: depicted through his cavorting with nymphs and the display of enjoyment in music. Pan is often depicted as a flautist. The term 'Panic', the sensation of fear so strong as to negate cerebral logic or reason, replacing it with the 'animalistic' fight-or-flight activation of the sympathetic nervous system, derives from Pan.[196] Panic is the moment calm rationalism or stoic recourse

[194] Republic quoted by Dolar, *A Voice and Nothing More*, 45.

[195] Plato, *The Collected Dialogues of Plato (Bollingen Series)*, 1295.

[196] That is, not the Platonic pursuit of expedient action via reason and language.

to logic gives way to impulse. In Pan the 'animal in man' is conveyed; in panic man's wont is animal over recourse to lofty reason.

There is a further horrifying incursion of the natural in the figure of Pan, a resonance between infectious voice that worms inside the ear and Pan's cavorting. Pan is rapacious: libido unleashed. Recalling the rehearsed insidiousness of voice, its potential to incur, unwanted: both Pan and voice always, at least in the array of Western registers surveyed thus far, threaten an unwanted dissemination (to be read with frank etymological connotations) in and through bodies.

Adriana Cavarero begins the chapter 'Some Irresistible (and Somewhat Dangerous) Flute Playing' in *For More Than One Voice: Toward a Philosophy of Vocal Expression* with a quotation from Plutarch's *Life of Alcibiades*: "He refused to play the flute, considering it a contemptible instrument unworthy of free men."[197] Although Plutarch is not the focus of the chapter, the sentiment about Alcibiades neatly expresses a theme running throughout her exploration of how he (Alcibiades) is used, ventriloquized through, by Plato in *Symposium*. The gist is that flutes are not for men; they are, as Emperor Chun might say, 'devoid of sense and effeminate'.[198] They are also dangerous, a *Pandora's Box*, that threatens to unleash the chaos of nature: desire, frenzy, bacchanalia. Not right for men of order. We shall come back to Cavarero's commentary shortly, but first, by way of Dolar, let's consider the flute and its mechanics as Plato and Aristotle deem it contraband.

Musical instruments and their mechanics are not exempt from Plato's scrutiny. The lesser the capacity to wander from prescribed modes the more acceptable the instrument; the antithesis of such an ideal is, of course, the flute, which can freely flutter through sensuous, infectious and corrupting sounds. One can suppose that flutes, slide whistles and stringed instruments without frets would all go to the pyre under Plato to save the players' temptation to stray into blasphemous and corrupting musical modes or into sonic expressions of no fixed mode. Aristotle parrots Plato's fear and disdain for sound not yoked to *logos*, citing the flute as being inherently corruptive, intoxicating and dangerous. He aligns it with femininity, bacchic revelry and unchecked passions.

Dolar, in 'The Metaphysics of the Voice', quotes Plato's record of Eryximachus' comment in *Symposium*—a request for the 'flute girl' to be

[197] Adriana Cavarero, *For More Than One Voice: Toward a Philosophy of Vocal Expression*, 68.
[198] Dolar, *A Voice and Nothing More*, 43.

removed: 'I would like to make a further motion: let us dispense with the flute-girl who just made her entrance; let her play for herself or, if she prefers, for the women in the house. Let us instead spend our evening in conversation' (Plato, 1978, Symposium 176e).[199] Tom Griffith's translation is slightly more contemporary in tone. It is worth presenting here because of the sumptuous italicization that underscores the gender division within the scene and the self-congratulatory backslapping machismo of the men's group. It reads: 'I've another suggestion to make. I don't think we need the flute girl who's just started playing. She can play for herself, or to the women upstairs, if she feels like it, but for this evening I suggest *we* stick to conversation.'[200]

Dolar summarizes the line, emphasizing how flutes and their music are to be played by and for women, whereas men engage in philosophy, conversation.[201] He then presents two texts from Aristotle's *Politics* that further 'endorse' this view. We shall return to Plato soon, for now there is more to be said about the passage from *Politics* than just an endorsement of Eryximachus' suggestion in the *Symposium*.

Aristotle argues for the reasons why the flute and certain modes of music are more undesirable, vulgar and less expedient than others. Curiously the closing sentiments of the section contradict Socrates' insistence on restricting licence to two modes of music and accept there is a place for the 'vulgar' instruments and other modes. To begin, Aristotle tackles the question of musical pedagogy. He asks: if music is taught, how best and which instruments should be involved so as to not corrupt or vulgarize?

> As to the vulgarizing effect which music is supposed to exercise, this is a question which we shall have no difficulty in determining, when we have considered to what extent freemen who are being trained to political virtue should pursue the art, what melodies and what rhythms they should be

[199] Dolar, *A Voice and Nothing More*, 46. This differs from the Hamilton and Cairns' edited edition I have access to which reads: 'I also propose that we dispense with the services of the flute girl who has just come in, and let her go and play to herself or to the women inside there, whichever she prefers, while we spend our evening in discussion of a subject which, if you think fit, I am prepared to name.' Plato. *The Collected Dialogues of Plato (Bollingen Series)*, 531. The 1978 edition Dolar cites from the same editors might well use a different translation.

[200] Plato, *Symposium and Phaedrus*, Trans. Tom Griffith (New York, USA: Alfred A Knopf/ Random House, 2000), 13.

[201] Dolar, *A Voice and Nothing More*, 46.

allowed to use, and what instruments should be employed in teaching them to play; for even the instrument makes a difference.[202]

Aristotle here, in contrast to Plato, is not as vehemently opposed to all music. He is not even opposed to musical enjoyment. But there is a question of which aspects of music are right to be indulged in. Because, as the following section evidences, without being conducted into following the proper modes and methods of musical endeavour, there is the risk of succumbing to the side of musical enjoyment that is base—that same sound that animals find pleasure in: 'Let the young practice even such music as we have prescribed, only until they are able to feel delight in noble melodies and rhythms, and not merely in that common part of music in which every slave or child and even some animals find pleasure.'[203] It is at this juncture where Aristotle turns his attention to the flute, directly after a paragraph that draws equivalence between a certain form of common music that gives pleasure to animals and humans alike. 'From these principles we may also infer what instruments should be used. The flute, or any other instrument which requires great skill, as for example the harp, ought not to be admitted into education, but only such as will make intelligent students of music.'[204] He continues, 'Besides, the flute is not an instrument which is expressive of moral character; it is too exciting. The proper time for using it is when the performance aims not at instruction, but at the relief of passions.'[205] In the following line, Aristotle complains of a further issue of flute playing—its mechanical denial of voice being used for educational and expedient ends: speech, words—one cannot play a flute and speak words. He writes: 'And there is a further objection; the impediment which the flute presents to the use of the voice detracts from its educational value. The ancients therefore were right in forbidding the flute to youths and freemen.'[206]

Not only does it deny the mouth used in the articulation of consonants for building speech, but its playing results in an amplified and modulated emission of voice-imbued breath. In a sense, it is incompatible with speech: it disallows any just, moral or expediency-orientated vocalization and instead sounds an augmented voice.

[202] Aristotle, *The Basic Works of Aristotle (Modern Library)*, Ed. Richard McKeon (New York, USA: The Modern Library, 2001), 1313.
[203] Ibid., 1313.
[204] Ibid.
[205] Ibid., 1313–1314.
[206] Ibid., 1314.

Song could be tolerated, provided it sticks to an approved musical mode, but the flute, because of its pneumatic and mechanical method of sounding notes, has an irksome tendency to stray off scale. The played flute relishes in everything that Plato argues to be corrupting, insidious, immoral and dangerous: it indulges in non-signifying voice and capriciously blasphemes in sound. It appeals to the baser passions. Aristotle states, in the closing segment of *Politics VIII*, in his discussion of the musical modes: 'Bacchic frenzy and all similar emotions are most suitably expressed by the flute, and are better set to the Phrygian than to any other mode. The dithyramb, for example, is acknowledged to be Phrygian.'[207]

Let's return to Plato's *Symposium*. Cavarero notes precisely this Platonic gripe of the flute's doubled vocal corruption:

> the flute lets itself, dangerously, represent the phone in the double sense of the term: voice and sound. Whoever plays it renounces speech and evokes a world in which the acoustic sphere and expressions of corporeality predominate. It is the world of the Dionysian dithyramb, where the flute modulates rhythms that accompany an orgiastic dance.'[208]

The flute is the doubling up of the qualities Plato (subsequently and Aristotle) wished to deny of voice. Not only does the flute veto the articulation of language or words, but, additionally, it amplifies breath into sonorous song. The flute and various wind instruments are prolongations of the mouth: 'they are all too similar to voice.'[209] Flutes 'require breath and thus impede the flutist from *speaking*'.[210] Flutes project an infectious musicality and cast a spell on those who listen whilst silencing any verbal expression of expedient speech. Words, *logos*, sense and rationality are denied, leaving only the resounding possibility of intoxicating, sensuous, sound.

Cavarero's analysis in 'Some Irresistible (and Somewhat Dangerous) Flute Playing' draws out further nuances of the presence of the flutes and voices. The issue of the flute is, within the diegesis, framed in a theological register qua the figure of Marsyas. On another level, Cavarero offers a more biographical reading of Plato's text. The flute comes to be heard in a symptomatic context of Plato's desires: which to say it is an object of

[207] Aristotle, *The Basic Works of Aristotle (Modern Library)*, 1316.
[208] Cavarero, *For More Than One Voice: Toward a Philosophy of Vocal Expression*, 69.
[209] Ibid., 69.
[210] Ibid., emphasis added.

repulsion, a phobia, for Plato. Cavarero's commentary (of Alcibiades' comments about Socrates, Plato's teacher) does not employ these terms but most certainly drives to suggest Alcibiades is voicing a personal sentiment of Plato in regard to his teacher.

The passage can be read as a curious chink in Plato's stoic aversion to voice and sound and his privileging of text and language. Plato, it almost goes without saying, was scribe to his teacher, Socrates. Socrates was an orator, not a scribe like Plato and, later, Aristotle. The briefest glance over Plato's texts yields evidence that he was anxious and fearful of the intoxicating sonic aspect of voice apart from language and the spellbinding abilities of music. Yet, he cannot, in the final instance, deny the influence and power of the sound of his master's—Socrates'—voice. Is the textual voice of Alcibiades Plato's veiled concession to his elder, a chink in his pathology of *phone*-denial?

Let's turn to the scene in question. At first Alcibiades' presence is acousmatic: 'Almost at once we heard Alcibiades' voice from the courtyard. He was very drunk and shouting at the top of his voice, asking 'where Agathon was', and demanding 'to be taken to Agathon'.'[211] Moments later he enters drunkenly. Cavarero writes: 'he is in the grips of a bacchic frenzy, the Dionysian inebriation that is linked to the orgiastic rhythm of the flute. In keeping with this rhythm, Alcibiades stumbles his way into the room "half-carried by the flute girl".'[212] Alcibiades' sonic and raucous debut immediately couches him contextual harmony with Pan, and the Bacchic frenzy of the dithyramb. It is apt that 'the flute girl' carries Alcibiades' rambunctiousness and intoxicated zeal into the Symposium.[213] But 'carried' should be read here in the double sense—he might well be physically supported by a young flautist, but he might well be carried off, carried away, intoxicated, compelled to revelry, also, by the flute. What is really carrying into the Symposium? Is he carried in as he has become *carried away*? This passage concerns more than the arrival of drunkenness. It is as close to literal symbolic array of all that Plato disparages. The flute, revelry, enjoyment, feminine and natural passions arrive in Bacchic form.[214]

[211] Plato, *Symposium and Phaedrus*, 68–69.

[212] Cavarero, *For More Than One Voice: Toward a Philosophy of Vocal Expression*, 69.

[213] Ibid.

[214] There is a further case for suggesting Alcibiades' inebriation is a departure from upright bipedalism that itself further inscribes the Bacchic into the scene. Pan did not have man's legs either.

After Alcibiades is seated, he notices Socrates beside him. To begin he is a touch abrasive towards Socrates and explains he is trying to avoid him. He then orders a large cup, but grabs a bucket and drains the wine. He orders Socrates to do the same but admits that 'It doesn't matter how much you give him to drink, he'll drink it and be none the worse for wear.'[215] Heed these two sentiments: Alcibiades wishes to avoid Socrates and Socrates cannot get drunk.

After some discussion Alcibiades announces his intention to 'praise Socrates using similes'.[216] Alcibiades likens Socrates to a Silenus figure: 'I think he's very like one of those Silenus-figures sculptors have on their shelves. They're made with flutes or pipes. You can open them up, and when you do you find little figures of the gods inside. I also think Socrates is like the satyr Marsyas.'[217] Alcibiades, by likening the old man to a flute or a pipe, is, by extension, suggesting that Socrates' voice is not only intoxicating and spellbinding but that his external appearance betrays his inner-worth. To put it bluntly, Socrates' 'face and body are ugly' but his soul is beautiful, and it is through his voice that his soul is conveyed and transported to others.[218] Alcibiades recounts:

> You may not play the pipes, like Marsyas, but what you do is much more amazing. He had only to open his mouth to delight men, but he needed a musical instrument to do it. The same goes for anyone nowadays who plays music—I count what Olympus played as really Marsyas', since he learned it from him. His is the only music which carries people away (…) Such is its divine power, and it makes no difference whether it's played by an expert, or by a mere flute girl.[219]

There are several themes nestled within this passage. Firstly, the shadow of pederast homosexuality 'as a model of cultural and political formation in the Greek aristocracy' is alluded to (in part by double entendres).[220] The backstory is Alcibiades' spurned love for Socrates. His torment stems from his military service with Socrates in Potidaea, where they were mess-mates. Alcibiades hoped that Socrates would 'improve him' and wined and

[215] Plato, *Symposium and Phaedrus*, 69–70.
[216] Ibid., 72.
[217] Ibid., 73.
[218] Cavarero, *For More Than One Voice: Toward a Philosophy of Vocal Expression*, 69.
[219] Plato, *Symposium and Phaedrus*, 73.
[220] Cavarero, *For More Than One Voice: Toward a Philosophy of Vocal Expression*, 68.

dined him more than once. One evening, after plying Socrates with wine, Alcibiades suggested he stay, arguing that it was too late an hour for him to leave. Socrates agreed. Alcibiades then details what happened after the slaves had fallen asleep and the lights were put out. He goes on, in vino veritas: 'I decided it was time to abandon all subtlety, and say plainly what I was after. So I nudged him. "Socrates, are you asleep?" "No." "Do you know what I've decided?" "What?" "I think you're the ideal person to be my lover, but you seem to be a bit shy about suggesting it."'[221] Alcibiades hoped to satisfy Socrates because he (Socrates) improves him (Alcibiades), and he wanted nothing more than his own improvement. Socrates, however, delicately declines, and Alcibiades sleeps next to him. Alcibiades admits that he 'slept with Socrates all night, but absolutely nothing had happened. It was just like sleeping with one's father or elder brother.'[222] Alcibiades, rejected but still full of admiration for Socrates, declares how he 'went around infatuated with the man, No one's ever been so infatuated.'[223]

This monologue of Alcibiades is a duet. Alcibiades speaks not only for himself but voices Plato's admiration of his teacher. Plato is ventriloquizing here. This is Cavarero's point on the opening page of the chapter—a sentiment she traces from Martha Nussbaum's more visual comment in *The Fragility of Goodness*: 'The enamoured Alcibiades speaks for himself, but he also speaks for the author: "the Symposium's portrait of Alcibiades is in some sense Plato's own self-portrait."'[224]

Alcibiades also tells the story of Marsyas and Olympus (or Zeus). Marsyas challenged Olympus to a musical duel. Challenging the Gods is doomed to failure: he lost, and his punishment was to be flayed alive, leaving only his screaming mouth. But 'Alcibiades' adds a twist; his thesis here is that Olympus was really playing Marsyas' music, not his own music. Alcibiades, running the same conceptual likening of speech and voice being as intoxicating and compelling as flutes and voices, feels he is just as transported and beguiled by the voice of Socrates even when others are poorly parroting his arguments:

[221] Plato, *Symposium and Phaedrus*, 77–78.

[222] Ibid., 79.

[223] Ibid.

[224] Cavarero, *For More Than One Voice: Toward a Philosophy of Vocal Expression*, 68, see note 2, 249.

> You have the same effect on people. The only difference is that you do it with word alone, without the aid of any instrument. We can all listen to anyone else talking, and it has virtually no effect on us, no matter what he is talking about, or how good a speaker he is. But when we listen to you, or to someone else using your arguments, even if he's a hopeless speaker, we're overwhelmed and carried away.[225]

Alcibiades, in likening Socrates to Marsyas and in the echo of his confession of his unrequited love, is plagued by Socrates's voice—even voices come from others' recounting Socrates' arguments and wisdom. Like the contagious laughter that travels from body to puppet, or like infectious music that earworm victims hum and pass on to others, Socrates' voice is everywhere; it sounds in the conversations and voices of others. Socrates voice is a ubiquitous and inescapable torment for the spurned Alcibiades, who is nevertheless fascinated and captivated:

> When I hear him, it's like the worst kind of religious hysteria. My heart pounds, and I find myself in floods of tears, such is the effect of his words. I used to listen to Pericles and other powerful speakers, and I thought they spoke well. But they never had the effect on me of turning all my beliefs upside down, with the disturbing realization that my whole life is that of a slave. Whereas this Marsyas here has often made me feel that, and decide that the kind of life I lead is just not worth living.[226]

Socrates voice, Alcibiades argues, torments, infects, plagues and is disseminated by others, through the bodies of others. There is a theme of contagion, insidious voice, in this love story. In this textual duet to Socrates, Alcibiades and Plato rehearse the age-old plague of love. Specifically, it is love for another's voice, an explication of which runs into multiple equivalences of voice and love with earworms and parasites.[227] Corporeal modulation, a horrifying stripping of agency, is even evidenced by the love-stricken Alcibiades: his heart quickens, and he becomes tearful at the disseminated voice of Socrates in others. Socratean arguments and words cast a spell of distinctly physical consequence when piped though others', even if they are poor orators.

[225] Plato, *Symposium and Phaedrus*, 73.
[226] Ibid., 74.
[227] Such as *Ophiocordyceps unilateralis* and *Sacculina carcini*.

Alcibiades, in the Griffith translation provided above, likens hearing Socrates' voice to hysteria, a mania like the extreme literary example of earworms detailed in 'Slimy & Wormy', "Crazy" and 'Parasites & Earworms' sections of this chapter. Alcibiades torment is echoed in contemporary popular music songs such as Britney Spears' *(You Drive Me) Crazy* (1999), *Toxic* (2004), *I'm a Slave 4 U* (2001) and Kylie Minogue's 2001 hit *Can't Get You Out of My Head*, whereby voice and love are framed as pernicious agents of mania. Alcibiades 'feels his heart flutter in his breast, and he becomes a slave to what he hears.'[228] He is plagued by a love that strips him of agency and bodily control and equally a voice manifesting in similar symptoms. The infectious and intoxicating spell of love is analogous to the compelling musical voice, the earworm that drives the victim 'crazy'.[229]

Alcibiades' solution is to resort to the same aural evasion as Odysseus does when his voyage takes him within earshot of the Sirens. He mentions the Homeric poem and references the irresistibility of voice: 'Even now I know in my heart of hearts that if I were to listen to him, I couldn't resist him. (…) So I tear myself away, as if stopping my ears against the Sirens; otherwise I would spend my whole life sitting there at his feet. (…) So I run for my life, and avoid him, and when I see him.'[230]

Plato's response to such a captivating speaker and his voice is very different to Alcibiades' reaction. Plato, unlike Alcibiades, stayed to listen to Socrates. In a sense, Alcibiades can be read as a Janus-faced representation of how Plato feels (the love for his master's enchanting sonorous voice) and what he does not (unlike Alcibiades) succumb to (the avoidance of the beguiling voice). Whereas the flighty, charming and handsome Alcibiades flees the spellbinding voice of Socrates' voice, Plato, by contrast, is

[228] Cavarero, *For More Than One Voice: Toward a Philosophy of Vocal Expression*, 70.

[229] To take the similarities further, Alcibiades' detailing of the virulent dissemination of Socrates' voice (in others) is also reflected in modern music's earworms: the endless replays of records, synthetic resoundings of the vocal performance that lodge in one's consciousness and torment. In addition to contemporary popular music's technological and consumerist reproduction and dissemination, the analogy between Alcibiades' torment and modern pop can be identified in popular music's proclivity for 'cover' versions, remixes, karaoke and tribute bands. Just as Alcibiades may hear others parroting the arguments of Socrates we too may be inadvertently exposed to poor reproductions. The contemporary hit record's contagion and infectiousness mirrors Alcibiades' torment in modality and symptom.

[230] Plato, *Symposium and Phaedrus*, 74.

prepared to stay and take notes.[231] Plato, textually speaking through Alcibiades, is describing by-proxy his love for his teacher's spellbinding speech whilst also describing the solution of avoidance he admirably refused. Cavarero details:

> Alcibiades not only functions as the double face of himself and Plato, but also as the one from whom Plato wishes to distinguish himself. Alcibiades—who is beautiful, famous and charming—is an ambiguous figure on whom hangs, among other things, an accusation of sacrilege. (…) Alcibiades turned his back on Socrates; he stopped his ears in order to extract himself from the teaching of Socratic logoi. On the other hand Plato, the legitimate heir, stayed to listen—all the while worrying about to eliminate precisely the enchanting aspect of this listening. Plato, in other words, found his own way to stop his ears—namely, through the devocalizing of logos.[232]

In this rich section of Plato's *Symposium* there are two modes of confronting and/or dealing with the horrifying, contagious, infectious and captivating voice. Alcibiades' (Plato's thinly veiled ode to his teacher's enchanting voice) 'incorrect' reaction is to flee and avoid the sonorous facet of speech. Plato, however, has a much more inventive and metaphysically drastic solution.

'Socrates does not write; he speaks. *Logos* comes out of his mouth and effectively enters the ears of his interlocutors.'[233] Plato, by writing down the words of Socratic speech, by setting to text the words and cleaving *logos*, language, soul and meaning away from the corrupt, unjust, inexpedient, feminine and enchanting sound of voice, devocalizes *logos*: Plato inscribes a method of having his teacher's words without having to bear his voice. The essence of Socratic *logoi* is recorded as silent masculine text without the corrupting sounds of voice. *Logos* sans *Phone*. Voice vivisected from language, thought and intellect without its messy viscera.

This is Plato's bifurcation (of himself and Socratean speech), his pathology of love and denial. On the one hand Plato must, albeit via textual proxy, admit Socrates' voice is wonderful, enchanting and unbearably

[231] To make a brief analogy with academia, Alcibiades is the exciting and engaging student who is first to speak to his teacher, glass in hand, at a soirée. Plato, by contrast, is the studious pupil who takes copious notes that are revisited, poured over and absorbed later on, in silence, in private.

[232] Cavarero, *For More Than One Voice: Toward a Philosophy of Vocal Expression*, 70.

[233] Ibid., 70.

captivating (like love). Yet he does not wish to be so captivated, because for him, or at least the ideal and political side of him, it is a despicable and dishonourable enjoyment, an enjoyment of voice he disdains. It is precisely because of this corrupting sonic-beauty that he likens voice to the ugly and flute-like exterior of the Silenus-statues. For Plato, Socrates' speech (logos housed within a beguiling voice) is akin to his ugly external appearance containing wonderful internal knowledge and wisdom. The Silenus-statue, with their blasphemous flute-like outside but God-like interior, is Plato's analogy of Socrates' speech. Plato's operation of devocalizing *logos* is akin to getting to the gods housed within the Silenus-statue whilst doing away with the presence of the corrupting external flute. This is one of the wonderful insights Cavarero draws out; the

> rhetorical surface of the Socratic logoi is ugly, but the content is beautiful. Alcibiades stops here. His drunken discourse has reached its end. The whole platonic philosophy, however, without a drop of wine in its veins, goes well beyond this. It devocalizes logos. It cuts off its sonorous skin and founds in its place an order rooted in the videocentric and noetic sphere of thought. It makes speech an acoustic shell of an idea.[234]

Plato, regarding voice and music as the undesirable, corrupting and distracting sonic shell of noetic thought, sought to flay this troublesome external *phone* from the *logos* it harboured. The likening of Socrates to Marsyas (who was flayed as punishment) reveals Plato's metaphysical operation of separating thought, *logos*, from voice, *phone*. It is this annexing of voice from thought, sound from order, *phone* from *logos* that underpins the previously detailed regulations of voice.

Horror, the unbearable, intoxicating and corrupting horror of voice, is a constant theme threaded through such operations. Both Alcibiades and Plato sought to be free from such a contagious voice. Alcibiades (throwing the proverbial 'baby out with the bath water') couldn't bear Socratic *logoi* wrapped up in voice and denied himself both: he fled from both logos and its sonic shell, the voice. The canny scribe Plato however, in his devocalizing flaying of his master's voice, sought to isolate knowledge from its corrupting sonic shell. Plato sought to preserve Socratic *logoi* by partitioning speech and separating logos from its vocal skin and receding into the

[234] Ibid., 70.

silent textual realm of language. Alcibiades and Plato are equally troubled and plagued by the contagious and spellbinding nature of voice. Both are tormented by Socrates' insidious voice that can rob the listener of agency, but both cannot help but fall for such a voice. It is an unbearable love. Each has their solution to the dangers, the horrors, of beguiling voice.

Conclusion

A different account of voice, object *a* voice contra 'the object voice', is presented here. The second chapter, which most forcefully levels criticism and elaborates departures from Dolar's account of voice, is at times nigh on a retort to the widely referenced yet seldom critiqued *A Voice and Nothing More*. Indeed, this project is at times an intervention. The contention laid out is to confront the body where Dolar does not, seeking not only to provide an alternative conception of the Lacanian voice qua object but also, by addressing the body, arguing for an implicit horror.

Dolar's methodology of is one of veils. He argues that meaning and aesthetics obfuscate the object voice. He considers voices from hidden sources, the acousmatic voice, at length. He praises the Pythagorean curtain that allows a voice to be heard without the body seen, as 'a stroke of genius' that stands at the 'very origin of philosophy'. Like a magician's cloak, Dolar tends to conceal the bodies from which voice issues and places voice in a mysterious context, analogous to the unknown object of horror. The horror vocabulary that peppers his arguments is perhaps symptomatic of this tendency. This book, by seeking corporeality, by going beyond the veil of language and aesthetics, articulates voice, qua object *a*, as an object of at once the body, from without the body, and one of horrors.

Within the second chapter, 'Beyond the Veil of This World', there are several questions simmering. The intervention, the retort to Dolar's *A*

T. Adams, *Horrors of* a *Voice (object* a*)*,
https://doi.org/10.1007/978-3-031-62050-8_6

Voice and Nothing More, is the most explicit here. Hopefully this, at times robust, critique will elicit more creative and constructive readings of both Lacan's work and contemporary commentaries (such as Dolar's). Additionally, it is hoped that the significance of role of the body is given more thought by future readers of Lacan and contemporary commentaries because of this. Quite how readers of this text may take this up is not prescribed here, because the fundamental argument, the aim (that is impressed throughout), is that the body is at least afforded some attention and considered. That said, this book does offer some examples of how this could be conducted. Essentially, if the second chapter argues *why* the body should be afforded attention in terms of object *a* voice and horror, the later chapters certainly continue this argument whilst also demonstrating *how* such projects might be conducted. There is a definite difference between the second chapter and the following three. 'Violence', 'Ch*a*nges' and 'Insidious' all demonstrate areas where a strict recourse to the question of the body is not only appropriate but can be the basis of a methodology that can uncover and explore rich and urgent questions relating to anthropocentricism, popular music, film and re-readings of classics (to name but a few). This triptych of demonstrations could be developed and broken out, and individually developed into standalone titles, were it not for the necessity that the claims in chapter "Beyond the Veil of Our World" are provided the essential presuppositions that these demonstrative trio of chapters rest on.

The role of voice in Lacan's life is a particularly rich avenue to pursue. Roudinesco has commented on several biographical-theoretic parallels. The plainest of which is the influence of legal troubles preventing Lacan from giving his name to his daughter, Judith, with Sylvia Bataille while he (Lacan) was still married to Malou and under French law was not allowed to recognize a child born to another woman.[1] Lacan's daughter never had his name albeit for a brief period before acquiring the Miller name. Roudinesco writes: 'There can be no doubt that one of the origins of Lacan's theory of the name-of-the-father, a key element in his teaching, lay in this imbroglio.'[2]

A continuation of this praxis (that of understanding Lacan's theoretical, psychoanalytical and philosophical work and Lacan's life, as a parallax view) might be to consider the significance of a man whose fame was built

[1] Roudinesco, *Jacques Lacan*, 163–164.
[2] Ibid., 163.

upon his voice, its proximity to the elusive archive of his thought, but whose voice ate itself in later life. Indeed, there are many threads of voice in Lacan one can follow in this manner. Incidentally, and it is surprising Dolar does not touch on this in his ruminations on *The Wizard of Oz*, does not mention that Lacan inaugurated the *École freudienne de Paris* (EFP) by way of a recorded message played in tape recorder, after which he then burst into the room and added several additional points on top of his own recording. This is one of many obvious biographical details that, surprisingly given the re-emergence of the question of voice in psychoanalysis, is, thus far, afforded scant attention.

There is a rich seam to explore, in terms of the silent object *a* voice, how Lacan's thought was 'heard' and how his health deteriorated. Roudinesco details, in the sad chapter 'Psychoanalysis Reduced to Zero', how Lacan receded into *knot*-speaking: receding into a habit of silently playing with rings and knots, supposedly in deep thought, during a period of increasingly erratic behaviour, a strange amalgamation of eccentricity, capriciousness, childlike impatience and—perhaps more worrying—forgetfulness. In this period Lacan's silence and mutterings were regarded as deep thought but may well have been symptoms of a brain tumour. There are accounts of this in 'Tomb for a Pharaoh'. [3] Late in life Lacan continued public appearances but spoke little; the few odd words or exclamations he did 'say' were subject to over-interpretation. As were the silences, as they always were considered rich in meaning. Much like the interruptions of speech, the throat clearing, the huffing, etc. Yet, as one cannot but conclude from the final chapters of Roudinesco's biography, the absences of speech, the distances, the departures, the lacunae of engagement were very likely not due to thought, or a creative and rich interpretation, concerning what was said to him, but symptoms of an ill man, close to death. In this sense, one can see Lacan's final period as a scene of malady as costume, a reverse of the emperor's new clothes fable. Lacan was smothered by those finding significance in what he did not say, by his non-verbal vocalizations, his silences and daydreams. But rather than these same absences carrying meaning pertaining to literature, philosophy or psychoanalysis, they were the symptoms of a very present corporeal malady. I explore this, at great length in a future project considering the concept, the sense or feeling, of masks.

[3] Ibid., 403.

'Violence' provides an acute focus on vocalization, what it means to give voice—what is required of the body to do so? Certainly, the opening section 'Army, Opera, Flesh' is a bridging text that follows the drive of the second chapter (providing a focus on the question of the body where Dolar does not) whilst also exploring meaning and signification. This section, in terms of drive, is closer to the interventionist tone of the second chapter, but the specific question it leads to is the focus on the chapter it is situated in: what language requires of the body from which it issues. The answer to this question is the chapter title.

Provided here is a focus on vocalization, not voice. Many voice texts explore the quality or aural experience of voice—but texts that examine and consider how voice is made are certainly in the minority. A key drive in the research of this chapter was to draw voice away from any human privilege and horrific by virtue of the decentred subject. Here, the notion of the human animal is presented. The trajectory of this thought was to articulate voice as a register of the inhuman in us; or to parse this sentiment out in lay terms, to impress the thought that we humans are not that special. The move intends to frame object *a* voice as silent, inhuman, horrific and confounding, but also active, of agency and autonomy indifferent to our myopically human view of the world. This drive certainly is indebted to the work of Lynn Turner and many others exploring animal studies. 'Violence' is most certainly the most ambitious chapter in term of discipline and owes some of this energy to the work of CCRU and the many writers that emerged from it, most immediately my first supervisor and friend, Mark Fisher. Despite this energy and enthusiasm, the text is certainly wary of wading too far, too imprudently, into the sciences' academic debates, though it does provide some context to the scientific arguments and narratives by recourse to divergent positions, opinions and counter arguments. If there is one hope for this chapter, it is that it can show how an interdisciplinary argument can engage creatively, thoughtfully and respectfully with more empirical fields of research whilst still exploring novel questions through the privileging of discourse, questioning, articulation and a touch of narrative flair (that the humanities tend to exercise more readily). This may well read as a rather bold claim, but it is also an ambition absolutely rooted in psychoanalysis. Without being too grand, and without being too partisan in terms of discipline, it should be said that psychoanalysis, in so many ways, picked up where scientific evidence fell short: theorizing and later philosophizing, always with a sustained recourse fiction literature and philosophy, upon the unknown maladies that haunt us. It is in this sense that 'Violence' does not interlope in the scientific debates it utilizes but builds something more, finds new questions, stakes and urgencies. It is also in this sense that the chapter exercises a certain liberty to evoke and affect. The violence of language is communicated, and the array of scientific texts support this angle, with (or at least with an aim for) impressing a level of vividness and *viscerality*. It is here where genre horror, philosophy, psychoanalysis and the body amalgamate most forcefully and with most fealty to psychoanalysis proper. This keenness for the blood and sweat of psychoanalysis and philosophy is rooted in a much broader project. Thoughts, emotions, questions—these have physical consequences. An unanswered question may conjure horror, elicit a flush or palpitation; speculating about the consequences of a question may well yield dread. In this sense, as has been reiterated throughout the book with recourse to both Lacan and Thacker, it is the lack, the unknown, that is so troubling. Make no mistake; the question mark can often be a macabre jester, grinning, taunting, goading. Questions yield physical reactions. This is developed at length in my next project concerning the sense and feelings—or suspicions—of masks. Philosophy is not entirely cerebral but inextricably linked to the body. This is the reason the chapter indulges in imagery and metaphor to a degree that may be misconstrued as effusiveness, poetic ambitions or indulgent flair. Much like effective genre horror, the text does indeed seek to make the heart flutter, to bring forth a bead of sweat. It is in this sense the chapter aims to be a heady (which is to say of great consequence to the body!) mix of scientific texts, psychoanalysis, metaphysics, philosophy and fiction literatures. This is to convey the tangibility of questions, concerns and stakes: to communicate concepts with some sensation, without being too breathlessly sensational.

Between the first two chapters there is a thread of dancing with commentaries around Freudian and Lacanian psychoanalysis and the sciences. 'Beyond *Beyond the Pleasure Principle*' and 'Spinal Trauma and Throats Torn with the Talk Sickness' could certainly be developed as new threads and produce a number of standalone articles. The former is a robust examination of Freud, and the latter is a zealously interdisciplinary dance through vocalization, evolution, phylogenetics and infant development to explicate Lacan's notion of the human organism's imprisonment in the torture house of language, the mutilations of meaning. Beyond the overriding engagement and intervention with Dolar's work, these sections are some of the more novel, ambitious and accomplished components of this book. Certainly, by contemporary 'standards' the breadth of materials and disciplines explored is notable. Whether these are imprudent and naïve or otherwise is not the author's prerogative to pass judgement on (this is why therapy takes two). However, it is worth recalling and underscoring the modality of Freud and Lacan's work here: these disciplines are evident in the texts and voices of both. As is the persistent utilization of the reanimating power of fiction literature. Does this methodology, this flamboyant or ostentatious fashion of methodology still offer a unique way to develop thought and productively explore questions that more reserved, more disciplined or more cautious texts might not? Perhaps some may read this is too youthful, too bold, a question? Perhaps that should not be the first question asked. These more vibrant, fizzier passage sections were produced with the conceit that this—perhaps giddy, perhaps capricious—approach still offers something other modes of approach do not. A kaleidoscope of empirical disciplines remixed with Freud, Lacan, Irigaray and CCRU may well be regarded as a touch loud too or cavalier in some circles. There is no apology. For one drive in producing the texts presented here was the concern that projects of this nature felt to be in stark minority (and still are).

'Ch*a*nges' explores the significance of voice in sounding out horrific change from a lacuna, sounding a changing body or psychology (or *soul*) through a corporeal vessel. Much of the focus riffs around voice as a register of corporeal change in terms of horror, puberty and what voice betrays of the vocalizer. Using lycanthropy as a frame or allegory for exploring the development of an adult sexual desire during puberty and using lycanthropy similarly to explore the effects of puberty on the developing human body is, perhaps, among the less novel takes in the book. But amalgamating these moves with concerns of gender, race and sexuality do contribute one of the more immediately powerful arguments in the book, albeit centred around the famously idiosyncratic figures (plurality well intended) of Michael Jackson. The figure(s) of Michael Jackson in the text, as bodies of multiplicities, flux and horror, has emerged to be prescient. Indeed, the reading is more apt for biographical parallels than one thought possible some years ago. What began as an excavation of latent horrors has, by the time of editing, been retroactively glossed into an explicit register. Once again, there is a closer more biographically determined reading that could be drawn out. There is reticence to pursue this angle over and above the concern of being too eager to fold a person's work and its commentaries into biographical details. Not least because Jackson's voice does not need representation: others' do.

This chapter is the most acute in terms of focus. It is also a slightly, but only slightly, less ambitious chapter in terms of interdisciplinary modality. Some scientific texts about vocal tract development and studies about psychological and physiological tells in voice are employed, but largely it provides close readings Jackson's work with recourse to scholars from the humanities (Barthes, Mercer, Jefferson, etc.). That said, the text does effectively riff across voice studies texts, to furnish the moves between vocal 'grain', noise, and corporeal transformation. Certainly, this is the chapter that engages most with the established field of voice studies and performance studies. In terms of horror and psychoanalysis, it is the double meaning of *thrill*, and the plurality of voice, that is the main question.

This double meaning of *thrill* does mark out a watershed in the project. The second chapter, 'Beyond the Veil of Our World', was interventionist and critical, and the second, 'Violence', continued exploring via myriad disciplines the significance of the body in terms of the violence and torture language imposes upon the human organism. These early chapters do not afford space for voice and/or vocalization to be considered as joyous, exciting, sensual or enchanting. 'Ch*a*nges' broadly follows a similar tone and thematic palette of horror, dread, trauma, violence in examining Jackson's works, but it does acknowledge and explore (certainly in the readings of Barthes) the prospect of thrill as a positive sensation, of delight, frisson, jouissance. These moments are the beginning of horror, voice and object *a* voice to be questions not only of negative valence but also of positive valence. This emergent turn towards positive valence, or the unfurling of a rich ambiguousness of horror and voice, is given more sustained focus in the last chapter. Nonetheless, it is worth keeping in mind that the Janus nature of *thrill* in terms of voice is first touched on here in a context of at once horror, eroticism, dance and a porous and amorphous conception of the human body. Pluralism and ambiguity in voice are framed not as positive or negative valence but as both, intrinsically both: an *extimacy*, one could say. Similarly, it is also here where the de-anthropocentrized figures of Jackson's personas are framed as at once horrifying and delightful, scary and exciting: thrilling. Not only is this a fold from a more traditional approach—examining what human horror may be—but it also casts interspecies pluralities as prospects to *enjoy* and, in doing so also, offers the prospect of interpretating object *a* voice as potentially emerging from enjoyment and desire too. These are certainly questions that warrant further consideration in future projects. Persecution, repression, suppression, anxiety, fear, horror are considered or at least touched upon in the many commentaries around object *a* voice (or object voice)—but asking what role object *a* voice plays in terms of enjoyment—enjoyment as a positive thing, a goal, an aim—is not a question afforded much focus. Dolar certainly explores enjoyment in various turns in *A Voice and Nothing More*, but the enjoyment is seldom couched as something good or acceptable; it is an enjoyment that is a problem, a guilt or an issue in many of the examples he works mostly through a gendered dichotomy of signifier/reason/meaning and aesthetics/nature/beauty. Dolar's position on enjoyment and voice is never quite given away. What does object *a* voice have to do with a positive enjoyment? It would be worth revisiting Poizat's *An Angel's Cry* (passages of which are close to blueprints for some parts of *A Voice and Nothing More*) with an ear for this question. Can object *a* voice be explored without a presupposition or framing that enjoyment is on some level problematic or part of a problematic dynamic or knot? Certainly, this is the most striking difference between Barthes' *grain*, a candid and earnest exploration of enjoyment, contra commentaries around 'object voice'. It is apt to ask; does object *a* voice *have to be* considered as part of a problem to be untangled?

These are certainly questions not squarely confronted in the chapter. But their importance can be underscored by returning to the anecdote Lacan recounts in 'On a Question Preliminary to Any Possible Treatment of Psychosis'. A woman maintaining two relationships mutters to herself 'I've just been to the pork butcher's.' At which point a neighbour, supposedly, shouts verbal abuse at her, calling her a 'Sow!' [4] The intraspecies nature of this episode is plain enough, of course. Lacan's thesis is that the woman's aural hallucination (a form or register of object *a* voice) ties up her utterance, making sense of her strange non-sequitur, and betrays a yearn to be fragmented (a register of her yearning for plurality). Lacan writes that she is 'prisoner of a dual relationship', but rather than read this anecdote as one of horror and persecution might one also read it as voicing an intraspecies desire to be in two places at once, to maintain a polyamorous relationship without the need for vivisection? Rather than a question of psychosis and persecution, might one read the scene as offering a very plain solution: why *not* have both? Pigs do. Of course, this reading is anathema to French cultures of that period (and many contemporary cultures within and without France still), but it is an attempt, a beginning, of interpreting object *a* voice as being as much about enjoyment and

[4] Lacan, *Écrits: A Selection*, 201.

desire (and voicing what enjoyment is) rather than framing it in a palette of negative valence. For obvious reasons a development of this thought including further readings of Jackson's work would be insensitive and uncomfortable. Nonetheless, plurality and interspecies figures are common in popular music and art; there are many opportunities for rich and productive re-readings in terms of this thought. What is of great future possibility is the ambition to explore object *a* voice—in terms of interspecies figures and narratives and pluralities *or not*—as an exciting way towards enjoyment and less stymied flows of desires (whatever the arbitrary objects may be).

'*In*sidious' adds to several commentaries that will continue to garner foci in various disciplines. The figures of the Sirens, how voice is treated in ancient Greek texts, and themes of contagion and slime all add most directly to sound studies. The chapter examines the question of the body within the dynamics of contagion and incursion whilst also adding a gloss concerning species and gender. It should be said that this chapter was produced years before the Covid-19 crisis, and not as a response, commentary or reaction to the pandemic. Of course, Covid-19 impacted (and ended) many lives, in many ways. There is no desire to diminish its significance. But contagion is a greater question than virology. The sections around INMI in popular music highlight this. Being crazy, being possessed, realizing one no longer has the agency of mind and body one presumed: such prospects and questions apply to and riff around anxieties of viral contagion, but they also resonate on a much deeper philosophical register: contagion and exposure are unignorable facets of horror philosophy. Certainly, in this very specific, or niche, sub-discipline the text contributes a resolutely voice-focused commentary that was largely lacking. This goes back to one of the main impetuses for the project: that almost thrown-away line of Thacker's 'that demons choose to present themselves via voice and sound—at once present and absent—is noteworthy'. It is more than noteworthy. There is a great deal more to explore; hopefully this text contributes some initial momentum for these lines of thought in future works.

'*In*sidious' is the chapter that most explicitly addresses gender and most directly engages with the metaphysics of voice examined by Dolar and Cavarero. The degree of novelty offered within the passages concerning the Sirens is perhaps a moot point. Also, much of the commentary offered around music and song (e.g. the Dionysian dithyramb) draw from the materials of Dolar and Cavarero survey as much as they add. The passages concerning Socrates, Alcibiades, Marsyas and Silenus figures do contribute in a very specific way. Desire was always a component of Cavarero's thesis around Alcibiades, despite the brevity of focus. What the latter parts of '*In*sidious' aim for is to reanimate and reconcile desire with a patrician's horror of voice, enjoyment and the body. This is one of the richest seams of thought struck upon. Although the examinations are lengthy, and deal with multiple commentaries and narratives, the sections do yield an unlikely alloy. Love is seldom a focus in explorations of horror, and texts focusing on love do not tend to afford much space to the question of horror. '*In*sidious' draws up an argument, building on the previous chapters, that love and horror are apt to be considered as part of a dynamic. The second chapter underscored the body as part of its critique of Dolar, the second explored speech and language and how the infant becomes trapped in the torture house of language in calling for care; the examinations of Jackson weave the double valence of *thrill* across voice and body, where anger and lust implode in a funk. '*In*sidious' builds on all these threads. It is a culmination that not only asks what the difference between desire and horror is, but also, in a Lacanian spirit, presumes there is a relationship between desire and horror, and sets out to explore the topology of such a relation.

The prospect of a desire/horror Mobius strip is a question running through much of this book and culminates in the final chapter. A further question is that of love: where and how does love fit into this schema? Desire and love have been brushed up against at each turn. [5] From analyses of Lacan's 'Sow!' example, to the click in Freud's 'A Case of Paranoia Running Counter to the Psychoanalytic Theory of the Disease', to Clorinda in Tasso's *The Liberation of Jerusalem,* to Michael Jackson, to the vocalization of Ernst away from the breast, desire and love percolate the contexts of the materials explored. The notion of love in the classic Greek texts, the leitmotif of spell, enchantment and intoxication in the Sirens, even the common phrase 'lovesick'—echoing pathogens introduced to bodies—all these seams could be applied to questions of voice and horror in terms of love and desire. Thus, I shall end on a question: if, in terms of voice, horrors are confrontations with the unthinkable and unknown, then perhaps love and desire are vectors of hope, not fear, in there being other voices, equally lost, in the mist?

[5] Dolar's previous texts concerning voice come within *Gaze and Voice as Love Objects.*

Bibliography

Acharya, Sourya and Samarth Shukla. 'Mirror neurons: Enigma of the metaphysical modular brain'. *Journal of Natural Science, Biology and Medicine*. Vol. 3, No. 2, July–December (2012): 118–124. https://doi.org/10.4103/0976-9668.101878

Adams, Tristam. "Accelerations and speed limits: An essay on the vocal limits of semiocapitalism" *Journal of Interdisciplinary Voice Studies*, Vol 3, Issue 1, 2018.

Adorno, Theodor. *Essays on Music*, California: University of California Press, 2002.

Aickman, Robert. *The Wine-Dark Sea*. London, UK: Faber & Faber, 2014.

Aickman, Robert, ed. *The 6th Fontana Book of Great Ghost Stories*. London, UK: Fontana/Collins, 1974.

Anderson, John P. *Kafka's Last Pipes: The Burrow and Josephine The Singer, or the Mouse Folk*, Boca Raton, Florida, USA: Universal Publishers, 2016.

Anthon, Charles. *A Classical Dictionary: Containing Account of the Principal Proper Names Mentioned in Ancient Authors, and Intended to Elucidate All the Important Points Connected with the Geography, History, Biography, Mythology, and Fine Arts of the Greeks and Romans*, New York: Harper & Brothers, 1848.

Anzieu, Didier. *The Skin Ego*, New Haven and London: Yale University Press, 1989.

Ammer, Christine. *The American Heritage Dictionary of Idioms: American English Idiomatic Expressions and Phrases (2nd Revised Edition)*. USA: Houghton Mifflin Harcourt Publishing Company, 2018.

Aristotle. *De Anima (On the Soul)*. Translated by Hugh Lawson-Tancred. London, UK: Penguin, 1986.

T. Adams, *Horrors of a Voice (object a)*,
https://doi.org/10.1007/978-3-031-62050-8

Aristotle. *The Basic Works of Aristotle (Modern Library)*. Edited by Richard McKeon. New York, USA: The Modern Library, 2001.

Aristotle. *The History of Animals*. Translated by D'Arcy Wentworth Thompson. Adelaide, Australia: The University of Adelaide, 2015. https://ebooks.adelaide.edu.au/a/aristotle/history/complete.html

Aristotle. *Politics: A New Translation*. Translated by C.D.C. Reeve. Indianapolis/Cambridge, USA: Hackett Publishing, 2017.

Avenanti, A., Paluello, L. M., Bufalari, I., & Aglioti, S. M. "Stimulus-driven modulation of motor-evoked potentials during observation of others' pain." *Neuroimage*, 32 (2006): 316–324. https://doi.org/10.1016/j.neuroimage.2006.03.010

Azar, Beth. "How mimicry begat culture: Researchers from varied disciplines look to mirror neurons to explain many aspects of human evolution" *American Psychological Association*, October, 2005, Vol 36, No. 9. Accessed 10 August 2017. http://www.apa.org/monitor/oct05/mimicry.aspx

Baken, R. J. *Clinical Measurement of Speech and Voice*. London: Taylor and Francis Ltd, 1987.

Barratt, Emma L. and Nick J. Davis. "Autonomous Sensory Meridian Response (ASMR): a flow-like mental state." *Peer J*, March, 2015, Vol. 3. Accessed June 11, 2017. https://www.ncbi.nlm.nih.gov/pmc/articles/PMC4380153/

Barthes, Roland. *Image-Music-Text*, London: Fontana, 1977

Barthes, Roland. *Mythologies*, New York: The Noonday Press, 1991

Batson, C. Daniel. "These Things Called Empathy: Eight Related but Distinct Phenomena" in *The Social Neuroscience of Empathy*. Edited by J. Decety and W. Ickes. 3–15. Cambridge, MA: MIT Press, 2011.

Baum, Lyman Frank. *The Wonderful Wizard of Oz*. Feedbooks. Available at: http://www.feedbooks.com/book/197/the-wonderful-wizard-of-oz (Accessed 10 July 2016).

Bekker, de Charissa; Martha Merrow and David P. Hughes. "From Behavior to Mechanisms: An Integrative Approach to the Manipulation by a Parasitic Fungus (Ophiocordyceps unilateralis s.l.) of Its Host Ants (Camponotus spp.)" In *Integrative and Comparative Biology*, Volume 54, Issue 2, 1 July 2014, Pages 166–176. Accessed July 19, 2018. https://academic.oup.com/icb/article/54/2/166/2797855

Berardi, Franco. *Precarious Rhapsody: Semiocapitalism and the pathologies of the post-alpha generation*. London, UK: Minor Compositions, 2009.

Bergland, Christopher. "The Neuroscience of Speaking With Your Hands: Scientists discover why we gesticulate when speaking." *Psychology Today*, July 5, 2013. Accessed August 11, 2017. https://www.psychologytoday.com/blog/the-athletes-way/201307/the-neuroscience-speaking-your-hands

Berke, G.S. and Long, J.L. "Functions of the larynx and production of sounds" In *Handbook of Mammalian Vocalization: An Integrative Neuroscience Approach*

(Handbook of Behavioral Neuroscience). Edited by Brudzynski, S. 419–426. USA. Academic Press, 2010.

Bernhard, Thomas. *The Voice Imitator*. Translated by Kenneth J. Northcott. Chicago, USA: Chicago University Press: 1997.

Bester, Alfred. *The Demolished Man (SF Masterworks Series)*. London, UK: Gollancz, 1999.

Bradbury, Ray ed. *Timeless Stories for Today and Tomorrow*. New York, USA: Bantam Books, 1952.

Brennan, Teresa ed. *Between Feminism & Psychoanalysis*. Abingdon, UK, New York, USA: Routledge, 1989.

Brudzynski, Stefan, M ed. *Mammalian Vocalization: An Integrative Neuroscience Approach (Handbook of Behavioral Neuroscience)*. USA: Academic Press, 2010.

Butler, Shane. *The Ancient Phonograph (Zone Books)*. Cambridge, Massachusetts, USA: The MIT Press, 2015.

Burgess, Anthony. *A Clockwork Orange*. London, UK: Penguin Books, 1972.

Burgin, Victor; James Donald & Cora Kaplan. *Formations of Fantasy*. London/ New York: Routledge, 1986.

Burroughs, William. *The Soft Machine*. London, UK: Fourth Estate, 2010.

Burroughs, William. *The Ticket That Exploded*. London, UK: Penguin, 2014.

Calvino, Italo. "A King Listens" in *Under The Jaguar Sun (Penguin Modern Classics)*. London, UK: Penguin Books, 2009.

Campbell, Ramsey. *Dark Feasts: The World of Ramsey Campbell*. London, UK: Robinson Publishing, 1987.

Carr, L., Iacoboni, M., Dubeau, M. C., Mazziotta, J. C., & Lenzi, G. L. "Neural mechanisms of empathy in humans: A relay from neural systems for imitation to limbic areas." in *Proceedings of the National Academy of Sciences of the United States of America*, 100(9), 5497–5502. USA: National Academy of Science, May 2003. https://doi.org/10.1073/pnas.0935845100

Carroll, Lewis. *Through The Looking Glass, And What Alice Found There*. London, UK: Macmillan, 1980.

Caruth, Cathy. *Unclaimed Experience: Trauma, Narrative, and History*. Baltimore, Maryland, USA: Johns Hopkins University Press, 2016.

Cavarero, Adriana. *For More Than One Voice: Toward a Philosophy of Vocal Expression*. Translated by Paul A. Kottman. Stanford, California: Stanford University Press, 2005a.

Cavarero, Adriana. *Horrorism: Naming Contemporary Violence*. Translated by William McCuaig. New York, USA: Columbia University Press, 2005b.

Charlton, Benjamin D. "Why female deer like a stag to be a big noise in the forest". University of Sussex, June 6, 2007. Accessed April 12, 2017. http://www.sussex.ac.uk/newsandevents/pressrelease/media/media625.html

Charlton, Benjamin D., Reby, David and McComb, Karen. "Female red deer prefer the roars of larger males." in *Biology Letters,* Vol. 3, Issue 4 (2007) 382–386. London, UK. https://doi.org/10.1098/rsbl.2007.0244

Charlton, Benjamin D., Reby, David and McComb, Karen. "Female perception of size-related formant shifts in red deer, Cervus elaphus" in *Animal Behaviour* Vol.74, Issue 4, October (2007) 707–714. https://doi.org/10.1016/j.anbehav.2006.09.021.

Chion, Michel. *Audio-Vision: Sound on Screen.* Translated by Claudia Gorbman. New York, USA: Columbia University Press, 1994.

Chion, Michel. *The Voice in Cinema.* Translated by Claudia Gorbman. New York, USA: Columbia University Press, 1999.

'Choking Prevention and Rescue Tips' *National Safety Council.* Accessed April 2, 2019, https://www.nsc.org/home-safety/safety-topics/choking-suffocation

Choudhury, Suparna and Slaby, Jan eds. *Critical Neuroscience: A Handbook of the Social and Cultural Contexts of Neuroscience.* Chichester, Sussex, UK. Wiley-Blackwell, 2011.

Christ, Hans D., Iris Dressler, and Christine Peters, eds. *Acts of Voicing.* Stuttgart, Germany: Spector Books, 2015.

Chu, Jennifer, "Software Listens for Hints of Depression" *MIT Technology Review,* November 4, 2009, accessed July 20, 2017, https://www.technologyreview.com/s/416131/software-listens-for-hints-of-depression/

Connor, Steven. *Dumbstruck: A Cultural History of Ventriloquism.* Oxford, UK: Oxford University Press, 2001.

Connor, Steven. *Beyond Words: Sobs, Hums, Stutters and other Vocalizations.* London, UK: Reaktion Books, 2014.

Conrad, Joseph. *Heart of Darkness (Everyman's Library Classics).* New York, USA: Alfred A Knopf/Random House. 1993.

Cox, Michael and R. A. Gilbert, eds. *The Oxford Book of Ghost Stories.* Oxford, UK: Oxford University Press, 2008.

Dante, Alighieri. *Inferno: The Divine Comedy I (Penguin Classics).* Translated and edited by Robin Kirkpatrick. London, UK: Penguin Books, 2006.

Davies, Sam. "Glove, socks, zombies, puppets: The unheimlich maneuvers and undead metonyms of Michael Jackson" in *The Resistible Demise of Michael Jackson,* edited by Mark Fisher, 233–243. Winchester, UK: Zero Books, 2009.

Davis, Colin. "Hauntology, Spectres and Phantoms" in *French Studies,* Volume 59, Issue 3, 1 July 2005, Pages 373–379.

Dayal, Geeta, "Japanese Speech-Jamming Gun Designers Reveal Details, Inspiration" *Wired,* March 6, 2012. Accessed July 22, 2017. https://www.wired.com/2012/03/speech-jamming-gun-inspiration/

Deleuze, Gilles. *Cinema I: The Movement Image (Continuum Impacts).* London, UK: Continuum, 2005a.

Deleuze, Gilles. *Cinema II: The Time Image (Continuum Impacts)*. London, UK: Continuum, 2005b.
Deleuze, Gilles. *The Logic of Sense (Continuum Impacts)*. London, UK. Continuum, 2001.
Deleuze, Gilles and Guattari, Felix. *A Thousand Plateaus: Capitalism and Schizophrenia (Continuum Impacts)*. London, UK: Continuum, 2004.
Derrida, Jacques. *Cinders*. Translated by Ned Lukacher. Minnesota, Minneapolis, USA: University of Minnesota Press, 2014.
Derrida, Jacques. *Of Grammatology*. Translated by Gayatri Chakravorty Spivak. Baltimore, USA: The John Hopkins University Press, 1997.
Derrida, Jacques. *Points...: Interviews 1974–1994 (Meridian Crossing Aesthetics)*. Edited by Elisabeth Weber. Translated by Peggy Kamuf & Others. Stanford, California, USA: Stanford University Press, 1995.
Derrida, Jacques. *Speech and Phenomena: And Other Essays on Husserl's Theory of Signs*. Evanston, Illinois, USA: Northwestern University Press, 1973.
Derrida, Jacques. *The Animal That Therefore I Am (Perspectives in Continental Philosophy)*. Edited by Marie-Louise Mallet. Translated by David Wills. New York, USA: Fordham University Press, 2008.
Derrida, Jacques. *Voice and Phenomena: An Introduction to the Problem of the Sign in Husserl's Phenomenology*. Translated by Leonard Lawlor. Evanston, Illinois, USA: Northwestern University Press, 2011.
Descartes, René. *Meditations and Other Metaphysical Writings (Penguin Classics)*. Translated by Desmond M Clarke, London, England: Penguin, 2000.
Dews, Peter B. *Caffeine: Perspectives from Recent Research*. Berlin, Heidelberg, New York, Tokyo: Springer-Verlag, 1984.
Dick, Philip K. *Selected Stories of Phillip K Dick*. New York, USA: Houghton Mifflin Harcourt, 2013.
Dick, Philip K. *The Three Stigmata of Palmer Eldritch (SF Masterworks)*. London, UK: Gollancz, 2003.
Dick, Philip K. *Do Androids Dream of Electric Sheep?*. London, UK: Gollancz, 2007.
Dickens, Charles. *A Christmas Carol and Other Christmas Books (Everyman's Library Classics)*. New York, USA: Alfred A Knopf/Random House, 2009.
Dickens, Charles. *Great Expectations (Everyman's Library Classics)*. New York, USA: Alfred A Knopf/Random House. 1992.
Dickens, Charles. *The Signal Man and Other Ghost Stories*. Stroud, UK: Alan Sutton Publishing Ltd, 1990.
Dickens, Charles. *Supernatural Short Stories*. Richmond, UK: Alma Classics Ltd, 2012.
"Did Thriller Really Sell a Hundred Million Copies?," *New Yorker*, accessed April 2, 2019. https://www.newyorker.com/culture/culture-desk/did-thriller-really-sell-a-hundred-million-copies.

Dolar, Mladen. *A Voice and Nothing More (Short Circuits)*. Massachusetts, USA: MIT Press, 2006.

Dolar, Mladen. "The Object Voice" in *Gaze and Voice as Love Objects*, edited by Renata Salecl and Slavoj Žižek, 7–31. Durham and London, UK: Duke University Press, 1996.

Dolar, Mladen. "The Voice and the Stone: From Hegel to Beckett" in *Theory@ Buffalo*, Issue 12. edited by Gorlick, N. and Kerr, L.R. 2008.

Dolar, Mladen, "The burrow of sound" *Salt Online*. Accessed 12 May 2019. http://www.saltonline.org/media/files/232.pdf.

Dolar, Mladen. "His Master's Voice." *The Symptom*, 13. 2012. Edited by Jacques-Alain Miller. Accessed 20 July 2017. http://www.lacan.com/symptom13/his-masters.html.

Dolar, Mladen. "What's in a Voice? (Transkript)" 17 February 2014a. Transcribed by Kathrin Batko. Accessed 12 March 2018. http://philosovereign.blogspot.co.uk/2014/02/mladen-dolar-whats-in-voice-transkript.html.

Dolar, Mladen. *What's in a Name?* Edited by Janez Janša. Ljubljana, Slovenia: Aksioma—Institute for Contemporary Art, 2014b.

"Don't you understand trying to stammer?" *The Vox Lab*. Accessed July 21, 2017. http://thevoxlab.org/dont-you-understand-trying-to-stammer/

Du Maurier, Daphne. *Don't Look Now: Short Stories (Virago Modern Classics)*. London, UK: Virago, 2015.

Du Maurier, Daphne. *Rebecca (Virago Modern Classics)*. London, UK: Virago, 2003

Du Maurier, Daphne. *The Breaking Point*. London, UK: Victor Gollancz Ltd, 1971.

Dunbar, Robin. *Grooming, Gossip and the Evolution of Language*. London, UK: Faber & Faber, 1996.

Dunn, Leslie C. and Nancy A. Jones. *Embodied voices: Representing female vocality in western culture*. Cambridge, UK: Cambridge University Press, 1996.

Eidsheim, Nina Sun. *Sensing Sound: Singing & Listening as Vibrational Practice*. Durham and London, UK: Duke University Press, 2015.

Eidsheim, Nina Sun. *Voice as a technology of selfhood: towards an analysis of racialized timbre and vocal performance*. Ph.D UC San Diego, 2008.

Ellgring, Heiner and Klaus R. Scherer. "Vocal indicators of mood change in depression." *Journal of Nonverbal Behavior*. June 1996, Vol. 20, Issue 2, 83–110

Erickson, Robert. *Sound Structure in Music*. California, USA: University of California Press, 1975.

Ettinger, Bracha. The Matrixial Borderspace (Theory Out of Bounds). Minneapolis, USA: Minnesota University Press, 2006.

Fant, Gunnar. *Acoustic Theory of Speech Production*. The Hague, Netherlands: Mouton & Co, 1960.

Fisher, Mark. *The Weird and The Eerie*. London, UK: Repeater Books, 2016.

Fitch, W. Tecumseh "Comparative Vocal production in nonhuman mammals: Implications for the evolution of speech." In *The Evolutions of Language: Proceedings of the 3rd International Conference*, 102–103, 2000.

Freeman, John, ed. *Granta: The Magazine of New Writing, Vol 117: Horror*. Autumn 2011. London, UK: Granta, 2011.

Freud, Sigmund. *Complete Works*. Compiled by Ivan Smith, 2010. Accessed Jan. 10, 2019. https://www.valas.fr/IMG/pdf/Freud_Complete_Works.pdf

Freud, Sigmund. *Beyond the Pleasure Principle*. Connecticut, USA: Martino Publishing, 2009.

Freud, Sigmund. *The Interpretation of Dreams (The Penguin Freud Library Volume 4)*. Edited by Angela Richards. Translated by James Strachey. London, UK: Penguin Books, 1991.

Freud, Sigmund. *The Uncanny*. Translated by David McLintock. London, UK: Penguin Books, 2003.

Freud, Sigmund. *On Aphasia: A Critical Study*. London, UK: Literary Licensing, 2011.

Gallagher, Shaun. 'Scanning the Lifeworld: Toward a Critical Neuroscience of Action and Interaction' in *Critical Neuroscience: A Handbook of the Social and Cultural Contexts of Neuroscience*, edited by Suparna Choudhury and Jan Slaby, 85–110. Chichester, Sussex, UK: Wiley-Blackwell, 2011.

Gelder, Ken, ed. *The Horror Reader*. London, UK: Routledge, 2000.

Gilman, Sander L. "Jewishness Denied: Kafka's Tumor and "Ein Landarzt"" in *A Companion to the Works of Franz Kafka*. Edited by James Rolleston, 263–279. Rochester, NY and Woodbridge, Suffolk, UK: Camden House, 2002.

Goode, Lauren. "Deborah Landis, Designer of the Red Jacket Michael Jackson Wore in "Thriller"" *The Wall Street Journal*. June 30, 2009. https://blogs.wsj.com/speakeasy/2009/06/30/deborah-landis-designer-of-the-red-jacket-michael-jackson-wore-in-thriller/

Grimm, The Brothers. *The Original Folk & Fairy Tales of The Brothers Grimm*. Translated & Edited by Jack Zipes. Princeton, New Jersey, USA: Princeton University Press, 2014.

Guattari, Felix. *Chaosmosis: An ethico-aesthetic paradigm*. Indiana, USA: Indiana University Press, 1995.

Guzman, Maria J. "Grace Jones in One Man Show: Music and Culture" MA. College of Fine Arts of Ohio University, 2007.

Habermas, Jürgen. 'The Language Game of Responsible Agency and the Problem of Free Will: How can epistemic dualism be reconciled with ontological monism?' in *Philosophical Explorations*, Vol 10, No. 1, (2007): 13–50. https://doi.org/10.1080/13869790601170128.

Hardy, Thomas. *The Mayor of Casterbridge (Oxford World's Classics)*. Oxford, UK: Oxford University Press, 2008.

Hardy, Thomas. *The Supernatural Tales of Thomas Hardy*. Edited by Peter Haining. Slough, UK: W. Foulsham and Company Ltd, 1988.

Hatfield, Elaine; Lisamarie Bensman, Paul D. Thornton, Richard L. Rapson. 'New Perspectives on Emotional Contagion: A Review of Classic and Recent Research on Facial Mimicry and Contagion' *Interpersona: An International Journal on Personal Relationships*. Vol 8. No. 2 (2014). https://doi.org/10.5964/ijpr.v8i2.162

Hewitson, Owen. 'What Does Lacan Say About … The Signifier?' *LacanOnline.Com*, June 20, 2010. Accessed January 14, 2019. http://www.lacanonline.com/index/2010/06/what-does-lacan-say-about-the-signifier/

Hoffman, E. T. A. *The Sandman*. Commapress: Online Short Stories. Accessed July 7, 2017, http://commapress.co.uk/resources/online-short-stories/the-sandman

Homer. *The Odyssey (Oxford World's Classics)*. Translated by Walter Shewring. Oxford, UK: Oxford University Press, 2008.

Homer. *The Odyssey*. Translated by Samuel Butler, Based on public domain edition, revised by Timothy Power and Gregory Nagy. A.C. Fifield, London. 1900. Accessed December 18, 2018, http://www.perseus.tufts.edu/hopper/text?doc=urn:cts:greekLit:tlg0012.tlg002.perseus-eng2:1.1-1.1

Hooton, Christopher. 'Fabric review board actually considered lowering BPMs to get the kids off drugs,' *Independent*, Sept 7, 2016, https://www.independent.co.uk/arts-entertainment/music/news/fabric-review-board-actually-considered-lowering-bpms-to-get-the-kids-off-drugs-a7229511.html

Horowitz, Eli, Matthew Derby, and Kevin Moffett. *The Silent History*. London, UK: Jonathan Cape, 2014.

Ihde, Don. *Listening and Voice: Phenomenologies of Sound, Second Edition*. New York, USA: State University of New York Press, 2007.

Irigaray, Luce. "The gesture in psychoanalysis" Translated by Elizabeth Gould, in *Between Feminism & Psychoanalysis*, ed. Teresa Brennan, 127–138. Abingdon, UK, New York, USA: Routledge, 1989.

Irigaray, Luce. *The Forgetting of Air in Martin Heidegger*. Translated by Mary Beth Mader. London, UK: The Athlone Press, 1999.

Jackson, Shirley. *The Sundial (Penguin Modern Classics)*. London, UK: Penguin, 2014.

Jakubowski, K. and Finkel, S. and Stewart, L. and Mullensiefen, D. 'Dissecting an earworm: Melodic features and song popularity predict involuntary musical imagery.' *Psychology of Aesthetics, Creativity, and the Arts*. Vol 11 (2), May 2017, 122–135.

Jarman-Ivens, Freya. "I Feel a Song Coming on: Vocal Identification and Modern Subjectivity". *Anglistica: Special Issue—Voicings*, edited by Serena Guarrancino and Marina Vitale (2010): 45–57. Access April 18 2017: http://sebinaol.

unior.it/sebina/repository/catalogazione/documenti/2009%2013.2%20 Anglistica%20Guarracino%20Vitale.pdf

Jeans, James H. *Science & Music*. New York, USA: Dover Publications, 1968.

Jefferson, Margo. *On Michael Jackson*. New York, USA. Vintage Books/Random House, 2007.

Joshi, S. T, ed. *American Supernatural Tales (Penguin Classics)*. New York, USA: Penguin Books, 2007a.

Joshi, S. T, ed. *Icons of Horror and the Supernatural: An Encyclopedia of Our Worst Nightmares, Volumes 1 & 2*. Westport, Connecticut, USA: Greenwood Press, 2007b.

Kafka, Joseph. *Collected Stories (Everyman's Library Classics)*. Translated by Willa and Edwin Muir. Edited by Gabriel Josipovici. New York, USA: Alfred A. Knopf, 1993.

Kafka, Joseph. "Josephine the Songstress or The Mouse Folk" available at http://www.kafka.org/pdfdocuments/JosephineMY.pdf accessed 8 August, 2017.

Kahn, Douglas. *Noise, Water, Meat: A History of Sound in the Arts*. Cambridge, Massachusetts, USA: The MIT Press, 2001.

Kane, Brian. *Sound Unseen: Acousmatic Sound in Theory and Practice*. Oxford, UK: Oxford University Press, 2014.

Kane, Reid. "The King of Pop's two bodies, or Thriller as allegory' in *The Resistible Demise of Michael Jackson*, edited by Mark Fisher, 233–243. Winchester, UK: Zero Books, 2009.

Karpf, Anne. *The Human Voice: A Story of Remarkable Talent*. London, UK: Bloomsbury, 2007.

Keetley, Dawn and Angela Tenga (eds.). *Plant Horror: Approaches to the Monstrous Vegetal in Fiction and Film*. London, UK: Palgrave Macmillan, 2017.

King, Stephen. *The Shining; Carrie; Misery: Three Novels In One Volume*. London, UK: Chancellor Press, 1992.

King, Stephen. 'Stephen King on songs that stick in your head' *Entertainment Weekly*. April 17, 2009. Accessed June 6, 2018. http://www.ew.com/article/2009/04/17/stephen-king-songs-stick-your-head/

Kreiman, Jody and Siditis, Diana. *Foundations of Voice Studies: An Interdisciplinary Approach to Voice Production and Perception*. Chichester, UK: Wiley-Blackwell, 2013.

Kolker, Robert. (ed.) *Stanley Kubrick's 2001: A Space Odyssey: New Essays*. New York, USA: Oxford University Press, 2006.

Konnikova, Maria. "Anatomy of an Earworm" *The New Yorker*, February 28, 2014. Accessed 6 June 2018. https://www.newyorker.com/tech/elements/anatomy-of-an-earworm

Koelb, Clayton. "Kafka Imagines His Readers: The Rhetoric of "Josefine die Sängerin" and "Der Bau"" in *A Companion to the Works of Franz Kafka*. Edited by James Rolleston, 347–360. Rochester, NY and Woodbridge, Suffolk, UK: Camden House, 2002.

LaBelle, Brandon. *Lexicon of the Mouth: Poetics and Politics of Voice and The Oral Imaginary.* New York, USA/London, UK: Bloomsbury Academic, 2014.

Lacan, Jacques. *Television: A Challenge to the Psychoanalytical Establishment.* Translated by Denis Hollier, Rosalind Krauss, Annette Michelson and Jeffrey Mehlman. Edited by Joan Copjec. New York, USA: W. W. Norton & Company, 1990.

Lacan, Jacques. *The Seminar of Jacques Lacan: Book II The Ego in Freud's Theory and in the Technique of Psychoanalysis 1954–1955.* Translated by Sylvana Tomaselli, Edited by Jacques-Alain Miller. New York, USA: W.W. Norton and Company, 1991.

Lacan, Jacques. *The Psychoses: The Seminar of Jacques Lacan Book III 1955–1965.* Translated by Russell Grigg. Edited by Jacques-Alain Miller. London, UK: Routledge, 1993.

Lacan, Jacques. *The Seminar of Jacques Lacan: Book XI The Four Fundamental Concepts of Psychoanalysis.* Translated by Alan Sheridan, Edited by Jacques-Alain Miller. New York, USA: W.W. Norton and Company, 1998.

Lacan, Jacques. "The Subversion of the Subject and the Dialectic of Desire" in *Écrits: A Selection.* Translated and Edited by Alan Sheridan. London: Tavistock/Routledge, 1977. 293–325.

Lacan, Jacques. *Écrits: A Selection.* Translated and Edited by Alan Sheridan. London: Routledge, 1989.

Lacan, Jacques. *The Seminar of Jacques Lacan: Book VI Desire and its Interpretation.* Translated by Cormac Gallagher. Accessed January 14, 2019a. http://www.lacaninireland.com/web/wp-content/uploads/2010/06/THE-SEMINAR-OF-JACQUES-LACAN-VI.pdf

Lacan, Jacques. *The Seminar of Jacques Lacan: Book VIII Transference.* Translated by Cormac Gallagher. Accessed 19 January 2019b. https://www.valas.fr/IMG/pdf/THE-SEMINAR-OF-JACQUES-LACAN-VIII_le_transfert.pdf

Lagaay, Alice. "Between Sound and Silence: Voice in the History of Psychoanalysis". *E-pisteme* Vol. 1, 2008. 53–62. ISSN 1756-8226. Accessed 30 July 2017. http://research.ncl.ac.uk/e-pisteme/issues/issue01/contents/e-pisteme%20Vol.%201(1)%20-%20Alice%20Lagaay%20(Full%20Text).pdf

Lanchester, John. *The Debt to Pleasure.* London, UK: Picador, 1997.

Land, Nick. *Fanged Noumena: Collected Writings 1987–2007.* Falmouth, UK: Urbanomic/Sequence Press, 2011.

Landis, John. "John Landis on the making of Michael Jackson's Thriller: 'I was adamant he couldn't look too hideous'," *The Guardian*, August 31, 2017, accessed March 20, 2019, https://www.theguardian.com/film/2017/aug/31/john-landis-on-the-making-of-michael-jacksons-thriller-i-was-adamant-he-couldnt-look-too-hideous

Lastra, James. *Sound Technology and the American Cinema: Perception, Representation, Modernity*. New York, USA: Columbia University Press, 2000.

Lazzarato, Maurizio. *Signs and Machines: Capitalism and the Production of Subjectivity (Semiotext(e) Foreign Agents Series)*. Cambridge, Massachusetts, USA: The MIT Press, 2014.

Ligotti, Thomas. *Songs of a Dead Dreamer and Grimscribe*. London, UK: Penguin Classics, 2015.

Ligotti, Thomas. *The Spectral Link*. Burton, USA: Subterranean Press, 2014.

Ligotti, Thomas. *Teatro Grottesco*. London, UK: Virgin Books Ltd, 2008.

Ligotti, Thomas. *The Conspiracy Against the Human Race: A Contrivance of Horror*. New York, USA: Hippocampus Press, 2010.

"Limus", *Wikipedia*, accessed June 2, 2018, https://en.wiktionary.org/wiki/limus

Luckhurst, Roger. *The Shining (BFI Film Classics)*. London, UK: Palgrave Macmillan, 2013.

Lyotard, Francois. *Libidinal Economy*. Translated by Iain Hamilton Grant. London, UK. Continuum, 2004.

M. Cara. "Speech Jammers: When you need someone to just stop talking." *Audify: Hearing. Technology. Life*, March 1, 2017. Accessed July 21, 2017.

Mackay, Robin, ed. *Collapse: Philosophical Research and Development, Vol IV*. Falmouth, UK: Urbanomic, 2008.

MacKendrick, Karmen. *The Matter of Voice: Sensual Surroundings*. New York, USA. Fordham University Press, 2016.

Magnani, Lorenzo. *Understanding Violence, The Intertwining of Morality, Religion and Violence: A Philosophical Stance*. Berlin-Heidelberg, Germany: Springer-Verlag, 2011.

Manninen, Sandra; Lauri Tuominen, Robin I. Dunbar, Tomi Karjalainen, Jussi Hirvonen, Eveliina Arponen, Riitta Hari, Iiro P. Jääskeläinen, Mikko Sams and Lauri Nummenmaa. "Social Laughter Triggers Endogenous Opioid Release in Humans", *Journal of Neuroscience*, Volume 37 Issue 25, June (2017): 6125–6131. https://doi.org/10.1523/JNEUROSCI.0688-16.2017

McCauley, Kirby ed. *Dark Forces: New Stories of Suspense and Supernatural Horror*. London, UK: MacDonald Futura Publishers, 1980.

McCullough Campbell, Stephanie and Elizabeth Hellmuth Margulis. 'Catching an Earworm Through Movement' *Journal of New Music Research*, Vol. 44, Issue 4, 2015. 347–358.

Mercer, Kobena. "Monster Metaphors: Notes on Michael Jackson's *Thriller*" in *Sound and Vision: The Music Video Reader*, edited by Simon Frith, Andrew Goodwin and Lawrence Grossberg. London, UK: Routledge, 1993. 26–43.

Migone, Christof. *Sonic Somatic: Performances of the Unsound Body (Errant Bodies Press Audio Issues Vol. 5)*. Los Angeles/Berlin: Errant Bodies Press, 2012.

Millot, Catherine. *Life With Lacan*. Translated by Andrew Brown. Cambridge, UK: Polity Press, 2018.

Mills, Matthew and Stoneham, Gillie. *The Voice Book for Trans and Non-Binary People: A Practical Guide to Creating and Sustaining Authentic Voice and Communication*. London, UK: Jessica Kingsley Publishers, 2017.

McGettigan, Caroline, Walsh, E; Jessop, R ; Agnew, Z. K.; Sauter, D.A.; Warren, J.E.; Scott, S. K., "Individual Differences in Laughter Perception Reveal Roles for Mentalizing and Sensorimotor Systems in the Evaluation of Emotional Authenticity". *Cerebral Cortex,* Volume 25, Issue 1, January (2015): 246–257. https://doi.org/10.1093/cercor/bht227. Access April 17, 2017. https://academic.oup.com/cercor/article/25/1/246/371629/Individual-Differences-in-Laughter-Perception

Meillassoux, Quentin. *The Number and the Siren: A Decipherment of Mallarmé's Coup De Dés*. Falmouth, UK/New York, USA: Urbanomic/Sequence Press, 2012.

Merleau-Ponty, Maurice. *Phenomenology of Perception*. Translated by Colin Smith. London/New York: Routledge, 2005.

"Michael Jackson's Thriller," *Wikipedia*, accessed March 4, 2019, https://en.wikipedia.org/wiki/Michael_Jackson%27s_Thriller_(music_video)

"Michael Jackson, "Thriller"," *1980s Music Video Closet*, accessed March 19, 2019, https://videoclosetblog.wordpress.com/michael-jackson-thriller/

Morell, Rebecca. "Speech lab: Unlocking the secrets of the human voice." BBC News, Science & Environment, April 24, 2012. Accessed July 20, 2017. http://www.bbc.co.uk/news/science-environment-17790595

Morill, Ryan J. et al. "Monkey lipsmacking develops like the human speech rhythm" in Developmental Science, 2012. 1–12. Accessed 11 August 2017. http://old.unipr.it/arpa/mirror/pubs/pdffiles/ferrari/2012/2012_Morrill_etal_DevSci.pdf

Moses, Paul J. *The Voice of Neurosis*. New York, USA: Grune & Stratton, 1954

Mowitt, John. *Sounds: The Ambient Humanities*. Oakland, California, USA: University of California Press, 2015.

Mowitt, John. *Radio: Essays in Bad Reception*. Berkeley, California, USA: University of California Press, 2011.

Mowitt, John. 'Tune Stuck in the Head' *Parallax*, Vol. 12, Issue 4 (2006): 12–25 https://doi.org/10.1080/13534640600955976

Neumark, Norie; Ross Gibson and Theo van Leeuwen, eds. *Voice: Vocal Aesthetics in Digital, Arts and Media*. Cambridge, Massachusetts/London, England: The MIT Press. 2010.

Nesbit, E. *Horror Stories*. London, UK: Penguin/Random House, 2016.

Nietzsche, Friedrich. *Daybreak: Thoughts on the Prejudices of Morality (Cambridge Texts in the History of Philosophy)*. Edited by Maudemarie Clark and Brian Leiter. Cambridge, UK: Cambridge University Press, 1997.

Nietzsche, Friedrich. *The Birth of Tragedy And Other Writings (Cambridge Texts in the History of Philosophy)*. Edited by Raymoud Geuss and Ronald Speirs. Translated by Ronald Speirs. Cambridge, UK: Cambridge University Press, 2007.

'Number of choking deaths by place of occurrence and age, registered in England and Wales, 2014 to 2016,' *Office for National Statistics*, accessed April 3, 2019. https://www.ons.gov.uk/peoplepopulationandcommunity/birthsdeathsandmarriages/deaths/adhocs/007747numberofchokingdeathsbyplaceofoccurrenceandageregisteredinenglandandwales2014to2016

"On A Soundstage All Along," *TV Tropes*, accessed September 10, 2018. http://tvtropes.org/pmwiki/pmwiki.php/Main/OnASoundstageAllAlong

Ovid. *Metamorphoses (Oxford World's Classics)*. Translated by A.D. Melville. Oxford, UK: Oxford University Press, 2008.

Pawley, Alisun and Daniel Müllensiefen. 'The Science of Singing Along: A Quantitative Field Study on Sing-Along Behavior in the North of England.' in *Music Perception: An Interdisciplinary Journal*. Vol 30, No. 2 (2012) 129–146. University California Press. https://doi.org/10.1525/mp.2012.30.2.129

Pettman, Dominic. *Sonic Intimacy: Voice, Species, Technics (Or, How to Listen to the World)*. Stanford, California, USA: Stanford University Press, 2017.

"Phlegmatic," *Merriam-Webster*, accessed June 2, 2018, https://www.merriam-webster.com/dictionary/phlegmatic

Pinker, Steven. *The Language Instinct*. London, UK: Penguin Books, 1994.

Plato. *Symposium and Phaedrus*. Translated by Tom Griffith. New York, USA: Alfred A Knopf/Random House, 2000.

Plato. *The Collected Dialogues of Plato (Bollingen Series)*. Translated by Lane Cooper. Edited by Edith Hamilton and Huntington Cairns. Princeton, New Jersey, USA: Princeton University Press, 1961.

Plato. *The Republic*. Translated by Desmond Lee. London, UK: Penguin, 2007.

Plato. *Plato: Complete Works*. Edited by John M. Cooper. Indianapolis, Indiana, USA: Hackett Publishing Company, 1997.

Poe, Edgar Allen. *The Black Cat: And Other Stories*. Cologne, Germany: Könemann, 1995.

Poe, Edgar Allen. *Tales, Poems and Essays*. London and Glasgow, UK: Collins, 1952.

"Principles of Audio-Psycho-Phonology". *Atlantis-VZW*. Accessed June 20, 2017. http://www.atlantis-vzw.com/app-bases.html

Prochazkova, Eliska, Mariska E. Kret. 'Connecting minds and sharing emotions through mimicry: A neurocognitive model of emotional contagion'. *Neuroscience and Biobehavioral Reviews*. Vol. 80, September (2017): 99–114. https://doi.org/10.1016/j.neubiorev.2017.05.013

Propp, Vladimir. *Theory and History of Folklore*. Translated by Ariadna Y. Martin and Richard P Martin. Edited by Anatoly Liberman. Minneapolis, USA: University of Minnesota Press, 1997.

Prud'homme, Johanne and Lyne Légaré, "Semanalysis. Engendering the Formula," *Signo: Theoretical Semiotics on the Web*, accessed April 10, 2019, http://www.signosemio.com/kristeva/semanalysis.asp

Rabaté, Jean-Michel. *The Cambridge Companion to Lacan*. Cambridge, UK: Cambridge University Press, 2003.

Rank, Otto. *The Trauma of Birth*. Connecticut, USA: Martino Publishing, 2010.

Rée, Jonathan. *I See A Voice: Language, Deafness & The Senses—A Philosophical History*. Hammersmith, London, UK: HarperCollins, 1999.

Reik, Theodor. *The Haunting Melody: Psychoanalytic Experiences in Life and Music*. New York, USA: Farrar, Straus and Young, 1953.

Reynolds, Simon. *Audio Culture: Readings in Modern Music*, edited by Christopher Cox and Daniel Warner, 55–59. New York/London: Bloomsbury Academic, 2007.

Roudinesco, Élisabeth. *Jacques Lacan*. Translated by Barbara Bray. New York, USA: Colombia University Press, 1997.

Roudinesco, Élisabeth. *Lacan: In Spite of Everything*. Translated by Gregory Elliot. London, UK: Verso, 2014.

Royle, Nicholas. *The Uncanny*. Manchester, UK. Manchester University Press. 2003.

"Sacculina carcini". *Animal Diversity Web*. Accessed January 20, 2019. https://animaldiversity.org/accounts/Sacculina_carcini/

Sacido-Romero, Jorge and Sylvia Mieszkowski. *Sound Effects: The Object Voice in Fiction*. Leiden, The Netherlands: Koninklijke Brill/ Rodopi, 2015.

Sacks, Oliver. *Musicophilia: Tales of Music and the Brain*. New York/Toronto: Alfred A. Knopf, 2007.

Salecl, Renata and Slavoj Žižek eds. *Gaze and Voice as Love Objects*. Durham and London, UK: Duke University Press. 1996.

Scarry, Elaine. *The Body In Pain: The Making and Unmaking of the World*. Oxford, UK: Oxford University Press, 1985.

Schafer, R. Murray. *The Soundscape: Our Sonic Environment and the Tuning of the World*. Rochester, USA: Destiny Books, 1994.

Schneider, Steven Jay, ed. *Horror Film and Psychoanalysis: Freud's Worst Nightmare*. Cambridge, UK: Cambridge University Press, 2004.

Schnupp, Jan; Israel Nelken and Andrew King, eds. *Auditory Neuroscience: Making Sense of Sound*. Cambridge, Massachusetts, USA: The MIT Press, 2012.

Schwartz, Hillel. *Making Noise: From Babel to the Big Bang & Beyond (Zone Books)*. Brooklyn, New York/Cambridge, Massachusetts, USA/London, UK: Zone Books/The MIT Press, 2011.

Sconce, Jeffrey. *Haunted Media: Electronic Presence from Telegraphy to Television (Console-ing Passions)*. Durham and London, UK: Duke University Press, 2000.

Scott, Sophie. "The Science of Laughter" in *BBC Health*, September 11, 2016. Accessed 17 April 2017. http://www.bbc.co.uk/news/health-37311320.

Scott, Sophie; Lavan, Nadine; Chen, Sinead and McGettigan, Caroline "The Social Life of Laughter". *Trends in Cognitive Neuroscience*, Volume 18, No. 12, December, 2014. 618–620 doi: https://doi.org/10.1016/j.tics.2014.09.002.

Scott, Sophie. "Laughter—the ordinary and the extraordinary". *The Psychologist*, April 2013. Accessed April 17, 2017. https://thepsychologist.bps.org.uk/volume-26/edition-4/laughter-ordinary-and-extraordinary.

Schaeffer, Pierre, "Acousmatics" in *Audio Culture: Readings in Modern Music*, edited by Christopher Cox and Daniel Warner, 76–81. New York/London: Bloomsbury Academic, 2007.

Schaeffer, Pierre. "Solfrege de l'objet Sonore" *UbuWeb Papers*. Accessed January 29, 2019. http://www.ubu.com/papers/schaefer_solfege.pdf

Schnable, Tom. "Rhythm Planet: Coltrane, Nicolas Slonimsky, Modal Music and Trance". *KCRW*. June 15, 2011. Accessed 6 July 2018. http://blogs.kcrw.com/music/2011/06/coltrane-nicolas-slonimsky-modal-music-and-trance/

"Seirênas". *Suda Online: Byzantine Lexicography*. Accessed December 8, 2018. http://www.stoa.org/solbin//search.pl?search_method=QUERY&login=&enlogin=&searchstr=sigma,280&field=adlerhw_gr&db=REAL

Silverman, Kaja. *The Acoustic Mirror: The Female Voice in Psychoanalysis and Cinema*. Bloomington and Indianapolis, USA: Indiana University Press, 1988.

Singer T, Seymour B, O'Doherty J, Kaube H, Dolan RJ, Frith CD. "Empathy for pain involves the affective but not sensory components of pain". *Science*, Vol. 303, Issue 5661 (2004): 1157–1162. https://doi.org/10.1126/science.1093535.

Sjogren, Britta. *Into the Vortex: Female Voice and Paradox in Film*. Urbana and Chicago, USA: University of Illinois Press, 2006.

Skipper, Jeremy I et al. "Speech-associated gestures, Broca's area, and the human mirror system" in Brain and Language, Vol 101, Issue 3, June 2007, 260–277. Accessed 10 August 2017. http://www.sciencedirect.com/science/article/pii/S0093934X07000442?via%3Dihub

"Slime," *Etymology Online*, accessed June 2, 2018, https://www.etymonline.com/word/slime

Slonimsky, Nicolas. *Thesaurus of Scales and Melodic Patterns*. New York, USA: Schirmer Books, 1975.

Sloterdijk, Peter. *Terror from the Air (Semiotext(e) Foreign Agents Series)*. Translated by Amy Patton and Steve Corcoran. Cambridge, Mass and London: MIT Press, 2009.

Sloterdijk, Peter. *Bubbles: (Spheres Volume 1: Microspherology) (Semiotext(e) Foreign Agents Series)*. Translated by Wieland Hoban. Cambridge, Mass and London: MIT Press, 2011.

Spadoni, Robert. *Uncanny Bodies: The Coming of Sound Film and Origins of the Horror Genre*. California, USA: University of California Press, 2007.

"Species of the week: The parasitic barnacle Sacculina" Royal Society of Biology Blog. Accessed January 20, 2019. https://blog.rsb.org.uk/sacculina-parasite/

Sterne, Jonathan. *The Audible Past: Cultural Origins of Sound Reproduction*. Durham and London, UK: Duke University Press, 2003.

Sterne, Jonathan. *The Sound Studies Reader*. Oxford, UK: Routledge, 2012.

Stewart, L., Müllensiefen, D., Finkel, S. and Jakubowski, K. "Dissecting an Earworm: Melodic Features and Song Popularity Predict Involuntary Musical Imagery" in *Psychology of Aesthetics, Creativity and the Arts*. Vol. 11, No. 2, 2017, 122–135. *American Psychological Association*. https://doi.org/10.1037/aca0000090

Stubbs, David. "The "King" is dead; long live everything else" in *The Resistible Demise of Michael Jackson*, edited by Mark Fisher, 69–80. Winchester, UK: Zero Books, 2009.

Summers, Montague, ed. *The Supernatural Omnibus: Volume 1: Hauntings and Horror*. Aylesbury, UK: Penguin, 1976.

Swales, Stephanie S. *Perversion: A Lacanian Psychoanalytical Approach to the Subject*. New York, USA: Routledge, 2012.

Tasso, Torquato. *The Liberation of Jerusalem (Oxford World Classics)*. Translated by Max Wickert. Oxford, UK: The Oxford University Press, 2009

Tennyson, Alfred. "The Voyage of Maeldune". *Words*. Accessed December 14, 2018. https://www.telelib.com/authors/T/TennysonAlfred/verse/ballads/maeldune.html

Titze, I.R. *Principles of Voice Production*, Boston, USA: Allyn & Bacon, 1994

Thacker, Eugene. *In the Dust of this Planet: Horror of Philosophy Vol. 1*. Winchester, UK: Zero Books, 2011.

Thacker, Eugene. *After Life*. Chicago, USA: Chicago University Press, 2010.

Thacker, Eugene. "Cryptobiologies" in *Artnodes*, Issue 6, Barcelona, Spain: Universiat Oberta de Catalunya: 2006. Available at *Posthuman Destinies: Science, Culture and Integral Yoga*. Accessed July 19, 2018. http://www.sciy.org/?p=5631

Thomas, Erik R, ed. *Sociophonetics: An Introduction*. Basingstoke, UK: Palgrave Macmillan, 2011.

Tomatis, A. Alfred. *The Ear and Language*. Ontario, Canada: Moulin Publishing, 1996.

Tomatis, A. Alfred. *The Ear and the Voice*. Translated by Roberta Prada and Pierre Sollier. Lanham, Maryland, USA: The Scarecrow Press, 2005.

Tomlinson, Gary. *A Million Years of Music: The Emergence of Human Modernity (Zone Books)*. Cambridge, Massachusetts, USA: The MIT Press, 2015.

Tompkins, Dave. *How to Wreck a Nice Beach: The Vocoder World War II to Hip-Hop: The Machine Speaks*. Brooklyn, New York, USA: Melville House Publishing, 2011.

Toop, David. *Sinister Resonance: The Mediumship of the Listener.* London, UK/ New York, USA: Continuum, 2010.

Trigg, Dylan. *The Thing: A Phenomenology of Horror.* Winchester, UK: Zero Books, 2014.

Twain, Mark. *The Best Short Stories of Mark Twain (Modern Library Classics).* New York, USA. Modern Library/Random House, 2004.

Van Thal, Herbert, ed. *The Fourth Pan Book of Horror Stories.* London, UK: Pan Books, 1963

Van Thal, Herbert, ed. *The 12th Pan Book of Horror Stories.* London, UK: Pan Books, 1971.

Van Thal, Herbert, ed. *The 13th Pan Book of Horror Stories.* London, UK: Pan Books, 1972.

Vanheule, Stijn. *The Subject of Psychosis: A Lacanian Perspective.* London, UK: Palgrave Macmillan, 2011.

Vernallis, Carol. *Unruly Media: Youtube, Music Video, and The New Digital Cinema.* New York, USA: Oxford University Press, 2013.

Vasse, Denis. *L'ombilic et la voix: Deux enfants en analyse.* Paris, France: Editions du Seuil, 1974.

Virno, Paolo. *When The Word Becomes Flesh: Language and Human Nature (Semiotext(e) Foreign Agents Series).* Cambridge, Massachusetts, USA: The MIT Press, 2015.

Voruz, Véronique and Bogdan Wolf, eds. *The Later Lacan: An Introduction (SUNY series in Psychoanalysis and Culture).* Albany, New York, USA: State University of New York Press, 2007.

Wallin, Nils L., Björn Merker, and Steven Brown, eds. The Origins of Music. Cambridge, Massachusetts and London, England: MIT Press, 2000.

Warren, Jane E. et al. "Positive Emotions Preferentially Engage an Auditory-Motor "Mirror" System" in *The Journal of Neuroscience*, December 13, 2006. 13067–13075

Weber, Samuel. *The Legend of Freud (Expanded Edition).* Minnesota, USA: Stanford University Press, 2000.

Welsh, Louise, ed. *Ghost: 100 Stories to read with the lights on.* London, UK: Head of Zeus Ltd, 2015.

Weed, Elizabeth and Ellen Rooney eds. *The Sense of Sound (differences: A Journal of Feminist Cultural Studies).* Vol. 22, Issue 2–3. Durham, NC, USA: Duke University Press, 2011.

Weiss, Allen S. *Phantasmic Radio.* Durham, USA and London, UK: Duke University Press, 1995.

White, E. B. 'The Supremacy of Uruguay' in *Timeless Stories for Today and Tomorrow,* edited by Ray Bradbury. 200–203. New York, USA: Bantam Books, 1952. Originally published in *The New Yorker*, November 25, 1933. 18.

Wolf, Bogdan. *Lacanian Coordinates: From the Logic of the Signifier to the Paradoxes of Guilt and Desire*. London, UK: Karnac Books, 2015.

Woodward, Ben. *Slime Dynamics*. Winchester, UK: Zero Books, 2012. "Worm," Dictionary.com, accessed April 6, 2018. http://www.dictionary.com/browse/wormlike

"Wormlike," Merriam-Webster, accessed 6 April 2018, https://www.merriam-webster.com/dictionary/wormlike

"Worm-like," The Free Dictionary, accessed 7 April 2018, https://www.thefreedictionary.com/worm-like

Wray, Alison, ed. *The Transition to Language (Oxford Studies in the Evolution of Language)*, Oxford, UK: Oxford University Press, 2002.

"The Wriggly History of 'Earworm': I just can't get you out of my head". *Merriam-Webster, Word History*. Accessed June 6, 2018. https://www.merriam-webster.com/words-at-play/earworm-meaning-origin

Wyndham, John. *The Day of the Triffids (Penguin Modern Classics)*, London, England: Penguin, 2000.

Young, Rob, ed. *Undercurrents: The Hidden Wiring of Modern Music*. London, UK/New York, USA: Continuum, 2002.

Zanatta, Marcello. 'Voice as Difference in Aristotelian Zoology' in *Journal of Ancient Philosophy* Vol. 7, No. 1 (2013): 1–18: https://doi.org/10.11606/issn.1981-9471.v7i1p1-18

Žižek, Slavoj. *Less Than Nothing: Hegel and the Shadow of Dialectical Materialism*. London, UK: Verso, 2012.

Žižek, Slavoj. 'Preface to the New Edition: Why Lacan is not a Heideggerian' in *The Ticklish Subject: The Absent Centre of Political Ontology*. London, UK: Verso, 2008a. Available at: https://sites.google.com/site/psychoanalyticrecordings/home/resources/why-lacan-is-not-a-heideggerian

Žižek, Slavoj. *How to Read Lacan (How to Read)*. London, UK: Granta Books, 2006.

Žižek, Slavoj. *Interrogating the Real: Selected Writings*. London, UK: Continuum, 2005.

Žižek, Slavoj. "I Hear You With My Eyes". In *Gaze and Voice as Love Objects*, edited by Renata Salecl and Slavoj Žižek, 90–126. Durham and London, UK: Duke University Press. 1996.

Žižek, Slavoj. "Language, Violence and Non-Violence" In *International Journal of Žižek Studies*, Vol. 2, No. 3 (2008b): 1–12.

Žižek, Slavoj and Mladen Dolar. *Opera's Second Death*. New York, USA: Routledge, 2002.

Filmography

Alien Resurrection. Digital File. Directed by Jean-Pierre Jeunet. USA: Brandywine Productions/Twentieth Century Fox, 1997

An American Werewolf In London. Digital File. Directed by John Landis. UK/USA: PolyGram Filmed Entertainment/Lycanthrope Films, 1981

Battlestar Galactica. DVD. Directed by Various. USA: British Sky Broadcasting (BSkyB); David Eick Productions; NBC Universal Television (2004–2007); R&D TV; Stanford Pictures (II); Universal Media Studios (UMS) (2007–2009)

Blade Runner. Digital File. Directed by Ridley Scott. USA, Hong Kong, UK: Ladd Company, The; Shaw Brothers (in association with) (as Sir Run Run Shaw); Warner Bros. (through: A Warner Communications Company) (as Warner Bros.); Blade Runner Partnership (Jerry Perenchio and Bud Yorkin present), 1982

Hulk. Digital File. Directed By Ang Lee. USA: Universal Pictures (presents) (An Ang Lee Film); Marvel Enterprises (in association with); Valhalla Motion Pictures (as A Valhalla Motion Pictures/Good Machine Production); Good Machine (as A Valhalla Motion Pictures/Good Machine Production), 2003.

The Fly. Digital File. Directed by David Cronenberg. USA, UK, Canada: SLM Production Group; Brooksfilms, 1986

Thriller. Digital File. Directed by John Landis. USA: Optimum Productions, 1982a.

Wolf. Digital File. Directed by Mike Nichols. USA: Colombia Pictures Corporation, 1994.

White Noise. Digital File. Directed by Geoffrey Sax. UK, Canada, USA: Universal Pictures (presents); Gold Circle Films (presents); White Noise UK Ltd.; Brightlight Pictures; Endgame Entertainment (in association with); Corus (in association with); Movie Network, The (TMN) (in association with); Province of British Columbia Film Incentive BC (with the participation of); Canadian Film or Video Production Tax Credit (CPTC) (with the assistance of), 2005.

Jacobs Ladder. Digital File. Directed by Adrian Lyne. USA: Carolco Pictures, 1990.

The Forgotten. Digital File. Directed by Joseph Ruben. USA: Revolution Studios; Jinks/Cohen Company; Visual Arts Entertainment, 2004.

The Mask. Digital File. Directed by Chuck Russell (as Charles Russell). USA: New Line Cinema; Dark Horse Entertainment, 1994.

The Shining. Digital File. Directed by Stanley Kubrick. UK/USA: Warner Brothers/Hawk Films, 1980.

Whisper. Digital File. Directed by Stewart Hendler. USA, Canada: Universal Pictures (presents); Gold Circle Films (presents); H2F Entertainment; Deacon Entertainment; Yukon Film Incentive Program (produced with the participation of) (as Yukon Film Incentives Program); Province of British Columbia Production Services Tax Credit (produced with the participation of); Canadian

Film or Video Production Tax Credit (CPTC) (produced with the participation of), 2007.

The Conversation. Digital File. Directed by Francis Ford Coppola. USA: The Directors Company (presents); The Coppola Company (as A Coppola Company Production); American Zoetrope (through the facilities of); Paramount Pictures. 1974.

Blow Out. Digital File. Directed by Brian De Palma. USA: Cinema 77; Geria Productions (as Geria); Filmways Pictures; Viscount Associates (copyright holder), 1981.

Ghostbusters. Digital File. Directed by Ivan Reitman. USA: Colombia Pictures; Delphi Films; Black Rhino Productions, 1984

Dead of Night. Digital File. Directed by Alberto Cavalcanti; Charles Crichton; Basil Dearden and Robert Hamer. UK: Ealing Studios, 1945.

Spirits of the Dead. Digital File. Directed by Federico Fellini, Louis Malle and Roger Vadim. France, Italy: Les Films Marceau; Produzioni Europee Associati (PEA); Cocinor, 1968

Scream of the Banshee. Digital File. Directed by Steven C. Miller. USA: After Dark Films; Bomar ODD (Production Service), 2011

The Exorcist. Digital File. Directed by William Friedkin. USA: Warner Bros.; Hoya Productions, 1973.

The Fog. Digital File. Directed by John Carpenter. USA: Embassy Pictures (presents) (as AVCO Embassy); EDI (presents) (as E.D.I.); Debra Hill Productions, 1980.

Silent House. Digital File. Directed by Chris Kentis and Laura Lau. France, USA: Elle Driver; Tazora Films, 2011.

The Skeleton Key. Digital File. Directed by Iain Softley. USA, Germany: Universal Pictures (presents); ShadowCatcher Entertainment; Double Feature Films; Daniel Bobker Productions; Brick Dust Productions LLC; MFPV Film (in association with), 2005.

Discography

Bad (1987) Epic Records

Can't Get You Out of My Head (2001) Parlophone

Dangerous (1991) Epic Records

I'm a Slave 4 U (2001) Jive Records

Genie in a Bottle (1999) RCA

Off the Wall (1979) Epic Records/CBS

Thriller (1982b) Epic Records

Toxic (2004) Jive Records

(You Drive Me) Crazy (1999) Jive Records

Index[1]

[1] Note: Page numbers followed by 'n' refer to notes.

T. Adams, *Horrors of* a *Voice (object* a*)*,
https://doi.org/10.1007/978-3-031-62050-8

D

E

K

L

SPRINGER NATURE

GPSR Compliance

The European Union's (EU) General Product Safety Regulation (GPSR) is a set of rules that requires consumer products to be safe and our obligations to ensure this.

If you have any concerns about our products, you can contact us on ProductSafety@springernature.com

In case Publisher is established outside the EU, the EU authorized representative is:

Springer Nature Customer Service Center GmbH
Europaplatz 3
69115 Heidelberg, Germany

The manufacturer's authorised representative in the EU is Springer Nature Customer Service Centre GmbH, Europaplatz 3, 69115 Heidelberg, Germany. If you have any concerns regarding our products, please contact ProductSafety@springernature.com

Printed and bound by CPI Group (UK) Ltd, Croydon, CR0 4YY
30/09/2026
02225583-0009